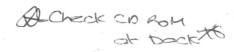

Microsoft® ASP.NET 3.5

Step by Step

George Shepherd

PUBLISHED BY
Microsoft Press
A Division of Microsoft Corporation
One Microsoft Way
Redmond, Washington 98052-6399

Library of Congress Control Number: 2007942085

Printed and bound in the United States of America.

2 3 4 5 6 7 8 9   QWT   3 2 1 0 9 8

Distributed in Canada by H.B. Fenn and Company Ltd.

A CIP catalogue record for this book is available from the British Library.

Microsoft Press books are available through booksellers and distributors worldwide. For further infor-
mation about international editions, contact your local Microsoft Corporation office or contact Microsoft
Press International directly at fax (425) 936-7329. Visit our Web site at www.microsoft.com/mspress.
Send comments to mspinput@microsoft.com.

Microsoft, Microsoft Press, ActiveX, BizTalk, Internet Explorer, MSN, Silverlight, SQL Server, Visual
Basic, Visual Studio, Win32, Windows, Windows NT, Windows Server, and Windows Vista are either
registered trademarks or trademarks of Microsoft Corporation in the United States and/or other countries.
Other product and company names mentioned herein may be the trademarks of their respective owners.

The example companies, organizations, products, domain names, e-mail addresses, logos, people, places,
and events depicted herein are fictitious. No association with any real company, organization, product,
domain name, e-mail address, logo, person, place, or event is intended or should be inferred.

This book expresses the author's views and opinions. The information contained in this book is provided
without any express, statutory, or implied warranties. Neither the authors, Microsoft Corporation, nor its
resellers, or distributors will be held liable for any damages caused or alleged to be caused either directly
or indirectly by this book.

Acquisitions Editor: Ben Ryan
Developmental Editor: Devon Musgrave
Project Editor: Kathleen Atkins
Editorial Production: P.M. Gordon Associates
Technical Reviewer: Kenn Scribner; Technical Review services provided by Content Master, a member
of CM Group, Ltd.
Cover: Tom Draper Design

Body Part No. X14-40155

Dedicated to
Darcy Gay Harrison and Pierre Nallet

Contents at a Glance

Table of Contents

What do you think of this book? We want to hear from you!

Microsoft is interested in hearing your feedback so we can continually improve our books and learning resources for you. To participate in a brief online survey, please visit:

www.microsoft.com/learning/booksurvey/

Part III Caching and State Management

What do you think of this book? We want to hear from you!

Microsoft is interested in hearing your feedback so we can continually improve our books and learning resources for you. To participate in a brief online survey, please visit:

www.microsoft.com/learning/booksurvey/

Introduction

This book will show you how to write Web applications using Microsoft's most current version of its HTTP request processing framework—ASP.NET 3.5. Web development has come a long way since the earliest sites began popping up in the early 1990s. The world of Web development offers several different choices as far as development tools go. During the past few years, ASP.NET has evolved to become one of the most consistent, stable, and feature-rich frameworks available for managing HTTP requests.

ASP.NET, together with Visual Studio, includes a number of features to make your life as a Web developer easier. For example, Visual Studio starts you off with several useful project templates from which to develop your site. Visual Studio also supports a number of development modes, including using Internet Information Services (IIS) directly to test your site during development, using a built-in Web server, or developing your site over an FTP connection. The debugger in Visual Studio lets you run the site and step through the critical areas of your code to find problems. The Visual Studio designer enables effective user interface development, allowing you to drop control elements onto a canvas to see how they appear visually. These are but a few of the features built into the ASP.NET framework when paired with Visual Studio.

While ASP.NET and Visual Studio offer excellent tools for writing Web applications, Web development on the Microsoft platform hasn't always been this way. The road to ASP.NET 3.5 has been nearly a decade in the making.

The Road to ASP.NET 3.5

ASP.NET has been available for nearly a decade. ASP.NET represents a quantum leap over previous methods of Web development. ASP.NET provides an object-oriented development environment centered around a well-defined pipeline.

ASP.NET 1.0 and 1.1

Microsoft's .NET framework introduces a whole new way of programming the Microsoft platform. Microsoft developers are primarily concerned with threads and memory (that's basically the API programming model). This model carried over to all areas of development, including Web development, placing a heavy burden on programmers.

ASP.NET introduces runtime services and a well-engineered class library for greatly enhancing Web development. In a way, classic ASP was sort of "taped onto" the IIS/ISAPI architecture without any real organic thought as to how early design decisions would affect developers later on. Well, now it's later on and classic ASP.NET's warts have become fairly obvious.

ASP.NET 1.0 and 1.1 provided a significant number of features, including

- An object-oriented framework for defining applications
- Separation of user interface declarations (HTML) and application logic
- Compiled code for executing application logic
- Configurable session state management
- Built-in data caching
- Built-in content caching
- A well-defined user interface componentization architecture
- High-level components for managing data formatting (grids, lists, text boxes)
- Built-in program tracing and diagnostics
- Built-in user input validation
- An easy-to-use custom authentication mechanism
- Solid integration with ADO.NET (the .NET database story)
- Excellent support for Web Services
- Zero reliance on the Component Object Model
- An extensible pipeline with many places in which a request can be intercepted

ASP.NET 1.0 set the stage for many developers both moving into Web development and moving to the Microsoft platform.

ASP.NET 2.0

Which brings us to ASP.NET 2.0. ASP.NET 2.0 builds on ASP.NET 1.0 and 1.1 by providing a number of new features in addition to what already existed with ASP.NET 1.0. These features include

- Master Pages and Skins
- Declarative data binding
- Site navigation and site map support
- Provider pattern model
- New cache features

- Membership controls

- Personalization controls

- Support for Web Parts

- Programmable configuration

- Administration tools

- New compilation model

All the features of ASP.NET 1.0/1.1 are still there. However, these new features make ASP.NET an even more compelling platform for creating Web sites.

ASP.NET 3.5

The primary features introduced by ASP.NET 3.5 include support for Asynchronous Java and XML (AJAX)-style programming and support for Windows Communication Foundation (WCF). In addition, the support for ASP.NET within Visual Studio has increased dramatically. The designer has improved significantly, and Visual Studio includes new templates for generating AJAX and WCF applications.

Using This Book

The purpose of this book is to weave the story of ASP.NET development for you. Each section presents a specific ASP.NET feature in a digestible format with examples. The stepwise instructions should yield working results for you immediately. You'll find most of the main features within ASP.NET illustrated here with succinct, easily duplicated examples. I made the examples rich to illustrate the feature without being overbearing. In addition to showing off ASP.NET features by example, you'll find practical applications of each feature so you can take these techniques into the real world.

Who Is This Book For?

This book is targeted at several developers:

- **Those starting out completely new with ASP.NET**   The text includes enough back story to explain the Web development saga even if you've developed only desktop applications.

- **Those migrating from either ASP.NET 1.x or 2.0, or even classic ASP**   The text explains how ASP.NET 3.5 is different from ASP.NET 1.x and 2.0. It also includes references explaining differences between ASP.NET and classic ASP.

- **Those who want to consume ASP.NET how-to knowledge in digestible pieces**   You don't have to read the chapters in any particular order to find the book valuable. Each chapter stands more or less on its own (with the exception of the first chapter, which details the fundamentals of Web applications—you may want to read it first if you've never ventured beyond desktop application development). You may find it useful to study the chapters about server-side controls (Chapters 3 to 5) together, but it's not completely necessary to do so.

Organization of This Book

This book is organized so that each chapter may be read independently, for the most part. With the exception of Chapter 1, about Web application essentials, and the three server-side control chapters (Chapters 3 to 5), which make sense to tackle together, each chapter serves as a self-contained block of information about a particular ASP.NET feature.

Getting Started

If you've gotten this far, you're probably ready to begin writing some code. Before beginning, make sure that Visual Studio 2008 is installed on your machine. As long as you've installed the development environment, you can be sure the .NET runtime support is installed as well.

The first few examples will require nothing but a text editor and a working installation of IIS. To start, we'll begin with some basic examples to illustrate ASP.NET's object-oriented nature and compilation model. In addition to letting you see exactly how ASP.NET works when handling a request, this is a good time to lay out ASP.NET's architecture from a high level. We'll progress to Web form programming and soon begin using Visual Studio to write code (which makes things much easier!).

After learning the fundamentals of Web form development, we'll break apart the rest of ASP.NET using examples to understand ASP.NET's features such as server-side controls, content caching, writing custom handlers, caching output and data, and debugging and diagnostics, all the way to ASP.NET's support for Web Services.

Finding Your Best Starting Point in This Book

This book is designed to help you build skills in a number of essential areas. You can use this book whether you are new to Web programming or you are switching from another Web development platform. Use the following table to find your best starting point in this book.

If you are	Follow these steps
New	
To Web development	1. Install the code samples.
	2. Work through the examples in Chapters 1 and 2 sequentially. They will ground you in the ways of Web development. They will also familiarize you with ASP.NET and Visual Studio.
	3. Complete the rest of the book as your requirements dictate.
New	
To ASP.NET and Visual Studio	1. Install the code samples.
	2. Work through the examples in Chapter 2. They provide a foundation for working with ASP.NET and Visual Studio.
	3. Complete the rest of the book as your requirements dictate.
Migrating	
From earlier versions of ASP.NET	1. Install the code samples.
	2. Skim the first two chapters to get an overview of Web development on the Microsoft platform and Visual Studio 2008.
	3. Concentrate on Chapters 3 through 20 as necessary. You may already be familiar with some topics and may only need to see how a particular feature differs between earlier versions of ASP.NET and ASP.NET 3.5. In other cases, you may need to explore a feature that's completely new for ASP.NET 3.5.
Referencing	
The book after working through the exercises	1. Use the Index or the Table of Contents to find information about particular subjects.
	2. Read the Quick Reference sections at the end of each chapter to find a brief review of the syntax and techniques presented in the chapter.

Conventions and Features in This Book

This book presents information using conventions designed to make the information readable and easy to follow. Before you start the book, read the following list, which explains conventions you'll see throughout the book and points out helpful features in the book that you might want to use:

Conventions

- Each chapter includes a summary of objectives near the beginning.
- Each exercise is a series of tasks. Each task is presented as a series of steps to be followed sequentially.

- Notes labeled "Tip" provide additional information or alternative methods for completing a step successfully.

- Text that you type appears in bold, like so:

```
class foo
{
    System.Console.WriteLine("HelloWorld");
}
```

- The directions often include alternate ways of accomplishing a single result. For example, adding a new item to a Visual Studio project may be done from either the main menu or by clicking the right mouse button in the Solution Explorer.

- The examples in this book are written using C#.

Other Features

- Some text includes sidebars and notes to provide more in-depth information about the particular topic. The sidebars might contain background information, design tips, or features related to the information being discussed. They may also inform you about how a particular feature may differ in this version of ASP.NET.

- Each chapter ends with a summary and a Quick Reference section. The Quick Reference section contains concise reminders of how to perform the tasks you learned in the chapter.

System Requirements

You'll need the following hardware and software to complete the practice exercises in this book:

 Note The Visual Studio 2008 software is *not* included with this book! The CD-ROM packaged in the back of this book contains the code samples needed to complete the exercises. The Visual Studio 2008 software must be purchased separately.

- Microsoft Windows Vista, Microsoft Windows XP Professional with Service Pack 2, or Microsoft Windows Server 2003 with Service Pack 1

- Microsoft Internet Information Services (included with Windows)

- Microsoft Visual Studio 2008 Standard Edition or Microsoft Visual Studio 2008 Professional Edition

- Microsoft SQL Server 2005 Express Edition (included with Visual Studio 2005) or Microsoft SQL Server 2005

- 1.2 GHz Pentium or compatible processor

- 384 MB RAM (758 MB or more for Vista)

- Video (1024 × 768 or higher resolution) monitor with at least 256 colors

- 5400 RPM hard drive (with 2.2 GB of available hard-disk space)

- CD-ROM or DVD-ROM drive

- Microsoft mouse or compatible pointing device

- 2.79 MB of available hard disk space to install the code samples

You will also need to have Administrator access to your computer to configure SQL Server 2005 Express Edition.

Using Microsoft Access

Chapter 11, "Data Binding,", and Chapter 15, "Application Data Caching," both use Microsoft Access. If you want to look at the databases and modify them, you need to have installed Microsoft Access on your machine. If you have Microsoft Office, you probably already have it. There is nothing special you need to do to set it up, and there is nothing special you need to do to use the databases within the ASP.NET applications.

Code Samples

The companion CD inside this book contains the code samples, written in C#, that you'll use as you perform the exercises in the book. By using the code samples, you won't waste time creating files that aren't relevant to the exercise. The files and the step-by-step instructions in the lessons also let you learn by doing, which is an easy and effective way to acquire and remember new skills.

Installing the C# Code Samples

Follow these steps to install the C# code samples on your computer so that you can use them with the exercises in this book:

> **Note** The code sample installer modifies IIS, so you must have Administrator permissions on your computer to install the code samples.

1. Remove the companion CD from the package inside this book and insert it into your CD-ROM drive.

Note An end user license agreement should open automatically. If this agreement does not appear, open My Computer on the desktop or the **Start** menu, double-click the icon for your CD-ROM drive, and then double-click **StartCD.exe**.

2. Review the end user license agreement. If you accept the terms, select the accept option and then click **Next**. A menu will appear with options related to the book.

3. Click **Install Code Samples**.

4. Follow the instructions that appear.

 Note If IIS is not installed and running, a message will appear indicating that the installer cannot connect to IIS. You can choose to ignore the message and install the code sample files; however, the code samples that require IIS will not run properly.

The code samples will be installed to the following location on your computer:

\My Documents\Microsoft Press\ASP.NET 3.5 Step by Step

The installer will create a virtual directory named *aspnet35sbs* under the Default Web Site. Below the aspnet35sbs virtual directory, various Web applications are created. To view these settings, open the Internet Information Services console.

Using the Code Samples

Each chapter in this book explains when and how to use any code samples for that chapter. When it's time to use a code sample, the book will list the instructions for how to open the files. Many chapters begin projects completely from scratch so you can understand the entire development process. Some examples borrow bits of code from previous examples.

Here's a comprehensive list of the code sample projects:

Project	Description
Chapter 1	
HelloWorld.asp, Selectnoform.asp, Selectfeature.htm, Selectfeature2.htm, Selectfeature.asp	Several Web resources illustrating different examples of raw HTTP requests.
WebRequestor	A simple application that issues a raw HTTP request.
Chapter 2	
HelloWorld, HelloWorld2, HelloWorld3, HelloWorld4, HelloWorld5, partial1.cs, partial2.cs	Web resources illustrating ASP.NET's compilation models and partial classes.

Project	Description
Chapter 3	
BunchOfControls.htm, BunchOfControls.asp, BunchOfControls.aspx	Web resources illustrating rendering control tags.
ControlORama	Visual Studio–based project illustrating Visual Studio and server-side controls.
Chapter 4	
ControlORama	Illustrates creating and using rendered server-side controls.
Chapter 5	
ControlORama	Illustrates creating and using composite server-side controls and User controls.
Chapter 6	
ControlPotpourri	Illustrates control validation, the *TreeView*, and the *MultiView/View* controls.
Chapter 7	
UseWebParts	Illustrates using Web Parts within a Web application.
Chapter 8	
MasterPageSite	Illustrates developing a common look and feel throughout multiple pages within a single Web application using Master Pages, Themes, and Skins.
Chapter 9	
ConfigORama	Illustrates configuration within ASP.NET. Shows how to manage the web.config file, how to add new configuration elements, and how to retrieve those configuration elements.
Chapter 10	
SecureSite	Illustrates Forms Authentication and authorization within a Web site.
Login.aspx, OptionalLogin.aspx, Web.Config, Web.ConfigForceAuthentication, Web.ConfigForOptionalLogin	Web resources for illustrating Forms Authentication at the very barest level.
Chapter 11	
DataBindORama	Illustrates databinding to several different controls, including the *GridView*. Also illustrates loading and saving data sets as XML and XML schema.
Chapter 12	
NavigateMeSite	Illustrates ASP.NET's navigation features.

Project	Description
Chapter 13	
MakeItPersonal	Illustrates ASP.NET's personalization features.
Chapter 14	
SessionState	Illustrates using session state within a Web application.
Chapter 15	
UseDataCaching	Illustrates caching data to increase performance.
Chapter 16	
OutputCaching	Illustrates caching output to increase performance.
Chapter 17	
DebugORama	Illustrates debugging and tracing Web applications.
Chapter 18	
UseApplication	Illustrates using the global application object and HTTP modules as a rendezvous point for the application. Illustrates storing globally scoped data and handling applicationwide events.
Chapter 19	
CustomHandlers	Illustrates custom HTTP handlers, both as separate assemblies and as ASHX files.
Chapter 20	
QuoteService	Illustrates a Web service that serves up random quotes.
Chapter 21	
WCFQuotesService	Illustrates a WCF-based service that serves up random quotes.
Chapter 22	
AJAXORama	Illustrates using AJAX to improve the end user's experience.
Chapter 23	
XAMLORama	Illustrates including XAML content within an ASP.NET site.
Chapter 24	
DeployThis	Illustrates how to make an installation package to deploy a Web site.

All these projects are available as complete solutions for the practice exercises (in case you need any inspiration).

Uninstalling the Code Samples

Follow these steps to remove the code samples from your computer:

1. In the Control Panel, open Add Or Remove Programs.

2. From the list of Currently Installed Programs, select **Microsoft ASP.NET 3.5 Step by Step**.

3. Click **Remove**.

4. Follow the instructions that appear to remove the code samples.

Software Release

This book was reviewed and tested against Visual Studio 2008. This book is expected to be fully compatible with the final release of Visual Studio 2008.

Support for This Book

Every effort has been made to ensure the accuracy of this book and the contents of the companion CD. As corrections or changes are collected, they will be added to a Microsoft Knowledge Base article. Microsoft Press provides support for books and companion CDs at the following Web site:

http://www.microsoft.com/learning/support/books/

Questions and Comments

If you have comments, questions, or ideas regarding the book or the companion CD, or questions that are not answered by visiting the sites previously mentioned, please send them to Microsoft Press via e-mail to

mspinput@microsoft.com

Or via postal mail to

Microsoft Press
Attn: Step by Step Series Editor
One Microsoft Way
Redmond, WA 98052-6399

Please note that Microsoft software product support is not offered through the preceding addresses.

Acknowledgments

A couple years ago I got a great Father's Day card from my son. When I opened it up, I saw that he had written the greeting in HTML!

```
<html>
   <head> <title> Father's Day Card </title> </head>
   <body> Happy Father's Day!!! </body>
</html>
```

After wiping away the tears, seeing Ted's card reinforced for me the increasing importance of Web-based applications. The Web permeates our social infrastructure. Whether you're a businessperson wanting to increase the visibility of your business, an avid reader trying to find an out-of-print book, a student fetching homework assignments from a school Web site, or any other producer or consumer of information, you touch the Internet.

Publishing a book is a huge effort. My name's on the lower right corner of the cover as the author, but I did only some of the work. I have so many people to thank for helping get this book out.

Thank you, Claudette Moore, for hooking me up with Microsoft Press again. Claudette has acted as my agent for all my work with Microsoft Press, handling the business issues associated with this work so I can be free to write. Thank you, Kathleen Atkins, for managing the project. It's always great working with you. Thank you, Charlotte Twiss and Angie Karp, for getting the code samples onto the CD. Thank you, Linnea Hermanson and the staff at P. M. Gordon Associates, for editing my work and making it appear that I can actually write coherent sentences. You all did a wonderful job on the editing, production, and layout. Thank you, Kenn Scribner, for providing the best technical objective eye I've ever worked with. Thank you, Ben Ryan, for accepting the book proposal and hiring me to create it.

Thank you, Jeff Duntemann, for buying and publishing my first piece ever for *PC Tech Journal*. Thank you, JD Hildebrand, for buying my second writing piece ever and for the opportunity to work with you all at Oakley Publishing. Thank you, Sandy Daston, for your support and guidance early in my writing career. Thank you to the folks at DevelopMentor for being an excellent group of technical colleagues and a great place for learning new technology.

Thank you, Christine Shooter, for all your love and support. You're the best. No one else even comes close. Thanks to my evil Java twin, Pat Shepherd, and his family, Michelle, Belfie, and Bronson, for the best trip to Michigan ever this summer. It was a welcome break in the middle of this project. Thank you, Ted Shepherd, you're the best son ever. Thank you, George Robbins Shepherd and Betsy Shepherd. As my parents you guided me and encouraged me to always do my best. I miss you both dearly.

Finally, thank you, Reader, for going through this book and spending time learning ASP.NET. May you continue to explore ASP.NET and always find new and interesting ways to handle HTTP requests.

George Shepherd
Chapel Hill, NC
January 2008

Part I
Fundamentals

Chapter 1
Web Application Basics

After completing this chapter, you will be able to

- Interpret HTTP requests
- Use the .NET Framework to make HTTP requests without a browser
- Interpret HTML
- Work with IIS
- Produce dynamic Web content without using ASP.NET yet

This chapter covers the fundamentals of building a Web-based application. Unlike the development of most desktop applications, in which many of the parts are available locally (as components on the user's hard disk drive), developing a Web application requires getting software parts to work over a widely distributed network using a disconnected protocol. The technologies underlying ASP.NET have been around for a long time. Of course, ASP.NET makes use of this technology underneath, while making it very approachable at the same time.

Although ASP.NET makes developing Web applications far easier than ever before, you must have a solid understanding of how the plumbing is actually working during the development of an ASP.NET application. A good example of such a time might be when you're tracking down a stray HyperText Transfer Protocol (HTTP) request or trying to figure out why a section of your page is appearing in the wrong font within a client's browser. Another such time might occur while you're writing a custom control for a Web page. Custom controls often require that the rendering code be written manually. That is, you must carefully ensure that the HyperText Markup Language (HTML) tags emitted by your control occur in exactly the right order. For that, you need to understand HTML.

This chapter covers three things necessary to allow you to work with ASP.NET:

- How HTTP requests work
- How HTML works
- How HTTP requests are handled on the Microsoft production Web server platform, Internet Information Services (IIS)

Understanding these three technologies underlying ASP.NET frames the rest of the system. As you study ASP.NET, these pieces will undoubtedly fall into place.

HTTP Requests

The communication mechanism by which Web browsers talk to Web sites is named the *Hyper-Text Transfer Protocol* (HTTP). The World Wide Web as we know it today began as a research project at CERN in Switzerland. In those days, the notion of hypertext—documents linked together arbitrarily—was becoming increasingly popular. Applications such as Hypercard from Apple Computer Inc. introduced hypertext applications to a wider audience. Now, if documents could be linked over a network, that would revolutionize publishing. That's the reason for the HyperText Transfer Protocol, which lies on top of TCP/IP as an application layer.

In its original form, HTTP was meant to transfer hypertext documents. That is, it was originally intended simply to link documents together without consideration for anything like the Web-based user interfaces that are the staple of modern Web sites. The earliest versions of HTTP supported a single GET request to fetch the named resource. It then became the server's job to send the file as a stream of text. After the response arrived at the client's browser, the connection terminated. The earliest versions of HTTP supported only transfer of text streams and did not support any other sort of data transfer.

The first formal specification for HTTP found itself in version 1.0 and was published in the mid-1990s. HTTP 1.0 added support for more complex messaging beyond a simple text transfer protocol. HTTP grew to support different media (specified by the Multipurpose Internet Mail Extensions). The current version of HTTP is version 1.1.

As a connection protocol, HTTP is built around several basic commands. The most important ones we'll see in developing ASP.NET applications are GET, HEAD, and POST.

GET retrieves the information identified by the Uniform Resource Identifier (URI) specified by the request. The HEAD command retrieves only the header information identified by the URI specified by the request (that is, it does not return a message body). You use the POST method to make a request to the server that may cause side effects, such as sending information to the server for it to process. You make most initial contacts to a page using a GET command, and you commonly handle subsequent interactions with POST commands.

HTTP Requests from a Browser

As an example, look at the request that is sent from a browser to fetch the helloworld.htm resource from the virtual directory aspnet2sbs running on localhost. (I'll cover the concept of a "virtual directory" later, but for now just imagine it as the location of a Web application everyone can access.) Here is a sample (fictitious) HTTP server request:

```
GET /aspnet2sbs/helloworld.htm HTTP/1.1
Accept: image/gif, image/x-xbitmap, image/jpeg, image/pjpeg, ... , */*
Accept-Language: en-us
Accept-Encoding: gzip, deflate
User-Agent: Mozilla/4.0 (compatible; MSIE 7.0; Windows NT 5.1; ... .NET CLR 3.0.04506.30)
Host: localhost:80
Connection: Keep-Alive
```

If you would like to see the actual data going back and forth, there are several TCP monitors available. A good one is TcpTrace, found at *http://www.pocketsoap.com/tcptrace/*. You'll find instructions for its use there as well. For simple TCP tracing, you may also use TELNET to send GET Requests to the server, which we'll look at now.

To send an HTTP request to a server using TELNET, follow these steps:

1. Open the Visual Studio command prompt. To do this, from the Start button select All Programs, Microsoft Visual Studio 2008, Visual Studio Tools, and then finally Microsoft Visual Studio 2008 Command Prompt. The command prompt tool should appear.

2. At the prompt, type the following:

```
TELNET localhost 80
```

3. After the TELNET client connects, type the following GET command (assuming you have a virtual directory named aspnet2sbs on your machine, containing a file named *HelloWorld .HTM*, or you may also use a file already installed with IIS, such as postinfo.html):

```
GET //aspnet2sbs/helloworld.htm
```

4. You should see the file's contents returned to the command line.

When a browser wants to make an HTTP request, it needs to process the HTTP request including the URI along with other information (such as header information and the requested file name). The header information in the request includes details about the operating environment of the browser and some other information that is often useful to the server. When the server receives this request, it returns the requested resource as a text stream. The browser then parses it and formats the contents. The following shows the response provided by the server when asked for the HelloWorld.htm file. Normally, you don't see all the header information when viewing the resource through a browser. A good TCP tracing utility will show it to you. When we look at ASP.NET's tracing facilities later on, this header information will be visible.

```
HTTP/1.1 200 OK
Server: Microsoft-IIS/5.1
X-Powered-By: ASP.NET
Date: Thu, 01 Nov 2007 23:44:04 GMT
Content-Type: text/html
Accept-Ranges: bytes
Last-Modified: Mon, 22 Oct 2007 21:54:20 GMT
ETag: "04e9ace185fc51:bb6"
Content-Length: 130
<html>
    <body>
        <h1> Hello World </h1>
        Nothing really showing here yet, except some HTML...
    </body>
</html>
```

The first line indicates the protocol (HTTP, version 1.1) and the return code (200, meaning "OK"). The rest of the response (until the first *<html>* tag) is information about the time of the request, the last time the file was modified, and what kind of content is provided. This information will be useful later when we examine such issues as page caching and detecting browser capabilities. The content following the response header information is literally the HTML file sent back by the server.

Making HTTP Requests without a Browser

In addition to being a framework for building Web applications, the .NET development environment includes classes for making HTTP requests in the raw. The *WebRequest* class includes a member named *GetResponse* that will send a request to the address specified by the Uniform Resource Locator (URL). To get a feeling as to how to make direct requests to a Web server without a browser, try compiling and then running this short program that fetches the home page for *Microsoft.com*.

Build a simple HTTP requestor

1. Start Visual Studio.NET. Select **New**, **Project** from the main menu. In the **New Project** dialog box, select a Console application and name it *WebRequestorApp*, as shown in the following graphic.

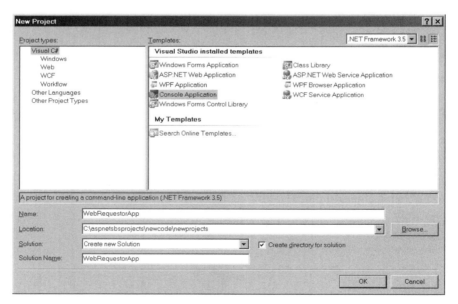

Visual Studio will generate a blank Console program for you.

2. Add the code necessary to make a Web request to the program. Visual Studio places the entry point of the Console application into a file named *Program.cs*. (This file is the code that shows up in the code window by default.) The code you add for making a Web request is shown in bold in the following lines of code:

```
using System;
using System.Collections.Generic;
using System.Linq;
using System.Text;
using System.Net;
using System.IO;
namespace WebRequestorApp
{
    class Program
    {
        static void Main(string[] args)
        {
            WebRequest req =
                WebRequest.Create
                    ("http://www.microsoft.com");
            WebResponse resp = req.GetResponse();
            StreamReader reader =
                new StreamReader(resp.GetResponseStream(),
                    Encoding.ASCII);
            Console.WriteLine(reader.ReadToEnd());
        }
    }
}
```

3. Run the application. You may do this by choosing **Debug**, **Start Without Debugging** from the main menu. Visual Studio will start up a Console for you and run the program. After a couple of moments, you'll see some HTML spewed to your screen.

Of course, the HTML isn't meant for human consumption. That's what a browser is for. However, this example does show the fundamentals of making a Web request—and you can see exactly what comes back in the response.

In this case, the request sent to the server is much smaller. *WebRequest.GetResponse* doesn't include as much information in the request—just the requisite GET followed by the URI, host information, and connection type:

```
GET /aspnet2sbs/helloworld.htm HTTP/1.1
Host: localhost:80
Connection: Keep-Alive
```

The fundamental jobs of most browsers are (1) to package a request and send it to the server represented in the URI and (2) to receive the response from the server and render it in a useful way. The response usually comes back as a text stream marked up using HTML tags. Let's take a look at HTML.

HyperText Markup Language

In the course of looking at ASP.NET, we'll see quite a bit of HTML. Most of it will be generated by the ASP.NET server-side controls. However, it's important to understand HTML because you may want to write your own server-side control from scratch, and at other times you may need to tweak or debug the output of your ASP.NET application.

Most HTTP requests result in a stream of text coming back to the program issuing the request. The world has pretty much agreed that HTML is the language for formatting documents, and all browsers understand HTML.

The first release of HTML worth using was version 2.0. Version 3.2 introduced new features, such as tables, text flow, applets, and superscripts and subscripts, while providing backward compatibility with the existing HTML 2.0 Standard.

The bottom line is that given a competent browser and well-structured HTML, you had the beginnings of a user interface development technology. And because HTML was understood by browsers running on a variety of platforms, the door was open for implementing a worldwide interactive computing platform. The other key that made this happen (besides a mature version of HTML) was the ability of servers to adapt their output to accommodate the requests of specific users at runtime.

For example, the following HTML stream will render an HTML page containing a button and a combo box filled with options. (This file is named *SelectNoForm.htm* in the collection of examples for this chapter.)

```html
<html>
 <body>
   <h2>Hello there. What's your favorite .NET feature?</h2>
   <select name='Feature'>
    <option> Type-Safety</option>
    <option> Garbage collection</option>
    <option> Multiple syntaxes</option>
    <option> Code Access Security</option>
    <option> Simpler threading</option>
    <option> Versioning purgatory</option>
   </select>
   <br/>
   <input type=submit name='Lookup' value='Lookup'></input>
   <br/>
 </body>
</html>
```

See Figure 1-1 for an example of how the page looks when rendered by the browser.

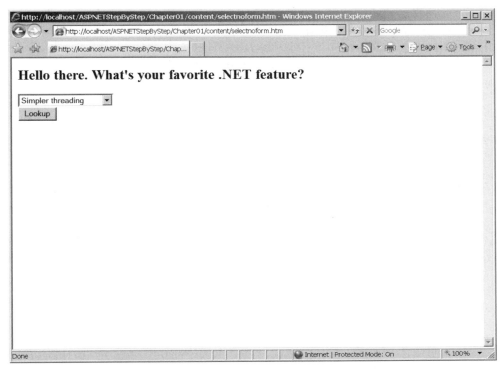

FIGURE 1-1 A simple HTML page showing a selection tag (rendered here as a Windows combo box) and a submission button

Note We'll actually surf to an HTML file that you write in subsequent chapters. Getting to that point is a bit involved, so for now, you can trust that the HTML will render in this fashion.

This is a static page. Even though it has a combo box and a button, they don't do anything worthwhile. You can pull down the combo box and work with it inside the browser. You can click the button, but all the action happens locally. That's because the server on the other end needs to support dynamic content.

Dynamic Content

The earliest Web sites were built primarily using static HTML pages. That is, you could surf to some page somewhere and read the HTML document living there. While at that time being able to do this was pretty amazing, HTML eventually evolved to be capable of much more than simply formatting text.

For example, HTML includes tags such as *<select></select>* that browsers interpret as a combo box, called a *drop-down list* in ASP.NET. The first tag, *<select>*, is called the *opening tag* while the second, *</select>*, is called the *closing tag*. Tags can contain other tags, which you saw with the *<option></option>* tags that provide content for the drop-down list. Tags also can have *attributes*, which are used to modify or tailor the behavior of the tag. Various attributes applied to the *<input></input>* tag cause browsers to draw text boxes and buttons. HTML provides a special tag, the *form*, that groups other tags designed to return information to the server for processing.

HTML Forms

HTML includes the *<form></form>* opening and closing tags for notifying the browser that a section of HTML includes tags representing controls the user will interact with to eventually return information to the server. This is how you specify a Web document will be handling input from the end user (not just output). The contents of the form, which is to say the data contained in the input controls, will be "posted back" to the server for processing. It's common to combine the words and call this action a *postback*. This is why the typical HTTP use case for an HTML document is GET, to initially retrieve the document, and then POST (or a modified form of GET), to return data to the server, if any.

The *<form>* tag usually sandwiches a set of tags specifying user input controls. The following shows the same feature selection page, but with the form tag added (the code is from the file named *SelectFeature2.htm* in the book's accompanying examples):

```
<html>
 <body>
   <form action="http://localhost/HttpHandlers/selectfeature.htm"
     method="get">
      <h2>Hello there. What's your favorite .NET feature?</h2>
      <select name='Feature'>
         <option> Type-Safety</option>
         <option> Garbage collection</option>
         <option> Multiple syntaxes</option>
         <option> Code Access Security</option>
         <option> Simpler threading</option>
         <option> Versioning purgatory</option>
      </select>
   <br/>
   <input type=submit name='Lookup' value='Lookup'></input>
   <br/>
   </form>
 </body>
</html>
```

If you'd like to see this work right away, type this into a file named *SelectFeature2.htm* and save it into the directory c:\inetpub\wwwroot and surf to the file by typing **http://localhost/ selectfeature2.htm** into your browser's navigation field.

The form tag includes several attributes that you may set to control how the page behaves. In the preceding example, notice the *<form>* tag sets the *action* attribute, which indicates the server that will receive the form's contents. In its absence, the current document URL will be used.

The other attribute used in the HTML is the *method* attribute. The *method* attribute specifies the HTTP method used when submitting the form and therefore dictates how the form data are returned to the server. The method employed in the example is GET because it's the first request to the server. Assuming you select the last option ("Versioning purgatory") and then click Lookup, the form's GET method causes the form's input control contents to be appended to the URL, like so:

```
http://localhost/SelectFeature2.htm?Feature=Versioning+purgatory&Lookup=Lookup
```

This modified URL, often called a *query string*, is then sent to the server.

The form's POST method causes the form contents to be sent to the server in the body of a returned HTTP packet, as you see here:

```
POST /SelectFeature2.htm HTTP/1.1
Accept: image/gif, image/x-xbitmap, image/jpeg, image/pjpeg, ... , */*
Accept-Language: en-us
Content-Type: application/x-www-form-urlencoded
Accept-Encoding: gzip, deflate
User-Agent: Mozilla/4.0 (compatible; MSIE 7.0; Windows NT 5.1; ... .NET CLR 3.0.04506.30)
Host: localhost:80
Content-Length: 42
Connection: Keep-Alive
Cache-Control: no-cache

Feature=Versioning+purgatory&Lookup=Lookup
```

Adding the form tag to the body of the document gets us part of the way to having an HTTP application that actually interacts with a user. Now we need a little more support on the server end. When you click the Lookup button, the browser will actually force another round-trip back to the server (although in this case, it will only perform an HTTP GET command to refetch the document since we specified this in the form's *method* attribute).

At this point, a normal HTTP GET command will only return the document. For a truly interactive environment, the server on the other end needs to modify the content as requests go back and forth between the browser and the server.

For example, imagine that the user does an initial GET for the resource, selects a feature from the combo box, and then clicks the Lookup button. For an interactive application to work, the browser will need to make a second round-trip to the server with a new request that includes the user's inputs for processing. The server will need to examine the request coming from the browser and figure out what to do about it. This is where the server begins to play a much more active role. Depending on the platform involved, there are several different ways in which a server can handle the postback—through such programs as the Common Gateway Interface or Internet Information Services.

Common Gateway Interface (Very Retro)

The earliest Web servers supporting "dynamic Web content" did so through the Common Gateway Interface (CGI). CGI was the earliest standard for building Web servers. CGI programs execute in real time and change their output based on the state of the application and the requests coming in. Each request coming into a Web server running CGI runs a separate instance of a program to respond. The application can run any sort of operation, including looking up data in a database, accepting credit card numbers, and sending out formatted information.

The Microsoft Platform as a Web Server

On the Microsoft platform, it's too expensive to start up a new process for each request (à la CGI). Microsoft's solution is to have a single daemon process (which in Windows we call a *service*) monitor port 80 for incoming network packets and load DLLs to handle separate requests when the content needs to change. Microsoft's standard Web platform is based on the Internet Information Services (IIS).

> **Note** When you create and edit Web applications using Visual Studio 2008, you can load them "from the file system" and "from IIS" (as well as by a few other means). If you load your Web application using IIS, then IIS acts as the Web server as you'd expect. But what about loading a Web application from the file system? What application is serving HTML (or ASP.NET) documents in that case? As it happens, starting with Visual Studio 2005, a special development Web server can be used to simplify debugging and administration. Based on a Web server named *Cassini*, it can serve HTML and ASP.NET pages just as effectively as IIS for development purposes. However, keep in mind that for robustness and security IIS is Microsoft's professional grade Web server and is the intended target for your ASP.NET Web application.

Internet Information Services

All Web application environments work fundamentally the same way. No matter what hardware/software platform you use, some piece of software is required on the server to monitor port 80 (typically) for incoming HTTP requests. When a request arrives, it's the server's job to somehow respond to the request in a meaningful way. On the Microsoft platform, IIS is the watchdog intercepting HTTP requests from port 80—the normal inbound port for HTTP requests. Internet servers use other ports as well. For example, HTTPS (Secure HTTP) happens over port 443. However, right now we're mostly interested in normal Internet traffic over port 80.

When a browser makes a call to a server running on the Microsoft platform, IIS intercepts that request and searches for the resource identified by the URL. IIS divides its directory space into manageable chunks called *virtual directories*. For example, imagine someone tries to get to a resource on your server using this URL:

http://www.aspnetstepbystep.com/examples/showfeatures.htm

The domain "aspnetstepbystep" is fictitious and used here for illustration. However, if there were a server registered using this name, the URL would identify the entire resource. Within this URL, *http://www.aspnetstepbystep.com* identifies the server and will direct the request through a maze of routers. Once the request reaches the server, the server will look for the *showfeatures.htm* resource in some directory-type entity named *examples*. If the server is running IIS, *examples* refers to a virtual directory.

IIS divides its working space into multiple *virtual directories*. Each virtual directory typically refers to a single application and is used to map a physical directory on your server's hard drive to an Internet URL. Using virtual directories, one per application, IIS can serve multiple applications. Each virtual directory includes various configuration properties, including such things as security options, error handling redirections, and application isolation options. The configuration parameters also include mappings between file extensions and optionally configured IIS extension DLLs, called *ISAPI DLLs* (ISAPI stands for *Internet Services Application Programming Interface*). (ASP.NET itself is handled by one of these ISAPI DLLs!)

While it's not critical for initially writing ASP.NET applications, knowing a bit about how IIS works is tremendously important when you need to fully debug, test, and deploy your Web application. The built-in Visual Studio Web server (Cassini) is fine for most things, but it lacks much that IIS offers. True ASP.NET developers understand this and often become quite adept at administering IIS. If you want to get going writing applications straightaway, you may skip the section on IIS, but we'll be looking at various aspects of IIS operations and administration throughout the book. To begin, here's a brief look at ISAPI and how it extends IIS.

Internet Services Application Programming Interface DLLs

On the Microsoft platform, creating a process space is an expensive proposition (in terms of system resources and clock cycles). Imagine trying to write a server that responds to each request by starting a separate program. The poor server would be bogged down very quickly, and your e-commerce site would stop making money.

Microsoft's architecture prefers using DLLs to respond to requests. DLLs are relatively inexpensive to load, and running code within a DLL executes very quickly. The DLLs handling Web requests are named *ISAPI DLLs*.

While we won't dive all the way into the inner workings of ISAPI DLLs, we'll take enough of a look at their architecture so you can see how they relate to ASP.NET.

ISAPI DLLs handling normal HTTP requests define an entry point named *HttpExtensionProc*. Although ISAPI extension DLLs define more entry points than *HttpExtensionProc*, it is by far the most important method in an ISAPI DLL. The point to realize about ISAPI extension DLLs is that they all implement this singular function when responding to HTTP requests. However, they may all respond differently.

The *HttpExtensionProc* method takes a single parameter—an EXTENSION_CONTROL_BLOCK structure. EXTENSION_CONTROL_BLOCK includes the entire context of a request. We don't need to see the whole structure here. However, we will see the managed equivalent in ASP.NET when we look at the *HttpContext* class.

Upon receiving a request, IIS packages the information into the EXTENSION_CONTROL_ BLOCK. IIS then passes the structure into the ISAPI DLL through the *HttpExtensionProc* entry point. The ISAPI extension DLL is responsible for parsing the incoming request and doing something interesting with it. The ISAPI extension DLL is completely at liberty to do whatever it wants with the request. For example, the client might make a request that includes param- eters in the query string (perhaps the client is performing a customer lookup or something similar). The ISAPI extension DLL uses those query string parameters to create a database query specific to the site. If the site is a commerce site, the database query might be for the current inventory. After processing the request, the ISAPI DLL streams any results back to the client.

You may have had some experience working with classic ASP, in which case much of this structure will appear familiar to you. For example, calling *Write* through ASP's intrinsic *Response* object eventually ends up executing the method indicated by the EXTENSION_ CONTROL_BLOCK's *WriteClient* property value.

We've taken a quick glance at the inner structure of an ISAPI DLL. Let's see how these DLLs fit into IIS. This is interesting because ASP.NET requests do pass through an ISAPI DLL.

Internet Information Services

The user interface to IIS is available through the Control Panel. To get a feel for how to admin- ister IIS, let's take a short tour. It's important to have some facility with IIS because ASP.NET relies on it to service Web requests in a real Web application. IIS 5.x, 6.0, and 7.0 work similarly as far as dividing the server's application space into virtual directories. IIS 6.0 and 7.0 include many other features such as application isolation and recycling to help control runaway re- quests and limit memory consumption if something untoward happens during a request.

Running IIS

1. Run IIS. To get to IIS, first go to **Administrative Tools**. On Windows Vista, you can do this through the Control Panel. Run Internet Information Services. You should see the IIS user interface on your screen. The following graphics show the Features View and the Content View—both running under Vista.

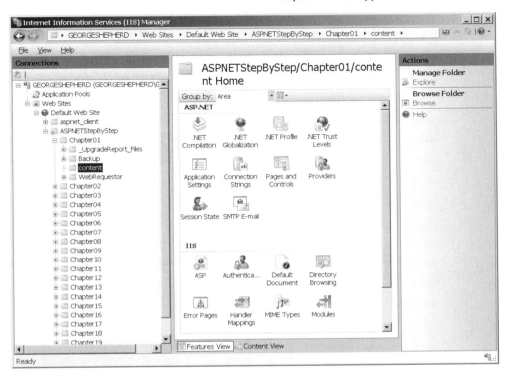

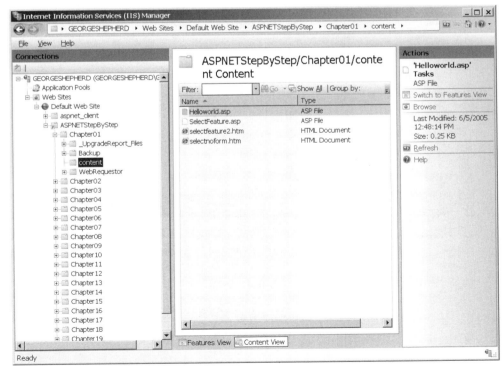

On the left-side of the screen is an expandable tree showing the Web sites and virtual directories available through IIS on your machine. IIS 5.x and 6.0 show the virtual directories on the left pane, with the directory contents on the right-side. The IIS 7 management console includes two views: the Features View and the Content View. The Features View includes various icons for managing specific aspects of IIS for the item selected from the list on the left side. The Content View shows the files contained within the selected item. Let's explore the Features View and the Content View.

2. View configuration for a specific virtual directory. The Features View lets you see how a specific virtual directory is configured. To find out more about the directory's configuration, try clicking on the various icons in the Features View. For example, to see how IIS figures out the correct default file to show (in the absence of a specific file extension), click on the **Default Document** icon. You'll see the list of default file names that IIS will try to load:

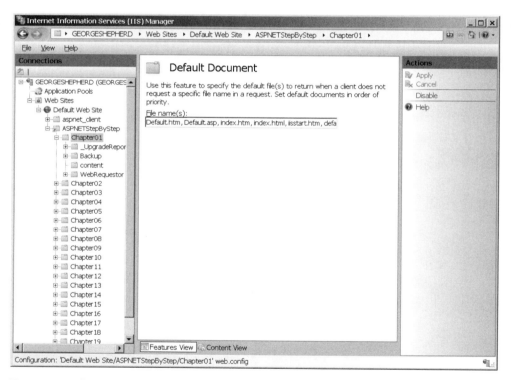

You can configure a number of features within IIS, and they're all represented by the icons presented in the Features View. The feature set is fairly extensive, covering all aspects of how the directory is accessed from the outside world. We won't spend a lot of time here because ASP.NET takes care of most of these issues (rather than leaving them up to IIS). Before discussing how IIS 7.0 handles ASP.NET requests, let's take a look at how IIS 7.0 handles other types of requests for the sake of completeness.

3. View module mappings for a virtual directory. Static file types such as HTM are transmitted directly back to the client. However, dynamic pages whose contents can change
between posts require further processing, so they are assigned to specific handlers. As
you'll see in a moment, IIS 7.0 prefers to handle most requests via managed code. For
those developers who wish to write native code, IIS 7.0 includes a new C++/native core
server API. This new API works with IIS 7.0 through the IsapiModule to expose classic
ISAPI extension DLLs. Another module, the IsapiFilterModule, replaces the traditional
ISAPI filter API from earlier releases of IIS. To view the IIS 7.0 module mappings, click on
the **Module Mappings** icon within the Features View. You should see a listing of the
IIS 7.0 modules that intercept requests:

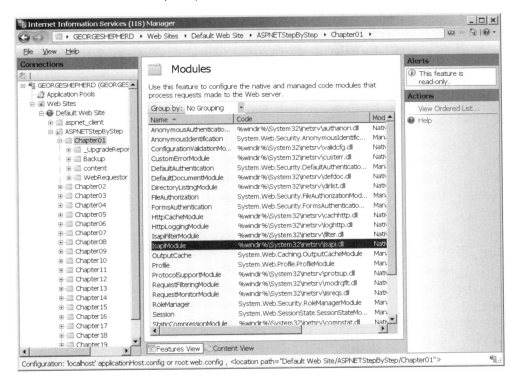

4. View file mappings for a virtual directory. For those applications that handle requests using managed code, IIS pipes them through the handlers listed on the Handler Mappings page. To view the file mappings for a specific virtual directory, click the **Handler Mappings** icon within the Features View. IIS responds by listing the file mappings for the directory:

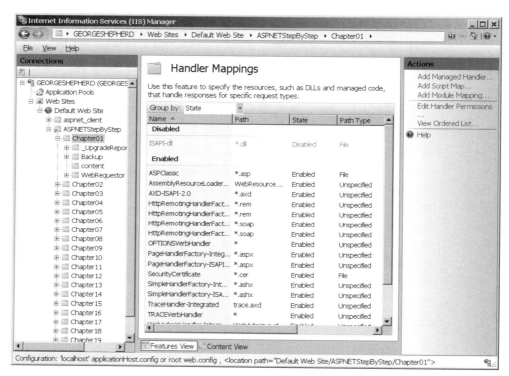

These mappings tell IIS how to handle specific requests. As you can see, most requests are handled through managed code via ASP.NET. Notice that at the top of the list, there's a handler for classic ASP files, named *ASPClassic*. This handler takes care of requests bearing the .ASP file extension (earlier versions of IIS piped these requests directly to the ASP.DLL handler).

Note If for some reason you find yourself with a need to run classic ASP, note that IIS 7.0 does not install ASPClassic by default—you must add this feature deliberately. In the Control Panel, select **Programs** and **Features** from the list. Then select **Turn Windows Features On and Off**. Select **Internet Information Services** from the dialog box that appears. Expand the **World Wide Web Services** node, and then the **Application Development Features** node. Check the ASP box to install classic ASP handling, as shown here:

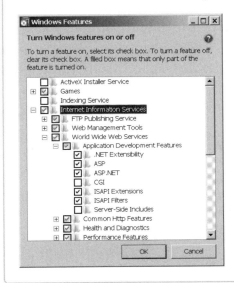

Classic ASP (Putting ASP.NET into Perspective)

While this book is really about ASP.NET, understanding classic ASP is usually helpful. By contrasting classic ASP and ASP.NET, you get a good idea as to why things are the way they are in ASP.NET. You can also gain an appreciation for all that ASP.NET does for you.

Microsoft originally developed Active Server Pages (ASP) to encourage a larger number of developers than just those using C++ to undertake Web development. When IIS came out, it was certainly a feasible environment for developing Web sites on the Microsoft platform compared to other platforms. In fact, you can still see some sites today deployed as pure ISAPI DLL sites; just look in the query strings going between the browser and the server for clues (eBay for one). For example, you might see a file name such as *ACMEISAPI.DLL* embedded within the query string.

However, writing an entire site using ISAPI DLLs can be daunting. Writing ISAPI DLLs in C or C++ gives you complete control over how your site will perform and makes the site work. However, along with that control comes an equal amount of responsibility because developing software using C or C++ presents numerous challenges.

So in delivering ASP, Microsoft provided a single ISAPI DLL named *ASP.DLL*. ASP Web developers write their code into files tagged with the extension .asp (for example, somefile .asp). ASP files often contain a mixture of static HTML and executable sections (usually written in a scripting language) that emit output at runtime. For example, the code in Listing 1-1 shows an ASP program that spits out the HelloWorld page, which contains both static HTML and text generated at runtime. (The file name is *HelloWorld.asp* in the book's accompanying examples.)

LISTING 1-1 A Classic ASP File

```
<%@ Language="javascript" %>
<html>
 <body>
   <form>
    <h3>Hello world!!! This is an ASP page.</h3>

    <% Response.Write("This content was generated");%>
    <% Response.Write("as part of an execution block");%>
   </form>
 </body>
</html>
```

The code shown in Listing 1-1 renders the following page. IIS monitored port 80 for requests. When a request for the file Helloworld.asp came through, IIS saw the .asp file extension and asked ASP.DLL to handle the request (that's how the file mapping was set up). ASP.DLL simply rendered the static HTML as the string "Hello world!!! This is an ASP page." Then when ASP.DLL encountered the funny-looking execution tags (<% and %>), it executed those blocks by running them through a JavaScript parser (note the language tag in the first line of code). Figure 1-2 shows how the page renders in Internet Explorer.

This book is about developing ASP.NET software, so we'll focus most of the attention there. However, before leaving the topic of classic ASP, Listing 1-2 shows the SelectFeature.htm page rewritten as a classic ASP page. Looking at this simple ASP application presents some of the core issues in Web development and illustrates why Microsoft rewrote its Web server technology as ASP.NET. (The accompanying file name is *SelectFeature.asp*.)

LISTING 1-2 The SelectFeature.htm Page Rewritten as a Classic ASP Page

```
<%@ Language="javascript" %>
<html>
 <body>
   <form>
      <h2>HelloWorld<h2>

      <h3>What's your favorite .NET feature?</h3>
      <select name='Feature'>
         <option> Type-Safety</option>
         <option> Garbage collection</option>
         <option> Multiple syntaxes</option>
         <option> Code Access Security</option>
```

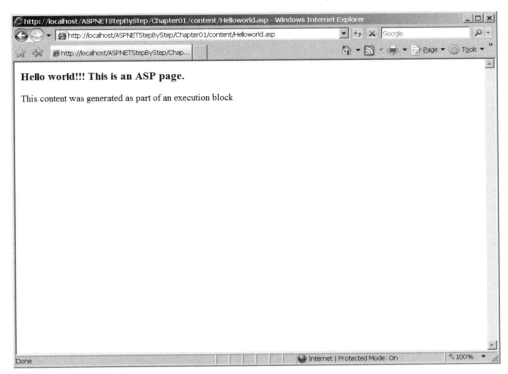

FIGURE 1-2 The results of a request made to the ASP program from Listing 1-1

```
        <option> Simpler threading</option>
        <option> Versioning purgatory</option>
    </select>
    </br>
    <input type=submit name="Submit" value="Submit"></input>
    <p>
        Hi, you selected <%=Request("Feature") %>
    </p>
  </form>
 </body>
</html>
```

Much of the text in SelectFeature.asp looks very similar to SelectFeature.htm, doesn't it? The differences lie mainly in the first line (that now specifies a syntax for executable blocks) and the executable block marked by <% and %>. The rest of the static HTML renders a selection control within a form.

Take note of the executable blocks and how the blocks use the *Response* object (managed by the ASP infrastructure) to push text out to the browser. The executable block examines the *Feature* control (specified by the *<select>* tag) and prints out the value selected by the user.

Figure 1-3 shows how SelectFeature.asp renders in Internet Explorer.

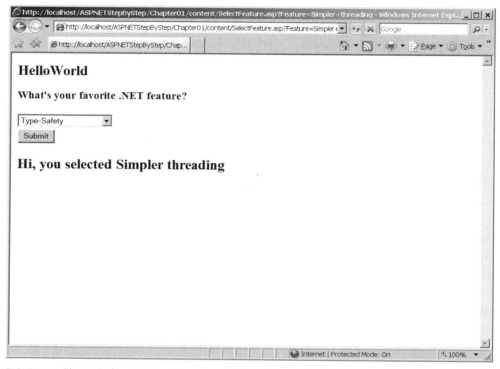

FIGURE 1-3 The code from Listing 1-2 as viewed using Internet Explorer

The screen in Figure 1-3 may look a bit odd because the drop-down list box shows "Type-Safety" while the rendered text shows "Simpler threading." Without doing anything extra, the drop-down list box will always re-render with the first element as the selected element. We'll see how ASP.NET fixes this later when we look at server-side controls. That's enough background information to help you understand the core concepts associated with developing Web applications.

Web Development Concepts

In the end, developing Web applications forces you to deal with two significant issues—managing user interfaces (UI) using HTML over a disconnected protocol and managing the state of your application. These fundamental activities separate Web development from other types of application development.

In many ways, the programming model has gone back to the model that dominated the mid-1970s, when large mainframes served output to terminals connected directly to them. Users would submit jobs to the mainframe and get output to their terminals. So, what's changed here? First, the terminal is a lot fancier—it's a powerful PC running a browser that interprets HTML. The endpoint to which the browser connects is a Web server (or perhaps a server farm). Finally, the connection protocol used by the client and the server is indirect (and a request can quite literally cross the globe before the user sees a result).

In Web application development, the program's primary job is to receive requests from "out there" and to provide meaningful responses to the requestors. That often means generating complex HTML that renders in a form humans can read on the client's browser. That can be fairly involved, for example, in a modern commercial Web site supporting commerce. Customers will undoubtedly ask about current pricing, request inventory levels, and perhaps even order items or services from the Web site. The process of "generating meaningful HTML for the client" suddenly means doing things such as making database accesses, authenticating the identity of the client, and keeping track of the client's order. Imagine doing all this from scratch!

While frameworks such as classic ASP go a long way toward making Web development more approachable, many features are still left for developers to create on their own (mostly related to the two issues mentioned at the beginning of this section). For example, building a secure but manageable Web site in classic ASP usually meant writing your own security subsystem (or buying one). Managing the state of the UI emitted by your Web site was often a tedious chore as well.

ASP.NET

All of this brings us to ASP.NET. A common theme you'll see throughout this book is that ASP.NET takes features usually implemented (over and over again) by developers and rolls them into the ASP.NET framework.

ASP.NET has been evolving steadily since it was first released. ASP.NET 1.0 introduced a well-defined pipeline, a viable extensibility model, a server-side control rendering model, and numerous other features to make developing Web sites very doable. ASP.NET 2.0 took ASP.NET 1.x to the next level and pushed even more commonly implemented features into the framework. An example of how ASP.NET 2.0 improved upon ASP.NET 1.x is the authentication and authorization services provided by ASP.NET 1.x. ASP.NET 1.x included a reasonable and easy-to-manage authentication model. However, developers were often left with the task of rolling their own authentication systems into their Web sites. ASP.NET 2.0 adds an authorization subsystem. We'll cover ASP.NET Forms Authentication and other security features in-depth in Chapter 10.

ASP.NET 2.0 has been in use for more than two years. Even with all the improvements provided by the release of version 2.0, there's still room for more. ASP.NET 3.5 delivers a couple of significant new features. The first one is support for Asynchronous Java and XML-style programming (commonly known as AJAX). The second main feature is support for Windows Communication Foundation application hosting via IIS/ASP.NET.

In the following chapters, we'll cover the most important ASP.NET features. By the end of the last chapter, you'll be well equipped to develop a Web site based on ASP.NET.

Summary

This chapter covers the basics of Web applications. Programming for the Web is different from programming desktop applications because, in effect, you're trying to create user interfaces for a distributed client base over a stateless, connectionless protocol. Clients making requests to a server using a browser issue HTTP requests to the server and wait for a response. The earliest Web applications were simply collections of HTML files or other resources. As HTML evolved to include tags representing standard user interface controls, so came the ability to create interactive applications allowing users to carry on a conversation with the server.

The modern Microsoft Web platform is based on ASP.NET, which has evolved over the years and has improved after several other technologies ran their course (raw ISAPI DLL programming and classic ASP). The job of any Web server is to receive requests from the users and do something meaningful with them. The rest of this book examines how to do that using ASP.NET.

Chapter 1 Quick Reference

To	Do This
Start Internet Information Services console	Go to the Control Panel
	Select **Administrative Tools**
	Select **Internet Information Services**
Create a new virtual directory	Open the IIS Console
	Open the **Web Site**s node
	Open the **Default Web Site** node
	Click the right mouse button on the **Default Web Site** node
	Select **New Virtual Directory**
	Follow the wizard
Surf to a resource from IIS	Click the right mouse button on the resource
	Select **Browse**
See what file types are supported in an IIS virtual directory	Select the virtual directory
	Select the **Features View**
	Browse the Handler Mappings and the Module Mappings pages

Chapter 2
ASP.NET Application Fundamentals

After completing this chapter, you will be able to

- Create IIS Virtual Directories

- Develop an HTML page into an ASP.NET application

- Mix HTML with executable code and work with server-side script blocks

- Locate and view the assembly compiled by ASP.NET from an ASPX file

- Work with code-behind and code-beside execution models

- Use Visual Studio 2008 to create Web projects

This chapter covers the fundamentals involved in building an ASP.NET application. From a syntactical point of view, writing .NET code is similar to writing the classic ASP code that you may have seen during the late dot-com era. Many of the key symbols remain the same, and even some of the syntax survives directly. However, the entire underlying execution model changed dramatically between classic ASP and ASP.NET. Whereas executing classic ASP pages was primarily an exercise in rendering HTML, interpreting script code, and calling Component Object Model (COM) code, ASP.NET introduces an entirely new object-oriented execution model. ASP.NET execution centers around Common Language Runtime (CLR) classes that implement an interface named *IHttpHandler*. ASP.NET includes a number of classes that already implement *IHttpHandler*, and you may actually write your own implementation from scratch. Typically, though, you'll write ASP.NET pages that, under the covers, are generated by an ASP.NET-provided *IHttpHandler*.

In this chapter, we'll examine the ASP.NET execution model to see how ASP.NET enables its features. We'll take a bottom-up approach, showing how the simplest ASP.NET page executes. Along the way, we'll introduce various ASP.NET programming techniques, including code behind. We'll see how ASP.NET's compilation model works. Finally, we'll observe how ASP.NET's Web Form architecture operates and how it's all nicely wrapped up by Visual Studio 2008.

Let's start by studying a simple page to discover how we can evolve it using ASP.NET's programming techniques.

The Canonical Hello World Application

Nearly all programming texts start by using the technology at hand to present the classic string "Hello World" to the end user. This time, our job is to send the statement "Hello World" to the awaiting browser.

To see how ASP.NET works, we'll take the simplest Web page and develop it into an ASP.NET Web application. We won't use Visual Studio (or at least its full capabilities) quite yet. Visual Studio is such a rich development environment that building and running Web applications with it seems almost like magic. This will be a bare-bones example built from scratch so you can see exactly what's going on before we bring Visual Studio's full capabilities into the picture. We'll examine each iteration along the way to see what ASP.NET is doing.

Building the HelloWorld Web Application

1. Create a directory to hold the Web application files. Using either a command shell or Windows Explorer, create a new folder to hold the Web application files. Although the name of the directory is unimportant to Internet Information Services (IIS), call it something meaningful. I used c:\aspnetstepbystepexamples.

2. Map a virtual directory to hold the files. To start, we need a virtual directory in which to hold the source code. As we saw earlier when examining the Web Application architecture imposed by the Windows platform, IIS divides the applications on your server using virtual directories. There's nothing really magic about this scheme—it's mostly just a mapping between requests coming in over port 80 and some real directory on your machine. Virtual directories show IIS where to find the code you want to execute in your application.

   Run the **Control Panel**, and then go to **Administrative Tools** and start **Internet Information Services**. Expand the nodes in the tree on the left side to expose the Default Web Site node under the Web Sites node, as shown in the following illustration:

Then click the right mouse button on the **Default Web Site** node and select **Add Virtual Directory** from the context menu. (The illustration shows how to perform this operation in IIS 7.0. If you're using IIS 5.x or IIS 6.x, the screen will look slightly different—though you can add new virtual directories in the same way.) IIS will ask you to provide a name for the virtual directory:

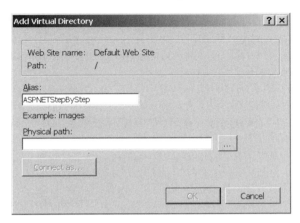

Call the Web site *ASPNETStepByStep*. This is the name by which your Web application will be known to the world. For example, when someone surfs to your Web site, they'll use the following URL:

http://www.mysite.com/ASPNETStepByStep

The name *mysite.com* is a fictitious site, only here for illustration. When you surf to this site on this computer, the server name will be *localhost*.

The wizard will ask you to provide a physical path for the virtual directory. Either browse to the physical directory you just created or type the name of the directory. Leave the IIS administration tool open. We'll be using other features in the following steps.

![Add Virtual Directory dialog box showing Web Site name: Default Web Site, Path: /, Alias: ASPNETStepByStep, Example: images, Physical path: C:\aspnetstepbystepexamples, with Connect as..., OK, and Cancel buttons]

Click **OK** to create the virtual directory.

3. Start with a simple HTML page. The easiest way to implement HelloWorld as a Web application is to store some text in an HTML file and browse to it.

   At this point we need a text editor. Notepad will work fine, or you can use Visual Studio to create the HTML file. If you use Visual Studio, then start Visual Studio and select **File**, **New**, and then **File**. Select **Text File** as the file type and then click **Open**. A new, blank file will be opened in Visual Studio's editor.

   Type the following HTML text between the body's opening and closing tags. Save the file as *HelloWorld.htm* within your new physical directory (the one that's been mapped to a virtual directory from the previous step).

   ```
   <!DOCTYPE html PUBLIC "...">

   <html xmlns="http://www.w3.org/1999/xhtml">
     <head>
       <title>Untitled Page</title>
     </head>

     <body>
       <h1> Hello World </h1>
       Nothing really showing here yet, except some HTML...
     </body>
   </html>
   ```

4. Browse to the page. There are two ways to do this. First, you may browse to the page by selecting the file from within IIS. Navigate to the directory in IIS (the IIS control panel should still be open if you haven't closed it). Select the **Content View** tab near the bottom of the main pane. You'll see the files in the directory. Click the right mouse button on the HelloWorld.htm file and select **Browse**. Alternatively, you may type the entire URL into the browser navigation bar:

   http://localhost/ASPNETStepByStep/helloworld.htm

   The browser will send an HTTP request to the server. On the Microsoft platform, IIS will see the HTM file extension and simply return the contents of the file to the browser. Because the text is marked using standard HTML tags, the browser understands it and displays it correctly.

Here's how the file appears to the end browser:

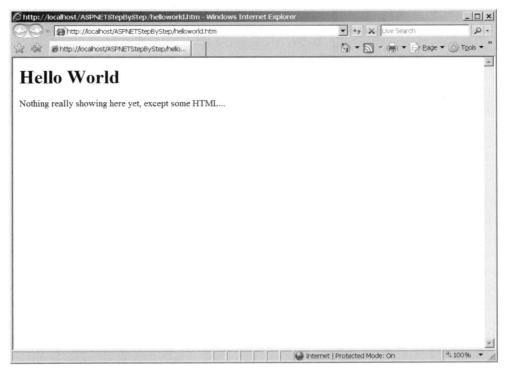

5. Convert the HTML file to an ASP.NET application. Take the HelloWorld.htm file that you were working on and convert it into an ASP.NET application. Turning this file into an ASP.NET application involves two small steps: adding a single line to the top of the file (the *Page* directive) and renaming the file to *HelloWorld.aspx*. This text represents an implementation of HelloWorld that works within the ASP.NET framework (be sure to save the file as *HelloWorld.aspx* by choosing **Save HelloWorld.htm As** from the **File** menu):

```
<%@ Page Language="C#" %>
<!DOCTYPE html PUBLIC "...">

<html xmlns="http://www.w3.org/1999/xhtml">
  <head>
    <title>Untitled Page</title>
  </head>

  <body>
    <h1> Hello World </h1>
    Nothing really showing here yet, except some HTML...
  </body>
</html>
```

When you fire up your browser and surf to this file within the virtual directory on your computer, you'll see the following in your browser.

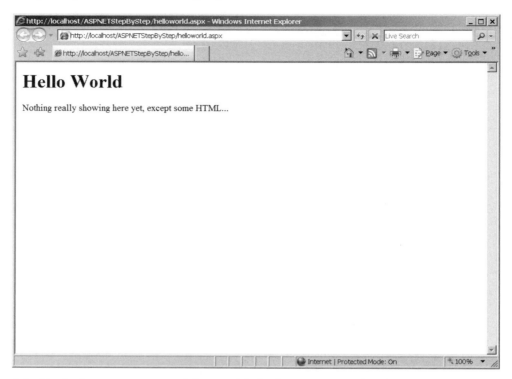

Admittedly, it may seem a small feat to simply show some text in a browser. However, it shows how a simple ASP.NET application works when using IIS.

6. View the HTML source that the browser is interpreting. While the content from the previous step is showing in your browser, use the **View**, **Source** menu to show the HTML source text being processed by the browser. It should look like this:

```
<!DOCTYPE html PUBLIC "-//W3C//DTD XHTML 1.0 Transitional//EN" "http://www.w3.org/TR/
xhtml1/DTD/xhtml1-transitional.dtd">
<html xmlns="http://www.w3.org/1999/xhtml" >
<head>
    <title>Untitled Page</title>
</head>
<body>
        <h1> Hello World </h1>
        Nothing really showing here yet, except some HTML...
</body>
</html>
```

Notice this text is almost identical to the text in Hello.aspx (without the *Page* directive: *<%@ Page Language="C#" %>*). In this case, you can see that the page-processing logic is fairly simple. That is, the ASP.NET runtime is simply spitting out the text within the file.

A Note about Application Pools

IIS 6.x and 7.0 support a feature called application pooling. One of the primary purposes behind application pooling is to support application isolation. For example, imagine you wanted to isolate the Web applications running in the same computer from other software managed by IIS. By creating a separate application pool for each Web application, you tell IIS to run the application in its own worker process. If anything bad happens in one application pool, the other applications will continue to run unaffected.

Application pooling also lets you govern the security aspects of a Web application. Some applications may need a higher degree of security, whereas others may not.

IIS 5.x runs the ASP.NET worker process as LocalSystem. LocalSystem has system administrator privileges. This has interesting implications because the account can access virtually any resource on the server. IIS 6.x and 7.x allow you to set the identity of the worker process to be the same as that of the application pool level. Application pools operate under the NetworkService account by default—which does not have as many access rights as LocalSystem.

The *Page* directive appearing at the top of the code is used by the ASP.NET runtime as it compiles the code. The *Page* directive shown above is fairly simple—it tells the runtime to compile this code and base it on the *Page* class and to treat any code syntax it encounters as C# code. ASP.NET supports integrating ASPX files with assemblies, which we'll see shortly. In subsequent examples, we'll see how ASP.NET compiles code on the fly and stores the assemblies in a temporary directory. There's no C# code in HelloWorld.aspx, so let's add some.

Mixing HTML with Executable Code

Classic ASP had an interesting way of marking code segments within a page. ASP always supported the classic script tag (*<script> </script>*) where anything found between the script tags was treated as executable code. However, in classic ASP, the script blocks were sent to the browser, and it became the browser's job to run the script. In addition to client-side script blocks, a classic ASP Web page could define script blocks to be interpreted on the server. These methods often performed tasks such as database lookups. Causing code to execute on the server involved marking executable segments with angle braces and percent signs like this:

```
<% ExecuteMe() %>
```

ASP.NET also supports server-side code execution. To write code that executes inline, simply mark it with the <% %> tags as well. When ASP.NET parses the file to manufacture the runtime class representing the page (more on that shortly), it will insert whatever code it finds between the execution tags as executable code. The only requirement is that the code between the execution tags is valid C# (because that's the language specified in the *Page* directive).

Adding executable code inline

1. Add executable code to the Web application. Create a new blank text file from within Visual Studio. Type the following code into the text file and save it as *HelloWorld2.aspx*.

```
<%@ Page Language="C#" Debug="true" %>
<html>
    <body>
        <h1>Hello World!!!</h1>
        <%
            // This block will execute in the Render_Control method
            Response.Write("Check out the family tree: <br/> <br/>");
            Response.Write(this.GetType().ToString());
            Response.Write(" which derives from: <br/> ");
            Response.Write(this.GetType().BaseType.ToString());
            Response.Write(" which derives from: <br/> ");
            Response.Write(this.GetType().BaseType.BaseType.ToString());
            Response.Write(" which derives from: <br/> ");
            Response.Write(
              this.GetType().BaseType.BaseType.BaseType.ToString());
            Response.Write(" which derives from: <br/> ");
            Response.Write(
              this.GetType().BaseType.BaseType.BaseType.BaseType.ToString());
        %>
    </body>
</html>
```

This code is almost exactly identical to code you'd see in a classic ASP application—including references to the *Response* object. In classic ASP, the *Response* object was one of those intrinsic objects, perennially available to the page's execution block. For the sake of a complete explanation, the *Response* object in classic ASP was a *COM* object that hung off the thread managed by the lower level components (the Internet Services Application Programming Interface DLL, or the ISAPI DLL). Notice that ASP.NET also has a *Response* object. However, this *Response* object is part of the *HttpContext* managed by the ASP.NET pipeline and is in no way related to the classic ASP object except in name.

2. Browse to the ASP.NET page. Surf to the Web page using Internet Explorer. The page should look like this in the browser:

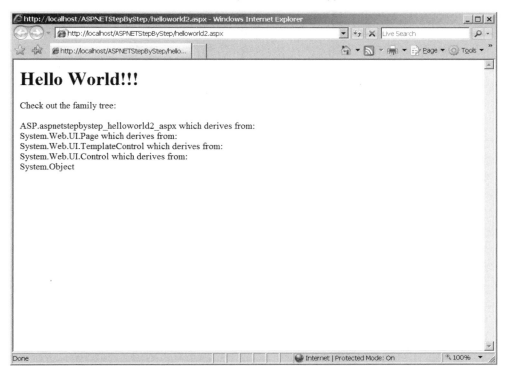

The output produced by HelloWorld2.aspx shows a very important aspect of ASP.NET's execution model. Before moving on, take a look at the inline code listed in the previous exercise and compare it to the output appearing in the browser. Notice the code includes statements like

```
Response.Write(this.GetType().BaseType.ToString());
```

Of course, the C# *this* keyword specifies an instance of a class. The code that's executing is clearly part of a member function of a class instance. The output shown by the browser indicates the class rendering the HTML to the browser is named *ASP.aspnetstepbystep_HelloWorld2_aspx*, and it derives from a class named *System.Web.UI.Page*. We'll learn more about this later in the chapter.

Server-Side Executable Blocks

ASP.NET also supports server-side code blocks (not just inline execution tags). ASP.NET adds a new *runat* attribute to the script tag that tells ASP.NET to execute the code block at the server end.

Adding Executable Code via a Script Block

1. Add an executable script block to the page. Create a new text file in Visual Studio. Type the following code into Visual Studio's editor. Note that the code separates rendered HTML from the script block that runs at the server. Save the file as *HelloWorld3.aspx* in your virtual directory.

```
<%@ Page Language="C#" Debug="true" %>
<script runat="server">
    void ShowLineage()
    {
        Response.Write("Check out the family tree: <br/> <br/>");
        Response.Write(this.GetType().ToString());
        Response.Write(" which derives from: <br/> ");
        Response.Write(this.GetType().BaseType.ToString());
        Response.Write(" which derives from: <br/> ");
        Response.Write(this.GetType().BaseType.BaseType.ToString());
        Response.Write(" which derives from: <br/> ");
        Response.Write(
          this.GetType().BaseType.BaseType.BaseType.ToString());
        Response.Write(" which derives from: <br/> ");
        Response.Write(
          this.GetType().BaseType.BaseType.BaseType.BaseType.ToString());
    }
</script>
<html>
    <body>
        <h1>Hello World!!!</h1>
        <%
            ShowLineage();
        %>
    </body>
</html>
```

As with the inline execution blocks, the most important criterion for the contents of the script block is for its syntax to match that of the language specified in the *Page* directive. The example above specifies a single method named *ShowLineage()*, which is called from within the page.

2. Surf to the page. Notice that the output of HelloWorld2.aspx and HelloWorld3.aspx is identical.

Marking the <script> tag containing the *ShowLineage* method with the *runat=server* attribute causes ASP.NET to execute the code on the server. But while classic ASP interprets the script block using the designated script language, ASP.NET has an entirely different execution model—the whole page is actually compiled into a class that runs under the Common Language Runtime (CLR). Here's how the ASP.NET compilation model works.

A Trip through the ASP.NET Architecture

When it arrives on the Web server, the HTTP request/response is routed through many server-side objects for processing. Once a request ends up at the server, it winds its way through the IIS/ASP.NET pipeline. The best way to understand the path of an HTTP request through ASP.NET is to follow a request as it originates in the browser and is intercepted by Internet Information Services and your Web application.

After an end user hits the Return key after typing in a URL, the browser sends an HTTP GET request to the target site. The request travels through a series of routers until it finally hits your Web server and is picked up on port 80. If your system has software listening to port 80, then the software can handle the request. On the Microsoft platform, the software most often listening to port 80 is IIS. For the time being, ASP.NET works with three versions of IIS: version 5.x (if you are using Windows XP Pro), version 6.x (if you are using Windows Server 2003), and version 7.0 (if you are using Windows Vista or Windows Server 2008).

The general flow of the requests is the same, regardless of which version of IIS you choose. IIS maintains a mapping between file extensions and binary components capable of interpreting the request (we'll see more about the binary components later). When a request comes in, IIS reads the file name named in the request and routes the request to the appropriate component.

Earlier versions of IIS (prior to version 7.0) implemented such features as client authentication and output caching independently of ASP.NET. That is, IIS and ASP.NET each implemented their own versions of these features. IIS 7.0 now integrates the ASP.NET versions of these features (some of which we'll see in future chapters). As far as IIS 7.0's ramifications to ASP.NET developers, running in Integrated mode makes .NET functionality part of the core pipeline. Features such as forms authentication can now be applied to a wide range of content—not just ASP.NET forms. For example, this helps when trying to secure an entire Web site using a uniform authentication method.

For the purposes of illustration, the following pictures show how IIS 7.0 routes requests of various types. The following shows IIS 7.0's module mappings when running Integrated mode.

Also for illustration purposes, the following shows IIS 7.0 handler mappings when running Integrated mode:

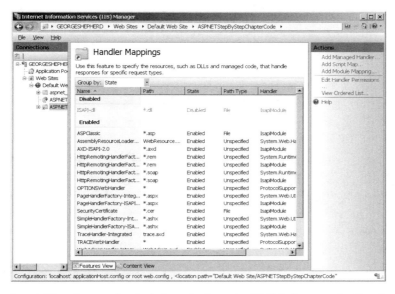

In addition to running in Integrated mode, IIS 7.0 also runs in Classic mode to support backward compatibility. When running in Classic mode, IIS 7.0 uses the module and handler architecture to pass processing to specific traditional binary components (that is, ISAPI DLLs).

To illustrate how mappings work in Classic mode, the following graphic shows IIS 7.0 module mappings running in Classic mode:

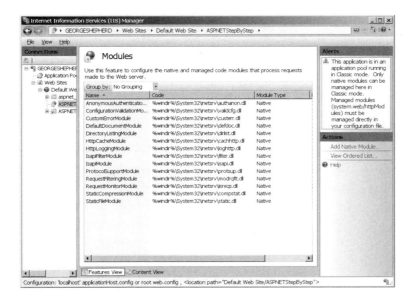

The following graphic shows IIS 7.0 running in Classic mode and its module mappings:

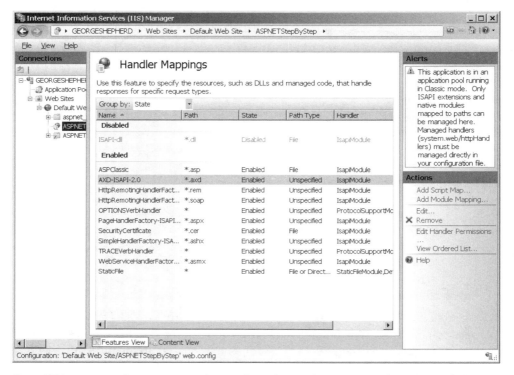

Once IIS intercepts the request and maps it to the worker process, the request follows a very specific path through the pipeline. We'll look at each part of the pipeline in more detail in coming sections. The outline of the request's path through IIS 5.x and 6.x is this:

1. The request lands in IIS.

2. IIS routes the request to aspnet_isapi.dll.

   2.1. If IIS 5.x is running, IIS asp_isapi.dll routes the request through a pipe to aspnet_wp.exe.

   2.2. If IIS 6.x is running, the request is already in the worker process.

3. ASP.NET packages the request context into an instance of *HttpContext*.

4. ASP.NET pipes the request through an instance of an *HttpApplication* object (or an *HttpApplication*-derived object).

5. If the application object is interested in receiving any of the request preprocessing events, *HttpApplication* fires the events to the application object. Any *HttpModules* that have subscribed to these events will receive the notifications as well.

6. Runtime instantiates a handler and handles the request.

Figure 2-1 shows how IIS version 5.x and ASP.NET work together to handle HTTP requests. Figure 2-2 shows how IIS version 6.x works with ASP.NET to handle requests.

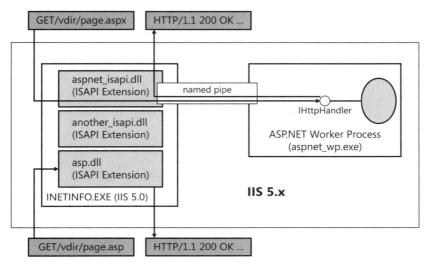

FIGURE 2-1 IIS 5.x working in concert with ASP.NET

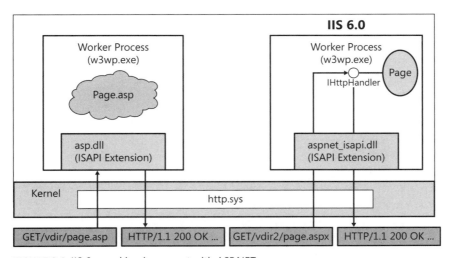

FIGURE 2-2 IIS 6.x working in concert with ASP.NET

By contrast, the request path through IIS 7.0 is slightly different. Here's a request's path through IIS 7.0:

1. The browser makes a request for a resource on the Web server.

2. HTTP.SYS picks up the request on the server.

3. HTTP.SYS uses the WAS to find configuration information to pass on to the WWW Service.

4. WAS passes the configuration information to the WWW Service, which configures HTTP.SYS.

5. WAS starts a worker process in the application pool for which the request was destined.

6. The worker process processes the request and returns the response to HTTP.SYS.

7. HTTP.SYS sends the response to the client.

Figure 2-3 shows the relationship between IIS 7.0 and ASP.NET.

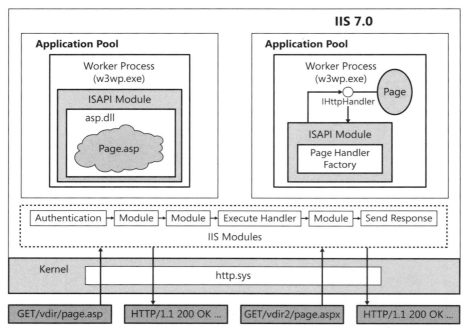

FIGURE 2-3 ASP.NET and IIS 7.0

Throughout the forthcoming chapters, we'll follow a request through the ASP.NET pipeline. You can plug into the ASP.NET pipeline at a number of distinct points to deal with various aspects of handling the requests. For example, if you'd like to do any preprocessing, you can either override event handlers in the *HttpApplication* class or you may write HTTP modules and plug them into the pipeline. While the *System.Web.UI.Page* class provides as much functionality as you'll ever need for building Web-based user interfaces, the pipeline is flexible enough that you can easily write your own custom handlers.

The ASP.NET Compilation Model

One of the most important improvements Microsoft has made to the ASP development environment is to build the Web request handling framework out of classes. Pushing request processing into a class-based architecture allows for a Web-handling framework that's compiled. When ASP.NET pages are first accessed, they are compiled into assemblies.

This is advantageous because subsequent access loads the page directly from the assembly. Whereas classic ASP interpreted the same script code over and over, ASP.NET applications are compiled into .NET assemblies and ultimately perform better and are safer. Because the code is compiled, it runs more quickly since it doesn't have to be interpreted. In addition, the managed runtime is a type-safe environment; you won't see the same sorts of errors and anomalies that you'd encounter in a scripting environment (as was the case for classic ASP).

In addition, compiling the Web request framework allows for more robust and consistent debugging. Whenever you run an ASP.NET application from Visual Studio, you can debug it as though it were a normal desktop application.

ASP.NET compiles .aspx files automatically. To get an .aspx page to compile, you simply need to surf to the .aspx file containing the code. When you do so, ASP.NET compiles the page into a class. However, you won't see that assembly containing the class anywhere near your virtual directory. ASP.NET copies the resulting assemblies to a temporary directory.

The .NET versions of Microsoft Visual Studio have always included a tool named Intermediate Language Disassembler (ILDASM) that uses reflection to reverse compile an assembly so you may view its contents. The result is an easily negotiated tree view you may use to drill down to the contents of the assembly. Right now, that's the important thing. (If you want to peer any more deeply into the assembly and see the actual Intermediate Language, ILDASM will show you that as well.)

Viewing the ASP.NET assemblies

Here's how to view the assemblies generated by ASP.NET.

1. To run ILDASM, open the Visual Studio .NET 2008 command prompt and type **ILDASM.**

2. Select **File**, **Open.**

3. Find the assembly compiled by the ASP.NET runtime. Go to C:\WINDOWS\Microsoft .NET\Framework\v2.0.50727\Temporary ASP.NET Files\aspnetstepbystep\. The subdirectory is named *v2.0.50727* at the time of this writing. The final subdirectory may be slightly different. You'll see some oddly named directories underneath. For example, on my machine, the subdirectory names generated by ASP.NET are *110a3860* and *9bf9cc39*. The directory name(s) will most likely be different on your machine. There's no easy way to figure out which directories have the code that just executed (though looking at the dates and times of the file creation may help), so you'll need to drill

down into the directories until you unearth some DLL files. Depending on how many times you've run the application, you may see several files. Open the files one at a time until ILDASM displays something similar to what's shown in Figure 2-4.

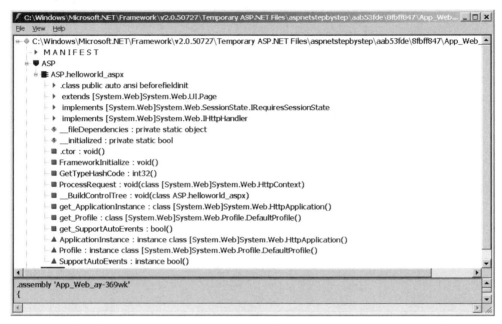

FIGURE 2-4 ILDASM showing the contents of the assembly generated by ASP.NET after surfing to HelloWorld.aspx

ASP.NET has used this temporary directory strategy since version 1.0. The reason ASP.NET copies these files to a temporary directory is to solve a long-standing problem that plagued classic ASP. Classic ASP Web sites often depended on *COM* objects to do complex operations such as database lookups and transactions. When you deploy a classic ASP site and clients begin accessing it, those files become locked. Of course, that's not really a problem—until you decide to upgrade or modify part of the Web site.

Classic ASP locked files during execution, meaning you couldn't copy new files into the virtual directory without shutting down the Web site. For many Web deployment scenarios, this is a bad option. Because ASP.NET copies the files and the components to the temporary directory and *runs them from there*, they're not locked. When it is time to update a component, simply copy the new assembly into the virtual directory. You can do that because it's not locked.

Coding Options

In addition to supporting inline code (that is, including executable code directly inside a server-side script block), modern ASP.NET offers two other distinct options for managing code: ASP.NET 1.x code behind, and modern ASP.NET code beside. ASP.NET supports code behind for backward compatibility. Code beside is the style employed by Visual Studio 2008. Let's look at these.

ASP.NET 1.x Style

ASP.NET continues to support ASP.NET 1.x style code behind. This may be important to understand if you ever run into any legacy code from that era. Using the code-behind directives in the ASPX file, you provide the code to run behind the page in a separate class and use the *Page* directive to tell ASP.NET which class to apply to the page. Then you tell ASP.NET the name of the file containing the source code for the class. For example, imagine this code is placed in a file named *HelloWorld4Code.cs*:

```
using System.Web;
public class HelloWorld4Code : System.Web.UI.Page
{
    public void ShowLineage()
    {
        Response.Write("Check out the family tree: <br/> <br/>");
        Response.Write(this.GetType().ToString());
        Response.Write(" which derives from: <br/> ");
        Response.Write(this.GetType().BaseType.ToString());
        Response.Write(" which derives from: <br/> ");
        Response.Write(this.GetType().BaseType.BaseType.ToString());
        Response.Write(" which derives from: <br/> ");
        Response.Write(
          this.GetType().BaseType.BaseType.BaseType.ToString());
        Response.Write(" which derives from: <br/> ");
        Response.Write(
          this.GetType().BaseType.BaseType.BaseType.BaseType.ToString());
    }
}
```

An ASP.NET page that uses the *HelloWorld4Code* class to drive the page might then look like this:

```
<%@ Page Language="C#" Inherits="HelloWorld4Code"
    Src="HelloWorld4Code.cs" Debug="true" %>
<html>
    <body>
        <h1>Hello World!!!</h1>
        <%
            this.ShowLineage();
        %>
    </body>
</html>
```

With the ASP.NET 1.x style of code behind, ASP.NET sees the *Src* attribute in the directives and compiles that file. ASP.NET reads the *Inherits* attribute to figure out how to base the class that runs the page. In the example above, ASP.NET uses the *HelloWorld4Code* class to drive the page.

By using the *Src* attribute, you tell the ASP.NET runtime to compile the file named by the *Src* attribute value. The ASP.NET runtime will compile it into the temporary directory. Alternatively, you may also precompile the file into an assembly containing the *HelloWorld4Code* class. For this to work, the precompiled assembly must appear in the bin directory of your virtual directory. If you precompile the page class and put the assembly in the bin directory, you don't even need to mention the source code file. In the absence of an *Src* attribute, the ASP.NET runtime will search the assemblies in the bin directory looking for the class specified in the *Inherits* attribute.

Modern ASP.NET Style

The other coding option for ASP.NET is new starting with version 2.0. This model is sometimes referred to as code beside. Consider the following ASP.NET page:

```
<%@ Page Language="C#" CodeFile="HelloWorld5Code.cs"
    Inherits="HelloWorld5Code" %>
<html>
    <body>
        <h1>Hello World!!!</h1>
        <%
            // This block will execute in the Render_Control method
            ShowLineage();
        %>
    </body>
</html>
```

It references the code found in the HelloWorld5Code.cs file:

```
using System.Web;
public partial class HelloWorld5Code : System.Web.UI.Page
{
    public void ShowLineage()
    {
        Response.Write("Check out the family tree: <br/> <br/>");
        Response.Write(this.GetType().ToString());
        Response.Write(" which derives from: <br/> ");
        Response.Write(this.GetType().BaseType.ToString());
        Response.Write(" which derives from: <br/> ");
        Response.Write(this.GetType().BaseType.BaseType.ToString());
        Response.Write(" which derives from: <br/> ");
        Response.Write(
        this.GetType().BaseType.BaseType.BaseType.ToString());
        Response.Write(" which derives from: <br/> ");
        Response.Write(
        this.GetType().BaseType.BaseType.BaseType.BaseType.ToString());
    }
}
```

In this case, ASP.NET looks to the *CodeFile* directive to figure out what code to compile. ASP .NET expects to find a partial class to implement the page's logic. Partial classes let you split the definition of a type (*class, struct,* or *interface*) between multiple source files, with a portion of the class definition living in each file. Compiling the source code files generates the entire class. This is especially useful when working with generated code, such as that generated by Visual Studio. You can augment a class without going back and changing the original code. Visual Studio .NET 2008 prefers the code-beside/partial class code representation.

The following short listings, Listing 2-1 and Listing 2-2, show two files that implement a singular class named *SplitMe*.

LISTING 2-1 Partial1.cs

```
// Partial1.cs
using System;

public partial class SplitMe
{

    public void Method1()
    {
        Console.WriteLine("SplitMe Method1");
    }
}
```

LISTING 2-2 Partial2.cs

```
// Partial2.CS
using System;

public partial class SplitMe
{
    public static void Main()
    {
        SplitMe splitMe = new SplitMe();
        splitMe.Method1();
        splitMe.Method2();
    }

    public void Method2()
    {
        Console.WriteLine("SplitMe Method2");
    }
}
```

To compile the previous example, you may build the project with Visual Studio, or you may use the following command line in the Visual Studio Command Prompt (if these are just loose files):

```
csc /t:exe Partial1.cs Partial2.cs
```

This will generate an executable file named *Partial2.exe*.

After working with ASP.NET source code in the raw, it's time to look at how Visual Studio and ASP.NET work together. Visual Studio .NET 2008 brings many new features for creating and developing Web applications, as we'll see when working through subsequent examples.

The ASP.NET HTTP Pipeline

As soon as ASP.NET 1.0 was released, it offered a huge improvement over classic ASP by introducing well-defined code processing modules that together form the *ASP.NET HTTP pipeline*. Classic ASP was patched together from several disparate components (IIS, the Web Application Manager, and the ASP ISAPI DLL). The *Request* and *Response* objects were *COM* objects hanging off the threads owned by IIS. If you wanted to do any processing outside the context of ASP, you needed to write an ISAPI filter. If you wanted to write code to execute during processing, it had to occur within a *COM* object implementing *IDispatch* (severely limiting the available types of data you could use and negatively affecting performance). If you wanted to write any request-handling code (outside the context of ASP), you had to write a separate ISAPI DLL. The ASP.NET HTTP pipeline includes the facilities to do these things, but in a much more manageable way.

In ASP.NET, your application has the opportunity to perform preprocessing and postprocessing within *HttpModules*. If you use IIS 5.x or 6.x as your Web server, the ASP.NET pipeline stands by itself, and requests are processed completely by ASP.NET as soon as aspnet_isapi.dll hands control off to the ASP.NET worker process. If you're using IIS 7.0 as your Web server, the ASP.NET pipeline is integrated into the server, allowing you to apply most ASP.NET services to non-ASP.NET content. In any case, your application also has the opportunity to process application-wide events using the *HttpApplication* object. Because of ASP.NET's object model, the need for separate *COM*-based scripting objects on the server disappears. The endpoint of all requests is an implementation of *IHttpHandler*. ASP.NET already includes some useful implementations of *IHttpHandler* (that is, *System.Web.UI.Page* and *System.Web.Services .WebService*). However, you may easily write your own (as we'll see later).

The IIS 5.x and IIS 6.x Pipeline

Once a request comes into the *AppDomain* managed by the ASP.NET runtime, ASP.NET uses the *HttpWorkerRequest* class to store the request information. Following that, the runtime wraps the request's information in a class named *HttpContext*. The *HttpContext* class includes all the information you'd ever want to know about a request, including references to the current request's *HttpRequest* and *HttpResponse* objects. The runtime produces an instance of *HttpApplication* (if one is not already available) and then fires a number of application-wide events (such as *BeginRequest* and *AuthenticateRequest*). These events are also pumped through any *HttpModules* attached to the pipeline. Finally, ASP.NET figures out what kind of handler is required to handle the request, creates one, and asks the handler to process the request. After the handler deals with the request, ASP.NET fires a number of postprocessing events (like *EndRequest*) through the *HttpApplication* object and the *HttpModules*.

Figure 2-5 illustrates the structure of the ASP.NET pipeline inside the ASP.NET worker process using IIS 6.x (the only difference from IIS 5.x is the name of the worker process).

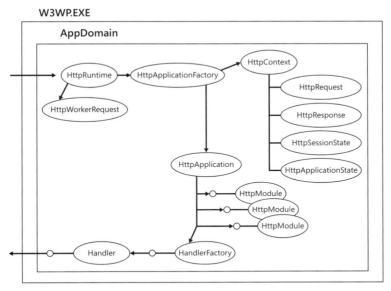

FIGURE 2-5 Main components of the HTTP pipeline within ASP.NET

The IIS 7.0 Integrated Pipeline

The Integrated IIS 7.0 pipeline is very similar to the ASP.NET HTTP pipeline that's been around since ASP.NET was first released (which you see in Figure 2-5). As you can see from earlier investigations using the IIS 7.0 management console, the IIS 7.0 Integrated pipeline employs modules and handlers just like earlier versions of the ASP.NET's HTTP pipeline. However, whereas ASP.NET's HTTP pipeline runs entirely within the ASP.NET worker process, IIS 7.0 runs the pipeline as directed by IIS. The Integrated pipeline in IIS 7.0 works in very much the same way as the ASP.NET pipeline, so the application-wide events exposed through the *HttpApplication* events work just as before (we'll discuss application-wide events in detail later). When running your application through IIS 7.0 in Integrated mode, your request no longer passes through aspnet_isapi.dll. IIS 7.0 pushes the request through the modules and handlers directly.

Tapping the Pipeline

While some of the parts within the pipeline are unavailable to you as a developer, several parts are available directly and provide a useful means of managing your request as it goes through the pipeline. The most important parts of the pipeline that you can touch include the *HttpApplication*, the *HttpContext*, the *HttpModule*, and the *HttpHandler*.

The following sections supply some details about these critical sections within the HTTP request path.

The *HttpApplication*

At this point, you understand the nature of a Web application as being very different from that of a normal desktop application. The code that you're writing is responsible for spitting some HTML response back to a client. In many ways, the model hearkens back to the terminal-mainframe model prevalent during the mid-1970s. In ASP.NET, the endpoint of a request is an implementation of *IHttpHandler* (even if that handler ultimately forms a Web page based on your ASP.NET Web Forms code).

HTTP handlers live for a very short period of time. They stick around long enough to handle a request, and then they disappear. For very simple applications, this model might be just fine. However, imagine the requirements of even a modest commercial-grade application. If all you had to work with was these ephemeral handlers, you'd have no way to achieve application-wide functionality. For example, imagine you wanted to cache data to avoid round-trips to the database. You'd need to store that data in a place where all the HTTP handlers could get to it.

The *HttpApplication* class exists for that purpose—to act as a rendezvous point for your request processing. During the lifetime of a Web application, the *HttpApplication* objects serve as places to hold application-wide data and handle application-side events.

The *HttpContext*

The *HttpContext* class acts as a central location in which you can access parts of the current request as it travels through the pipeline. In fact, every aspect of the current request is available through *HttpContext*. Even though the *HttpContext* components are really just references to other parts of the pipeline, having them available in a single place makes it much easier to manage the request.

Here is an abbreviated listing of *HttpContext*, showing the parts you'll be using most frequently in developing Web applications. The members are exposed as properties.

```
class HttpContext
{
    public static HttpContext Current {...};
    public HttpRequest Request {...};
    public HttpResponse Response {...};
    public HttpSessionState Session {...};
    public HttpServerUtility Server {...};
    public HttpApplicationState Application {...};
    public HttpApplication ApplicationInstance {...};
    public IDictionary Items {...};
    public IPrincipal User {...};
    public IHttpHandler CurrentHandler {...};
    public Cache Cache {...};
    ...
}
```

The static *Current* property gives you a means of getting to the current request at any time. Many times, the *HttpContext* is passed as a method parameter (as in the method *IHttpHandler .RequestProcess(HttpContext ctx)*); however, there may be times when you need the context even though it hasn't been passed as a parameter. The *Current* property lets you grab the current process out of thin air. For example, this is how you might use *HttpContext.Current:*

```
Public void DealWithRequest()
{
   HttpContext thisRequest = HttpContext.Current;
   thisRequest.Response.Write("<h3> Hello World</h3>");
}
```

As you can see from the previous snippet of the *HttpContext* object, the properties within *HttpContext* include such nuggets as

- a reference to the context's *Response* object (so you can send output to the client)
- a reference to the *Request* object (so you can find information about the request itself)
- a reference to the central application itself (so you can get to the application state)
- a reference to a per-request dictionary (for storing items for the duration of a request)
- a reference to the application-wide cache (to store data and avoid round-trips to the database)

We'll be seeing a lot more of the context—especially when we look at writing a custom *HttpHandler*.

HttpModules

While the *Application* object is suitable for handling application-wide events and data on a small scale, sometimes application-wide tasks need a little heavier machinery. *HttpModules* serve that purpose.

ASP.NET includes a number of predefined *HttpModules*. For example, session state, authentication, and authorization are handled via *HttpModules*. Writing *HttpModules* is pretty straightforward and is a great way to handle complex application-wide operations. For example, if you wanted to write some custom processing that occurs before each request, using *HttpModules* is a good way to do it. We'll see *HttpModules* up close later.

HttpHandlers

The last stop a request makes in the pipeline is an *HttpHandler*. Any class implementing the interface *IHttpHandler* qualifies as a handler. When a request finally reaches the end of the pipeline, ASP.NET consults the configuration file to see if the particular file extension is mapped to an *HttpHandler*. If it is, the ASP.NET loads the handler and calls the handler's *IHttpHandler.ProcessRequest* method to execute the request.

Visual Studio and ASP.NET

Visual Studio .NET 2008 expands your options for locating your Web sites during development. The Visual Studio .NET 2008 wizards define four separate Web site projects: local IIS Web sites, file system–based Web sites, FTP Web sites, and remote Web sites.

Here's a rundown of the different types of Web sites available using the project wizard. Each is useful for a particular scenario, and having these options makes it much easier to develop and deploy an ASP.NET application with Visual Studio 2008 than with earlier versions.

Local IIS Web Sites

Creating a local IIS Web site is much like creating a Web site using the older versions of Visual Studio .NET specifying a local virtual directory. This option creates sites that run using IIS installed on your local computer. Local IIS Web sites store the pages and folders in the IIS default directory structure (that is, \Inetpub\wwwroot). By default, Visual Studio creates a virtual directory under IIS. However, you may create a virtual directory ahead of time and store the code for your Web site in any folder. The virtual directory just needs to point to that location.

One reason to create a local Web site is to test your application against a local version of IIS, for example, if you need to test such features as application pooling, ISAPI filters, or HTTP-based authentication. Even though a site is accessible from other computers, it's often much easier to test these aspects of your application when you can see it interact with IIS on your computer. To create a local Web site, you need to have administrative rights. For most developers, this is not an issue.

File System–Based Web Sites

File system–based Web sites live in any folder you specify. The folder may be on your local computer or on another computer sharing that folder. File-system Web sites do *not* require IIS running on your computer. Instead, you run pages by using the Visual Studio Web server.

Visual Studio Web Server

Until Visual Studio 2005, the development environment used IIS directly to serve up pages. That meant that developers needed to have IIS fully enabled on their machines to be able to develop effectively. This created a possible security compromise. Visual Studio 2008 includes its own built-in Web server. This lets you develop Web applications effectively even if you don't have IIS installed on your development machine.

File-system Web sites are useful for testing your site locally but independently of IIS. The most common approach is to create, develop, and test a file-system Web site. Then when it is time to deploy your site, simply create an IIS virtual directory on the deployment server and move the pages to that directory.

Because file-system Web sites employ the Visual Studio Web server rather than IIS, you may develop your Web site on your computer even when logged on as a user without administrative rights.

This scenario is useful for developing and testing those features of your site that you develop. Because IIS is out of the picture, you won't be able to work with (or have to deal with) such IIS features as ISAPI filters, application pooling, or authentication (though in many cases you won't need to worry about that sort of thing during development).

FTP Web Sites

In addition to creating HTTP-based sites, you may use Visual Studio to manage Web sites available through an FTP server. For example, if you use a remote hosting company to host your Web site, an FTP server offers a convenient way to move files back and forth between your development location and the hosting location.

Visual Studio connects to any FTP server for which you have read and write privileges. Once connected, you then use Visual Studio to manage the content on the remote FTP server.

You would use this option to deploy your Web site to a server that lacks FrontPage 2002 Server Extensions.

Remote Web Sites

The final option for developing and managing Web sites through Visual Studio is to use the remote Web sites option. Remote Web sites use IIS on another computer that is accessible over a network. In addition to running IIS, the remote computer must have IIS installed and needs to have FrontPage 2002 Server Extensions installed. Pages and folders on a remote site become stored under the default IIS folder on the remote computer.

This option is useful if you decide you want to move he Web site to its actual deployment server. In addition, the entire development team can work on the site simultaneously. The downside of this approach is that debugging and configuring a Web site remotely can sometimes be tricky because it's slow and hard to control the site as a whole.

Hello World and Visual Studio

To get started, let's use Visual Studio to generate the HelloWorld Web application.

1. Create a new Web site. To create a new Web site, select the following menu combination: **File**, **New**, and then **Web Site**. Visual Studio will display a dialog box like this one:

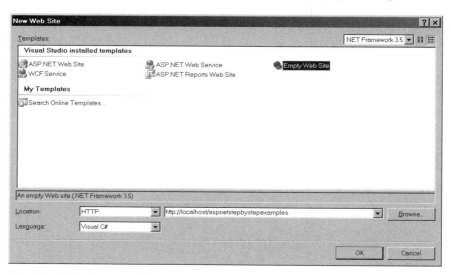

Give the Web site a useful name like *ASPNETStepByStepExamples*. Even though this is the same directory name used for the previous IIS examples, you can use it because Visual Studio will create the subdirectory under IIS's default subdirectory \inetpub\wwwroot.

Notice that several different kinds of sites are showing in the dialog box. Choose **Empty Web Site** for this example.

Choosing **Empty Web Site** causes Visual Studio to generate an ASP.NET solution file within a directory named Visual Studio 2008\Projects in your normal My Documents directory. Visual Studio will also create a new directory within your inetpub\wwwroot directory and map it as an IIS virtual directory. However, the virtual directory will be devoid of any files.

Selecting **ASP.NET Web Site** causes Visual Studio to generate a directory structure similar to the one generated by **Empty Web Site**. However, Visual Studio will throw in a default Web form and source code to go with (default.aspx and default.aspx.cs). You'll also get an App_Data directory that may contain data pertinent to your site (for example, a database file containing ASP.NET security information could be contained here).

2. Choose the language syntax. At this point, you have the option of choosing a syntax to use within your code. Choose among Visual Basic, C#, and J#. For this example, choose C#.

3. Create a local Web site. For this example, select **HTTP** from the location combo box to run this Web site locally on your machine. Visual Studio's default option is to create a Web site on your local machine file system. By using the HTTP project type, clients trying to access your Web site will have their requests directed through IIS. This is the best option to choose when learning how ASP.NET works with IIS because it gives you the chance to work with your Web site as an entire system, and you can use tracing and debugging on your local machine. Later examples that focus on specific ASP.NET features will use the more convenient file system–style project.

4. Add a HelloWorld page. To add the HelloWorld page to the new site, select **Website**, **Add New Item...** to reach the Add New Item dialog box:

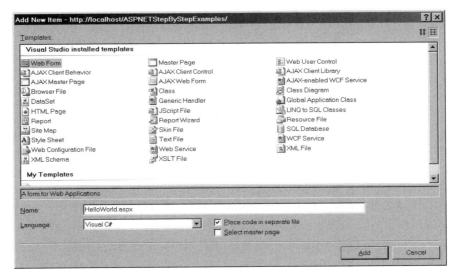

This dialog box lists all the various pieces you may add to your Web site. Topping the list is an item named *Web Form*. Select this option, and then type **HelloWorld.aspx** into the *Name* text box. Leave the other defaults the same.

Visual Studio will confront you with the pure ASP.NET code from the HelloWorld.aspx file.

Notice that the code generated by Visual Studio includes directives near the top connecting HelloWorld.aspx to the accompanying source file HelloWorld.aspx.cs (using the *CodeFile* and *Inherits* attributes in the *Page* directive). Following the directive is some initial HTML produced by Visual Studio.

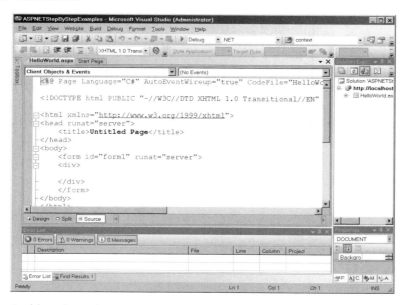

At this point, take a moment to explore the layout of Visual Studio. Along the top of the window, you'll see a number of toolbar buttons and menu options. We'll visit most of them throughout the course of this text. Directly beneath the code window, you'll see three tabs labeled **Design**, **Split**, and **Source** (the **Source** tab is selected by default). If you select the **Design** tab, you'll see what the page will look like in a browser. Right now, the page has no visible HTML tags or ASP.NET Web Forms controls, so the design view is blank.

To the right of the Source window, you'll see the Solution Explorer, which lists the components of your application that Visual Studio will compile into an executable code base. Along the top of the Solution Explorer, you'll find a number of buttons. By hovering your cursor over the buttons, you can see what they do. The following graphic shows how each button functions when an ASPX file is selected.

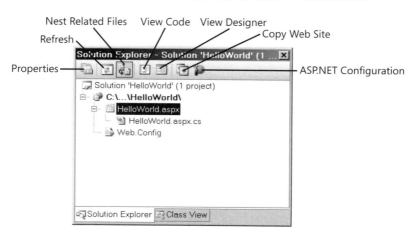

5. Write some code into the page. Select the HelloWorld.aspx file in Solution Explorer and then click the **View Code** button. This will show the C# code in the Source code window, like so:

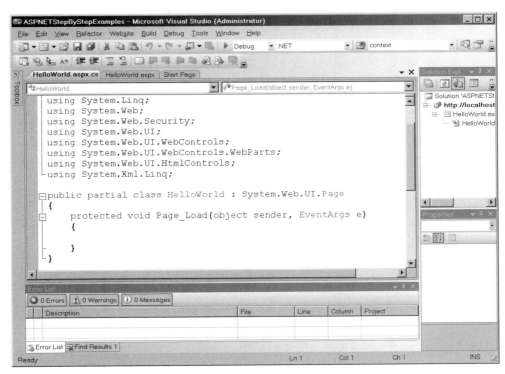

Add the following code to show the page's lineage (it's the same code from HelloWorld5 shown previously). The code you add should follow the *Page_Load* method:

```csharp
public void ShowLineage()
{
    Response.Write("Check out the family tree: <br/> <br/>");
    Response.Write(this.GetType().ToString());
    Response.Write(" which derives from: <br/> ");
    Response.Write(this.GetType().BaseType.ToString());
    Response.Write(" which derives from: <br/> ");
    Response.Write(this.GetType().BaseType.BaseType.ToString());
    Response.Write(" which derives from: <br/> ");
    Response.Write(
    this.GetType().BaseType.BaseType.BaseType.ToString());
    Response.Write(" which derives from: <br/> ");
    Response.Write(
    this.GetType().BaseType.BaseType.BaseType.BaseType.ToString());
}
```

The HelloWorld.aspx.cs file should look like the following:

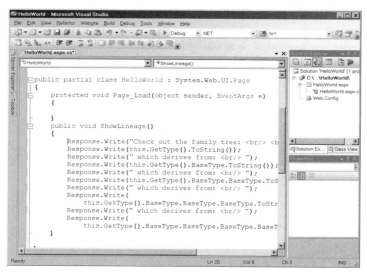

6. Call the *ShowLineage* method from the ASPX file. Select the **HelloWorld.aspx** tab atop the editor window to return to the visual designer and then select the **Source** tab near the bottom of the screen. With the HTML content showing, insert the following markup in the page. It should be placed between the opening and closing <div> tags:

```
<h2> Hello World!!!</h2>
<%
ShowLineage();
%>
```

The HelloWorld.aspx markup then would appear like the following:

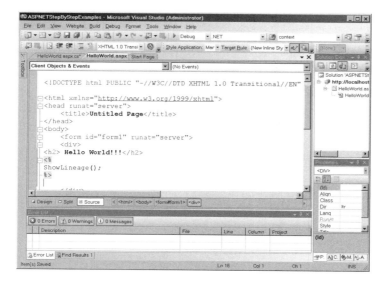

7. Now build the project and run the Web site from Visual Studio. To build the application, select **Build**, **Solution** from the main menu. If the source code has any errors, they'll appear in the Errors window in the bottom window.

To run the application, select **Debug**, **Start Without Debugging** (or press Ctrl-F5). Visual Studio will start up a copy of an Internet browser (Microsoft Internet Explorer by default) and browse the page. You should see a page like this (make sure the HelloWorld.aspx page is highlighted in the Solution Explorer):

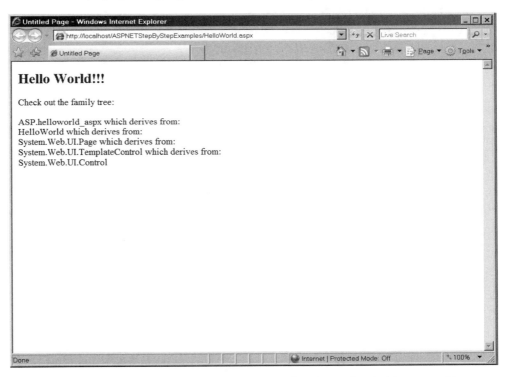

When you run this application, Visual Studio compiles the HelloWorld.aspx and its code-beside file, HelloWorld.aspx.cs, and moves them to the temporary ASP.NET directory. IIS is then called upon to activate the ASP.NET HTTP pipeline, which loads the compiled files (DLLs) and renders the page you just created.

Summary

We've just seen how ASP.NET works from a high level. When a client surfs to an ASPX file on your server, the request is pushed through IIS running on your server. IIS maps individual file extensions to specific ISAPI DLLs. When IIS sees the .aspx extension in the request, that ISAPI DLL is aspnet_isapi.dll. The request ends up within the ASP.NET worker process, which instantiates an HTTP handler to fulfill the request.

In the case of an ASPX file, ASP.NET instantiates a class derived from *System.Web.UI.Page* (which implements *IHttpHandler*). ASPX files are usually paired with source code files containing the source code for the page. The ASPX file behaves mainly as the presentation layer while the accompanying *Page* class contributes the logic behind the presentation layer.

Next up—all about *System.Web.UI.Page* and how Web forms work.

Chapter 2 Quick Reference

To	Do This
Create an FTP Web site in Visual Studio 2008	Select **File**, **New**, **Web Site** from the main menu. Select **FTP** from the *Locations* combo box.
	This option is useful for creating sites that will eventually be deployed by sending the bits to the site's host over FTP.
Create an HTTP Web site in Visual Studio 2008	Select **File**, **New**, **Web Site** from the main menu. Select **HTTP** from the *Locations* combo box.
	This option is useful for creating sites that use IIS as the Web server throughout the entire development cycle.
Create a file-system Web site in Visual Studio 2008	Select **File**, **New**, **Web Site** from the main menu. Select **File System** from the *Locations* combo box.
	This option creates sites that use Visual Studio's built-in Web server. That way, you may develop your own site even if you don't have IIS available on your machine.

Chapter 3
The Page Rendering Model

After completing this chapter, you will be able to

- Work directly with server-side control tags
- Work with Web forms and server-side controls using Visual Studio
- Work with postback events using Visual Studio
- Understand the ASP.NET Page rendering model

This chapter covers the heart of ASP.NET's Web Forms rendering model: controls. As we'll see here, *System.Web.UI.Page* works by partitioning the rendering process into small components known as server-side controls.

The entire tour of the ASP.NET control model will look at the fundamental control architecture. We'll start by looking at the HTML required to render controls in the browser. We'll take a very quick look at the classic ASP approach to displaying controls. Although you will probably never use classic ASP in your career, seeing it in this context will help you appreciate some of the problems ASP.NET has solved. This will lay the groundwork for following chapters in which we'll look at how controls can provide custom rendering, User controls, some of the standard user interface (UI) controls, and some of the modern, more complex controls. We'll start with the ASP.NET rendering model.

Rendering Controls as Tags

As we saw when looking at basic HTML Web forms, developing a Web-based UI is all about getting the right tags out to the browser. For example, imagine you wanted to have your application's UI appear in the client's browser as shown in Figure 3-1.

Getting this to appear on a client's browser means populating an HTML stream with the correct tags so the browser renders the screen using client-side controls. Listing 3-1 shows some HTML that does the job. If you would like to run this page, the file is named *BunchOfControls.htm*. You'll find it in the sample code for this chapter. To run the page, take the file and save it in a virtual directory and browse to it.

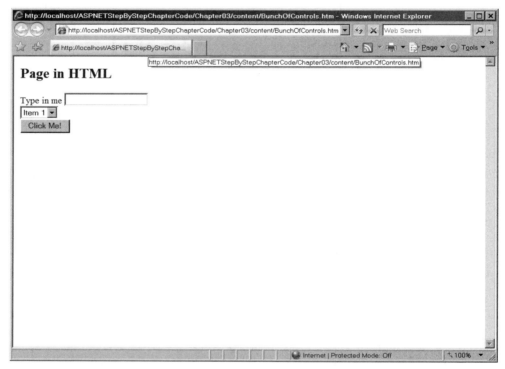

FIGURE 3-1 Some HTML tags rendered as controls in Internet Explorer

LISTING 3-1 Initial HTML Markup from BunchOfControls.htm

```html
<html>
<body>
<h2> Page in HTML </h2>
<form method="post" action="BunchOfControls.htm" id="Form1">
   <label>Type in me</label>
   <input name="textinfo" type="text" id="textinfo" />
   <br/>
   <select name="selectitems" id="ddl">
   <option value="Item 1">Item 1</option>
   <option value="Item 2">Item 2</option>
   <option value="Item 3">Item 3</option>
   <option value="Item 4">Item 4</option>

   </select>
   <br/>
   <input type="submit" name="clickme" value="Click Me!" id="clickme" />
</form>
</body>
</html>
```

Of course, using controls on a page usually implies dynamic content, so getting this HTML to the browser should happen dynamically, in a programmatic way. Classic ASP has facilities for rendering dynamic content. However, classic ASP generally relies on raw HTML for rendering its content. That means writing a page like the BunchOfControls.htm page shown in Listing 3-1 might look something like Listing 3-2 in classic ASP. Figure 3-2 shows how the ASP page renders in Internet Explorer.

LISTING 3-2 Source for BunchOfControls Page Using Classic ASP

```
<%@ Language="javascript" %>
<h2> Page in Classic ASP </h2>
<form>

    <label>Type in me</label>
    <input name="textinfo" type="text" id="textinfo" />
    <br/>
    <select name="selectitems" id="ddl">
    <option value="Item 1">Item 1</option>
    <option value="Item 2">Item 2</option>
    <option value="Item 3">Item 3</option>
    <option value="Item 4">Item 4</option>

</select>
    <br/>
    <input type="submit" name="clickme" value="Click Me!" id="clickme" />
<p>
    <% if (Request("textinfo") != "") { %>
        This was in the text box: <%=Request("textinfo") %> <br/>
        And this was in the selection control: <%=Request("selectitems") %>
    <% } %>
</p>

</form>
```

When you select an item from the selection control, notice that the page responds by telling you what you selected. This demonstrates ASP's support for dynamic content.

Notice that even though classic ASP offers a way to decide your page's content at runtime, you still have to create much of it using raw HTML. Also, the state of the controls is always reset between posts (we'll look at that when we examine ASP.NET's *ViewState* later). ASP.NET adds a layer of indirection between the raw HTML and the rendered page—that layer of indirection is provided by ASP.NET's collection of server-side controls. Server-side controls eliminate much of the tedium necessary to develop a Web-based UI in classic ASP.

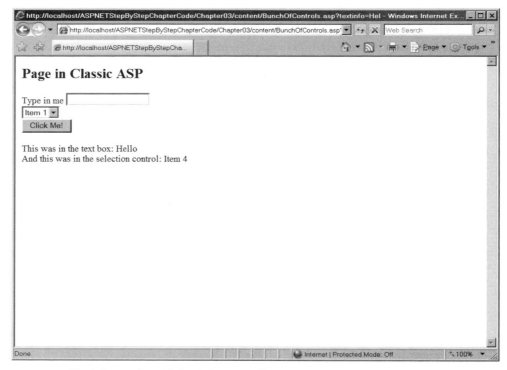

FIGURE 3-2 The ASP page from Listing 3-2 appears like this in Internet Explorer.

Packaging UI as Components

Being able to assemble the UI from component parts is one of the most-cited benefits of producing components. The earliest technologies for building components in Windows was to write custom Windows Procedures, to use the owner draw capabilities of controls like list boxes or buttons, or to subclass an existing window. In the early 1990s, Windows employed VBXs (Visual Basic Controls) as a viable UI technology. Of course, that was more than a decade ago. Throughout the mid- and late 1990s and early 2000s, ActiveX controls represented the graphical user interface (GUI) componentization technology of the day. Windows Forms controls are the current standard for modular GUIs if you're writing a rich client application.

In the late 1990s, ActiveX controls also emerged as a way to render a Web-based GUI as components. The idea was that by using an ActiveX control in your page, the control would be downloaded as users surfed to the page. During the mid-1990s, Java applets also gained some popularity as a way to package GUI components for distribution over the Web. However, both of these techniques depend on some fairly extensive infrastructure on the client machine (the Component Object Model infrastructure to support ActiveX and a Java Virtual Machine to support Java applets). When you're developing a Web site, you may not be able to count on a specific infrastructure's being available on the client machine to support your GUI. To support the greatest number of clients, represent your GUI using only HTML. That means GUI componentization needs to happen on the server side.

Now that modern client platforms are becoming more homogeneous, Web UIs are beginning to lean increasingly toward the Asynchronous Java And XML programming model (AJAX). We'll see how AJAX works a bit later. AJAX tends to push more intelligence back up to the browser. However, AJAX applications still have plenty of rendering to do. The ASP.NET UI componentization model makes developing AJAX applications very approachable. The AJAX programming model includes a lot of underlying plumbing code that fits perfectly within the server-side control architecture of ASP.NET.

As we saw earlier, ASP.NET introduces an entirely new model for managing Web pages. The infrastructure within ASP.NET includes a well-defined pipeline through which a request flows. When a request ends up at the server, ASP.NET instantiates a handler (an implementation of *IHttpHandler*) to deal with the request. As we'll see in a later chapter, the handling architecture is extraordinarily flexible. You may write any code you wish to handle the request. The *System.Web.UI.Page* class implements *IHttpHandler* by introducing an object-oriented approach to rendering. That is, every element you see on a Web page emitted by an ASP.NET page is somehow generated by a *server-side control*. Let's see how this works.

The Page Using ASP.NET

Try turning the previous Web page into an ASP.NET application. Doing so will introduce some canonical features of ASP.NET, including server-side controls and server-side script blocks.

1. Create a file named *BunchOfControls.aspx*. Follow the steps for creating a basic text file from the previous chapter. Since all of the code will be in a single file, do not create a full-fledged ASP.NET file for this step using the wizard.

2. Add the source code in Listing 3-3 to the file.

   LISTING 3-3 Source Code for BunchOfControls Page Using ASP.NET

```
<%@ Page Language="C#" %>

<script runat="server">
  protected void Page_Load(object sender, EventArgs ea)
  {
     ddl.Items.Add("Item 1");
     ddl.Items.Add("Item 2");
     ddl.Items.Add("Item 3");
     ddl.Items.Add("Item 4");
  }
</script >
<h2> Page in ASP.NET </h2>
```

```
<form id="Form1" runat="server" >
    <asp:Label Text="Type in me" runat="server" />
    <asp:TextBox id="textinfo" runat="server" />
    <br/>
    <asp:DropDownList id="ddl" runat="server" />
    <br/>
    <asp:Button id="clickme" Text="Click Me!" runat="server" />
</form>
```

3. Save the file in a virtual directory (either create one or use the one from the previous chapter).

Many of the same elements seen in the classic ASP page also appear here. There's a top-level *Page* directive. The *Language* attribute is new for ASP.NET, stipulating that any code encountered by the ASP.NET runtime should be interpreted as C# code. There's a server-side script block that handles the *Page_Load* event. Following the script block is an HTML *<form>* tag. Notice the *<form>* tag has an attribute named *runat*, and the attribute is set to *server*. The *runat=server* attribute tells the ASP.NET runtime to generate a server-side control to handle that UI element at the server. We'll see this in detail thoughout the chapter.

By including the *runat=server* attribute in page control tags, the ASP.NET runtime implicitly creates an instance of the control in memory. The resulting assembly includes a member variable of the same type and name (tied to the control's ID value) as the control listed on the page. Notice the ASP.NET code specifies the *DropDownList* named *ddl* to run at the server. To access the control programmatically, the code block (expressed inline in this case) simply needs to refer to the *DropDownList* as *ddl*. The example above accesses the member variable to add items to the drop-down list.

If you needed to access the control using code beside you'd explicitly declare the *DropDownList* variable as *ddl* in the associated code file. This is required because ASP.NET derives the code-beside class from *System.Web.UI.Page*. Visual Studio will do this for you automatically, as we'll see shortly.

Further down the ASP.NET code, you'll see that the other elements (the label, the text box, the selection control, and the button) are also represented as server-side controls. The job of each of these controls is to add a little bit of HTML to the response. Each time you add a server-side control to the page, ASP.NET adds an instance of the control to a control tree the page maintains in memory. The control tree acts as a container that collects every single element encapsulated by one of these server-side controls—including the title text that seems to be floating near the top of the page even though there is no explicit *runat=server* attribute associated with the *<h2>* tag.

The Page's Rendering Model

To get a good idea as to how ASP.NET's *Page* model works, we'll run the page again, but this time we'll turn on the tracing mechanism. We'll examine tracing in more detail when we look at ASP.NET's diagnostic features. For now, you simply need to know that ASP.NET will dump the entire context of a request and a response if you set the page's *Trace* attribute to *true*. Here's the *Page* directive with tracing turned on:

```
<%@ Page Language="C#" Trace="true" %>
```

Figure 3-3 shows what the page looks like with tracing turned on.

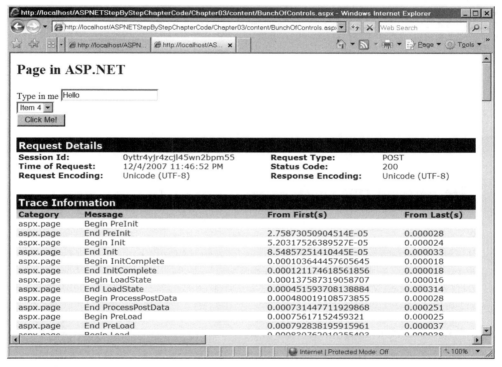

FIGURE 3-3 The ASPX file from Listing 3-3 rendered in Internet Explorer

If you look at the raw text of the response (by selecting **View**, **Source** from the Internet Explorer menu), you see that ASP.NET responds with pretty straightforward run-of-the-mill HTML. There's a bit extra near the top—the hidden _*VIEWSTATE* field—which we'll cover later. After that, the rest is familiar HTML describing a form. Listing 3-4 shows the raw HTML emitted by the ASP.NET code from Listing 3-3. Be sure to turn tracing off first!

LISTING 3-4 Raw HTML Produced by the BunchOfControls.ASPX File

```
<h2> Page in ASP.NET </h2>
<form method="post" action="BunchOfControls.aspx" id="Form1">
<div>
<input type="hidden" name="__VIEWSTATE" id="__VIEWSTATE"
value="/wEPDwUJODQ1ODEz ... " />
</div>

    <span>Type in me</span>
    <input name="textinfo" type="text" id="textinfo" />
    <br/>
    <select name="ddl" id="ddl">
    <option value="Item 1">Item 1</option>
    <option value="Item 2">Item 2</option>
    <option value="Item 3">Item 3</option>
    <option value="Item 4">Item 4</option>

</select>
    <br/>
    <input type="submit" name="clickme" value="Click Me!" id="clickme" />
</form>
```

You don't see any of the *runat=server* attributes anywhere in the rendered page. That's because the *runat=server* attributes are there to instruct ASP.NET how to construct the page's control tree.

The Page's Control Tree

After turning the page's *Trace* property to *true*, ASP.NET will spew a ton of information your way in the form of a page trace. If you scroll down just a bit, you can see that part of ASP .NET's page trace includes the page's control tree. Figure 3-4 shows what the previous page's trace looks like with the focus on the control tree.

The first line in the page's control tree trace is an item named __Page. This is in fact the *System .Web.UI.Page* object running in memory. Beneath that are a whole host of other items. You'll recognize some of their names as they were named in the ASP.NET source code. Notice the *Form1, textinfo,* and *clickme* items. Those names came from the tags in the original ASPX file.

What's happening here is that ASP.NET is breaking down the page rendering architecture into small, easily managed pieces. Every item in the control tree shown in Figure 3-4 derives from the *System.Web.UI.Control* class. Every time the *System.Web.UI.Page* needs to render the page, it simply walks the control tree, asking each control to render itself. For example, when the ASP.NET runtime asks the *TextBox* server-side control to render itself, the *TextBox* control adds the following HTML to the output stream heading for the browser:

```
<input name="textinfo" type="text" id="textinfo" />
```

FIGURE 3-4 The ASP.NET page's control tree shown in the page trace

This works similarly for the other controls. For example, the *DropDownList* is responsible for emitting the select and option tags (the option tags represent the collection of items held by the *DropDownList* control).

```
<select name="ddl" id="ddl">
    <option value="Item 1">Item 1</option>
    <option value="Item 2">Item 2</option>
    <option value="Item 3">Item 3</option>
    <option value="Item 4">Item 4</option>
</select>
```

Now that you see how these tags work, let's see how to manage them in Visual Studio.

Adding Controls Using Visual Studio

Visual Studio (in concert with ASP.NET) is very good at fooling you as to the real nature of Web-based development. As you saw from earlier chapters, Web-based development hearkens back to the old terminal–mainframe days of the mid-1970s. However, this time the terminal is a sophisticated browser, the computing platform is a Web server (or perhaps a Web farm), and the audience is worldwide. When a client browser makes a round-trip to the server, it's really getting only a snapshot of the state of the server. That's because Web user interfaces are built using a markup language over a disconnected protocol.

When you build Web applications in Visual Studio, it's almost as if you're developing a desktop application. With Visual Studio, you don't have to spend all your time typing ASP-style code. The designer is a great environment for designing a Web-based UI visually.

Building a Page with Visual Studio

To see how this works, let's develop a simple page that uses server-side controls. The page will look roughly like the ones we've seen so far.

1. Create a Web site to experiment with controls. Use Visual Studio to create a new file system–based ASP.NET Web site. Call the Web site *ControlORama*, as shown here:

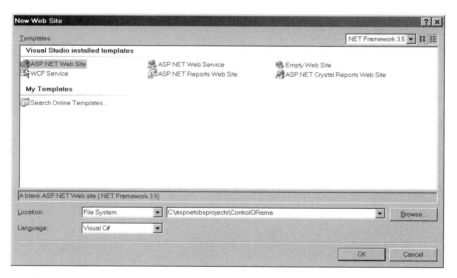

2. Use the Designer. Visual Studio starts you off editing the markup in the Default.aspx file. If you don't see the page layout designer mode, switch to the Design view as shown here by clicking on the **Design** tab near the bottom of the edit window.

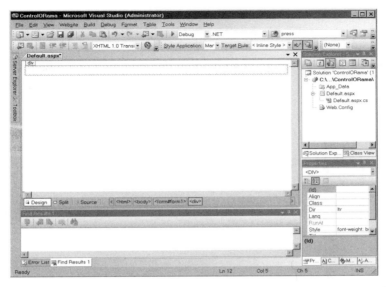

The ASP.NET code generated by Visual Studio includes an HTML *<div>* tag in the body of the page. To see the code generated by Visual Studio as you modify elements in the designer, select the *Source* tab near the bottom of the design window. Visual Studio now includes a handy **Split** tab that allows you to see both the design and source views at the same time.

If you simply start typing some text into the Design view, you'll see some text at the top of the page. The following graphic illustrates the Design view with some text inserted. To insert the text, click inside the box with the dashed blue border and type **Page in Visual Studio**:

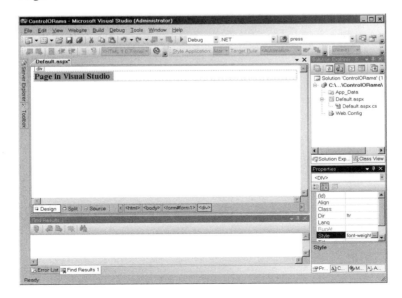

3. Format the text on the page. To edit the format of the text on the page, you need to view the page's properties. Highlight the text, click the right mouse button the text, and select **Properties** from the local menu. Then highlight the *Style* property in the **Property** dialog box. You'll see a small button appear in the *Property* field with an ellipsis (. . .). Click the button to reveal the **Modify Style** dialog box. The **Modify Style** dialog box sets the attributes for the *<div>* tag where you can set the font face and style. The following graphic shows the **Modify Style** dialog box. Make the selections for font-family, font-size, and font-weight you see in the graphic and click **OK**:

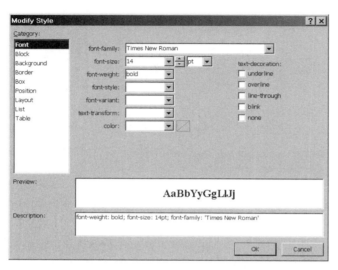

4. Open the Control toolbox. Next add a label to the page. Move the cursor to the Toolbox tab on the far left side of Visual Studio. This will highlight the toolbox on the left as shown in the following graphic:

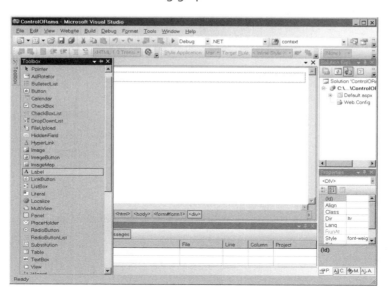

5. Add a label to the page. Drag a label from the Toolbar and drop it onto the page, then select it as shown in the following graphic (notice how Visual Studio 2008's designer adorns the label with a small tag right above it, helping you identify the label in the designer when you select it):

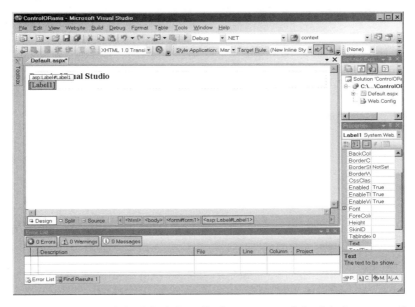

6. Edit the content of the label. To edit the content of the label, you need to view the control's properties. If the properties aren't showing, click the right mouse button on the label and select **Properties** from the shortcut menu. The following graphic illustrates the property window:

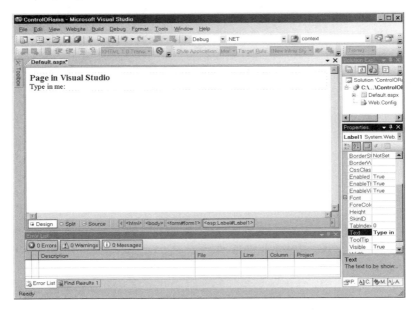

You can now manipulate the appearance of the label to your liking. The example label here uses a small Times New Roman font and the text in the label is **Type in me:**.

7. Add a text box. Next, pick up a *TextBox* from the toolbox and drop it next to the *Label* (you can pick up a *TextBox* from the toolbox—just as you did with the *Label*). Follow the *TextBox* with a line break tag (*
*).

8. Add a drop-down list. Next, add a *DropDownList* box by picking it up off the Toolbox and dropping it onto the page. The following graphic illustrates the drop-down list as it appears in the designer. Notice the local menu for editing the data source and for adding/editing items.

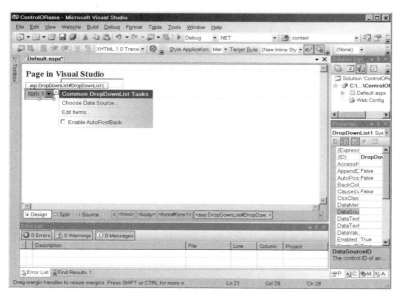

As soon as you drop the control onto the page, Visual Studio prompts you with the opportunity to add items to the *DropDownList*. Select **Edit Items** from the Common DropDownList Tasks window. You'll see the **ListView Collection Editor** dialog box as shown in the following graphic:

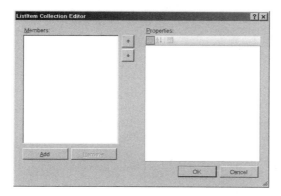

Each time you click the **Add** button, the ListView Collection Editor adds a new item to the *DropDownList* item collection. You can edit the display name (the Text property). You may add a corresponding value to associate with the text as well. For example, in an inventory-tracking application, you might include a product name as the *Text* property and an enterprise-specific product code in the *Value* field. You can retrieve either or both aspects of the item at runtime.

Add several of these items to the *DropDownList* as shown in the following graphic. When you've added several, click **OK**:

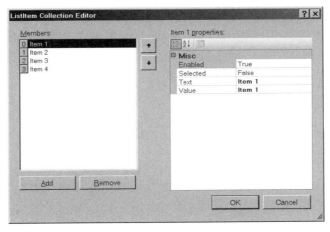

9. Add a button to the page. First, add a line break following the *DropDownList*. Then pick up a *Button* from the Toolbox and drop it on the page. The following graphic shows the controls in place:

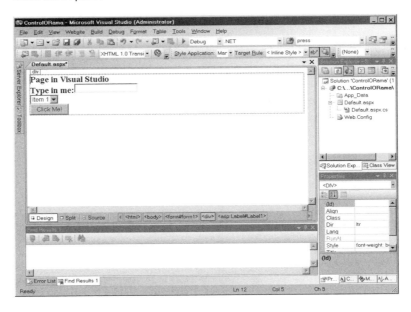

Add some meaningful text to the button by modifying its *Text* property.

Before moving on, take a minute to look at the source code generated by Visual Studio. In adding a *Label* control, a *TextBox* control, a *DropDownList* control, and a *Button* control, Visual Studio has added four new member variables to your code (implied through the *runat=server* attributes placed within the control tags). The contents of the ASPX file (starting with the form tag) look something like Listing 3-5 at this point.

LISTING 3-5 Final Default.aspx Markup

```
<form id="form1" runat="server">
<div style="font-weight: bold; font-size: 14pt; font-family: 'Times New Roman'">
    Page in Visual Studio<br />
    <asp:Label ID="Label1" runat="server"
      Text="Type in me:" >
    </asp:Label>
    <asp:TextBox
     ID="TextBox1" runat="server">
    </asp:TextBox>
    <br />
    <asp:DropDownList ID="DropDownList1" runat="server">
        <asp:ListItem>Item 1</asp:ListItem>
        <asp:ListItem>Item 2</asp:ListItem>
        <asp:ListItem>Item 3</asp:ListItem>
        <asp:ListItem>Item 4</asp:ListItem>
    </asp:DropDownList><br />
    <asp:Button ID="Button1"
     runat="server" OnClick="Button1_Click"
     Text="Click Me!" />
 </div>
</form>
```

Notice each ASP.NET tag that runs at the server is given an *ID* attribute. This is the identifier by which the control will be known at runtime. We'll make use of that shortly.

10. Add an event handler for the button. Finally, to make the button do something, you need to add an event handler to the page so it will respond when the button is clicked. The easiest way to do that is to double-click on the button in Design mode. Visual Studio will generate a handler function for the button click and then show that code in the Source code view. At this point, you can add some code to respond to the button click.

Add the source code in Listing 3-6 to the file.

LISTING 3-6 Button Handling Code

```
    protected void Button1_Click(object sender, EventArgs e)
    {
        Response.Write("Hello. Here's what you typed into the text box: <br/>");
        Response.Write(this.TextBox1.Text);

        Response.Write("<br/>");
        Response.Write("And the selected item is: <br/>");
        Response.Write(this.DropDownList1.SelectedItem.Text);
    }
```

The code shown above responds to the button click by sending some text to the output stream via the *Response* object. The text coming through *Response.Write* will be the first text the client browser will see, and so will appear at the top of the page.

Notice that the response code uses the *TextBox1* member variable in the page's class, showing that the controls are available programmatically at runtime. Here's how the page appears to the client browser. Notice how the text emitted by *Response.Write* is inserted before any of the controls are:

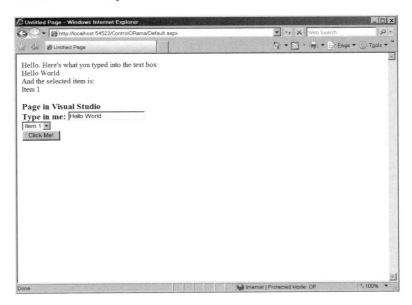

To test the controls on the page, browse to the page by selecting **Debug**, **Start Without Debugging** from the main menu. To see the HTML generated by all the server-side controls, you may view the source sent to the browser (if your browser is Microsoft Internet Explorer, choose **View**, **Source** from the menu). When you view the source, you should see something like that shown in Listing 3-7. Notice how the text emitted by *Response.Write* appears at the very top of the listing.

LISTING 3-7 HTML Resulting from Running Default.aspx

```
Hello. Here's what you typed into the text box: <br>

Hello World<br>

And the selected item is: <br>Item 1

<!DOCTYPE html PUBLIC "-//W3C//DTD XHTML 1.1//EN"
 "http://www.w3.org/TR/xhtml11/DTD/xhtml11.dtd">

<html xmlns="http://www.w3.org/1999/xhtml" >
<head><title>
        Untitled Page
</title></head>
```

```html
<body>
    <form name="form1"
     method="post"
     action="Default.aspx" id="form1">
<div>
<input type="hidden"
name="__VIEWSTATE"
id="__VIEWSTATE" value="/wEPDwULLTEyNDk3ODQyMjNkZDJq3IDR4Y6f3FKOG+2mn5C/b7d7" />
</div>

    <div
    style="font-weight: bold; font-size: 14pt;
    font-family: 'Times New Roman'">
        Page in Visual Studio<br />
    </div>
        <span id="Label1">
        Type in me:</span>
        <input name="TextBox1" type="text"
        id="TextBox1" /><br />
        <select name="DropDownList1"
        id="DropDownList1">
        <option value="Item 1">Item 1</option>
        <option value="Item 2">Item 2</option>
        <option value="Item 3">Item 3</option>
        <option value="Item 4">Item 4</option>

</select><br />
    <input type="submit"
    name="Button1" value="Click Me"
    id="Button1" />

<div>

        <input type="hidden"
    name="__EVENTVALIDATION"
    id="__EVENTVALIDATION"
    value="/wEWB4rGBnHVt17sGtxxk2ij1iXXWxOLHCUU" />
</div></form>
</body>
</html>
```

Notice that this is just pure HTML that the browser is viewing. ASP.NET generated it using its page rendering model, but the browser is none the wiser.

Layout Considerations

You may have noticed when building the last page that the layout of the page flowed. That is, every time you dropped a control onto the page, the designer forced it up against the placement of the previous control. If you've worked with earlier versions of Visual Studio, you'll notice this is different default behavior. Visual Studio 2003 started off with absolute positioning for elements on a page (which is what you're used to if you've done rich client or standard Windows development).

Although Visual Studio 2008 does not let you set positioning styles directly in the designer, you may apply positioning options via a style that applies to the whole page or to singular elements in the page. To add a new style to the page, make sure the designer is showing in the window and select **Formatting**, **New Style**. You'll see the following dialog box:

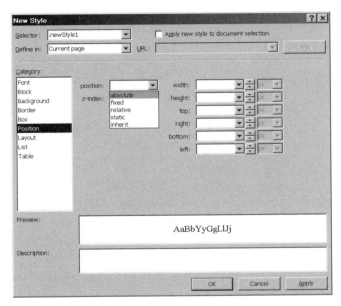

To change the layout options using the style, select **Position** from the Category list appearing on the left of the dialog. Notice the combo selection for setting positions. Once you've set up a style, you can apply it to various elements on the page by referring to the class name through the element's *CssClass* property.

Changing the positioning options allows you to apply various kinds of layout assignments to the page. Play around with them a bit. That's the only way to get a feel for how they work. We'll explore styles in greater depth when we discuss Master Pages.

Summary

The *System.Web.UI.Page* class includes a collection of server-side controls. Everything that ever makes its way out to the client browser was somehow generated by a server-side control. Even literal text on the page was rendered using a *LiteralControl*. When the ASP.NET runtime compiles a page, it scans the ASPX file for any tag that says *runat=server* and adds a member variable representing that control to the page's control tree. Nothing escapes being packaged as a control—when ASP.NET finds literal text on the page, ASP.NET packages that as a literal control. When it comes time for the page to render, ASP.NET walks the control list and asks each control in the list to render itself.

Visual Studio 2008 includes a useful designer that lets you drag and drop controls onto a page. This development environment makes you feel as though you're developing normal applications for a single machine, even though the UI is represented as HTML over HTTP.

We'll take a look at writing a custom control in the next chapter.

Chapter 3 Quick Reference

To	Do This
Switch between ASPX Source code mode and Designer mode	The **Design** and **Source** tabs usually appear near the bottom left side of the editor window. You may also use the **Split** tab to see both the code and the designer views at once.
Add a server-side control to a page	Show the Toolbox if it's not already showing by selecting **View**, **Toolbox** from the main menu (using the key combination Ctrl-W, X will also work). Click on the control from the Toolbox. Drag the control and drop it onto the page.
Change the properties of controls on a page	Make sure the page editor is in Design mode. Highlight the control whose property you want to change. Select the property to edit in the property window.
Turn tracing on	In Source code editing mode, edit the Page directive to include the attribute *Trace*="true" OR Select the *Document* element from the combo box near the top of the Properties window. Assign the Trace property to be *true*.
Change the size of a server-side control	Click on the control once to highlight it. Click on one of the handles appearing on the border of the control. Hold the mouse button down and drag the mouse until the control is the correct size.
Add a handler for a control's default event	Double-click on the control for which you want to handle the event.
Change the layout characteristics of a page	Add a new style to the page by selecting **Format**, **New Style** from the main menu. Select **Layout** from the main menu and develop a style (defining a style also includes other elements in addition to the layout options, such as font face, size, and margins). Apply the style to the page or to singular elements.

Chapter 4
Custom Rendered Controls

After completing this chapter, you will be able to

- Add a new project to the existing project within a Visual Studio solution file
- Create a server-side control that renders custom HTML
- Add a server-side control to the Visual Studio toolbox
- Place a server-side control on a Web form
- Manage events within the control
- Use ASP.NET to detect differences in client browsers and apply that information

In Chapter 3, "The Page Rendering Model," we saw the fundamental architecture behind the ASP.NET rendering model. *System.Web.UI.Page* manages a list of server-side controls, and it's the job of each server-side control to render a particular portion of the page. ASP.NET broadly classifies server-side controls into two categories:

- Rendering controls (controls that completely manage the rendering process)
- Composite controls (multiple server-side controls bundled into a single unit)

This chapter focuses on the first type: custom rendered controls. We'll see how the control works once it's part of a Web page. Along the way we'll cover topics such as how controls manage events and how they detect the differences in client browsers.

Let's start by looking at the heart of the ASP.NET server-side control architecture—the *System.Web.UI.Control* class.

The *Control* Class

ASP.NET server-side controls derive from a class named *System.Web.UI.Control*. In fact, the *Control* class is the core of almost every *User Interface* element within ASP.NET. Even *System .Web.UI.Page* is derived from the *Control* class. Table 4-1 shows a small sampling of the *System.Web.UI.Page* class.

The entries in Table 4-1 show a small cross section of the functionality available within *System.Web.UI.Control*. We'll visit all these members while investigating ASP.NET Web forms. Remember from the last chapter that ASP.NET Web forms manage a collection of controls as part of their internal structure. As you add controls to a Web page, they're placed within the collection. When it comes time for a page to render its content back to the client, *System.Web.UI.Page* iterates the collection of controls and asks each one of them to render

Table 4-1 Sampling of the Page's Properties, Methods, and Events

Member	Description
Application	Reference to the *HttpApplicationState* object associated with the current request
Cache	Reference to the application's cache—an in-memory dictionary of application-wide state (usually for optimization)
Controls	The *Page*'s control collection
CreateChildControls	Virtual method during which the page constructs its control tree
Init	Event indicating the page has initialized
IsPostBack	Distinguishes the request as either a new request or a POST
Load	Event indicating the page has been loaded
RenderControl	Virtual method during which the page renders its contents
Request	Reference to a stateful object representing the incoming request
Response	Reference to a stateful object representing the outgoing response
Session	Reference to a stateful object representing information specific to the current request
Unload	Event indicating the page has unloaded

themselves. If a control contains subcontrols (just as a page includes controls), ASP.NET will walk down those collections as well. You can see the *RenderContents* method in Table 4-1. *RenderContents* takes a single argument of type *HtmlTextWriter*. We'll examine that class later in this chapter. Right now, think of it as the conduit through which you send the page's response back to the client.

Other elements of the *Control* class include items such as

- Properties for managing the control's view state
- Properties for managing skins (to accommodate a consistent look and feel across multiple pages within a site)
- Properties for getting the parent control (in the case of composite controls) and the parent page
- Event handlers for the *Init, Load, PreRender*, and *Unload* events
- Methods for raising the *Init, Load, PreRender*, and *Unload* events
- Methods for managing child controls

We'll visit the most important topics in examining both rendered controls and composite controls. Although the *Page* class is sizable, there is a straightforward logic to it and it unfolds nicely in practice. The easiest way to start is to jump into building a custom control.

Visual Studio and Custom Controls

In this section, we'll build a simple control (the default control Visual Studio generates for you) and see how it fits on a Web form. Visual Studio will create a simple control that contains a single *Text* property, and it will render that *Text* property to the end browser. It's a good way to discover how server-side controls work.

Create a custom control

1. Begin by opening the ControlORama project from Chapter 3. Note: If you want to preserve the current state of ControlORama, make a copy of the whole project directory and work on the copy. This example will be built up over this chapter and the next chapter to demonstrate the different approaches to developing controls.

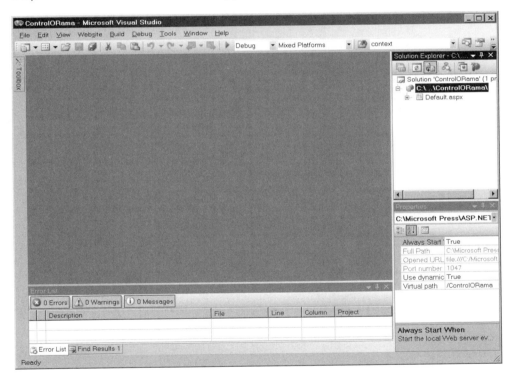

2. Add a new project to ControlORama. Highlight the solution node in the solution explorer, click the right mouse button, and select **Add**, **New Project** from the context menu. Name the new project *CustomControlLib*. Choose the project type to be a Web project, and select **ASP.NET Server Control** as the template, like so:

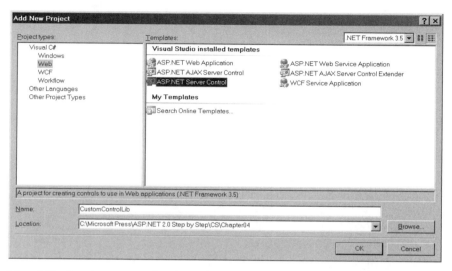

Visual Studio gives you a simple Web control to start with. Listing 4-1 shows the default code generated by Visual Studio for a Web Control Library.

LISTING 4-1 Default Custom Control Implementation

```
using System;
using System.Collections.Generic;
using System.ComponentModel;
using System.Linq;
using System.Text;
using System.Web;
using System.Web.UI;
using System.Web.UI.WebControls;

namespace CustomControlLib
{
    [DefaultProperty("Text")]
    [ToolboxData("<{0}:WebCustomControl1
     runat=server></{0}:WebCustomControl1>")]
    public class WebCustomControl1 : WebControl
    {
        [Bindable(true)]
        [Category("Appearance")]
        [DefaultValue("")]
        [Localizable(true)]
        public string Text
        {
            get
```

```
        {
            String s = (String)ViewState["Text"];
            return ((s == null) ? String.Empty : s);
        }

        set
        {
            ViewState["Text"] = value;
        }
    }

    protected override void RenderContents(HtmlTextWriter output)
    {
        output.Write(Text);
    }
  }
}
```

The code generated by Visual Studio includes a simple class derived from *System.Web .UI.WebControl*. *WebControl* (which derives from the standard *Control* class) adds some standard properties along the way. Notice that the code has a single property named *Text* and overrides *Control's RenderContents* method. This is a real, functioning control (although all it really does is act very much like a *Label*).

3. Build the project by selecting **Build**, **Build Solution** from the main menu.

4. Now find the control that Visual Studio just built. From the Tools menu select Choose Toolbox Items. Click the **Browse** button in the **Choose Toolbox Items** dialog box. Navigate to the ControlORama project directory and then go to the CustomControlLib directory. Then open the Bin\Debug directory. (Visual Studio builds debug versions by default.) Select the *CustomControlLib.DLL* assembly and click the **Open** button.

   WebCustomControl1 will appear in the Choose Toolbox Items dialog box. The check box will show it as selected.

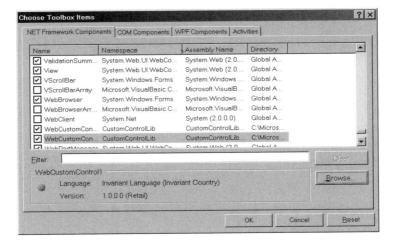

As soon as you click the **OK** button in the Choose Toolbox Items dialog box, the new *WebCustomControl1* will appear in the toolbox. To make it easier to find the control, click the right mouse button on the toolbox and select **Sort Items Alphabetically**.

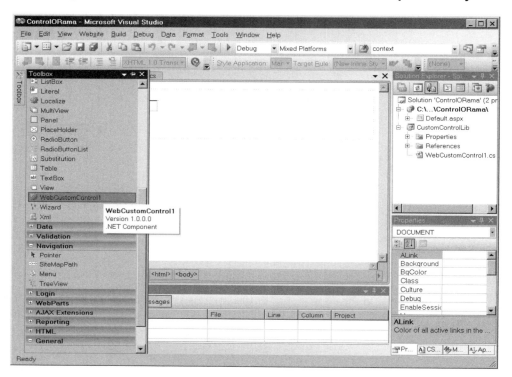

5. Place the control on a page. To see how the control works, you need to give it a home. Add a new page to the Web site. Select the ControlORama project from the Solution Explorer. Select **Web Site**, **Add New Item**, and add a Web Form. Name the Web Form *UseCustomControl.aspx*.

To place the control on the page, switch to Design mode. Drag the *WebCustomControl1* from the Toolbox and drop it onto the UseCustomControl design view.

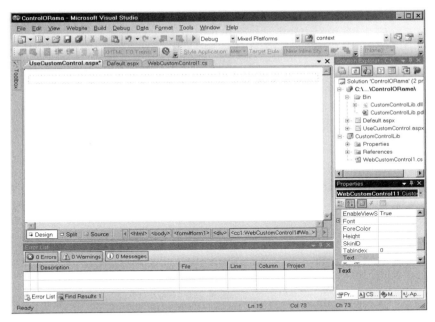

Although there will be no text showing within the control at this point, you'll see a very lightly colored dashed line showing where the control is placed on the page. You can select the new control using the drop-down list within the Property dialog in the lower right corner for Visual Studio. Change the *Text* property in the control and watch it show up in the designer.

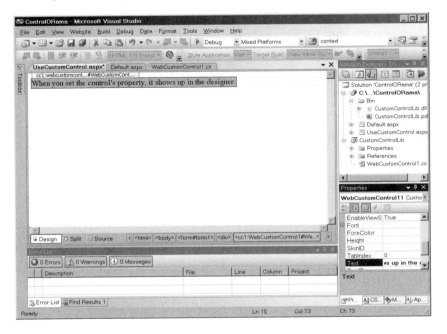

Take a look at the source code for the control again—specifically looking at the *RenderContents* method. Notice that the method simply uses the parameter (an *HtmlTextWriter*) to send the *Text* property to the browser. That's why the *Text* property is showing after you change it in the designer.

The following line of code is what Visual Studio added to the ASPX file to accommodate the control. You can see it by selecting the **Source** tab from the bottom of the code window in Visual Studio. The *Register* directive tells the ASP.NET runtime where to find the custom control (which assembly) and maps it to a tag prefix.

```
<%@ Register Assembly="CustomcontrolLib" Namespace="CustomcontrolLib" TagPrefix="cc1" %>
```

Listing 4-2 shows how the control is declared on the page when you set the control's *Text* property to the string value **When you set the control's property, it shows up in the designer.**

LISTING 4-2 UseCustomControl.aspx Markup with the Custom Web Control

```
<form id="form1" runat="server">
<div>

    <cc1:WebCustomControl1 ID="WebCustomControl11"
     runat="server"
     Text="When you set the control's property,
       it shows up in the designer." />

</div>
</form>
```

Now take a moment to change a few of the control's properties and see what happens in the designer (for example, changing the font is always very noticeable). The properties you see in the *Properties* page are all standard, and they show up because the control is derived from *System.Web.UI.WebControl*.

6. Now add a text box and a button to the Web page. After you drop them on the page, Visual Studio adds the code shown in Listing 4-3.

LISTING 4-3 Revised UseCustomControl.aspx Markup

```
<form id="form1" runat="server">
<div>
    <cc1:webcustomcontrol1 id="WebCustomControl11"
    runat="server"
    text="The control's Text property...">
    </cc1:webcustomcontrol1>
    <br />
    <br />
    <asp:Label ID="Label1"
    runat="server"
    Text="Type something here;">
    </asp:Label>
    <asp:TextBox ID="TextBox1" runat="server">
    </asp:TextBox>
```

```
        <br />
        <asp:Button ID="Button1"
        runat="server" OnClick="Button1_Click"
        Text="Set Control Text" />
        </div>
    </form>
```

Notice that the standard ASP.NET controls (the button, the text box, and the label) all begin with the *asp:* prefix while the new custom control uses the prefix *cc1:*. Visual Studio made up the tag *cc1:*, although you could change this for this page by modifying the TagPrefix attribute in the Register directive.

7. Add an event handler for the button by double-clicking the button in the designer. Once Visual Studio adds the event handler for you, have the button pull the text from the *TextBox* and use it to set your custom control's *Text* property. To do this, type in the code you see in boldfaced font:

```
protected void Button1_Click(object sender, EventArgs e)
{
    this.WebCustomControl11.Text = this.TextBox1.Text;
}
```

Now surf to the new page with the control. When you type something into the text box and click the button, the browser sends your request to the server. The server responds by taking the text from the *TextBox* and using it to set the *Text* property of the *WebCustomControl1*.

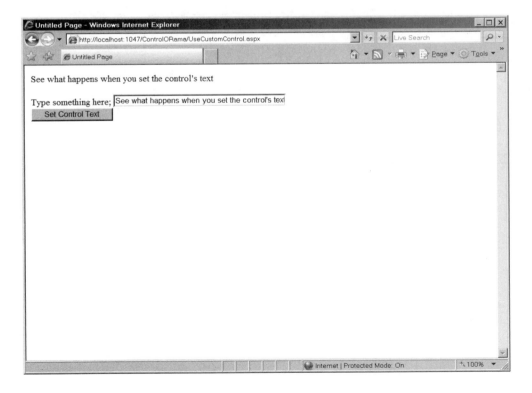

Notice how the new control appears in the control tree with tracing turned on. (You can turn on page tracing by setting the page's *Trace* property to *true*, as we did in the last chapter.)

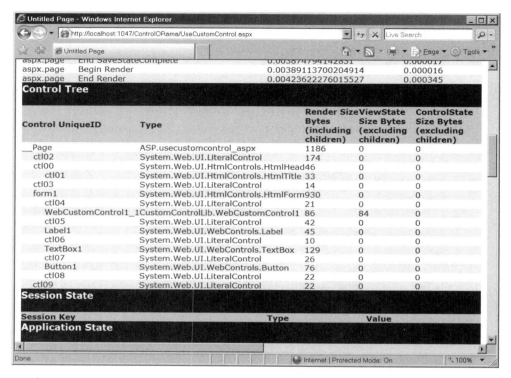

You have now built a simple control. The control framework is pretty flexible, and you can send out anything you want using the *RenderContents* method. Next, we'll develop a more sophisticated control that demonstrates more advanced control rendering.

A Palindrome Checker

The preceding exercise shows the fundamentals of writing a simple server-side control that renders client-side markup. However, ASP.NET already delivers a perfectly good *Label* control. Why do you need another one? To further illustrate rendered server-side controls, here's a simple control that checks to see if the string typed by the client is a palindrome. We'll observe some more advanced rendering techniques as well as how control events work.

The *Palindrome Checker* control

1. Create the *Palindrome Checker* control. In the Solution Explorer, highlight the **CustomControlLib** node. Click the right mouse button on the node and select **Add**, **New Item** from the shortcut menu. Be sure the Web category is selected and then

highlight the **ASP.NET Server Control** node. Enter **PalindromeCheckerRenderedControl** in the *Name* text box and click **OK** to generate the code.

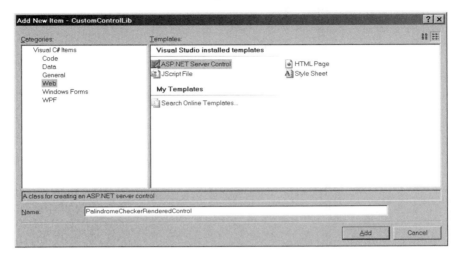

2. Add a method to test for a palindrome. A *palindrome* is a word, sentence, or phrase that reads the same forward as it does backward (for example, "radar"). Add a method to the control that checks to see whether the internal text is a palindrome. This is a simple test for a palindrome that converts the text to uppercase, reverses it, and then compares the result to the original text. You should also strip out nonalphanumeric characters. Listing 4-4 shows some code that does the trick.

LISTING 4-4 Stripping Alphanumerics

```
protected string StripNonAlphanumerics(string str)
{
    string strStripped = (String)str.Clone();
    if (str != null)
    {
        char[] rgc = strStripped.ToCharArray();
        int i = 0;
        foreach (char c in rgc)
        {
            if (char.IsLetterOrDigit(c))
            {
                i++;
            }
            else
            {
                strStripped = strStripped.Remove(i, 1);
            }
        }
    }
    return strStripped;
}
protected bool CheckForPalindrome()
```

```
{
   if (this.Text != null)
   {
      String strControlText = this.Text;
      String strTextToUpper = null;
      strTextToUpper = Text.ToUpper();
      strControlText =
                  this.StripNonAlphanumerics(strTextToUpper);
      char[] rgcReverse = strControlText.ToCharArray();
      Array.Reverse(rgcReverse);
      String strReverse = new string(rgcReverse);
      if (strControlText == strReverse)
      {
         return true;
      }
      else
      {
         return false;
      }
   }
   else
   {
      return false;
   }
}
```

3. Change the rendering method to print palindromes in blue and nonpalindromes in red. The *RenderContent* method takes a single parameter of type *HtmlTextWriter*. In addition to allowing you to stream text to the browser, *HtmlTextWriter* is full of other very useful features we'll see shortly. For now, you can treat it very much like *Response.Write*. Whatever you send through the *Write* method will end up at the client's browser.

```
protected override void RenderContent(HtmlTextWriter output)
   {

      if (this.CheckForPalindrome())
      {
         output.Write("This is a palindrome: <br>");
         output.Write(@"FONT size=5 color:blue;'>");
         output.Write("<B>");
         output.Write(Text);
         output.Write("</B>");
         output.Write("</FONT>");
      } else {
         output.Write("This is NOT a palindrome <br>");
         output.Write("<FONT size=5 color=red>");
         output.Write("<B>");
         output.Write(Text);
         output.Write("</B>");
         output.Write("</FONT>");
      }

   }
```

4. Build the project by selecting **Build**, **Build Solution** from the main menu.

5. Add the *PalindromeCheckerRenderedControl* to the toolbox if it's not already there. Visual Studio should add the *PalindromeCheckerRenderedControl* to the Toolbox. If not, you can add it manually. Click the right mouse button on the toolbox and select **Choose Item**. Use the **Browse** button to find the *CustomControlLib.DLL* assembly and select it. Visual Studio will load the new control in the toolbox.

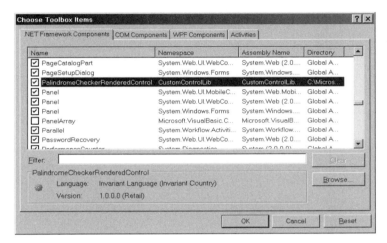

6. Add a page to use the palindrome checker control. Add a new Web Form to the ControlORama project and name it *UsePalindromeCheckerControls.aspx*. Drag the *PalindromeCheckerRenderedControl* and drop it on the page. Add a *TextBox* and a button so you can add a palindrome to the control and check it.

7. Add a handler for the button. Double-click on the button. Visual Studio will add a handler to the page. In the handler, set the *PalindromeCheckerRenderedControl*'s text property to the *TextBox.Text* property.

```
public partial class UsePalindromeCheckerControls : System.Web.UI.Page
{
    protected void Button1_Click(object sender, EventArgs e)
    {
        this.PalindromeCheckerRenderedControl1.Text = this.TextBox1.Text;
    }

}
```

8. Run the page and test for a palindrome. Palindromes should appear in blue and non-palindromes in red.

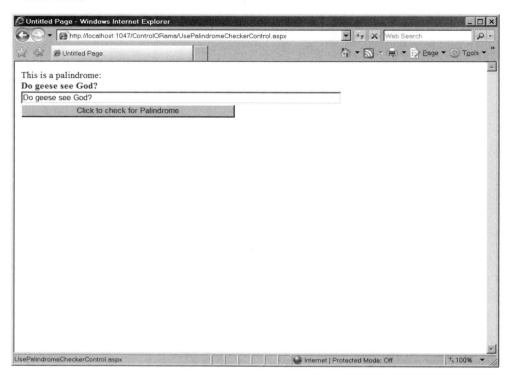

Controls and Events

The *PalindromeCheckerRenderedControl* shows how to render control content differently depending on the state of the *Text* property. While that's a very useful thing in itself, it's often helpful to also alert the host page to the fact that a palindrome was found. You can do this by exposing an event from the control.

Most of ASP.NET's standard server-side controls already support events. You've already seen how the *Button* control sends an event to the host page when it is clicked. You can actually do this type of thing with any control. Let's add a *PalindromeFound* event to the *PalindromeCheckerRenderedControl*.

Adding a *PalindromeFound* event

1. Open the PalindromeCheckerRenderedControl.cs file. To add a *PalindromeFound* event, type in the following line:

```
public class PalindromeCheckerRenderedControl : WebControl
{
    public event EventHandler PalindromeFound;
        // Other palindrome control code goes here
}
```

2. Once hosts have subscribed to the event, they'll want to know when the event fires. To
do this, fire an event on detecting a palindrome. The best place to do this is within the
Text property's setter. Add the boldfaced lines of code to the palindrome's *Text* property and rebuild the project:

```
[Bindable(true)]
[Category("Appearance")]
[DefaultValue("")]
[Localizable(true)]
public string Text
{
    get
    {
        string s = (string)ViewState["Text"];
        return ((s == null) ? String.Empty : s);
    }

    set
    {
        ViewState["Text"] = value;
        if (this.CheckForPalindrome())
        {
            if (PalindromeFound != null)
            {
                PalindromeFound(this, EventArgs.Empty);
            }
        }
    }
}
```

Notice that the code generated by Visual Studio 2008 stores the property in the control's *ViewState*. That way, the property retains its value between posts. We'll examine
ViewState more closely later in this chapter.

3. Now wire the event in the host page. Remove the current instance of the
PalindromeCheckerRenderedControl from the page and drop a new instance on the
page. This will refresh the *CustomControlLib.DLL* assembly so the changes (the new
event) will appear in Visual Studio. Select the *PalindromeCheckerRenderedControl* on
the page and click the **Events** button (the little lightning bolt) in the property page in
Visual Studio. Double-click on the text box next to the *PalindromeFound* event. Visual
Studio will create an event handler for you.

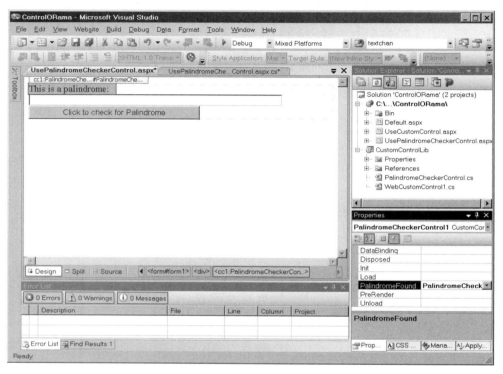

4. Respond to the *PalindromeFound* event. The example here simply prints some text out to the browser using *Response.Write*.

```
public partial class UsePalindromeCheckerControls : System.Web.UI.Page
{
    protected void Page_Load(object sender, EventArgs e)
    {
    }
    protected void Button1_Click(object sender, EventArgs e)
    {
        this.PalindromeCheckerRenderedControl1.Text =
                this.TextBox1.Text;
    }
    protected void PalindromeCheckerControl1_PalindromeFound(
        object sender, EventArgs e)
    {
        Response.Write("The page detected a PalindromeFound event");
    }
}
```

Run the page. You should see something like the following when you type a palindrome:

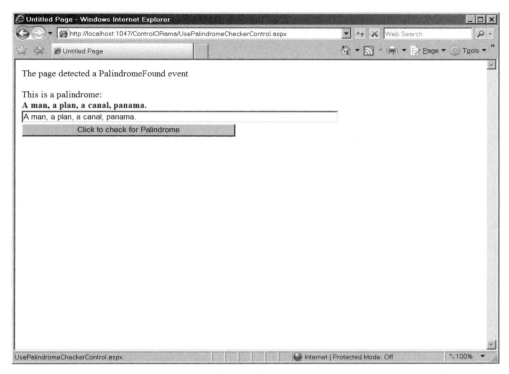

Now that the control renders palindromes correctly and has an event, let's take a closer look at the parameter passed in during the call to *Render: HtmlTextWriter*.

HtmlTextWriter and Controls

Go back and review the control's *RenderContents* method for a minute. Notice that the *RenderContents* method places literal font tags to change the color of the palindrome text. While this is certainly effective, this technique has a couple of downsides. For example, HTML is defined by multiple standards. That is, browsers running both HTML version 3.2 and version 4.0 occur in nature. Certain HTML elements have changed between version 3.2 and version 4.0. If you render all your HTML directly expecting requests from a certain kind of browser, your users may be taken by surprise if they browse to your page with a new browser that interprets HTML differently.

Note The .NET framework includes multiple versions of the *HtmlTextWriter* class: *Html32TextWriter*, *HtmlTextWriter*, *XhtmlTextWriter*, and *ChtmlTextWriter*. When a request comes from a browser, it always includes some header information indicating what kind of browser made the request. Most browsers these days are capable of interpreting the current version of HTML. In this case, ASP.NET passes in a normal *HtmlTextWriter* into the *RenderControl* method. However, if you happen to get a request from a lesser browser that understands only HTML 3.2, ASP.NET passes in an *Html32TextWriter*. The classes are similar as far as their use and may be interchanged. *Html32TextWriter* emits certain tags (such as table tags) in HTML 3.2 format, while *HtmlTextWriter* emits the same tags in HTML4.0 format. Information within machine.config and the browser capabilities configuration help ASP.NET figure out what kind of *HtmlTextWriter* to use. The browser capability information deduced by the ASP.NET runtime may be used for more than simply selecting the correct *HtmlTextWriter*. The *Request* property (available as part of the *HttpContext* and the *Page*) includes a reference to the *Browser* object. This object includes a number of flags indicating various pieces of information, such as the type of browser making the request, whether the browser supports scripting, and the name of the platform the browser is running on. This information comes down as part of the headers included with each request. The ASP.NET runtime runs the headers against some well-known regular expressions within the configuration files to figure out the capabilities. For example, here's a short listing illustrating how to figure out if the browser making the request supports Frames:

```
public class TestForFramesControl : Control
{
    protected override void RenderContents(HtmlTextWriter output)
    {
        if (Page.Request.Browser.Frames)
        {
          output.Write(
            "This browser supports Frames");
        }
        else
        {
            output.Write("No Frames here");
        }
    }
}
```

To get a feel for using the more advanced capabilities of *HtmlTextWriter*, replace the hard-coded font tags in the *RenderContents* method of the *PalindromeCheckerRenderedControl* with code that uses the *HtmlTextWriter* facilities.

Use the *HtmlTextWriter*

1. Open the PalindromeCheckerRenderedControl.cs file.

2. Update the *RenderContents* method to use the *HtmlTextWriter* methods. Use *HtmlTextWriter.RenderBeginTag* to start a font tag and a bold tag. Use *HtmlTextWriter* *.AddStyleAttribute* to change the color of the font to blue.

```
protected override void RenderContents(HtmlTextWriter output)
{
    if (this.CheckForPalindrome())
```

```
            {
                output.Write("This is a palindrome: <br/>");
                output.RenderBeginTag(HtmlTextWriterTag.Font);
                output.AddStyleAttribute(HtmlTextWriterStyle.Color, "blue");
                output.RenderBeginTag(HtmlTextWriterTag.B);
                output.Write(Text);
                output.RenderEndTag(); // bold
                output.RenderEndTag(); // font
            } else {
                output.Write("This is not a palindrome: <br/>");
                output.RenderBeginTag(HtmlTextWriterTag.Font);
                output.AddStyleAttribute(HtmlTextWriterStyle.Color, "red");
                output.RenderBeginTag(HtmlTextWriterTag.B);
                output.Write(Text);
                output.RenderEndTag(); // bold
                output.RenderEndTag(); // font
            }
        }
```

The *HtmlTextWriter* class and the enumerations include support to hide all the oddities of switching between HTML 3.2 and 4.0. Listing 4-5 shows how a table would be rendered using an HTML 4.0–compliant response. Listing 4-6 shows how a table would be rendered using an HTML 3.2–compliant response.

LISTING 4-5 HTML 4.0 Rendered Control

```
<br />
<br />
This is a palindrome: <br>
<b><font>Do geese see god?</font></b><br>
<table width="50%" border="1" style="color:blue;">
    <tr>
    <td align="left" style="font-size:medium;color:blue;">
A man, a plan, a canal, panama.</td>
    </tr>
<tr>
    <td align="left" style="font-size:medium;color:blue;">
Do geese see god?</td>
    </tr>
```

LISTING 4-6 HTML 3.2 Rendered Control

```
<br />
<br />
This is a palindrome: <br>
<b><font>Do geese see god?</font></b><br>
<table width="50%" border="1">
<tr>
<td align="left">
<font color="blue" size="4">A man, a plan, a canal, panama.</font>
</td>
</tr>
<tr>
<td align="left"><font color="blue" size="4">Do geese see god?</font>
</td>
</tr>
```

Controls and *ViewState*

Before leaving rendered controls, let's take a look at the issue of control state. If you go back to some of the classic ASP examples from earlier chapters, you may notice something disconcerting about the way some of the controls rendered after posting back. After you select something in the combo box and make a round-trip to the server, by the time the response gets back, the controls (especially selection controls) have lost their state. Recall that the basic Web programming model is all about making snapshots of the server's state and displaying them using a browser. We're essentially trying to perform stateful user interface (UI) development over a disconnected protocol.

ASP.NET server-side controls include a facility for holding onto a page's visual state—it's a property in the Page named *ViewState*, and you can easily access it any time you need. *ViewState* is a dictionary (a name-value collection) that stores any serializable object.

Most ASP.NET server-side controls manage their visual state by storing and retrieving items in the *ViewState*. For example, a selection control might maintain the index of the selected item between posts so that the control knows which item has its *selected* attribute assigned.

The entire state of a page is encoded in a hidden field between posts. For example, if you browse to an ASPX page and view the source code coming from the server, you'll see the *ViewState* come through as a BASE 64–encoded byte stream.

To get a feel for how *ViewState* works, add some code to keep track of the palindromes that have been viewed through the control.

Using *ViewState*

1. Open the PalindromeCheckerRenderedControl.cs file.

2. Add *System.Collections* to the list of using directives.

   ```
   using System;
   using System.Collections.Generic;
   using System.ComponentModel;
   using System.Text;
   using System.Web.UI;
   using System.Web.UI.WebControls;
   using System.Collections
   ```

3. Add an *ArrayList* to the control to hold the viewed palindromes. Update the *Text* property's setter to store text in the view state if the text is a palindrome.

   ```
   public class PalindromeCheckerRenderedControl : WebControl
   {
       public event EventHandler PalindromeFound; // public event
       ArrayList alPalindromes = new ArrayList();

       [Bindable(true)]
   ```

```
[Category("Appearance")]
[DefaultValue("")]
[Localizable(true)]
public string Text
{
    get
    {
        String s = (String)ViewState["Text"];
        return ((s == null) ? String.Empty : s);
    }
    set
    {
        ViewState["Text"] = value;
        string text = value;
        this.alPalindromes =
            (ArrayList)this.ViewState["palindromes"];
        if (this.alPalindromes == null)
        {
            this.alPalindromes = new ArrayList();
        }
        if (this.CheckForPalindrome())
        {
            if (PalindromeFound != null)
            {
                PalindromeFound(this, EventArgs.Empty);
            }
            alPalindromes.Add(text);
        }
        ViewState.Add("palindromes", alPalindromes);
    }
}
}
```

4. Add a method to render the palindrome collection as a table and update the *RenderContents* method to render the viewed palindromes.

```
protected void RenderPalindromesInTable(HtmlTextWriter output)
{
    output.AddAttribute(HtmlTextWriterAttribute.Width, "50%");
    output.AddAttribute(HtmlTextWriterAttribute.Border, "1");
    output.RenderBeginTag(HtmlTextWriterTag.Table); //<table>

    foreach (string s in this.alPalindromes)
    {
        output.RenderBeginTag(HtmlTextWriterTag.Tr); // <tr>
        output.AddAttribute(HtmlTextWriterAttribute.Align, "left");
        output.AddStyleAttribute(HtmlTextWriterStyle.FontSize, "medium");
        output.AddStyleAttribute(HtmlTextWriterStyle.Color, "blue");
        output.RenderBeginTag(HtmlTextWriterTag.Td); // <td>
        output.Write(s);
        output.RenderEndTag(); // </td>
        output.RenderEndTag(); // </tr>
    }

    output.RenderEndTag(); // </table>
}
```

```
protected override void RenderContents (HtmlTextWriter output)
{
  if (this.CheckForPalindrome())
  {
    output.Write("This is a palindrome: <br>");
    output.RenderBeginTag(HtmlTextWriterTag.Font);
    output.AddStyleAttribute(HtmlTextWriterStyle.Color, "blue");
    output.RenderBeginTag(HtmlTextWriterTag.B);
    output.Write(Text);
    output.RenderEndTag(); // bold
    output.RenderEndTag(); // font
  } else {
    output.Write("This is NOT a palindrome: <br>");
    output.RenderBeginTag(HtmlTextWriterTag.Font);
    output.AddStyleAttribute(HtmlTextWriterStyle.Color, "red");
    output.RenderBeginTag(HtmlTextWriterTag.B);
    output.Write(Text);
    output.RenderEndTag(); // bold
    output.RenderEndTag(); // font
  }

  output.Write("<br>");
  RenderPalindromesInTable(output);
}
```

5. Build and run the application. When you surf to the page holding the palindrome checker, you should see the previously found palindromes appearing in the table:

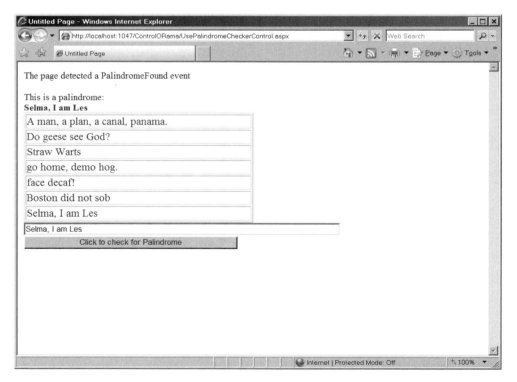

Now that the control is storing more information in the *ViewState*, the HTML response due to postbacks will increase in size as the _VIEWSTATE field within the response grows. Add a few more palindromes to the page, viewing the source that's sent to the browser each time. You'll see the VIEWSTATE hidden field grow in size with each postback. The caveat here is that introducing controls that use view state will increase the size of the HTTP payload coming back to the browser. Use the view state judiciously as overuse can bog down a site's performance.

Summary

ASP.NET's *Page* infrastructure is set up so that each page is broken down into smaller components (server-side controls) that are responsible for rendering a small amount of HTML into the page's output stream. After reading this chapter, you probably have a good idea as to how some of the standard ASP.NET controls are rendered. *Button* controls render as an input tag with a type of "submit." *TextBox* controls render as an input tag with a type of "text." You can actually see how each of the controls in a page renders by viewing the HTML that comes back to the browser.

Of course, because ASP.NET's *Page* infrastructure is set up this way, it leaves the door open for custom User controls. In this chapter, we looked at rendered custom controls. Custom controls that render have the ability to squirt anything they want into the output bound for the browser. Custom rendered controls usually manage a set of properties, fire events to their hosts, and render snapshots of themselves to their hosts. In this chapter, we built a palindrome checker as an example. Next, we'll see examples of the other kind of control you can create for your own needs—composite-style "User" controls.

Chapter 4 Quick Reference

To	Do This
Create a custom control that takes over the rendering process	Derive a class from *System.Web.UI.Control*. Override the *RenderContents* method. Visual Studio includes a project type, ASP.NET ServerControl, that fits the bill.
Add a custom control to the toolbox	Show the toolbox if it's not already showing by selecting **View**, **Toolbox** from the main menu. Click the right mouse button anywhere in the toolbox. Select **Choose Items** from the local menu. Choose a control from the list OR Browse to the assembly containing the control.

To	Do This
Change the properties of controls on a page	Make sure the page editor is in Design mode. Highlight the control whose property you want to change. Select the property to edit in the *Properties* window.
Manage events fired by controls on a page	Make sure the page editor is in Design mode. Highlight the control containing the event you want your page to handle. Select the event in the event window (you may highlight it by pressing the lightning bolt button in the *Properties* window). Double-click in the combo box next to the event to have Visual Studio insert the given handler for you OR Insert your own event handler name in the field next to the event name.
Store view state information that lives beyond the scope of the page	Use the *ViewState* property of the control (a name-value dictionary) that contains serializable types. Just be sure to use the same index to retrieve the information as you do to store the information.
Write browser version–independent rendering code	Use the *HtmlTextWriter* tag-rendering methods for specific tags instead of hard-coding them. The *RenderContents* method will have the correct *HtmlTextWriter* based on header information coming down from the browser.

Chapter 5
Composite Controls

After completing this chapter, you will be able to

- Create a binary composite custom control
- Create a composite User control
- Use both kinds of controls in an application
- Recognize when each kind of control is appropriate

The last chapter covered the details of controls that do custom rendering, and this chapter covers the other kind of control—composite controls. ASP.NET defines two broad categories of composite controls—binary custom controls and user custom controls. Each type of composite control has advantages and disadvantages, which we'll discuss. First, let's explore the primary differences between rendered controls and composite-style controls.

Composite Controls versus Rendered Controls

Recall that custom rendered controls completely form and tailor the HTML going back to the client via the *System.Web.UI.Control.RenderControl* method. Custom rendered controls take over the entire rendering process. With custom rendered controls, you have extraordinary flexibility and power over the HTML emitted by your Web site—all the way down to the individual control level.

However, with that power and flexibility also comes the need to keep track of an enormous amount of detail. For example, if you were to add an input button to a custom rendered control, you'd need to insert the correct HTML to describe the button within the response stream heading back to the client. Things get even more difficult when you decide to add more complex controls such as selection controls that may need to track collections of items. Even though input buttons and selection controls are easy to describe in HTML, we've seen that ASP.NET already includes server-side control classes that render the correct tags. The standard ASP.NET controls greatly simplify user interface (UI) programming for Web forms.

Composite controls take advantage of these server-side controls that have already been written. Composite controls are *composed* from other controls. To illustrate the utility of composite controls, imagine you're working on a number of projects whose login screens require a similar look and feel. On the one hand, you've already seen that it's fairly easy to build Web forms in Visual Studio. However, if you run into a situation that requires the same group of controls to appear together in several instances, it's pretty tedious to recreate those pages repeatedly. ASP.NET solves this problem with composite controls.

If you need common login functionality to span several Web sites, you might group user name/password labels and text boxes together in a single control. Then when you want to use the login page on a site, you simply drop the controls *en masse* on the new form. The controls (and the execution logic) instantly combine so you don't need to keep writing the same HTML over and over.

> **Note** Beginning with version 2.0, ASP.NET includes a set of login composite controls so you don't need to write new ones from scratch. However, they are mentioned here because they represent an excellent illustration for the power of composite controls.

Let's begin by looking at custom composite controls.

Custom Composite Controls

In Chapter 4, we saw how binary custom controls render custom HTML to the browser. The factor distinguishing this kind of control most is that these controls override the *RenderContents* method. Remember, the *System.Web.UI.Page* class manages a list of server-side controls. When ASP.NET asks the whole page to render, it goes to each control on the page and asks it to render. In the case of a rendering control, the control simply pushes some text into the stream bound for the browser. Likewise, when the page rendering mechanism hits a composite-style control, the composite control walks its list of child controls, asking each one to render—just as the *Page* walks its own list of controls.

Composite controls may contain an arbitrary collection of controls (as many children as memory will accommodate), and the controls may be nested as deeply as necessary. Of course, there's a practical limit to the number and depth of the child controls. Adding too many controls or nesting them too deeply will add complexity to a page, and it may become unsightly. In addition, adding too many nested controls will greatly inhibit the performance of the application. It does take time to walk the control collection and have each one render.

In Chapter 4, we created a control that checked for palindromes. When the control's *Text* property was set to a palindrome, the control rendered the palindrome in blue text, added it to an *ArrayList*, and then rendered the contents of the palindrome collection as a table. Let's build a similar control—however, this time it will be a composite control.

The palindrome checker as a composite custom control

1. Open the ControlORama project. Highlight the CustomControlLib project in the Solution Explorer. Click the right mouse button on the project node and select **Add**, **New Item**. Create a new class and name the source file *PalindromeCheckerCompositeControl.cs*. Use the ASP.NET Server Control template (as you did with the PalindromeCheckerRenderedControl from Chapter 4).

2. After Visual Studio creates the code, do the following:

❏ Edit the code to change the derivation from *WebControl* to *CompositeControl*. Deriving from the *CompositeControl* also adds the *INamingContainer* interface to the derivation list. (*INamingContainer* is useful to help ASP.NET manage unique IDs for the control's children.)

❏ Add the *PalindromeFound* event that the host page may use to listen for palindrome detections.

❏ Remove the *RenderContents* method.

❏ Add four member variables—a *TextBox*, a *Button*, a *Label*, and a *LiteralControl*.

The code should look something like this when you're finished:

```
public class PalindromeCheckerCompositeControl :
        CompositeControl
{
    protected TextBox textboxPalindrome;
    protected Button buttonCheckForPalindrome;
    protected Label labelForTextBox;
    protected LiteralControl literalcontrolPalindromeStatus;
    public event EventHandler PalindromeFound;
...
// RenderContents method removed.
}
```

Leave the *Text* property intact. We'll still need it in this control.

The control is very much like the one in Chapter 4. However, this version will include the palindrome *TextBox*, the *Button* to invoke palindrome checking, and will contain a literal control to display whether or not the current property is a palindrome.

3. Borrow the *StripNonAlphanumerics* and *CheckForPalindrome* methods from the *PalindromeCheckerRenderedControl*:

```
protected string StripNonAlphanumerics(string str)
{
    string strStripped = (String)str.Clone();

    if (str != null)
    {
    char[] rgc = strStripped.ToCharArray();

        int i = 0;

        foreach (char c in rgc)
        {
            if (char.IsLetterOrDigit(c))
            {
                i++;
            }
        }
```

```
            else
            {
                strStripped = strStripped.Remove(i, 1);
            }
        }
    }

    return strStripped;
}

protected bool CheckForPalindrome()
{
    if (this.Text != null)
    {
        String strControlText = this.Text;
        String strTextToUpper = null;

        strTextToUpper = Text.ToUpper();

        strControlText = this.StripNonAlphanumerics(strTextToUpper);

        char[] rgcReverse = strControlText.ToCharArray();
        Array.Reverse(rgcReverse);
        String strReverse = new string(rgcReverse);
        if (strControlText == strReverse)
        {
            return true;
        }
        else
        {
            return false;
        }
    }
    else
    {
        return false;
    }
}
```

4. Add an event handler to be applied to the *Button* (which we'll install on the page soon). Because this is a binary control without designer support, you'll need to add the event handler using the text wizard (that is, you'll need to type it by hand).

```
public void OnCheckPalindrome(Object o, System.EventArgs ea)
{
    this.Text = this.textboxPalindrome.Text;
    this.CheckForPalindrome();
}
```

5. Add an override for the *CreateChildControls* method. Overriding the *CreateChildControls* method is what really distinguishes composite controls from rendered controls. In the method, you'll need to create each *UI* element by hand, set the properties you want appearing in the control, and add the individual control to the composite control's list of controls.

```
protected override void CreateChildControls()
{
    labelForTextBox = new Label();
    labelForTextBox.Text = "Enter a palindrome: ";
    this.Controls.Add(labelForTextBox);

    textboxPalindrome = new TextBox();
    this.Controls.Add(textboxPalindrome);

    Controls.Add(new LiteralControl("<br/>"));

    buttonCheckForPalindrome = new Button();
    buttonCheckForPalindrome.Text = "Check for Palindrome";
    buttonCheckForPalindrome.Click += new EventHandler(OnCheckPalindrome);
    this.Controls.Add(buttonCheckForPalindrome);

    Controls.Add(new LiteralControl("<br/>"));

    literalcontrolPalindromeStatus = new LiteralControl();
    Controls.Add(literalcontrolPalindromeStatus);

    Controls.Add(new LiteralControl("<br/>"));

    this.tablePalindromes = new Table();
    this.Controls.Add(tablePalindromes);

    this.ChildControlsCreated = true;
}
```

Although the code listed above is pretty straightforward, a couple of lines deserve special note. First is the use of the *LiteralControl* to render the line breaks. Remember—every element on the page (or in this case the control) will be rendered using a server-side control. If you want any literal text rendered as part of your control, or if you need HTML markup that isn't included as a provided ASP.NET control (such as the *
* element), you need to package it in a server-side control. The job of a *LiteralControl* is to take the contents (the *Text* property) and simply render it to the outgoing stream.

The second thing to notice is how the event handler is hooked to the *Button* using a delegate. When you use Visual Studio's designer support, you can usually wire event handlers up by clicking on a UI element in the designer—at which point Visual Studio adds the code automatically. However, because there's no designer support here, the event hookup needs to be handled manually.

6. Show the palindrome status whenever the *Text* property is set. Modify the *Text* property to match the following bit of code. The *Text* property's setter will check for a palindrome and render the result in the *LiteralControl* we added in Step 2. It should also raise the *PalindromeFound* event.

```
private String text;

public string Text
{
```

```
get
{
  return text;
}
set
{
  text = value;

  if (this.CheckForPalindrome())
  {
    if (PalindromeFound != null)
    {
      PalindromeFound(this, EventArgs.Empty);
    }

    literalcontrolPalindromeStatus.Text =
      String.Format(
      "This is a palindrome <br/><FONT size=\"5\" color=\"blue\"><B>{0}</B></FONT>",
      text);
  }
  else
  {
    literalcontrolPalindromeStatus.Text =
      String.Format(
      "This is NOT a palindrome <br/><FONT size=\"5\" color=\"red\"><B>{0}</B></FONT>",
      text);
  }
}
}
}
```

7. Show the palindromes in a table, just as the rendered version of this control did. First, add an *ArrayList* and a *Table* control to the *PalindromeCheckerCompositeControl* class.

```
public class PalindromeCheckerCompositeControl :
Control, INamingContainer
{

    protected Table tablePalindromes;
    protected ArrayList alPalindromes;

}
```

8. Add a method to build the palindrome table based on the contents of the *ArrayList*. Check to see if the array list is stored in the *ViewState*. If it's not, then create a new one. Iterate through the palindrome collection and add a *TableRow* and a *TableCell* to the table for each palindrome found.

```
protected void BuildPalindromesTable()
{
    this.alPalindromes = (ArrayList)this.ViewState["palindromes"];
    if (this.alPalindromes != null)
```

```
      {
        foreach (string s in this.alPalindromes)
        {
           TableCell tableCell = new TableCell();
           tableCell.BorderStyle = BorderStyle.Double;
           tableCell.BorderWidth = 3;
           tableCell.Text = s;
           TableRow tableRow = new TableRow();
           tableRow.Cells.Add(tableCell);
           this.tablePalindromes.Rows.Add(tableRow);
        }
      }
   }
```

9. Update the *Text* property's setter to manage the table. Add palindromes to the *ArrayList* as they're found, and build the palindrome table each time the text is changed.

```
public string Text
{
  get
  {
    return text;
  }
  set
  {
    text = value;

    this.alPalindromes = (ArrayList)this.ViewState["palindromes"];
    if (this.alPalindromes == null)
    {
      this.alPalindromes = new ArrayList();
    }

    if (this.CheckForPalindrome())
    {
      if (PalindromeFound != null)
      {
        PalindromeFound(this, EventArgs.Empty);
      }

      alPalindromes.Add(text);

       literalcontrolPalindromeStatus.Text =
          String.Format(
          "This is a palindrome <br/><FONT size=\"5\" color=\"blue\"><B>{0}</B></FONT>",
          text);
    }
    else
    {
       literalcontrolPalindromeStatus.Text =
          String.Format(
          "This is NOT a palindrome <br/><FONT size=\"5\" color=\"red\"><B>{0}</B></FONT>",
          text);
    }
```

```
        this.ViewState.Add("palindromes", alPalindromes);
        this.BuildPalindromesTable();

    }
}
```

10. Build the project and add the *PalindromeCheckerCompositeControl* control to the ControlORama UsePalindromeCheckerControls.aspx page. If you are extending the example from the last chapter, add a line break (*
*) following the rendered control from the last chapter. Add a *label* to indicate that the next control is the composite control and one more line break. Then pick up the *PalindromeCheckerCompositeControl* control directly from the toolbox and drop it onto the page. When you run the page, it will check for palindromes and keep a record of the palindromes that have been found, like so (tracing is turned on in this example so we can see the control tree later). Note that this example extends the previous chapter and the page includes the controls added from the previous chapter:

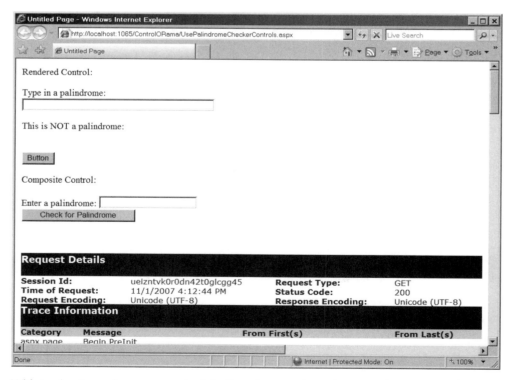

With tracing turned on, you can look further down and see the control tree. Notice how the *PalindromeCheckerCompositeControl* acts as a main node on the tree and that the composite control's child controls are shown under the **PalindromeCheckerCompositeControl** node.

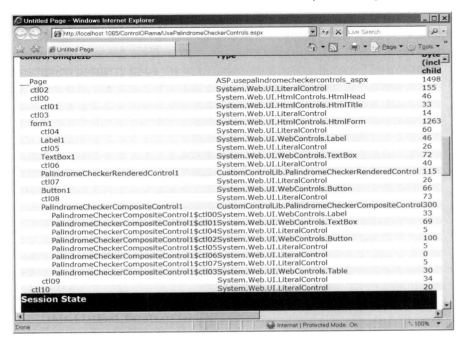

When you type palindromes and click the button, the control will detect them. The control displays the current *Text* property in red if it's *not* a palindrome and in blue if it *is* a palindrome. You can also see the table rendering, showing the currently found palindromes.

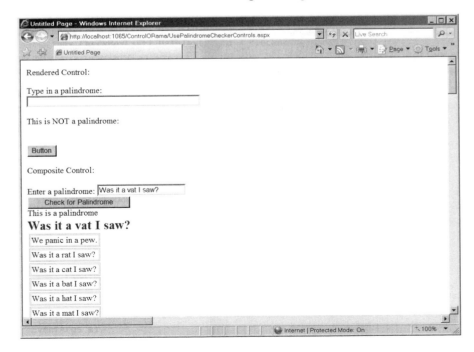

The palindrome checker is a good example of a binary composite control. The composite control lives entirely within the *CustomControlLib* assembly and does not have any designer support at present (we could add code to support high-quality design time support, but that's beyond the scope of this chapter). Here's an alternative to coding a composite control entirely by hand—the second way to create composite controls is via a *User* control.

User Controls

User controls are composite controls that contain child controls very much like binary composite controls do. However, instead of deriving from *System.Web.UI.CompositeControl*, they derive from *System.Web.UI.UserControl*. Perhaps a better description is that they're very much like miniature Web forms. The have a UI component (an .ascx file) that works with the Visual Studio designer, and they employ a matching class to manage the execution. However, unlike a Web form, they may be dragged onto the toolbox and then dropped into a Web form.

To get a good idea as to how Web *User* controls work, here's how to build the palindrome checker as a *User* control.

The palindrome checker as a *User* control

1. Open the ControlORama project (if it's not already open). Highlight the ControlORama Web site within the Solution Explorer. Click the right mouse button on the site and select **Add New Item**. Select the *Web User Control* template and name the control *PalindromeChecker UserControl.ascx*.

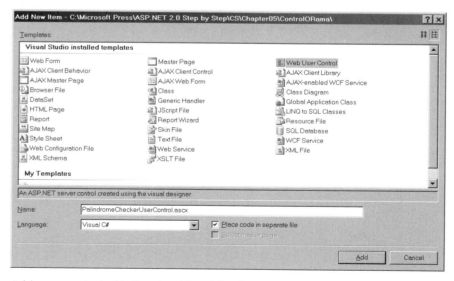

2. Add new controls. Notice that Visual Studio may drop you into the designer (if instead you're facing the code view, switch to the design view using the **Design** tab). User controls are designer friendly. Drag a *Label*, a *TextBox*, a *Button*, and another *Label* from

the toolbox. Drop them into the User control. Delete the *Text* property from the second label so that it will show its identifier. Format them as shown:

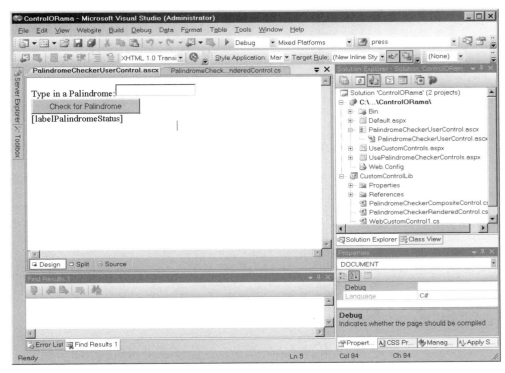

Name the second label *labelPalindromeStatus* to make it easier to use from within the code beside.

3. Borrow the *StripNonAlphanumerics* and *CheckForPalindrome* methods from the *PalindromeCheckerCompositeControl* class. Open the source code file PalindromeCheckerCompositeControl.cs. Copy these methods into the *PalindromeCheckerUserControl* class in the PalindromeCheckerUserControl.ascx.cs file.

```
protected string StripNonAlphanumerics(string str)
{
    string strStripped = (String)str.Clone();
    if (str != null)
    {
        char[] rgc = strStripped.ToCharArray();
        int i = 0;
        foreach (char c in rgc)
        {
            if (char.IsLetterOrDigit(c))
            {
                i++;
            }
            else
```

```
                {
                    strStripped = strStripped.Remove(i, 1);
                }
            }
        }

        return strStripped;
    }

    protected bool CheckForPalindrome()
    {
        if (this.Text != null)
        {
            String strControlText = this.Text;
            String strTextToUpper = null;

            strTextToUpper = Text.ToUpper();

            strControlText = this.StripNonAlphanumerics(strTextToUpper);

            char[] rgcReverse = strControlText.ToCharArray();
            Array.Reverse(rgcReverse);
            String strReverse = new string(rgcReverse);
            if (strControlText == strReverse)
            {
                return true;
            }
            else
            {
                return false;
            }
        }
        else
        {
            return false;
        }
    }
```

4. Add the *PalindromeFound* event to the control class.

```
public event EventHandler PalindromeFound; // public event
```

5. Open the code file and add a text member variable and a *Text* property, very much like the other composite control implemented. Unlike binary composite controls, User controls aren't generated with any default properties. (There are some minor changes, such as the use of a *Label* control instead of the *Literal* control for accepting the palindrome status, so be sure to make the necessary adjustments if cutting and pasting code from the previous control.)

```
private String text;

public string Text
{
  get
  {
```

```
      return text;
    }
    set
    {
      text = value;

      if (this.CheckForPalindrome())
      {
        if (PalindromeFound != null)
        {
          PalindromeFound(this, EventArgs.Empty);
        }

        this.labelPalindromeStatus.Text =
            String.Format(
            "This is a palindrome <br/><FONT size=\"5\" color=\"blue\"><B>{0}</B></FONT>",
            text);
      }
      else
      {
         this.labelPalindromeStatus.Text =
            String.Format(
            "This is NOT a palindrome <br/><FONT size=\"5\" color=\"red\"><B>{0}</B></FONT>",
            text);
      }
    }
  }
}
```

6. Now add support for keeping track of palindromes. Add an *ArrayList* to the control class.

```
ArrayList alPalindromes;
```

7. Add a *Table* to the control. Switch to the *PalindromeCheckerUserControl* Design view and drag a *Table* onto the form.

8. Add a method to build the table of palindromes. It's very much like the one in the *PalindromeCheckerCompositeControl*, except the name of the table has changed. *Table1* is the name given the table by Visual Studio.

```
protected void BuildPalindromesTable()
{
    this.alPalindromes = (ArrayList)this.ViewState["palindromes"];
    if (this.alPalindromes != null)
    {
       foreach (string s in this.alPalindromes)
       {
          TableCell tableCell = new TableCell();
          tableCell.BorderStyle = BorderStyle.Double;
          tableCell.BorderWidth = 3;
          tableCell.Text = s;
          TableRow tableRow = new TableRow();
          tableRow.Cells.Add(tableCell);
          this.Table1.Rows.Add(tableRow);
       }
    }
}
```

9. Add support for keeping track of the palindromes in the *Text* property's setter as well as calling *BuildPalindromesTable*.

```
public string Text
{
  get
  {
    return text;
  }

  set
  {
    text = value;

    this.alPalindromes =
            (ArrayList)this.ViewState["palindromes"];
    if (this.alPalindromes == null)
    {
      this.alPalindromes = new ArrayList();
    }

    if (this.CheckForPalindrome())
    {
      if (PalindromeFound != null)
      {
        PalindromeFound(this, EventArgs.Empty);
      }

      alPalindromes.Add(text);

      this.labelPalindromeStatus.Text =
          String.Format(
          "This is a palindrome <br/><FONT size=\"5\" color=\"blue\"><B>{0}</B></FONT>",
          text);
    }
    else
    {
      this.labelPalindromeStatus.Text =
          String.Format(
          "This is NOT a palindrome <br/><FONT size=\"5\" color=\"red\"><B>{0}</B></FONT>",
          text);
    }

    this.ViewState.Add("palindromes", alPalindromes);
    this.BuildPalindromesTable();

  }
}
```

10. Add a *Click* handler to the button by double-clicking on it in the designer. This will generate a handler in the associated code file. Within the handler, grab the control's *Text* property from the *TextBox.Text* property and call the method *CheckForPalindrome*. This will set the control's *Text* property and build the table of palindromes.

```
protected void Button1_Click(object sender, EventArgs e)
{
    this.Text = this.TextBox1.Text;
    CheckForPalindrome();
}
```

11. Now add the control to the page. Pick up the .ascx file from the Solution Explorer. Click and drag it onto the UsePalindromeCheckerControls.aspx page. You can add a line break between the last control on the page and this one to help the layout look okay.

12. Build and run the project. When you type palindromes into the *PalindromeCheckerUserControl*, it should look something like this:

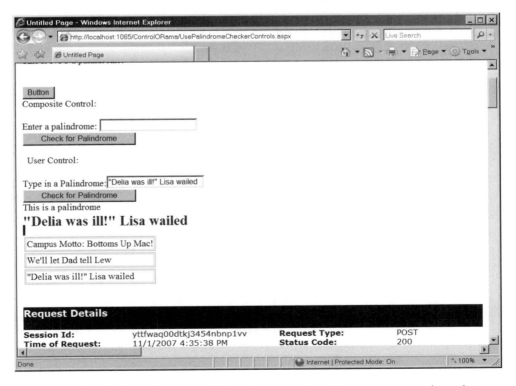

Before leaving, take a look at the page with tracing turned on. Here you can see how the page/control hierarchy is laid out in memory.

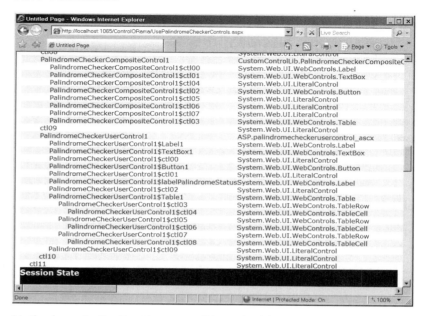

Notice how similar the *User* control is to the binary composite control. Both composite-style controls nest multiple single controls. They're very convenient ways of grouping rich Web-based user interface functionality into single units.

When to Use Each Type of Control

With binary composite controls and *User* controls having so many similarities, there seems to be some redundancy in the framework. Since *User* controls have such an affinity with the designer, perhaps it seems you don't need custom composite controls at all. However, each style of composite control has distinct advantages and disadvantages.

The major advantage of binary composite controls is that they are deployed as individual assemblies. Because binary composite controls are packaged in distinct assemblies, you may sign them and deploy them across the enterprise. You also may install them in the Global Assembly Cache. Signing and deploying global assemblies is an advanced topic—but I mention it here because this is one of the main reasons to choose a binary control over a User control. The primary downside to using binary composite controls is that they require more attention to detail in the coding process (there's no designer support as you write them since they're created entirely from code).

The primary advantage to *User* controls is that they *do* include designer support. That makes them very easy to design visually. However, *User* controls have a downside in their deployment—they go with the project in which they were created, and they are deployed that way. You can include them as part of other projects, but that requires copying the ASCX and the CS files to the new project. They are not deployed as signed, secure assemblies.

Summary

This look at composite-style controls wraps up ASP.NET's custom control story. Composite controls are a great way to package UI functionality into manageable chunks. Binary composite controls and User controls both maintain internal lists of controls and render them on demand. However, binary composite controls live entirely within an assembly, whereas User controls are split between ASCX files and a backing source code file and/or assembly.

In the next chapter, we'll take a look at some of the other controls available within ASP.NET.

Chapter 5 Quick Reference

To	Do This
Create a binary control composed of other server-side controls that lives in its own assembly	Derive a class from *System.Web.UI.Control*. Override the *CreateChildControls* method. Visual Studio includes a project type, *ASP.NET Server Control*, that fits the bill.
Add controls to a binary composite control	Instantiate the child control. Add the child control to the composite control's Control collection.
Add a custom control to the Toolbox	Show the Toolbox if it's not already showing by selecting **View, Toolbox** from the main menu. Click the right mouse button anywhere in the Toolbox. Select **Choose Items** from the local menu. Choose a control from the list OR Browse to the assembly containing the control.
Tell ASP.NET to assign unique IDs for the child controls within either type of composite control	Derive the binary composite control from ASP.NET's *CompositeControl* class. If you're creating a *User* control, this functionality is built in.
Raise events within either type of composite control	Expose the (public) events using the *event* keyword.
Create composite (*User*) controls using the Visual Studio Designer	Within a Visual Studio Web Site project, select **Web Site, Add New Item** from the main menu. Select the *Web User Control* template.

Chapter 6
Control Potpourri

After completing this chapter, you will be able to

- Use ASP.NET validation controls
- Use the *Image, ImageButton,* and *ImageMap* controls
- Use the *TreeView* control
- Use the *MultiView* control

ASP.NET has always evolved with the goal of reducing the effort developers must expend to get their Web sites up and running. One of the things you'll find as you tour ASP.NET is that Microsoft has done a great job of anticipating what the developer needs and putting it in the framework. In the three previous chapters, we saw the architecture behind ASP.NET Web Forms and controls. With this architecture in place, you can easily extend the framework to do almost anything you want it to do.

ASP.NET versions 1.0 and 1.1 took over much of the functionality developers were building into their sites with classic ASP. For example, server-side controls handled much of the arduous coding that went into developing Web sites displaying consistent user interfaces (such as combo boxes that always showed the last selection that was chosen).

Later versions of ASP.NET continued that theme by introducing new server-side controls that insert commonly desired functionality into the framework. In this chapter, we look at support provided by ASP.NET for validating the data represented by controls. We'll also look at a few other controls that are very useful: various flavors of the *Image* control, the *MultiView* control, and the *TreeView* control.

Let's start with the validation controls.

Validation

One of ASP.NET's primary goals has been to provide functionality to cover the most often used scenarios. For example, we'll see later that authorization and authentication requirements are common among Web sites. Most sites won't let you get to the real goodies until you authenticate as a valid user. ASP.NET now includes some login controls and an entire security infrastructure those controls work with to make authorization and authentication easier.

Another scenario you often find when surfing Web sites is that most sites include a page onto which you are to enter various types of information. For example, when applying for credentials to enter a Web site, you often need to enter things such as user names and passwords. If you want to have something e-mailed to you, you may be asked to enter your e-mail address.

When the company sponsoring a Web site wants some information from you, it wants to make sure it has accurate information. Although it can't guarantee that whatever you enter is 100 percent accurate, it can at least have a fighting chance of getting accurate information by validating the fields you've entered. For example, some fields may be absolutely required, and the Web site will ensure that data are entered into them. If you're asked to enter a phone number, the site may ask for it in a certain format and then apply a regular expression to validate that whatever you enter is at least formatted correctly. If you're asked to change your password, the site may ask you to enter it twice to be sure you really meant what you typed.

ASP.NET includes a host of validation controls that accompany standard controls (like a *TextBox*) on a Web Form. They work in concert with the standard controls and emit error messages (and alerts if configured to do so) if the user has typed in something that looks amiss.

ASP includes six validator controls:

- **RequiredFieldValidator**   Ensures that a field is filled in
- **RangeValidator**   Ensures the value represented by a control lies within a certain range
- **RegularExpressionValidator**   Validates that data within a control match a specific regular expression
- **CompareValidator**   Ensures that the data represented by a control compare to a specific value or another control
- **CustomValidator**   Provides an opportunity to specify your own server-side and client-side validation functions
- **ValidationSummary**   Shows a summary of all the validation errors on a page

The validation controls all work the same way. First define a regular control on the page. Then place the accompanying validators wherever you want the error messages to appear on the page. The validator controls have a property named *ControlToValidate*. Point the validator control to the control that needs validation and the rest works automatically. Of course, the validator controls have a number of properties you may use to customize the appearance of the error messages coming from the controls.

The ASP.NET validator controls work with the following server-side controls:

- TextBox
- ListBox
- DropDownList
- RadioButtonList

- HtmlInputText

- HtmlInputFile

- HtmlSelect

- HtmlTextArea

- FileUpload

To see how they work, follow the next example, which applies validation controls to a Web Form.

Creating a page that employs validation controls

1. Begin by creating a new Web site named *ControlPotpourri*.

2. Add a new Web Form named *ValidateMe.aspx*. This form will hold the regular server-side controls and their accompanying validation controls. The form will resemble a sign-in form that you often see on Web sites. It's the canonical example for employing user input validation.

3. Add a *TextBox* to hold the user's first name. Name the control *TextBoxFirstName*. It's important to give the controls meaningful names because they are attached to the validators by their names. If you use the defaults produced by Visual Studio (that is, TextBox1, TextBox2, TextBox3, etc.), you'll have a difficult time remembering what the text boxes represent. For each of the following steps, "adding a text box" also means adding an associated label and a *
* element to make the form look nice. In this case the label that precedes the *TextBoxFirstName* should say **First Name:**. The other labels should be self-evident. Note that you should also set the label's ControlToAssociate property to the text box the label precedes. This ties the label and text box together (actually the label renders using the *<label>* element rather than as simple text).

4. Add a last name *TextBox*. Name the control *TextBoxLastName*.

5. Add an address *TextBox*. Name the control *TextBoxAddress*.

6. Add a postal code *TextBox*. Name the control *TextBoxPostalCode*.

7. Add a phone number *TextBox*. Name the control *TextBoxPhone*.

8. Add *TextBoxes* to hold a password and a password confirmation. Name them *TextBoxPassword* and *TextBoxPasswordAgain*, respectively. Set the *TextMode* property for both of them to *Password* so that they don't display the text being typed by the end user. Using a secondary (or confirmative) *TextBox* ensures that the user types a password he or she really means to enter. (Setting the *TextMode* property to *Password* on the *TextBox* prevents the user from seeing the characters as they are keyed.)

9. Add a *TextBox* to hold the user's age. Name the control *TextBoxAge*.

10. Add a *Button* to submit the form. Give it the text **Submit Information**.

The form should look something like this when you're done:

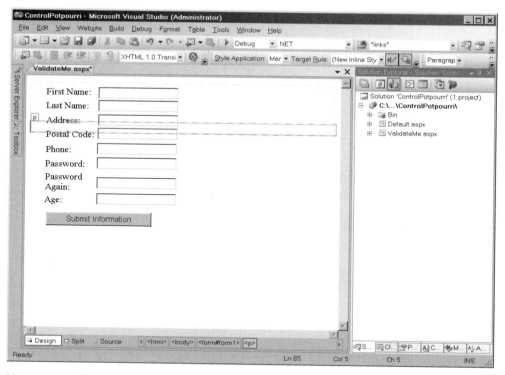

11. Now start adding validators. Add a *RequiredFieldValidator* control for the first name. Drag an instance of *RequiredFieldValidator* and drop it on the page just to the right of the *TextBoxFirstName*. In the properties for the first name validator control, pull down the combo box in the *ControlToValidate* property. Select the *TextBoxFirstName* control. Set the *ErrorMessage* property to a useful error message such as **Please give your first name**.

12. As with the first name text box, add a *RequiredFieldValidator* control for the last name. In the properties for the last name validator control, pull down the combo box in the *ControlToValidate* property. Select the *TextBoxLastName* control. Set the *ErrorMessage* property to a useful error message such as **Please give your last name**.

13. Add *RequiredFieldValidator* controls for the postal code, the phone number, the password, and the age text boxes.

14. In the properties for the postal code validator control, pull down the combo box in the *ControlToValidate* property. Select the *TextBoxPostalCode* control. Set the *ErrorMessage* property to a useful error message such as **Please give your postal code**.

15. In the properties for the phone validator control, pull down the combo box in the *ControlToValidate* property. Select the *TextBoxPhone* control. Set the *ErrorMessage* property to a useful error message such as **Please give your phone number so we may call you at dinner**.

16. In the properties for the first password validator control, pull down the combo box in the *ControlToValidate* property. Select the *TextBoxPassword* control. Set the *ErrorMessage* property to a useful error message such as **Please make up a password**.

17. In the properties for the second password validator control, pull down the combo box in the *ControlToValidate* property. Select the *TextBoxPasswordAgain* control. Set the *ErrorMessage* property to a useful error message such as **Please confirm your password**.

18. In the properties for the age required field validator control, pull down the combo box in the *ControlToValidate* property. Select the *TextBoxAge* control. Set the *ErrorMessage* property to a useful error message such as **Please give your age**.

19. Add a *ValidationSummary* to the form. This will show any errors occurring at once. If you want an alert to pop up in the browser, set the *ValidationSummary.ShowMessageBox* property to *true*. After all the validators have been added, the page should look something like this in the designer:

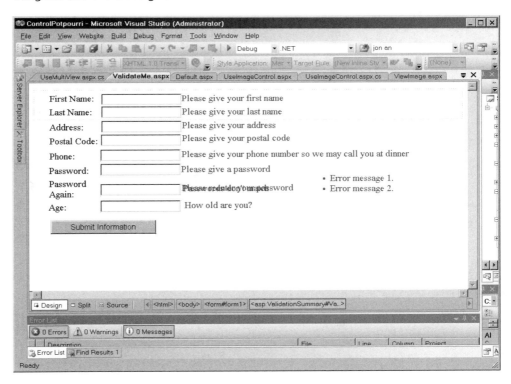

20. Compile the site and view the page. At first, all you'll see is a collection of input boxes. Before entering any fields, click the **Submit Information** button. Watch the error messages appear, as shown in the following graphic:

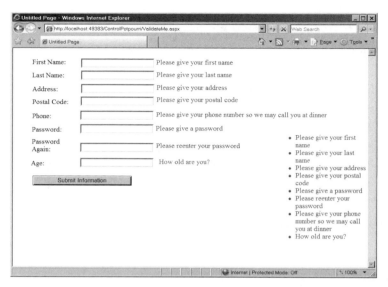

21. Type a first name and then press the **Enter** key. This will invoke the client-side JavaScript validation script. Watch what happens. The ASP.NET validator controls have inserted some JavaScript into the HTML sent to the browser (if the browser understands JavaScript, which the majority today do). With the client-side script in place, required field validators can manage their error messages without a round-trip to the server, as shown in the following graphic:

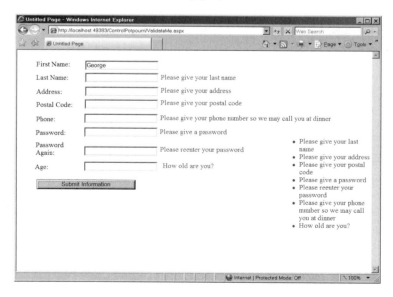

Before adding more validation controls, let's take a look at how ASP.NET user input validation works.

How Page Validation Works

ASP.NET's page validation is set up very cleverly—and it's all based on the page *server-side* control architecture. As with many other features in ASP.NET, the validation mechanism solves the most common use cases you encounter during Web site development. Most sites include both client-side and server-side validation. By supporting client-side validation, users are spared a round-trip when validating data input to the page. In addition to client-side validation, most sites also support server-side validation for two reasons: to make sure no data were garbled or modified during transmission and to support clients unable to support client-side scripting (perhaps the client browser doesn't support JavaScript). Let's start with a look at client-side validation.

Client-Side Validation

If you looked at the ASPX source code generated by Visual Studio as you placed controls on the page, you probably noticed the page became littered with even more tags, such as server-side control tags to support text boxes and selection controls. In addition, each validator control placed on the page corresponds to a separate tag. Validators are server-side controls, too. They render standard browser-interpretable code—similar to the regular server-side controls.

ASP.NET validator controls support client-side validation by linking a JavaScript file named *WebUIValidation.js* into the HTML sent to the browser. The file contains the client-side validation functions necessary to support client-side validation.

When the validation controls render to the browser, they add span elements with custom attributes to the rendered HTML. The validation handlers are hooked up when the HTML document is loaded in the browser.

Because client-side validation requires JavaScript support in the client, clients without JavaScript support will need to rely on server-side validation. If you want, you may disable the client-side script for each control by setting the *EnableClientScript* property on the validator to false.

Server-Side Validation

Once the client has passed the client-side validation tests, the request is posted back to the server and the server-side validation kicks in. Server-side validation is managed by infrastructure within the *Page* class. As you add validator controls to the page, they're added to a collection of validators managed by the page. Each validation control implements an interface named *IValidator*. The *IValidator* interface specifies a *Validate* method, an *ErrorMessage* property, and an *IsValid* property. Of course, each validator has its own custom logic to determine the validity of the data held within the control it's validating. For example, the

RequiredFieldValidator checks to see that there are data within the control it's associated with. The *RegularExpressionValidator* compares the data within a control to a specific regular expression.

During the postback sequence for a page, validation occurs just after the *Page_Load* event fires. The page checks each validator against its associated control. If validation fails, the server-side validation controls that failed render themselves as visible span elements.

The page itself has a property named *IsValid* that you can check to ensure your confidence in the data passed in from the client before you actually start using the data in the controls. In addition, the *Page* class implements a method named *Validate()*. *Validate* walks the list of validation controls, running each control's *Validate* method.

Add finer-grained validation

Once you've ensured that users fill the required fields, it's important to make sure that the data coming from users are likely to be correct. For example, you may not be able to ensure the veracity of the user's phone number, but at least you can make sure it is in the right format and doesn't contain garbage characters that could not possibly form a phone number. Let's add a validator that uses regular expressions to validate patterns. We'll add a couple of new validators to the page next.

1. Dismiss the browser and go back to the designer window. Now that you have controls that show error messages when the user forgets to type something, let's take a look at some finer-grained validation. When you look at the fields being entered, you can see a couple more opportunities for the user to enter bad data.

2. There's not much you can do for the first name, last name, and address fields except hope that the users type what they really mean to type. However, you might want to ensure the user types only numbers into the Postal Code field. The way to ensure that is to use a *RegularExpressionValidator* for the *TextBoxPostalCode* control. Drop a *RegularExpressionValidator* onto the page. Set the *ControlToValidate* property so it points to the postal code control. As for an error message, set the *ErrorMessage* property to **The postal code you provided is invalid**. Click the button associated with its *ValidationExpression* property, and from the resulting dialog box, select **U.S. ZIP Code** as the validation expression:

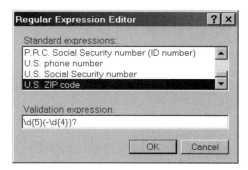

3. Add a regular expression validator for the *TextBoxPhone* control. Set the *ControlToValidate* property to *TextBoxPhone*. Assign its *ErrorMessage* property to be **The phone number you typed is invalid**. Bring up the Regular Expression Editor and choose **U.S. Phone Number** as the regular expression to validate, as shown in the following graphic:

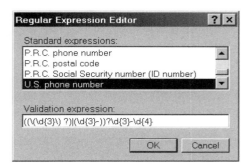

4. Add a *CompareValidator* for the *TextBoxPasswordAgain* control. In the properties for the password again validator control, pull down the combo box in the *ControlToValidate* property. Select the *TextBoxPasswordAgain* control. Set the *ControlToCompare* property to *TextBoxPassword*. Set the *ErrorMessage* property to a useful error message such as **The passwords provided do not match**.

5. Add another *CompareValidator* for the *TextBoxAge* control. Enter **30** for *ValueToCompare* and **Integer** as the data type to compare (the *Type* property). A possible error message here could be **You must be younger than 30 to submit data**. The operator property should be *LessThanEqual*.

6. Build and run the program. Enter some erroneous data. See what happens. You should see the error messages emitted by the validator controls. For example, if you type **33** as the age, the *CompareValidator* for the control should emit an error message. The *CompareValidator* should display an error in this case because the validator is looking for values less than or equal to 30.

Other Validators

In addition to the validators mentioned previously, ASP.NET includes two other validators: the *RangeValidator* and the *CustomValidator*. Let's take a quick look at each of those.

The *RangeValidator* is similar to the *CompareValidator* in that you may use it to check the data in a control against a value. However, the *RangeValidator's* purpose is to report an error if the data held in a control is out of a range. The validator specifies a minimum and a maximum value and reports the error if the value in the control falls beyond these thresholds.

You can try to fit any other kind of validation you might encounter into the *CustomValidator*. The *CustomValidator* fits on the page in the same way as the other validators. However, rather than predefining validation methods (on the server and within the client script), these pieces are left open. When you put a *CustomValidator* onto a page, you assign it an associated control. Then you refer to a validation function (that you write into the page). You may also specify a validation script block to be shipped to the client and run (along with the other client-side validation script).

Validator Properties

In looking through the validator controls, you can see that they contain the standard properties available to the other standard ASP.NET controls. For example, there's a *Text* property, a *Font* property, and various coloring properties. In addition, you'll find a couple of other properties useful for managing the error output sent to the browser.

The first property is the *Display* property. Its value may be either static or dynamic. This property manages the client-side rendering of the error message. *Static* (the default value) causes the span element emitted by the control to take up layout space in the HTML bound for the client, even when hidden. When the *Display* property is *Dynamic*, the span element emitted by the control changes the layout and dynamically expands when displayed.

ASP.NET has the ability to group validation controls. That is, each validation control may belong to a named group. The *ValidationGroup* property controls the name of the group. When a control belongs to a group, controls in that group only validate when one of the other validators in that group fires. This gives you a "multiple forms" effect within a single page.

Let's take a look at a few other interesting controls: the *Image* control and image-based controls, the *TreeView* control, and the *MultiView* control.

Image-Based Controls

Graphic images are often used within Web pages. HTML includes an image tag that tells the browser to fetch an image file (for example, a .GIF, .JPG, or .PNG file) and display it. When you need to get an image onto a page, HTML's *<img />* tag fits the bill. Naturally, ASP.NET wraps the *<img />* tag using a server-side control—the *Image* control.

Using the *Image* control is fairly straightforward. You pick it up out of the Toolbox like any other control and drop it onto the page. ASP.NET's *Image* control generates an *<img />* tag complete with the correct *src* attribute.

In addition to the normal *Image* control, ASP.NET includes an *ImageButton* control and an *ImageMap* control. The *ImageButton* control wraps the *<input type=image />* tag, giving you the ability to use an image as the background to a button. The *ImageMap* control shows a bitmap with hot spots on it that you can click.

The following exercise illustrates how the various ASP.NET image-based controls work.

Using image controls in a page

1. Add a new Web Form to the project to hold some image controls. Call the page *UseImageControls.aspx*.

2. Pick up an *Image* control from the Toolbox and drop it on the page.

3. Go to the Properties explorer and add a valid path to an image to the *ImageUrl* property. The image file may be on your own machine, or you can point the *ImageUrl* property to a valid image URL on the Web. To use an image on the Web, click the right mouse button on an image in the browser and select **Properties** from the local menu. Then copy the URL from the property dialog box and paste it into the *ImageUrl* in the property explorer. Try each option to see how it works. If the file is on your machine, you'll need to add it to your Web project. You can easily do so by dragging an image file from your local drive and dropping it onto the ControlPotpourri solution in Solution Explorer. If you'd like to organize your images in separate folders, simply create a new folder and drop them there. If you want to use an image from out on the Web you'll need to edit the *ImageUrl* property by hand in the Source view. Needless to say, no matter what image URL you use, if the image cannot be found (with a resulting error in the *<img/>* tag), you'll get the standard "image not found" image for your browser. In Internet Explorer that would be the image of the box with the red "X" in the center.

4. Run the site and see what the ASP.NET *Image* control produces (note your image URL will undoubtedly differ):

```
<img id="Image1" src="Images/sandiego.jpg" />
```

5. Now add an *ImageButton* to the page. The *ImageButton* gives you a way to decorate a normal input button so it shows a graphic. Your application can react to an *ImageButton* in one of three ways. First, the *ImageButton* behaves like a normal button to which you can attach a normal *Click* event handler on the server. Second, you may define a client-side script block and point the *ImageButton*'s *OnClientClick* property to the script. When you push the button, the button press runs the script on the browser. Finally, you may tell the *ImageButton* to redirect the next request to a specific page (even one on another site) using the *ImageButton*'s *PostBackUrl* property.

6. Run the page and examine the HTML produced by the *ImageButton*. It should look something like this (keeping in mind your image URL will be different):

```
<input type="image" name="ImageButton1" id="ImageButton1"
src="Images/goldengatebridge.jpg" style="border-width:0px;" />
```

7. Finally, add an *ImageMap* to the page. The *ImageMap* is useful for defining click-able areas on a bitmap. Pick an image available to you (download one from somewhere, or use one you have floating around on your hard drive). Set the *ImageMap*'s *ImageUrl* property to the image file.

8. Open the image that you have decided to use for the *ImageMap* using a picture editor such as Microsoft Paintbrush or Visual Studio's bitmap editor. The *ImageMap* in this example will define a hot spot that can be used to zoom into a portion of the image used in the map. Mark out a rectangular portion of the picture and make a new graphic file using the portion of the graphic. Make a note of the coordinates defining the section of the graphic you cut out. Enlarge the new image and save it to a new file.

9. Define some hot spots on the *ImageMap*. Among the *ImageMap*'s properties, you'll see one named *HotSpots*. Click on the button appearing in the property field to bring up the HotSpot Collection Editor, as shown in the following graphic:

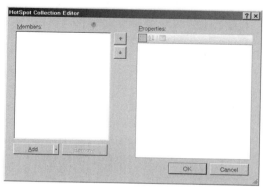

10. Add a hot spot to the collection. To do this, click the **Add** button. Notice that you can define circular, rectangular, or polygonal hot spots by clicking on the little arrow on the right side of the **Add** button. Create a rectangular hot spot using the coordinates of the portion of the image you just defined. Add some text to the *AlternateText* property—this will be the text that shows in the tool tip. Set the *HotSpotMode* property to *Navigate*, and use the NavigateUrl editor to set the *NavigateUrl* property to point to the new image file you just created (you may have to add the new image file to the project explicitly using the **Add Existing Item** menu after clicking the right mouse button on the project node in the Solution Explorer). The following graphic shows editing of the hot spot:

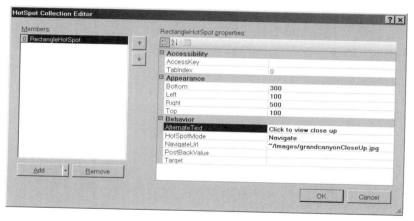

11. After adding the hot spot, run the new page. You should see something similar to the following graphic—the example here shows the Grand Canyon, and the hot spot is outlined in the image with a rectangle (that had to be added to the image by hand—the hot spot doesn't draw the rectangle for you). Notice how the tool tip pops up.

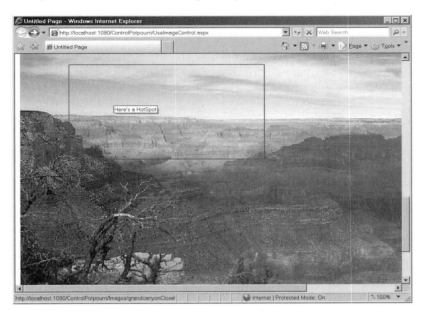

12. Click on the hot spot and notice how the application redirects to the "enlarged" image, as shown in the next graphic:

This section only scratches the surface of working with the image controls. However, you can see that you have much flexibility in defining how images look and behave.

TreeView

One of the most common user interface idioms in modern software is a hierarchy represented by expandable nodes. For example, whenever you browse for a file using Windows Explorer, you need to expand and contract various folders (subdirectories) to see what's inside. This type of control is generically known as a *tree control*.

Tree controls let users navigate hierarchies by representing expandable and collapsible nodes. For example, when you explore your C drive using Windows Explorer, the directories appear as closed folders with small plus signs to the left. When you click on a plus sign, Windows Explorer displays an open folder and then shows the subdirectories directly underneath. If there are further subdirectories, you may open them the same way.

ASP.NET provides this functionality via the *TreeView*. It's useful any time you want to represent a nested data structure and have a way of drilling down into it. To see how the *TreeView* works, let's look at an example.

Using the *TreeView* control

This exercise illustrates the *TreeView* control by showing a hierarchical, expandable list of 1970s bands that are still around today. The example will illustrate the hierarchical nature of the bands mentioned by showing the name of the band followed by a list of roles performed by each particular member.

1. Begin by adding a new Web form to the ControlPotpourri Web site. Name it *UseTreeView*.

2. Pick up a *TreeView* from the toolbox and add it to the default page. You'll find it under the Navigation controls.

3. Format your tree view. Visual Studio presents a number of options you can apply to the *TreeView*. Select the **Auto Format** option. Visual Studio presents a dialog box showing a number of styles for the *TreeView*. Browse through a few of them, highlighting them to see what the styles look like. The following graphic shows the local menu that you may use to bring up the **AutoFormat** dialog box:

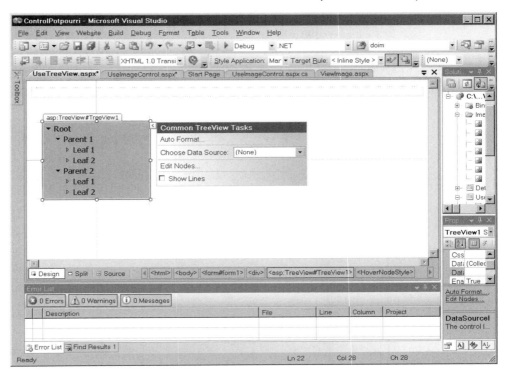

4. After selecting a style for the *TreeView*, select the **Edit Nodes** task. You may edit the nodes by clicking the right mouse button on the *TreeView* control and selecting **Edit Nodes** from the local menu. From this dialog box you may edit each of the nodes. The leftmost button adds new root nodes. In this example, the bands are represented as root nodes. The next button over is for adding child nodes. You may nest these nodes as deeply as necessary. In this example, the second layer of nodes represents the members of the bands, and the third layer represents their roles. The following graphic shows the *TreeView* node editor:

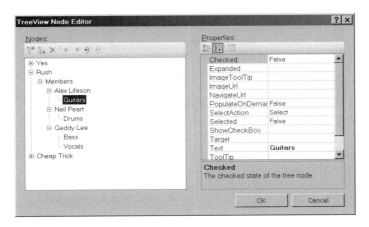

5. Add a border around the *TreeView* using the *BorderStyle* and *BorderColor* properties. Set the style to solid and the color to black. Of course, this is for visual aesthetics.

6. Build the project and browse to the page. You should be able to expand and contract the nodes. After running the page, take a quick look at the ASPX source code to see how the *TreeView* manages its nodes. The following graphic shows how the *TreeView* appears in the browser:

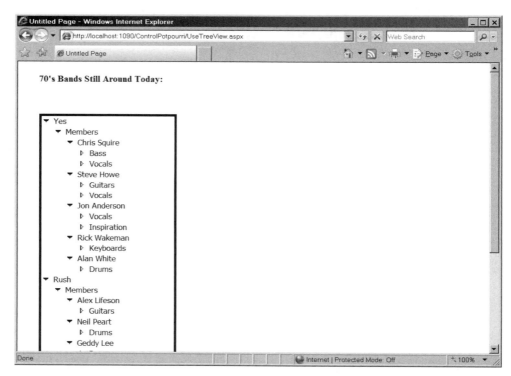

7. To make it a bit more interesting, add some functionality to handle some of the tree node events. First add a label to show the selected node. Name the label *LabelSelectedNode* so that you have programmatic access to it. Add a *TextBox* to show information about the selected node. Name it *TextBoxInfo*. Make the *TextBox* multiline. Then add an event handler for the *TreeView*'s *SelectedNodeChanged* event. Add the following code to interrogate the selected node to list information about the child nodes. Don't forget to add a *using* statement for *System.Text* (to identify *StringBuilder*):

```
protected void TreeView1_SelectedNodeChanged(object sender, EventArgs e)
{

    this.LabelSelectedNode.Text = String.Format("Selected Node changed to: {0}",
        this.TreeView1.SelectedNode.Text);
    TreeNodeCollection childNodes = this.TreeView1.SelectedNode.ChildNodes;
    if (childNodes != null)
```

```
    {
        this.TextBoxInfo.Text = String.Empty;
        StringBuilder sb = new StringBuilder();
        foreach(TreeNode childNode in childNodes)
        {
            sb.AppendFormat("{0}\n", childNode.Value);
        }
        this.TextBoxInfo.Text = sb.ToString();
    }

}
```

The following graphic shows how the selected details appear in the *ListBox*:

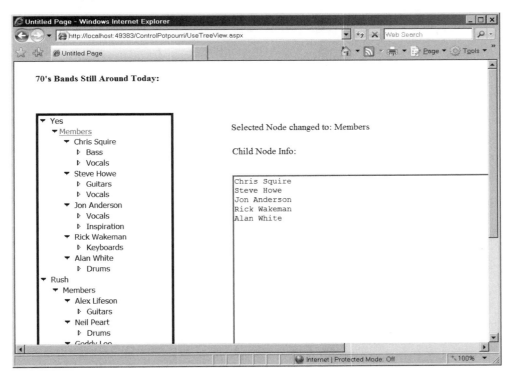

This is just a small illustration of what the *TreeView* is capable of doing. In addition to building nodes using the designer, you may build them programmatically. You may expand and contract nodes as well. Finally, the *TreeView* supports data binding, allowing you to throw a hierarchical data structure at the control so it will render properly for you.

Finally, let's take a look at ASP.NET's *MultiView* and *View* controls.

MultiView

From time to time, it's useful to gather controls together in several panes and give the user the opportunity to page through the panes. During the lifetime of ASP.NET 1.0, Microsoft released several rich dynamic (though officially unsupported) controls that emitted DHTML instead of regular HTML. A trio of these controls—the *TabStrip*, the *MultiView* (an older version), and the *PageView*—worked together to form essentially a set of tabbed panes.

These exact controls aren't available in later versions of ASP.NET; however, two controls— the *MultiView* and the *View*—go a long way toward providing similar functionality. The *MultiView* acts as a container for *Panel*-like controls (*View* controls). The *MultiView* includes support for paging through the various *Views* held within it. The *MultiView* shows a single *View* at a time.

The following exercise provides an example that shows how the *MultiView* and the *View* controls work together.

Using the *MultiView* and *View* controls

1. Add a new Web Form to the ControlPotpourri site. Name it *UseMultiview.aspx*. You'll add a *MultiView* to this form and then add some *Views* to it.

2. Add a *MultiView* control to this Web Form.

3. Add some views. The main purpose of the *MultiView* is to manage a set of *Views*. To add a *View* to a *MultiView*, pick up a *View* instance from the Toolbox and drop it *inside* the *MultiView*. Add three *Views* to the Web Form like so:

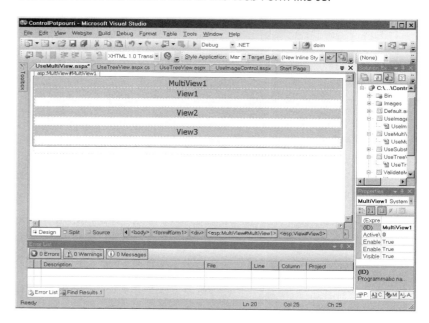

4. Add some content to each of the *Views*. You can think of the *Views* very much like panes. In this example, the views include labels that distinguish them. The following graphic illustrates how the *Views* look in the designer.

5. Activate the first pane. To cause the *MultiView* and the first *View* to show up, set the *MultiView*'s *ActiveViewIndex* property to **0** to show the first pane.

6. Add some controls to navigate between the *Views* in the *MultiView*. Add two buttons to the bottom of the form. Call them *ButtonPrev* and *ButtonNext*—they'll be used to page through the *Views*.

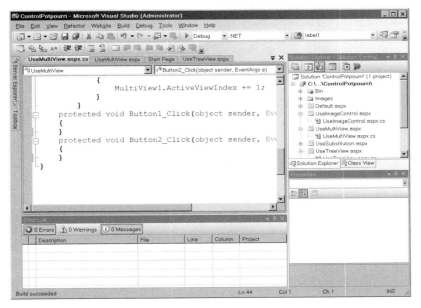

7. Add event handlers for the buttons by double-clicking on each of them.

8. Add code to the page through the *Views*. This code responds to the button clicks by changing the index of the current *View*.

```
protected void ButtonPrev_Click(object sender, EventArgs e)
{
    if (MultiView1.ActiveViewIndex == 0)
    {
        MultiView1.ActiveViewIndex = 2;
    }
    else
    {
        MultiView1.ActiveViewIndex -= 1;
    }
}
protected void ButtonNext_Click(object sender, EventArgs e)
{
    if (MultiView1.ActiveViewIndex == 2)
```

```
    {
        MultiView1.ActiveViewIndex = 0;
    }
    else
    {
        MultiView1.ActiveViewIndex += 1;
    }
}
```

9. Compile the project and browse to the Web page. Pressing the navigator buttons will cause postbacks to the server, which will render the individual views. The following graphic shows how the *MultiView* and *View* number 3 appear in a browser:

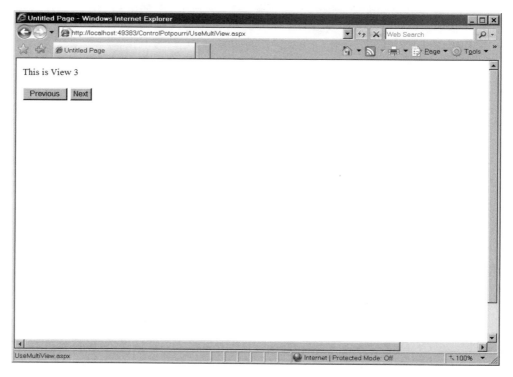

As you can see, the *MultiView* and the *View* classes act as panes that you can swap in and out. They represent a great way to manage the surface area involved in collecting large amounts of data. We'll see another version of this kind of control when we look at the *Wizard* control in conjunction with the session state.

Summary

In this chapter, we looked at both the ASP.NET validations and several of the controls available in ASP.NET. ASP.NET has always strived to lessen the drudgery of Web development by solving the most common use cases encountered during the development of Web sites.

Whenever you sign onto a commercial Web site, you almost invariably hit a form that asks you for information. When creating such forms, you will want to ensure that the data coming from the user are as accurate as possible. It's a good idea to check certain things, such as making sure that all the required fields are completed, that the fields have data in the correct format if formatting is important, and that certain data match specific values or fall within a stated range. ASP.NET validators perform this function.

The ASP.NET *TreeView* helps users browse hierarchical data structures (such as directories or Web site maps). The *TreeView* renders expandable and collapsible nodes that let users drill down into the data structures. The *MultiView* and the *View* work very much like panels that can be swapped in and out.

Next up: *Web Parts* (server-side controls on steroids).

Chapter 6 Quick Reference

To	Do This
Validate form input	ASP.NET includes a number of validator controls that check data entered via server-side controls. These controls include
	CompareValidator
	RangeValidator
	RequiredFieldValidator
	RegularExpressionValidator
	ValidationSummary
	CustomValidator
	To validate the input of a server-side control, drag the appropriate validator control onto the page and set the *ControlToValidate* property to the target control.
	Set the other validator properties appropriately.
Display hierarchical data sets in an intuitive way	Use the *TreeView* control.
	Either add items by hand or bind the *TreeView* control to a hierarchical data source. We'll see *TreeViews* again when we look at navigation controls in Chapter 12.
Swap between several pages of information on the same Web page	Use the *MultiView* and *View* controls.
	You can think of the *View* control as a miniature page managing controls.
	The *MultiView* manages a collection of *Views*.
	The *MultiView* supports swapping between *Views*.
Add an image to a Web page	Drop an *Image* control onto the Web page.
	Set the *Image* control's *ImageUrl* property to the URL of the image you'd like to show.
Add an image with clickable regions to the Web page	Drop an *ImageMap* onto the Web page.
	Use the hot spot editor to define clickable regions.

Part II
Advanced Features

Chapter 7
Web Parts

After completing this chapter, you will be able to

- Understand ASP.NET Web Parts
- Use standard Web Parts in a Web page
- Create a custom Web Part
- Use the custom Web Part in a Web page

In Chapters 4 and 5, we took a look at both rendered and composite controls. Chapter 6 covered a few of the controls already available within ASP.NET. Because rendering an ASP.NET Web Form is broken down into small, manageable chunks, arbitrarily extending the framework by adding new controls is a straightforward affair. Server-side controls offer very fine-grained control over the HTML rendered by your application.

In this chapter, we get a taste of Web Parts. The topic of Web Parts could take up an entire book—they represent a whole new level of interaction with Web sites. Web Parts are in many ways like custom controls. They give you a way to customize the HTML coming out of your Web site without having to hard-code the output of your page.

While custom controls derive either from *System.Web.UI.Control* or from *System.Web.UI .WebControl*, Web Parts derive from *Microsoft.SharePoint.WebPartPages.WebPart*. Although *WebPart* does inherit from *System.Web.UI.Control*, it goes beyond the regular control functionality by handling interactions with *WebPartPage* and *WebPartZone* classes to support adding, deleting, customizing, connecting, and personalizing Web Parts on a page.

Probably the largest difference between ASP.NET server-side controls and Web Parts is that Web Parts provide a way for *end users* to configure your site to their liking. By contrast, ASP.NET server-side controls are targeted to ASP.NET developers. ASP.NET allows lower-level developers to build interactive Web pages easily, whereas Web Parts allow users of a Web site a certain degree of flexibility in managing their view of your site.

Another way to get a good idea of the effectiveness of Web Parts is to consider the wave of social networking sites, such as Microsoft Live Spaces, that have emerged during the past few years. Although the main thrust of the site is governed back at the server, end users may create their own accounts and completely customize the presentation appearing on their screen. End users may add friends and associates, and they may build in links to other sites.

In addition to enabling Web sites that are customizable by end users, Web Parts can be very useful to lower-level site developers. Web Parts combine the flexibility of rendered custom controls with the drag-and-drop manageability of User controls. As a developer, you can drag completed Web Parts from Web Parts galleries and drop them onto Web Parts zones. You can modify the shared properties of a group of Web Parts and make them persistent. In addition to being a useful way to package user interface (UI) components, Web Parts can connect with each other via standard interfaces.

Web Part technology is very useful in building portals and collaboration sites. Microsoft SharePoint is an excellent example of this type of site. Rather than building document collaboration and sharing facilities into an application from the ground up, SharePoint already has high-level components that handle those sorts of features. Setting up a portal is about assembling high-level parts into an application.

A Brief History of Web Parts

In the early 2000s, SharePoint emerged as a highly leveraged way for organizations to build portals and collaboration environments. For example, coordinating large teams toward a common goal is an excellent reason for a portal. Team endeavors such as software development require systems such as version control and bug tracking. If the team is distributed geographically or in some other way not part of the office network, the next logical thing is to be able to share information over the Web.

Without a framework such as SharePoint, developers would likely duplicate much effort between them. SharePoint introduced some prefabricated components to ease building collaboration sites (rather than building them from scratch). SharePoint Web pages are based on a type of component named *Web Parts*. Web Parts are a way to package information and functionality for users.

Whereas SharePoint is a stand-alone framework dedicated to building collaboration portals, modern ASP.NET represents a broad-spectrum Web development framework that happens to have a built-in portal framework. That is, SharePoint represents a dedicated means to build portals, and ASP.NET includes some classes useful for building portal-like applications. However, even though they're different development environments, they do share a principal concept between them—Web Parts. Although ASP.NET Web Parts and SharePoint Web Parts aren't exactly the same animal, they operate similarly.

What Good Are Web Parts?

WebPart controls are useful for developing portal-type Web sites. Work flow and collaboration management is quickly becoming one of the most important application areas for Web site development. Because portals often have much of the same functionality from one to the other, it makes more sense to build portals from a framework than to build them completely from scratch. Much of this functionality includes such items as file transfers, implementing user profiles, and user administration.

ASP.NET offers three distinct Web Parts development scenarios: (1) building regular pages to consume Web Parts controls, (2) developing Web Parts controls, and (3) implementing Web Parts pages and Web Parts within a portal-type application.

Developing Web Parts Controls

Web Parts controls represent a superset of the existing ASP.NET server-side controls (including custom rendered controls, User controls, and composite controls), regardless of who wrote them. For maximum programmatic control of your environment, you can also create custom Web Parts controls that derive from the *System.Web.UI.WebControls.WebParts .WebPart* class.

Web Parts Page Development

Regular Web pages may use Web Parts. Visual Studio includes support for creating pages to host *WebPart* controls. Developing a *WebPart* page involves introducing a *WebPartManager* to the page, specifying a number of zones on the page, and then populating them with *WebPart* controls.

Web Parts Application Development

Finally, you may develop entire applications out of *WebPart* controls. For example, you may decide to build a portal. *WebPart* controls enable you to write personalized pages that are customizable. Web Parts are also ideal for building a commonly used application (such as sharing records or documentation) and shipping it as a unit so it can be deployed on another company's Web site wholesale.

The Web Parts Architecture

The Web Parts architecture serves multiple purposes. Given that the job of Web Parts is to behave as a bigger UI lever, the functional components have been broken into overall page management and zone management. *WebPart* controls need to be coordinated together. In addition, the different functional areas of a page often need to be handled as a group of controls (for managing layout, for example).

In terms of framework classes, Web Parts are nested within zones, which are managed by a singular *WebPartManager* that talks to the application data store. Figure 7-1 illustrates how the parts are related.

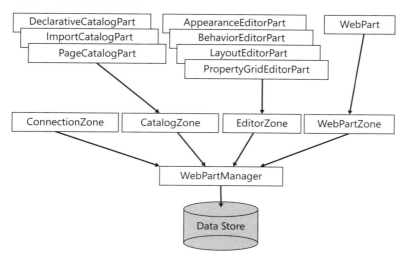

FIGURE 7-1 How Web Parts are managed within zones, which in turn are managed by an instance of *WebPartManager*

WebPartManager and *WebZones*

As Figure 7-1 illustrates, *WebPartManager* manages each *WebZone*, which in turn manages each individual *WebPart*. Any page using at least one *WebPart* needs an instance of *WebPartManager*. The *WebPartManager* is responsible for managing and coordinating the zone(s) and the controls lying within them. The *WebZone* also manages any extra *UI* elements that go with the group of controls.

Within the zone, the *ZoneTemplate* contains all Web Parts. If a regular ASP.NET control is in a *ZoneTemplate*, ASP.NET will wrap it as a Web Part.

Built-in Zones

Web Parts zones manage the layout for a group of controls. Out of the box, ASP.NET includes four built-in zones. These are

- **WebPartZone**   This class represents basic functionality for managing server-side controls within zones on a page. *WebPartZone* controls are responsible for hosting both normal server-side controls and *WebPart* controls. Normal controls become wrapped by the *GenericWebPart* control at run time to add *WebPart* qualities to them.

- **CatalogZone**   This zone hosts *CatalogPart* controls. Catalogs generally manage the visibility of parts on a page. The *CatalogZone* control shows and hides its contents based on the catalog display mode. Web Part Catalogs are named such because they act as catalogs of controls from which the end user may select.

- **EditorZone**   The *EditorZone* control represents the means through which end users may modify and personalize Web pages according to their preferences. Personalizing a Web site includes such things as setting up personal information (such as birthdays, gender-specific addressing, number of visits to the site, etc.). Other kinds of personalization involve setting up color schemes and layouts. The *EditorZone* helps manage this functionality as well as saves and loads those settings so they're available the next time the user logs on.

- **ConnectionZone**   Web Parts are often more useful when they're connected and communicate dynamically. The *ConnectionZone* manages this functionality.

Built-in Web Parts

In addition to including several zones straight out of the box, ASP.NET provides some ready-to-use *WebPart* controls as well. The *WebPart* controls fit into various functional categories. Some are for managing catalogs, whereas others are for managing editing. Each specific kind of *WebPart* fits within a particular zone. Here's a rundown of the currently available *WebPart* Toolbox:

- **DeclarativeCatalogPart**   When building a *WebPart* page, you may add parts dynamically or declaratively. Adding parts to a page dynamically means executing code that adds parts to the page at run time. For example, imagine you had a Web Part represented as a class named *MyWebPart* (ultimately derived from *System.Web.UI.Controls .WebParts*). You may add the part to the page by creating an instance of the part and adding it to the *WebPartManager* using *WebPartManager.AddWebPart*. Adding parts to a page declaratively means including tag declarations within the ASPX file representing the *WebPart* page. The *DeclarativeCatalogPart* control manages server-side controls added declaratively to a catalog on a Web page.

- **PageCatalogPart**   One way end users will probably want to customize a site is by opening and closing controls. The *PageCatalogPart* represents a page catalog for holding controls that were previously added to a page that is now closed. By managing the controls in a *PageCatalogPart*, the end user may add the controls back to the page.

- **ImportCatalogPart**   The *ImportCatalogPart* enables users to import a Web Part description from XML data.

- **AppearanceEditorPart**   The *AppearanceEditorPart* is used to edit the appearance properties of an associated *WebPart* or *GenericWebPart*.

- **BehaviorEditorPart**   To support editing the behavior of a *WebPart* or *GenericWebPart*, ASP.NET provides the *BehaviorEditorPart*.

- **LayoutEditorPart**   The *LayoutEditorPart* is for editing the layout properties and associated *WebPart* (or *GenericWebPart* control).

- **PropertyGridEditorPart**   To support users in editing custom properties of *WebPart* controls, ASP.NET provides the *PropertyGridEditorPart* (the other *EditorPart* controls only support editing existing properties from the *WebPart* class, however).

To get a feel as to how to use *WebPart* controls, let's run an example. The following exercise shows how to build a Web page from *WebPart* controls.

Using Web Parts

1. Create a new site. Name it *UseWebParts*.

2. In the default page, add a *WebPartManager* by dragging an instance from the Toolbox onto the page.

3. Drag a *WebPartZone* onto the page. Set the ID to **WebPartZoneLinks**. Set the *HeaderText* to *Links*. Set the *HeaderStyle* font *ForeColor* to a *Blue* (so you can see it better later during editing mode). Using the *AutoFormat* editor of the control itself, set the style to Professional. (To access *AutoFormat*, click the caret to the right of the control in the designer.)

4. Add some *HyperLinks* to the *WebPartZone*, as shown here. Feel free to add any hyperlink you like (these are just examples).

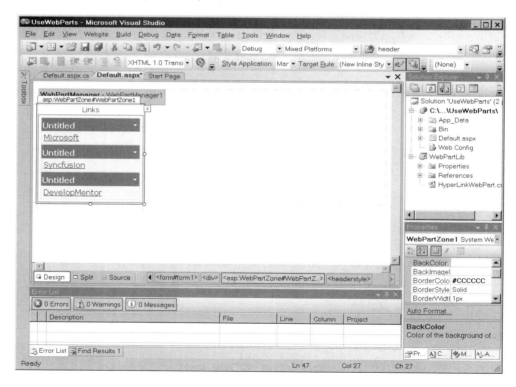

5. Run the page. You should see the links appear on the left side of the page.

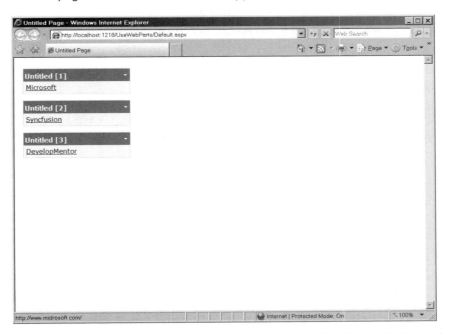

6. Add a *DropDownList* to the page. Name it *DropDownListDisplayModes* and set its *AutoPostBack* property to *true*. This will be used to switch the display mode back and forth.

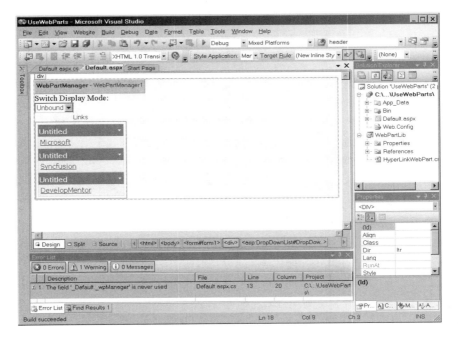

ASP.NET Web Parts support five separate display modes. We'll add code to support (some of) these display modes in the next step

❑ **BrowseDisplayMode**   This is normal mode. No personalization or editing is available here.

❑ **DesignDisplayMode**   This mode turns on drag-and-drop layout personalization.

❑ **EditDisplayMode**   This option turns on personalization or customization of *WebPart* properties and permits a user to delete Web Parts that have been added to the page dynamically.

❑ **ConnectDisplayMode**   This mode allows a user to connect Web Parts at run time.

❑ **CatalogDisplayMode**   This mode allows a user to add Web Parts into a *WebPartZone* at run time.

7. Update the *_Default* class to support switching modes. Add a *WebPartManager* member named *_wpManager* to the class to hold an instance of the current *WebPartManager*. Update the *Page_Init* method to attach an event handler to the page's *InitializationComplete* event. In the *InitializationComplete* handler, get the current *WebPartManager* and stash the reference in the *_wpManager* member, as shown in this listing:

```
public partial class _Default : System.Web.UI.Page
{
    WebPartManager _wpManager;
    protected void Page_Load(object sender, EventArgs e)
    {
    }

    void Page_Init(object sender, EventArgs e)
    {
        Page.InitComplete += new EventHandler(InitializationComplete);
    }

    public void InitializationComplete(object sender, System.EventArgs e)
    {
        _wpManager = WebPartManager.GetCurrentWebPartManager(Page);
        String browseModeName = WebPartManager.BrowseDisplayMode.Name;
        foreach (WebPartDisplayMode mode in
          _wpManager.SupportedDisplayModes)
        {
            String modeName = mode.Name;
            // Make sure a mode is enabled before adding it.
            if (mode.IsEnabled(_wpManager))
            {
                ListItem item = new ListItem(modeName, modeName);
                DropDownListDisplayModes.Items.Add(item);
            }
        }
    }
}
```

The code listed in the *InitializationComplete* handler interrogates the current *WebPartManager* for the supported display modes and puts them in the *DropDownList*.

8. Add a handler for the *DropDownListDisplayModes* drop-down list box when the *SelectedIndexChanged* event occurs. Have the handler switch the *WebPart* page into the selected mode. The following code shows how:

```
protected void
    DropDownListDisplayModes_SelectedIndexChanged(
            object sender, EventArgs e)
{
    string selectedMode = DropDownListDisplayModes.SelectedValue;
    WebPartDisplayMode mode =
     _wpManager.SupportedDisplayModes[selectedMode];
    if (mode != null)
    {
        _wpManager.DisplayMode = mode;
    }
}
```

9. Finally, override the *Page_PreRender* method to display the selected display mode in the drop-down list box.

```
void Page_PreRender(object sender, EventArgs e)
{
    ListItemCollection items = this.DropDownListDisplayModes.Items;
    int selectedIndex =
       items.IndexOf(items.FindByText(_wpManager.DisplayMode.Name));
    DropDownListDisplayModes.SelectedIndex = selectedIndex;
}
```

10. Run the site. Immediately (without doing anything else), you may enter *Design* mode, as shown in the following graphic:

You'll see more modes later as you add more zones. Notice how the title now shows up. You may pick up items on the page and move them around now. For example, you may pick up one of the links and move it around within the Links *WebPartZone*.

11. Now add some more functionality. Add an *EditorZone* to the page. Then in the *EditorZone*, add an *AppearanceEditorPart*, as shown in the following graphic (the designer's default layout is to lay out components one after the other—this example shows the *EditorZone* part with an absolute layout style set so it may placed anywhere on the form):

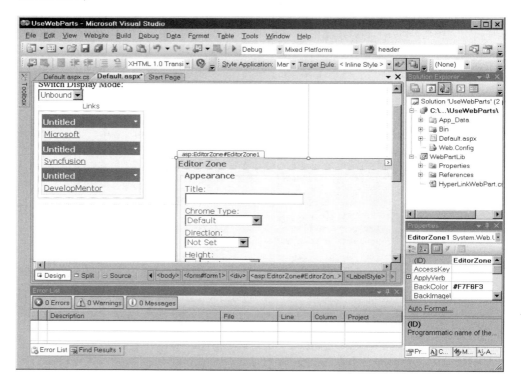

12. Now run the site. You'll see a new option in the display mode drop-down list box: the Edit mode.

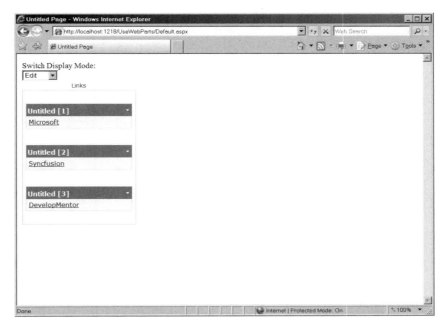

13. Now go back and add a *CatalogZone*. Drop a *DeclarativeCatalogPart* into the new *WebPartZone* and select **Edit Templates**.

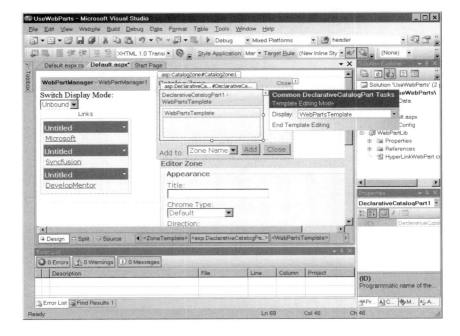

14. While in Template Editing mode, pick up a *TextBox* control from the Toolbox and drop it into the *DeclarativeCatalogPart*. Then update the actual markup to add a *Title* attribute, as shown:

```
<ZoneTemplate>
   <asp:DeclarativeCatalogPart
      ID="DeclarativeCatalogPart1" runat="server">
      <WebPartsTemplate>
        <asp:TextBox ID="TextBox1"
          Title="A TextBox"
          runat="server">
        </asp:TextBox>
      </WebPartsTemplate>
   </asp:DeclarativeCatalogPart>
</ZoneTemplate>
```

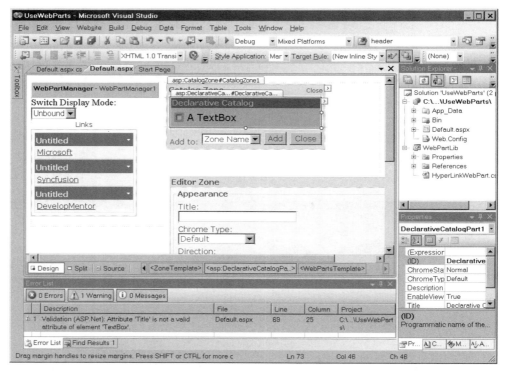

15. Now run the page again. Switch to Catalog Mode. Check the **A TextBox** check box and click **Add** to add a *TextBox* to the Links zone. (This may not seem too interesting yet. However, in the next exercise, you'll write a hyperlink Web Part that you may add to the links page from the catalog—and then update it with your own links and display names).

Here is the page with a new *TextBox* added from the catalog:

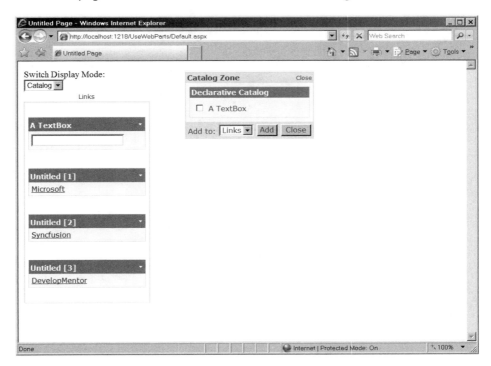

16. Run the page and shift to Edit mode. Select a local menu from one of the hyperlink Web Parts in the Links zone. (You can get to the local "verb" menu by clicking on the arrow symbol in the upper right-hand corner of each Web Part). Select **Edit**. You should see a collection of controls for editing the Web Part appearing in the Editor Zone, like so:

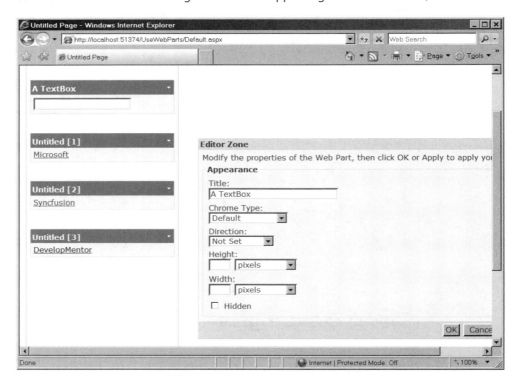

So there's an example of adding Web Part zones to a page and then using normal ASP.NET server-side controls as if they were Web Parts (the *HyperLink* controls). Let's take a look at how to develop a real Web Part.

Developing a Web Part

The previous example showed how to use Web Parts within a page and how to switch the page among various modes at run time. The catalog built into the page includes a *TextBox* control that you may add to a *WebPartZone* on the page. The example delivers a glimpse into the flexibility and power of Web Parts. However, simply dropping a *TextBox* onto a *WebPartZone* isn't very interesting. In this example, we'll build a hyperlink Web Part that you may use to augment the Links *WebPartZone*.

Developing a Web Part is actually fairly straightforward and quite similar to developing a custom control (like the ones from Chapters 4 and 5). Instead of deriving a class from

System.Web.UI.Controls.WebControl or *System.Web.UI.Controls.CompositeControl*, you derive a class from *System.Web.UI.WebControls.WebParts.WebPart*. From that point, you have the choice of either rendering HTML or composing a Web Part from other ASP.NET controls. The *WebPart* includes considerable functionality for integrating with the Web Part architecture. For example, in the next example, the navigation URL and display name properties of the hyperlink Web Part will be exposed as properties that the end user may modify through the *PropertyGridEditorPart*.

The following example illustrates how to create a hyperlink Web Part that you may add to the links *WebPartZone* in the UseWebParts project. Although you could add a regular *HyperLink* control to the catalog, normal controls don't have the same support for the user to modify the links. For example, when you edited the *HyperLink* controls in the previous example, all you could do was move them around in the Links Web Part. To provide your Web application users with additional properties they can configure, the links need to be represented as Web Parts in their own right.

Developing the *HyperLinkWebPart*

1. Add a new project to the UseWebParts solution. Make it a class library and name the library *WebPartLib*. Visual Studio asks you to name the file, and that also becomes the name of the first class being placed in the library. Name the file *HyperLinkWebPart.cs*. (Visual Studio will name the class *HyperLinkWebPart*.)

2. Make a reference to the System.Web assembly within the new child project. Click the right mouse button on the **WebPartLib** node in Solution Explorer and use the **Add Reference** option from the local menu to add the System.Web assembly.

3. Derive the new class from *System.Web.UI.WebControls.WebParts.WebPart* by adding it to the inheritance list, as shown here:

```
using System;
using System.Collections.Generic;
using System.Text;
using System.Linq;
using System.Web;
using System.Web.UI;
using System.Web.UI.WebControls;
using System.Web.UI.WebControls.WebParts;

namespace WebPartLib
{

    public class HyperLinkWebPart : WebPart
    {

    }
}
```

4. Add two string member variables to the *HyperLinkWebPart* class—one to represent the display name of the Web Part and the other to represent the actual URL. Initialize them with reasonable values:

```
using System;
using System.Collections.Generic;
using System.Text;
using System.Web;
using System.Web.UI;
using System.Web.UI.WebControls;
using System.Web.UI.WebControls.WebParts;

namespace WebPartLib
{

    public class HyperLinkWebPart :
    System.Web.UI.WebControls.WebParts.WebPart
    {

        string _strURL = "http://www.microsoft.com";
        string _strDisplayName = "This is a link";
    }
}
```

5. Add a member variable of type *HyperLink* to the class. The Web Part will leverage the already existing functionality of the *HyperLink* control. Override *CreateChildControls* to create an instance of *HyperLink* and add it to the *HyperLinkWebPart* controls collection. Initialize the *HyperLink.Text* property to the member variable representing the display name. Initialize the *HyperLink.NavigateUrl* property to the member variable representing the URL:

```
using System;
using System.Collections.Generic;
using System.Text;
using System.Web;
using System.Web.UI;
using System.Web.UI.WebControls;
using System.Web.UI.WebControls.WebParts;

namespace WebPartLib
{

    public class HyperLinkWebPart :
    System.Web.UI.WebControls.WebParts.WebPart
    {

        HyperLink _hyperLink;

        string _strURL = "http://www.microsoft.com";
        string _strDisplayName = "This is a link";
        protected override void  CreateChildControls()
        {
            _hyperLink = new HyperLink();
            _hyperLink.NavigateUrl = this._strURL;
```

```
        _hyperLink.Text = this._strDisplayName;
        this.Controls.Add(_hyperLink);
        base.CreateChildControls();
    }
  }
}
```

6. Finally, expose the URL and the display name as properties so that the Web Parts architecture can understand and work with them. To allow the exposed properties to work
with the Web Parts architecture through the *PropertyGridEditorPart* we'll add later, be
sure to adorn the properties with the attributes *Personalizable*, *WebBrowsable*, and
WebDisplayName, as shown here:

```
using System;
using System.Collections.Generic;
using System.Text;
using System.Web;
using System.Web.UI;
using System.Web.UI.WebControls;
using System.Web.UI.WebControls.WebParts;

namespace WebPartLib
{

    public class HyperLinkWebPart :
    System.Web.UI.WebControls.WebParts.WebPart
    {

        HyperLink _hyperLink;

        string _strURL = "http://www.microsoft.com";
        string _strDisplayName = "This is a link";
        [Personalizable(), WebBrowsable, WebDisplayName("Display Name")]
        public string DisplayName
        {
            get
            {
                return this._strDisplayName;
            }
            set
            {
                this._strDisplayName = value;
                if (_hyperLink != null)
                {
                    _hyperLink.Text = this.DisplayName;
                }
            }
        }
        [Personalizable(), WebBrowsable, WebDisplayName("URL")]
        public string URL
        {
            get
            {
                return this._strURL;
            }
```

```
            set
            {
                this._strURL = value;
                if (_hyperLink != null)
                {
                    _hyperLink.NavigateUrl = this.URL;
                }

            }
        }
        protected override void  CreateChildControls()
        {
            _hyperLink = new HyperLink();
            _hyperLink.NavigateUrl = this._strURL;
            _hyperLink.Text = this._strDisplayName;
            this.Controls.Add(_hyperLink);
            base.CreateChildControls();
        }
    }
}
```

7. Compile the WebPartLib project. Note that this will add the new *HyperLinkWebPart*
   Web Part to the Toolbox. You'll need that in the next step.

8. Now add the *HyperLinkWebPart* to the catalog. First, click the right mouse button in
   the Toolbox and select **Choose Item** (just as you did when adding custom controls to
   a page). Find the *WebPartLib.dll* assembly and load it into Visual Studio. You should see
   the *HyperLinkWebPart* appear in the Toolbox, as shown here:

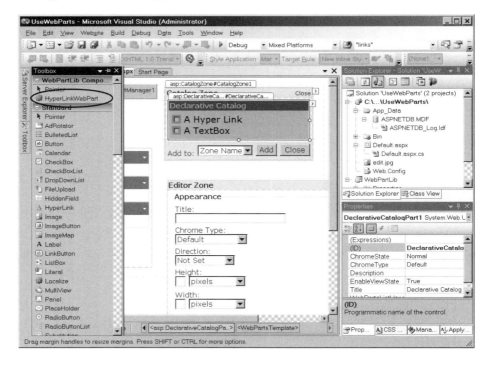

9. Put the *CatalogZone* into Edit Templates mode by clicking on the small arrow in the Web Template. Then drag the *HyperLinkWebPart* into the *CatalogZone*, just as you did earlier with the *TextBox*, as shown here:

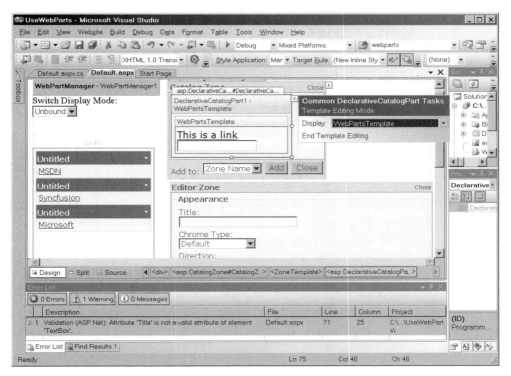

10. Add a title to the new catalog item. Switch to the source code window in Visual Studio. Within the source code, add a title to the new control:

```
<ZoneTemplate>
    <asp:DeclarativeCatalogPart
     ID="DeclarativeCatalogPart1" runat="server">
        <WebPartsTemplate>
            <cc1:HyperLinkWebPart
            Title="A HyperLink"
            ID="HyperLinkWebPart1"
            runat="server" />
            <asp:TextBox ID="TextBox1"
            Title="A TextBox"
            runat="server">
            </asp:TextBox>
        </WebPartsTemplate>
    </asp:DeclarativeCatalogPart>
</ZoneTemplate>
```

The *HyperLinkWebPart* should now appear in the catalog with a title, as shown here:

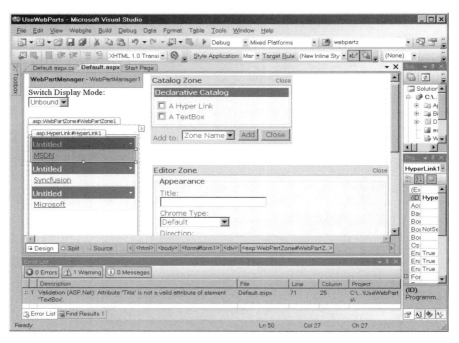

11. Add a *PropertyGridEditorPart* to the *EditorZone* on the page. Just pick one out of the Toolbox and drop it onto the *EditorZone*, as shown in the following graphic:

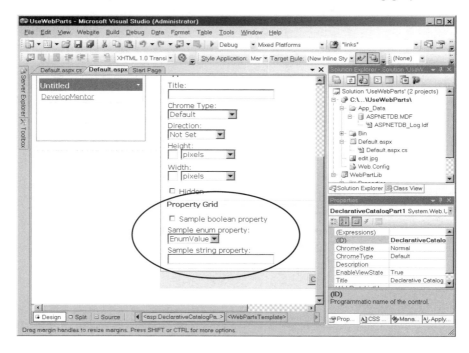

12. Surf to the Web site. Put the page in Catalog mode by selecting **Catalog** from the drop-down list box.

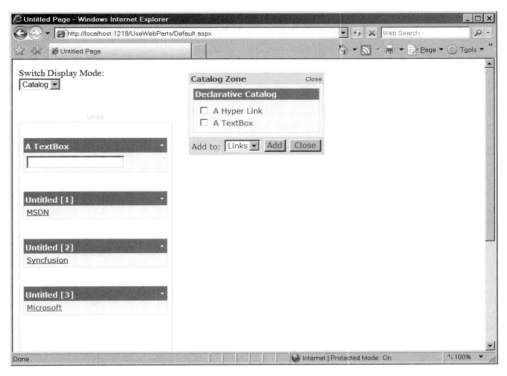

13. Select **A Hyper Link** from the catalog (by checking the check box) and add it to the Links Web Part Zone.

14. Put the Web Parts Page into Edit mode by selecting **Edit** from the drop-down list box. Click on the local menu area on the upper-right corner of the newly added link.

15. Select **Edit** to edit this link. You should see the Editor Zone appear, along with the new property grid showing text boxes for editing the *DisplayName* and the *URL* (the default *DisplayName* and *URL* will appear in the text boxes—just type new values in):

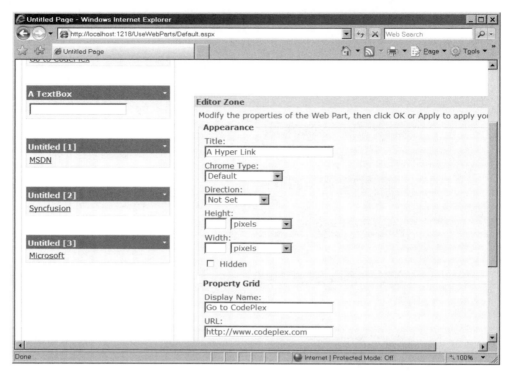

16. Type in a new *DisplayName* and a new *URL*. (The example points to *www.codeplex.com*.) Select **OK**.

The browser should now show the new properties for the *HyperLinkWebPart*.

You should be able to surf to the site represented by the link.

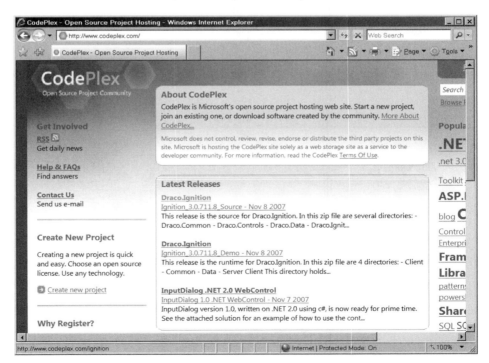

Summary

In this chapter, we took a brief look at Web Parts from an ASP.NET point of view. Web Parts are like server-side controls on steroids. They provide layout and control management above and beyond normal server-side controls. The Web Part architecture is built around four fundamental concepts: *WebPart* zones, Web Parts themselves, the server-side controls that may populate them, and the *WebPartManager* that orchestrates the whole thing. Web Parts are especially useful for portal-type applications because of their ability to leverage the personalization and customization facilities of ASP.NET.

Chapter 7 Quick Reference

To	Do This
Enable a Web page to use *WebPart* controls	Add a *WebPartManager* to the page on which you wish to use *WebPart* controls.
Add various editing capabilities to a Web Parts page	Add an *EditorZone* to the page.
Add a place in which to position server-side controls to be managed by the Web Part architecture	Add a *WebZone* to the page.
Allow users to dynamically add controls from a collection of controls	Add *CatalogZone* to the page. Add controls to the catalog while in Edit Templates mode.
Create a Web Part	Derive a class from *System.Web.UI.WebControls.WebParts.WebPart* and:
	Render some HTML in the Web Part's *Render* method OR Create ASP.NET child controls and add them to the Web Part's *Controls* collection for automatic rendering.

Chapter 8

A Consistent Look and Feel

After completing this chapter, you will be able to

- Use Master Pages to develop a consistent look and feel for your entire site
- Use Themes to apply a style to a page en masse
- Use Skins to stylize custom controls

This chapter covers one of ASP.NET's most useful features as far as developing a consistent look and feel for your site: Master Pages. A distinguishing characteristic of most well-designed modern Web sites is the consistent look and feel of each page within the site.

For example, many sites incorporate a specific color scheme and fonts. In addition, the way a well-designed site frames information and provides navigation tools is consistent from one page to another. Can you imagine visiting a site where each page appeared radically different from the previous page? At the very least, you'd probably be confused. At the very worst, you might even be repulsed.

ASP.NET includes Master Pages to help you make your site appear consistent as visitors move around it. In addition, ASP.NET features a way to stylize controls. Let's take a look at how they work.

A Consistent Look and Feel

Getting to the point where Web development tools support creating a common look and feel for all the pages in a site has been a long process. Classic ASP provided a very crude way of spreading a common look and feel throughout a site by incorporating a file inclusion mechanism that pulled one .asp file into another wholesale. It was brute force to say the least. Although it worked to a certain degree, you had very little control over the nuances of your site while clumping files together.

ASP.NET 1.0 went quite a bit further by composing the whole page-rendering mechanism out of smaller server-side controls and User controls. We saw this in Chapters 2 and 3. However, even though you could package portions of a Web application's user interface (UI) into separate modules, you still had some heavy lifting to do to implement a common look and feel among the pages in your application. User controls also support developing a common look and feel. For example, you can create a User control with specific navigation controls and links and use it in the same place on every page in your site. That in itself creates a common look and feel.

While using the custom control/User control approach to break apart a site's user interface is useful for developing a consistent UI, it falls short of being an ideal solution in a couple of ways. First, all the pages in an application need to include the surrounding code. That means that you have to apply the controls in the same way to *each page.* If you decide to change the placement of the controls (or some other aspect not governed by the controls), you have to change each page. Second, every page using a custom control needs a *Register* directive—and more code that needs to be copied. As a reuse model it went much further than earlier approaches (that is, classic ASP). What you really want is a single place in the site where you can lay out the look and feel of the page *once* and have it propagate across the site.

One way to accomplish this goal and avoid building pages one at a time is to build a primary class from which all the pages in your application will derive. Because ASP.NET is built on an object model based on the *Page* class, why not simply add a new layer to your application? Figure 8-1 shows a diagram illustrating how you might build a set of pages from a single base page.

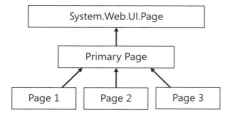

FIGURE 8-1 A base class to implement functionality common among several pages

All the ASPX pages inherit from the same code-behind class deriving from the primary class (which in turn derives from *System.Web.UI.Page*). The primary class takes responsibility for loading the controls necessary for the site's look and feel. Then each separate page is responsible for managing the rest.

This approach works, as long as you don't mind doing a lot of coding. In addition, there was no design support in ASP.NET 1.x for this sort of thing, and messing with the *Page* class hierarchy in Visual Studio sometimes would break the project.

ASP.NET 2.0 introduced *Master Pages* to support developing a common look and feel across your entire site.

ASP.NET Master Pages

Master Pages represent a sort of metapage. They have much the same structure as normal pages. However, they live in files named with the "master" extension. A Master Page serves as a template that renders a common appearance to all pages based on it. Master Pages use XHTML document tags (such as *<html>*, *<head>*, and *<body>*) that apply only to the

Master Page. When you surf to a page that has a Master Page applied to it, the request and response are filtered through the Master Page. The Master Page may not be served by itself. Instead, it ensures that each page has a common look and feel by (logically) acting as the "primary page" you see in Figure 8-1. ASP.NET merges the Master Page and the ASPX page (the content page) into a single class. At that point, the class processes requests and renders output like any other *System.Web.UI.Page*-derived class.

Because Master Pages are similar to normal ASPX pages, they may contain the same sort of content and functionality as normal pages. That is, they may contain server-side controls, User controls, and markup. In addition to markup and controls, a Master Page may contain instances of the *System.Web.UI.WebControls.ContentPlaceHolder* control. As its name implies, the content placeholder stands in place of the real content that will eventually appear in pages based on the Master Page. A Master Page renders all the elements it contains—that is, those elements not contained within a *System.Web.UI.WebControls.ContentPlaceHolder* control.

Because Master Pages play a part in how the final page handler is synthesized, they work a bit differently than the straight inheritance technique described previously (that is, writing a base class to implement common functionality via inheritance). As the page executes, the Master Page injects its own content into the ASPX page. Specifically, the Master Content ends up being represented by a control that is added to the ASPX page's *Controls* collection, where it's rendered in the same way as all other controls are rendered.

Like normal page attributes and functionality, Master Pages may contain the following attributes in their *MasterPage* directive:

- *AutoEventWireup*
- *ClassName*
- *CompilerOptions*
- *Debug Description*
- *EnableViewState Explicit*
- *Inherits*
- *Language*
- *Strict*
- *Src*
- *WarningLevel*
- *Master*

The following exercise illustrates developing a site around a Master Page.

Using a Master Page

1. Create a new site named *MasterPageSite*.

2. Add a new item to the page. Select **MasterPage** from the available templates. Accept the default and name it *MasterPage.master*. The following graphic shows adding a Master Page template:

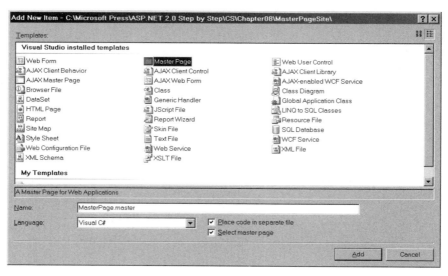

Visual Studio will pump out code like this in a file named *MasterPage.master*. Notice the *ContentPlaceholder* controls generated by Visual Studio:

```
<%@ Master Language="C#" AutoEventWireup="true"
CodeFile="MasterPage.master.cs"
Inherits="MasterPage" %>

<!DOCTYPE html PUBLIC "..." ><html xmlns="http://www.w3.org/1999/xhtml">
<head runat="server">
    <title>Untitled Page</title>
    <asp:ContentPlaceHolder id="head" runat="server">
    </asp:ContentPlaceHolder>
</head>
<body>
    <form id="form1" runat="server">
    <div>
        <asp:ContentPlaceHolder id="ContentPlaceHolder1" runat="server">

        </asp:ContentPlaceHolder>
    </div>
    </form>
</body>
</html>
```

This is what the Master Page looks like in Design mode:

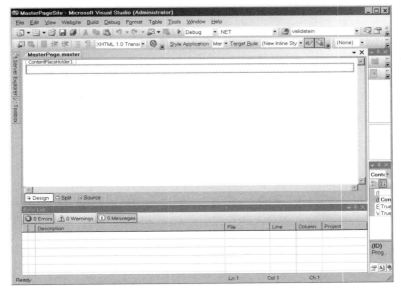

Notice how the Master Page looks very similar to a normal .aspx page. In fact, you may work with a Master Page in very much the same way you may work with a normal .aspx page.

3. Update the background color of the Master Page. In the **Properties** dialog box, select the *Document* element from the combo box and update the document's background color. The example here uses light gray. This will let you see that the Master Page is really being used in subsequent ASPX files.

4. Create a new form and name it *UseMaster.aspx*. Make sure the **Select Master Page** check box is checked, like so:

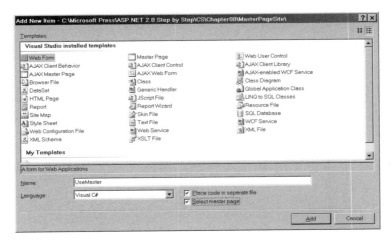

Visual Studio will ask you to select a Master Page, as shown in the following graphic:

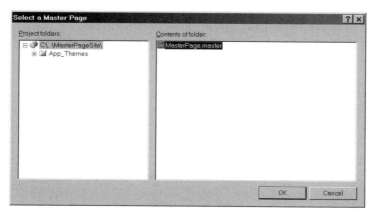

When you view UseMaster.aspx in the designer, it looks like the MasterPage.master file. Notice the grayish hue applied to the page. This lets you know the Master Page is really being applied here.

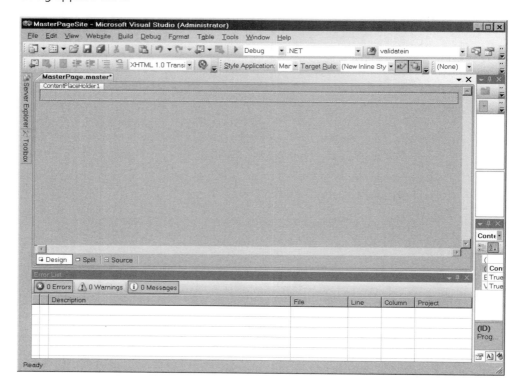

This is the code generated by Visual Studio to support using the Master Page:

```
<%@ Page Language="C#"
MasterPageFile="~/MasterPage.master"
AutoEventWireup="true"
CodeFile="UseMasterx.aspx.cs"
Inherits="UseMasterx"
Title="Untitled Page" %>

<asp:Content ID="Content1"
  ContentPlaceHolderID="head" Runat="Server">
</asp:Content>

<asp:Content ID="Content2"
    ContentPlaceHolderID="ContentPlaceHolder1"
    Runat="Server">
</asp:Content>
```

5. Now add some content to UseMaster.aspx. Add a label to the content placeholder. Have it say something so you can distinguish this as a separate page.

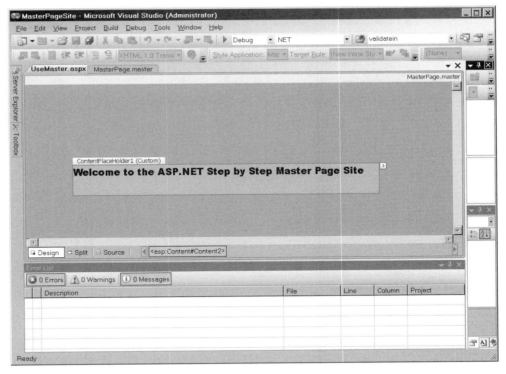

6. Add two more pages to the site. The example here includes a page describing the chapter content of this book and a second page describing the projects. You may use this or add your own content. Add some content to the two pages in the content placeholders. That way you can distinguish the pages (we'll add navigation support later).

The important thing is to add two more pages and apply the Master Page to them (that is, create the Web Forms with the **Select Master Page** box checked).

The following two graphics show the example site's pages containing a *ListBox* to select the topic and a *TextBox* to hold information about the topic. Setting the positioning of the items to *absolute* can make it easier to arrange items on the page. The examples here use absolute positioning. In addition, the example here populates the *ListBox* with project names (on the product page) and chapter names (on the chapter page). Each has a *ListBox* selection change handler that fills the *TextBox* with information about the projects and chapters. This is so that you can actually see the pages having functionality in addition to the consistent look and feel from the master page.

Here's how to add elements to the *ListBox* by hand (we'll see another technique—data binding—in Chapter 11). First, select the *ListBox* in the designer. Click on the small arrow on the right side of the *ListBox*. You'll see a dialog allowing you to add item/value pairs. The example here uses two *ListBoxes*—one holding project information for this book and the other holding chapter information for this book.

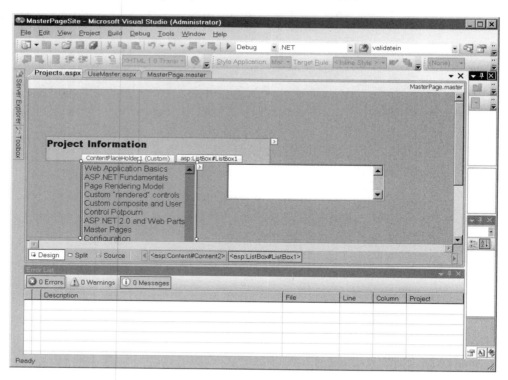

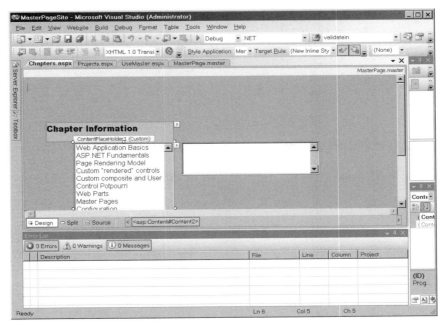

7. Go back to the MasterPage.master page and update it so it has a bit more content. Use the **Table**, **Insert Table** menu option to insert a table immediately above the content pane on the Master Page. Give the table one row and two columns. Size it so that the left cell is narrow and the right cell is wide. It should look something like this:

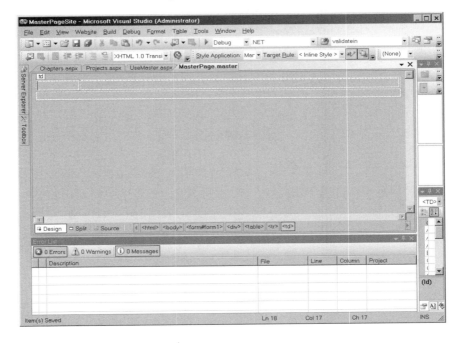

8. Add a menu to the leftmost cell in the table. In customizing the menu, add an *AutoFormat* style to it. The example here uses the *Classic* style. Add three items to the menu for navigating to the three pages in this site—the Home page, the Chapters page, and the Projects page. To add the menu items, select the menu in the designer and look for the small arrow prompt on the right side of the menu. Click the arrow and select **Edit Menu Items...** from the local menu. You'll see the following dialog box. Add the menu items here.

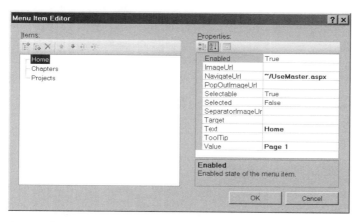

Set up the appropriate navigation for each menu option. That is, have the Home menu item navigate to the UseMaster.aspx page. Have the Chapters menu item navigate to the Chapters.aspx file. Finally, have the Projects menu item navigate to the Projects.aspx file. The navigation URLs are set up individually here—we'll look at using ASP.NET's site map support shortly. You may do this by clicking the navigation button in the *NavigateUrl* field of the *Property* page:

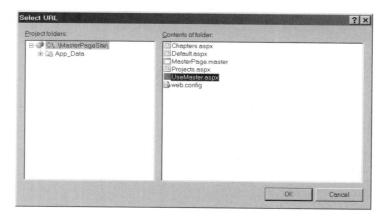

You should end up with something like this:

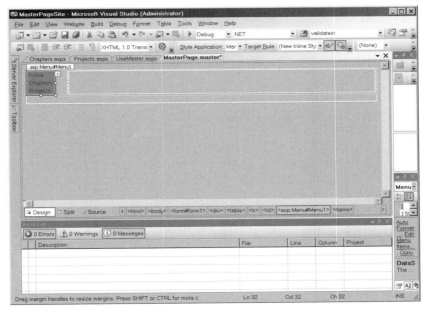

9. Finally, add a banner. In my opinion, no Master Page is complete without a banner. Use the bitmap editor (or Paintbrush—mspaint.exe) to draw a banner. The one in this example is approximately 1000 pixels wide by 90 pixels high. Drop the banner into the table cell on the right. Your Master Page should look something like this now:

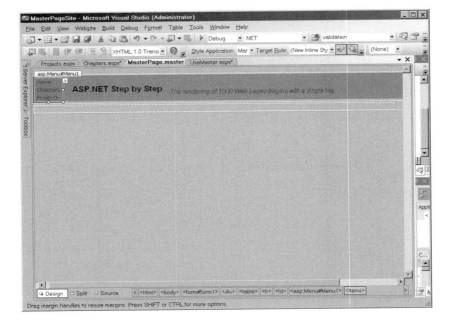

Because the UseMaster.aspx, Chapters.aspx, and Projects.aspx files were created using the Master Page, they have the menu and banner built in automatically. Surf to the UseMaster.aspx file and browse through the menu items. You should see that each page has a common look and feel, but with the correct content.

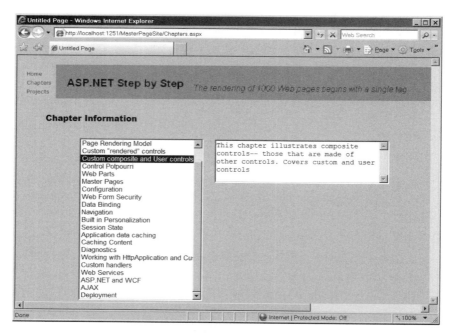

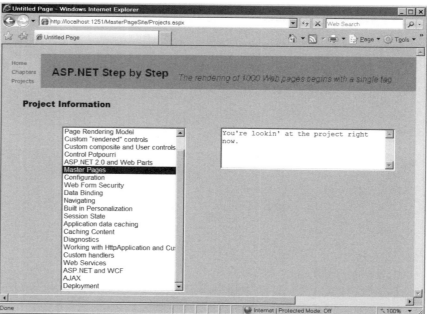

Master Pages offer significant improvements over earlier versions of classic ASP and ASP.NET for developing a common look and feel among all the pages in your application. Of course, you may use multiple Master Pages in a project, and you may also nest them.

A second way to help manage the look and feel of your application is ASP.NET Themes.

Themes

Master Pages control the general layout of a series of pages within an application. However, there are other elements (those that are subject to change between pages) that you might like to have remain constant. Themes provide a means of applying common styles to the elements on each page in your site.

If you're familiar with Cascading Style Sheets (CSS), you will feel very at home with Themes. The two techniques are similar because through both techniques you may define the visual styles for your Web pages. Themes go a step beyond CSS. You may use Themes to specify styles, graphics, and even CSS files within the pages of your applications. When available, you may apply ASP.NET Themes at the application, page, or server control level.

Themes are represented as text-based style definitions in ASP.NET. ASP.NET already includes a number of Themes straight out of the box. You'll find these Themes located at C:\WINDOWS\ Microsoft.NET\Framework\vxxxxx\ASP.NETClientFiles\Themes. ASP.NET includes some pre-defined Themes (note the "vxxxxx" indicates the current version of the .NET Framework you're using, most likely "v3.5" at the time this was written). In addition, you may define and use your own Themes.

The following exercise shows how to create and use a Theme.

Creating and using a Theme

1. Add a new form to the MasterPagesSite project. Name the page *UseThemes.aspx*. Turn off the **Select Master Page** check box if it happens to be turned on before you commit to creating the page.

2. Add a Theme folder to your project. Highlight the Web site node in the Solution Explorer. Click the right mouse button and select **Add ASP.NET Folder**. Select **Theme**. This will create an App_Themes directory for you.

3. Create a Default Themes folder under the App_Themes folder. Click the right mouse button on the **App_Themes** folder. Select **Add Folder**, and then select **Theme Folder** from the menu. Rename the folder from *Theme1* to *Default*.

4. Add a new style sheet to the Theme1 folder. Click the right mouse button on the **Theme1 folder** and select **Add New Item**. Select the Style Sheet template. Name the *Style sheet Default.css*.

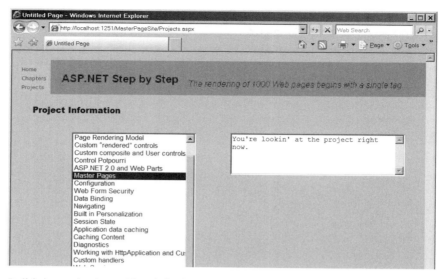

5. Build the style sheet. The default style sheet includes only a *body* tag. When the style sheet is open in Visual Studio, select **Add Style Rule** from the **Styles** menu. You may click the right mouse button on the **Elements** node to modify the style for the node. For example, if you want to change the style of the *<h1>* tag, you would click the right mouse button on the **Elements** node and select **Add Style Rule**. To add a style for the *<h1>* tag, select it from the list of elements and move it into the Style Rule Hierarchy by clicking the **>** button, as shown here. Then click **OK**.

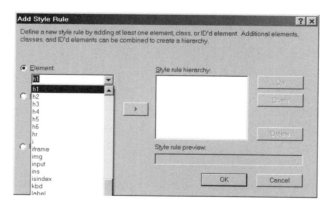

To modify the style, click on the **H1** node in the CSS outline page and select **Style** in the Properties window. Click the "**...**" button to activate the **Modify Style** dialog box:

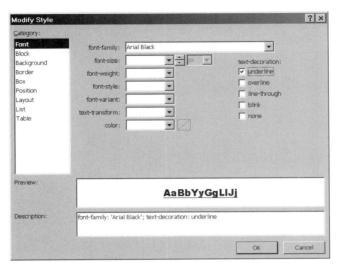

The sample application included with the CD sets the font to Arial Black with an underscore.

6. Now test the Theme by declaring it in the page and by typing a heading with *<h1>* tags, like so:

```
<%@ Page Language="C#" AutoEventWireup="true"
CodeFile="UseThemes.aspx.cs"

"Theme=Default"
trace="false" Inherits="UseThemes" %>
<%@ Register Src="Banner.ascx" TagName="Banner" TagPrefix="uc1" %>

<!DOCTYPE html PUBLIC "-//W3C//DTD XHTML 1.1//EN"
"http://www.w3.org/TR/xhtml11/DTD/xhtml11.dtd">

<html xmlns="http://www.w3.org/1999/xhtml" >
<head runat="server">
    <title>Untitled Page</title>
</head>
<body>
    <form id="form1" runat="server">
    <div>
    <h1> How does this look? </h1>
    </div>
    </form>
</body>
</html>
```

Here's how the themed page appears in the browser with the new theme (the *<h1>* tag set to the new font and set to use the underline in this example):

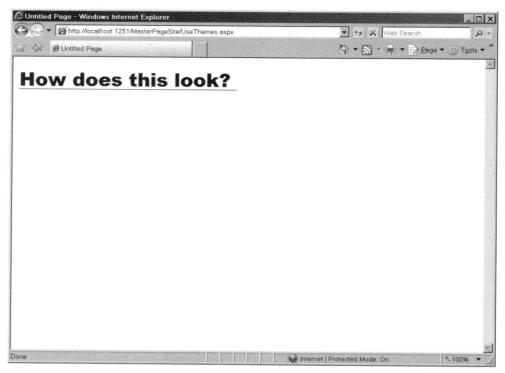

7. Add another Theme to the project. Name the Theme *SeeingRed*. That is, create a new Theme folder and add a new style sheet of the same name. Make the *<h1>* tag use a red color font this time. Then change the Theme used by the page to SeeingRed (you can also set the theme in the Properties window in Visual Studio):

```
<%@ Page Language="C#" AutoEventWireup="true"
CodeFile="UseThemes.aspx.cs"
Theme="SeeingRed"
trace="false" Inherits="UseThemes" %>
```

Surf to the page to see the *<h1>* tag printed in red.

This is just a taste of the kinds of things you can do by providing Themes for a page. Once a Theme is defined, you may apply it by declaring it as part of the *Page* declaration or by intercepting the *PreInit* event and changing the Theme property in the page to a valid Theme.

Going hand in hand with Themes are Skins. Let's look at those.

Skins

Skins complement Master Pages and Themes as a way to manage the style of your Web site. Using Skins is almost like combining *WebControl*-based controls with CSS. Another way to think of Skins is as a way to set certain properties of a control as a group. For example, you may want to define different coloring schemes for a control such as the *TextBox* control. The *Calendar* control is also a good example because it's so rich. By providing Skins for controls, you can have a number of different appearance options for various controls at your disposal without having to go into detail and manage the control properties one by one.

You have actually used Skins already. Many server-side controls already support style templates. For example, when working with the *TreeView* earlier, you saw that you could apply one of several styles to it. Earlier in this chapter, we looked at applying a set of color attributes to the *Menu* control when we chose the "classic" style from the *AutoFormat* control option menu. In this section, we'll see how Skins work and how to apply them.

Skin files define specific controls and the attributes that apply to them. That is, a .skin file contains server-side control declarations. The Skin file's job is to preset the style properties for the control. Skin files reside in named Theme folders for an application, accompanied by any necessary CSS files.

The following exercise illustrates how to create Skins for some controls on your Web site.

Create a Skin

1. Create a Skin file by clicking the right mouse button on the **SeeingRed** folder in the App_Theme node on the Solution Explorer and selecting **Add New Item**. Choose **Skin File** from the templates. Name the file *SeeingRed.skin*.

2. In the SeeingRed.skin file, pre-declare some controls for which you'd like to have default property values set. For example, the following SeeingRed.skin file declares default properties for some controls. These controls have their various colors defaulting to assorted shades of red.

```
<asp:Label runat="server" ForeColor="red"
Font-Size="14pt" Font-Names="Verdana" />

<asp:button runat="server" borderstyle="Solid"
borderwidth="2px" bordercolor="#ff0000" backcolor="#cc0000"/>

<asp:CheckBoxList runat=server ForeColor="#ff0000" />

<asp:RadioButtonList runat=server ForeColor="#ff9999" />
```

3. Now add those controls for which you've pre-declared attributes in the Skin file onto the UseThemes.aspx page to see how the SeeingRed.skin file applies. The effect in the following graphic shows the red colored controls as a lighter gray. You will no doubt see the effect when running the sample application.

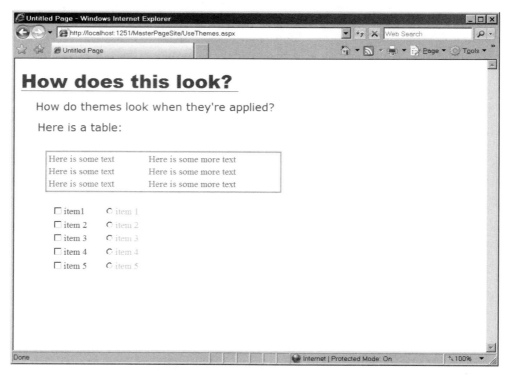

The SeeingRed.skin file will automatically be applied by declaring the SeeingRed Theme within the page. You may also prescribe different Skins at runtime within the page's *PreInit* handler, and you can apply separate Skins to each control.

Summary

One of the most often requested features for ASP.NET has been to support a common look and feel for a site. The Master Pages feature within ASP.NET pushes this capability to the forefront and makes developing a set of pages with similar aspects a very doable proposition. In addition to Master Pages, ASP.NET Themes represent a way to apply global style attributes to all the pages in your application.

ASP.NET also supports specifying default values for specific server-side controls through a Skin file. Skins offer a finer-grained approach to applying styles in a control-centric manner.

Chapter 8 Quick Reference

To	Do This
Define a page that will represent the consistent look and feel of a series of pages in a Web site	Add a Master Page to the site.
Create a page based on the Master Page	Check the **Select Master Page** check box when creating forms for a site.
Add elements to the Master Page that will show up in pages based on the Master Page	Place elements outside the area represented by the content pane.
Add individual elements to content pages	Add elements within the content page shown on the page.
Create a Theme for a page	Add a new Theme folder to the App_Themes folder within your application. Use a Cascading Style Sheet (CSS) to define styles and classes for the Theme.
Apply a Theme to a page	Set the Theme property within the *Page* Directive OR Set the Theme property within the page during the page's *PreInit* event.
Create a Skin	Create a text file within a Theme folder. Simply make the file have a .skin extension. Add control declarations with their properties set to default values.

Chapter 9
Configuration

After completing this chapter, you will be able to

- Understand the way .NET handles configuration
- Apply configuration settings to ASP.NET applications
- Manage ASP.NET configuration using the ASP.NET Administration tool
- Manage ASP.NET configuration using the MMC Snap-in

This chapter introduces how ASP.NET manages its configuration information. It gives a taste of how ASP.NET configuration works. We'll revisit ASP.NET configuration in later chapters. ASP.NET is a feature-rich system for developing and deploying Web sites. The features we'll see in more detail as we examine ASP.NET further include some of the following:

- Session state
- Caching content to help optimize your Web site's responses
- Tracing requests
- Mapping specific file extensions to custom handlers
- Authenticating users

Each of these features is controlled by a number of separate configurable parameters. For example, when you enable session state for your application, you may choose where to locate your application's session state (in process, on a separate machine using a Windows Service, or using SQL Server). You may also configure the lifetime of your session state and how your application tracks the session state (via a cookie or some other method).

A second feature controlled through the configuration file is caching output. When you cache the content of your site, you may vary the lifetime of your cached content and where it's cached (on the server, on the client, or on the proxy).

For both these features (and others), the configuration options are governed by configuration files. Here, we first examine the nature of Windows configuration and then look specifically at how ASP.NET handles configuration. In ASP.NET 1.x, modifying the configuration of your application meant editing the XML-based configuration file by hand. Fortunately, more recent ASP.NET versions offer two tools that make configuration a much easier proposition. One tool is the ASP.NET configuration tab available through the normal Internet Information Services (IIS) configuration panel. The second tool is the Web Site Administration Tool, available through the **Web Site**, **ASP.NET Configuration** menu in Visual Studio. We'll cover these tools as well.

Windows Configuration

Every computing platform needs a configuration mechanism to control the behavior of the platform. On any platform, a number of various parameters can govern how the operating system and programs operate. The parameters often need to be modified, perhaps to tune performance or tailor security or even just to control normal operation. For example, Windows provides an environment variable named *PATH* that controls the search path for executable programs. Other environment variables include one named *TEMP* (controls the location of temporary files) and *USERPROFILE* (identifies the location of the current user's profile information).

In addition to operating system variables, individual applications may require different settings specific to that program. For example, many applications require a specific version of Windows or that specific dynamic link libraries (DLLs) be available. These actions may vary from one installation to the next, and it's not a good idea to hard-code the settings into your application. Instead, you store values in a secondary file that accompanies the application.

During the early days of Windows, "initialization files" (.INI files) served to not only configure individual applications but also Windows itself; there is even a set of Windows Application Programming Interface (API) functions for managing configuration parameters. The files contain a name/value pair that dictates a property and its associated setting. For example, the name/value pair in Win.INI that turns on Object Linking and Embedding (OLE) messaging looks like

```
OLEMessaging=1
```

Now that we are a few years into the new millennium, XML is the way to go. .NET depends on XML files (machine.config and web.config) for its configuration.

> **Note** The second way in which applications have configured themselves in the past is through the Registry. The Registry is a centralized database that applications may use to store name/value pairs. The reason ASP.NET doesn't use the Registry to configure information is because global nature Registry is in direct conflict with ASP.NET's need for flexibility during deployment. Settings stored in the Registry would need to be copied through the Registry API, whereas Configuration files may simply be copied. In addition, the account that runs most ASP.NET sites is specifically configured to be opted out of the Registry to secure the site from hacks and attacks.

.NET Configuration

.NET configuration files are well-formed XML files whose vocabulary is understood by the .NET runtime. You can see a listing of all the configuration files by looking in the configuration directory. We'll see that directory in just a minute.

The .NET runtime reads these configuration files into memory as necessary to set the various .NET runtime parameters. For example, web.config is loaded when ASP.NET applications are started. The first configuration file we'll take a look at is machine.config.

Machine.Config

The default .NET configuration for your machine is declared within a file named *machine.config*. You can find machine.config within the directory C:\Windows\Microsoft .NET\Framework\vxxxxx\config. Machine.config sets the default .NET application behaviors for the entire machine.

Recent .NET versions made a number of improvements to the machine.config arrangement. .NET 1.x lumped all of machine.config into a single file—even comments and configuration information for systems not in use on the specific machine (browser information, for example, even though the machine may not have been hosting ASP.NET). The current version of machine.config is trimmed down substantially from version 1.x. The comments have been moved to a separate file named *machine.config.comments*, and separate browser definition capability files have been moved to separate configuration files. This is important to know because the machine.config comments are sometimes more useful as documentation for configuring .NET than the regular online documentation. As you configure your various ASP.NET applications, the machine.config comments should be the first place you look for information.

Configuration Section Handlers

At the top of machine.config you'll see a number of Configuration Section Handlers. Each of these handlers understands a specific vocabulary for configuring .NET (and ultimately ASP .NET). While machine.config controls the settings for the entire machine, ASP.NET applications rely on files named *web.config* to manage configuration. We'll see much more about web.config shortly. However, for now here is a small snippet that you might find in a web.config file for a specific application:

```xml
<?xml version="1.0" encoding="utf-8"?>
<configuration>
    <system.web>
        <authentication mode="Forms" />
        <sessionState mode="SQLServer" cookieless="UseUri" timeout="25" />
    </system.web>
</configuration>
```

This small segment tells the ASP.NET runtime to use Forms Authentication (one of ASP.NET's authentication options) to authenticate users of this site. The configuration information also tells ASP.NET to use SQL Server to manage session state, to allow session state information to expire after 25 minutes, and to track session information using a session ID embedded within the request Universal Resource Indicator (URI). We'll look at session state in detail in Chapter 14—for now it's a good example to illustrate some of the parameters ASP.NET configuration manages.

You can see from this example that configuring ASP.NET relies on the ability of the runtime to understand some keywords. In this case, the keywords *authentication*, *mode*, and *Forms* tell ASP.NET how to manage authentication. ASP.NET must correctly interpret *sessionState*, *mode*, *SQLServer*, *cookieless*, *UseURI*, and *timeout* to know how to manage an application's session state.

The .NET components that understand these vocabularies are listed near the top of machine.config.

```
<configuration>
  <configSections>
    <section name="appSettings"
     type="{entire strong assembly name here...}"
        restartOnExternalChanges="false" />
    <section name="connectionStrings"
      type="{entire strong assembly name here...}" />
    ...
    <sectionGroup name="system.web"
      type="{entire strong assembly name here...}">
      <section name="authentication"
        type="{entire strong assembly name here...}"
          allowDefinition="MachineToApplication" />
      <section name="sessionState"
        type="{entire strong assembly name here...}"
          allowDefinition="MachineToApplication" />
    ...
    </sectionGroup>
  </configSections>
</configuration>
```

The listing above is necessarily abbreviated. Go ahead and take a look at machine.config and you'll see the section handlers in their full glory. (On most systems, machine.config is located at C:\Windows\Microsoft.NET\Framework\vxxxxx\config.) In looking at the configuration handlers, you can see that the *sessionState* configuration settings are interpreted by an assembly with the strong name *System.Web.Configuration.SessionStateSection, System.Web, Version=2.0.0.0, Culture=neutral, PublicKeyToken=b03f5f7f11d50a3a*. A *strong name* fully specifies the name of an assembly including a version (to ensure version compatibility) and a public token (to ensure the assembly has not been tampered with). Even though we're looking at ASP.NET 3.5 in this book, and even to a degree version 3.5 of the .NET Framework itself, many .NET assemblies remain unchanged since version 2.0. It isn't surprising to look through machine.config and find references to older versions of Framework components for this reason. The strong name you've just seen is but one example.

Web.Config

While machine.config lays out the default setting for your machine (and ultimately for your applications), the default settings are generally targeted toward the most common use cases (rather than some special configuration you may need to apply to your application). For example, *sessionState* is configured to be handled in process by default. That's fine when you're developing, but almost certainly is not appropriate for a commercial-grade application that is servicing many diverse clients.

Because all your .NET applications depend on machine.config to configure them, making changes to machine.config could potentially affect your other applications. It's a bad idea to update machine.config directly.

Stand-alone .NET applications depend on configuration files modeled after the application name to configure themselves. For example, an application named *MyApp.EXE* would have a configuration file named *MyApp.EXE.config*. Of course, ASP.NET applications aren't named in that way. Instead, the ASP.NET runtime expects configuration information to be declared in a file named *web.config*.

To override the default settings, you simply need to include a file named *web.config* in your application's virtual directory. For example, the following code sets up the Web application to which it applies. The configuration file turns on Forms Authentication and tracing, for example.

```xml
<?xml version="1.0" encoding="utf-8"?>
<configuration>
    <system.web>
        <authentication mode="Forms" />
        <trace enable=true/>
    </system.web>
</configuration>
```

The configuration settings your application actually sees have been inherited from a (potentially) long line of other web.config files. The machine.config file sets up the default .NET configuration settings. The top-level web.config file (in the .NET configuration directory) sets up the initial ASP.NET configuration. Then, subsequent child web.config files within the request path have the opportunity to tweak the settings for a single application.

This way of managing configuration information works well. Many of the normal defaults apply in most situations, and you sometimes need to tweak only a few items. When you do, just drop a web.config in your virtual directory and/or subdirectory.

However, managing settings by littering your hard disk with web.config files can get a bit unwieldy if lots of different parts of your application need separate configurations. The ASP.NET configuration schema includes a *location* element for specifying different settings for different directories—but they can all go in a master configuration file for your application.

For example, the following configuration section will remove the ability for the AppSubDir directory to process standard ASP.NET Web Services. The *remove* instruction causes ASP.NET to have amnesia about all files with the extension .asmx.

```
<configuration>
  <location path="appSubDir">
    <system.web>
      <httpHandlers>
        <remove verb="*" path="*.asmx" />
      </httpHandlers>
    </system.web>
  </location>
</configuration>
```

You could also apply other specific settings to the subdirectory, such as for security. While we'll look at security in depth in the next chapter, you may not find it surprising to find that ASP.NET configuration files include terms to manage authorization and authentication. This is a perfect use for the *location* element. The following configuration snippet allows all users into the main (virtual) directory while requiring users wanting access to the PagesRequiringAuth subdirectory to be authenticated.

```
<configuration>
  <system.web>
    <authorization>
      <allow users="*" />
    </authorization>
  </system.web>
  <location path="pagesRequiringAuth">
    <system.web>
      <authorization>
       <deny users="?" />
      </authorization>
    </system.web>
  </location>
</configuration>
```

Managing Configuration in ASP.NET 1.x

Configuration within ASP.NET 1.x was done entirely by manually typing changes into a target web.config file. For example, if you wanted your application to use *SQLServer* as a session state database, you'd need to insert the correct verbiage into the application's web.config file keystroke by keystroke. Unfortunately, there was no configuration compiler to help ensure that the syntax was correct. If you typed something wrong, you usually wouldn't know about it until you ran the application, at which point ASP.NET would cough up a cryptic error message.

Managing Configuration in Later Versions of ASP.NET

ASP.NET 2.0 introduced some major improvements to the process of managing ASP.NET applications, and these improvements carry through to the current version of ASP.NET. Although you can still type configuration information into the web.config file manually, ASP.NET 2.0 and later versions provide some new configuration utilities. These tools include the Web Site Administration Tool (WSAT) available in Visual Studio and the ASP.NET configuration facilities available through IIS.

Configuring your application

In this exercise, you'll change some application settings within an application's configuration and see how they're reflected within web.config.

1. Begin by creating a new Web site named *ConfigORama*. Make it a regular ASP.NET site (not an empty one). It can be a file system–based Web site.

2. Run the ASP.NET Administration tool. After Visual Studio generates the application, select the **Web Site**, **ASP.NET Configuration** menu item. This will bring up the ASP.NET Administration tool.

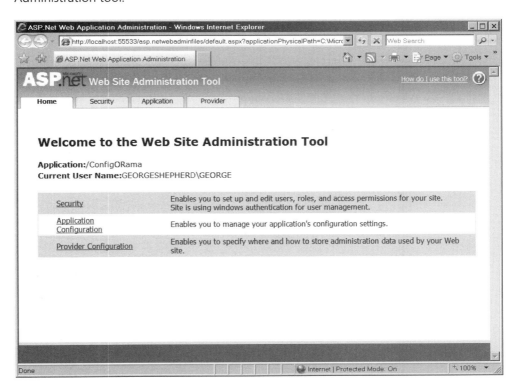

Note Notice that the Administration tool includes three tabs in addition to Home: Security, Application, and Provider. The Security tab manages authentication and authorization settings. That is, you may use the Security tab to add users and assign roles to them. We'll explore that process in detail in the next chapter.

The Application tab is for maintaining various settings related to your application. Some basic configuration settings are controlled here, including maintaining key-value pairs specific to your application, SMTP settings for defining how the site manages e-mail, and turning debugging and tracing on and off. You can also use the Application tab to take your application offline in case you need to perform maintenance.

Finally, the Provider tab is used to manage various data providers. Starting with ASP.NET 2.0, Microsoft introduced the concept of a "provider" designed to make data access for a given ASP.NET subsystem easier and more standardized. For example, your users might have personalized settings, and the *Membership* provider would retrieve those for your code to display to the user or otherwise manage. Roles your user might be granted when using your Web application are provided by the *Roles* provider. The various providers can be individually configured using the Provider tab. It's most likely you'll use the built-in providers that ASP.NET offers, which will access a database for data archival and retrieval, but you could use custom providers that you create, third party providers that someone else creates, or mix and match. The way the various providers are configured is administered in this Provider tab, including which provider to use (if you have more than one available) and database connection string settings if a database is to be used.

The Web Site Administration Tool lets you manage parts of web.config without having to type things by hand. It's accessible from Visual Studio. Visual Studio 2008 will create a web.config file by default. But if for some reason one isn't created, the Web Site Administration Tool will create a web.config file for you. The tool will also create a database suitable for consumption by SQL Server Express in the App_Data folder of your Web site for storing application data (we'll see more about that when we look at ASP.NET features such as personalization and authorization).

3. Continue working with configuration. Go to the **Application** tab and add a couple of application settings. Add a setting named *SomeString* and one named *AnotherString*. In this exercise, it doesn't matter what you type as the corresponding value.

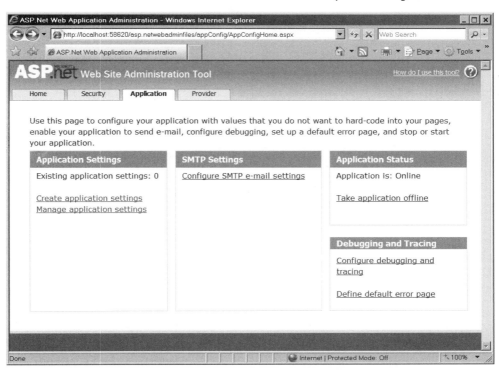

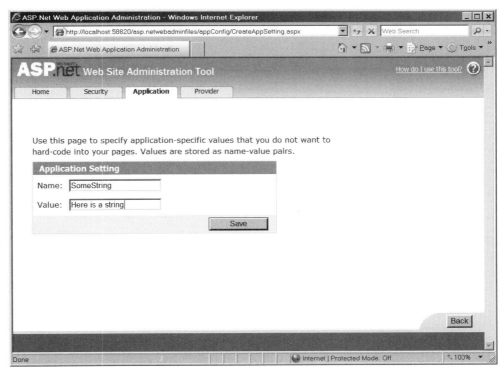

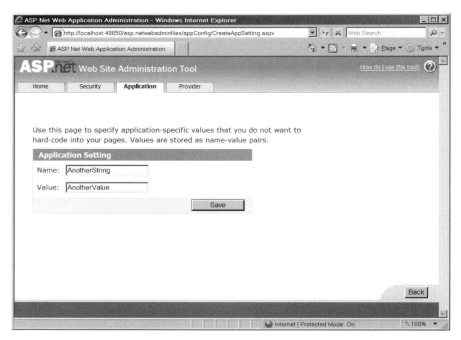

4. Open the application's web.config file. You should see entries for both *SomeString* and *AnotherString*.

   Web.config should look like this now (some entries inserted by Visual Studio have been omitted):

```xml
<?xml version="1.0" ?>
<configuration >

    <appSettings>
        <add key="SomeString" value="Here is a string" />
        <add key="AnotherString" value="AnotherValue" />
    </appSettings>

    <connectionStrings/>
</configuration>
```

5. Now write some code to access the application settings you just added. They're available via a class named *ConfigurationManager*. Add a drop-down list to the Default.aspx form to hold the application settings keys (with an ID of **DropDownListApplicationSettings**) and a label to display the values (with the ID **LabelSetting**). Add a button that will be used to look up the value associated with the application settings key. Give it the ID **ButtonLookupSetting**. In the *Page_Load* handler, interrogate the *ConfigurationManager* for all the application settings:

```csharp
public partial class _Default : System.Web.UI.Page
{
    protected void Page_Load(object sender, EventArgs e)
    {
```

```
    if (!this.IsPostBack)
    {
        foreach (String strKey
            in ConfigurationManager.AppSettings.AllKeys)
        {
            this.
                DropDownListApplicationSettings.
                Items.Add(strKey);
        }
    }

}
protected void ButtonLookupSetting_Click(object sender, EventArgs e)
{

    string strSetting;
    strSetting =
        ConfigurationManager.AppSettings[this.
            DropDownListApplicationSettings.
            SelectedItem.Text];
    this.LabelSetting.Text = strSetting;

}
}
```

6. Compile the program and run the site. When you start the page, it will load the drop-down list with all the keys from the *ConfigurationManager.AppSettings* collection. When you select the application settings using the key from the drop-down list, the code looks up the value of the application setting and displays it in the label:

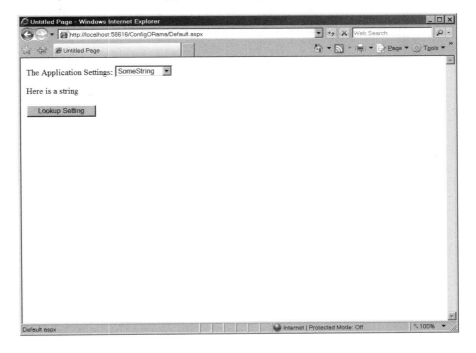

ASP.NET also supports another way to manage Application Settings. It's the ASP.NET configuration tab for your site when it's hosted in IIS.

Configuring ASP.NET from IIS

If your site is running from within a virtual directory (through IIS), you may use the features view within IIS to edit configuration information. To use this, you need to have your site managed by IIS.

Although configuring ASP.NET this way may be done only from the computer hosting the site, it is much more extensive in its ability to manage your ASP.NET application.

Here's an exercise to familiarize yourself with the ASP.NET configuration tab in IIS.

Use IIS to configure ASP.NET

1. Begin by creating a new Web site. Call it *ConfigORamaIIS*. Make it an HTTP site managed by IIS (that is, select HTTP in the Location combo box on the page). Run it from your own computer (*localhost*). Visual Studio will create a virtual directory for you and point itself to the virtual directory:

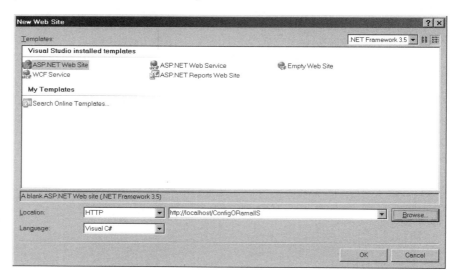

2. Open up the IIS Management Console. Look for the ConfigORamaIIS site. When you navigate to that virtual directory, you'll see the ASP.NET-related settings appear in the Features view:

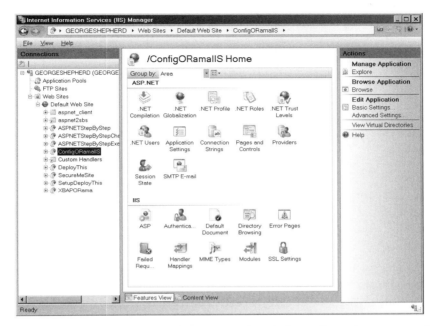

3. Double-click on some of the features to view their configuration screens. For example, clicking on the **Connection Strings** icon yields the connection strings screen:

4. Click the right mouse button in the middle of the connection strings user interface (UI) to add a connection string. The Configuration utility shows a user-friendly dialog box asking for connection string information:

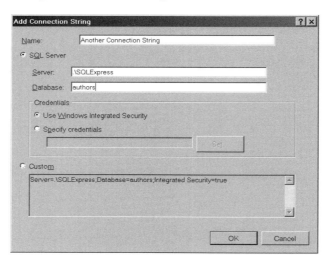

In addition to managing connection strings from the Features view, you can also manage application settings. Return to the Features pane. From there, select **Application Settings**. When the application settings screen is displayed, click the right mouse button in the middle of the screen to bring up the context menu. Here's where you may add application settings—just as you did with the ASP.NET Web Site Administration Tool. Clicking the **Add** menu option brings up the Add Application Settings editor. Add a key-value pair:

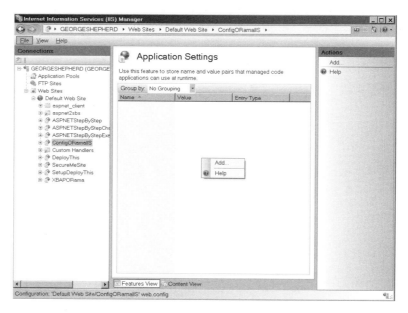

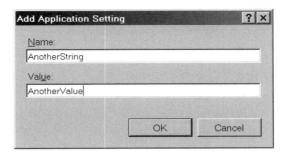

5. Open web.config within your application. It should now include an entry for
AnotherString.

```
<?xml version="1.0" encoding="UTF-8"?>
<configuration >
    <appSettings>
        <add key="AnotherString" value="AnotherValue" />
    </appSettings>
</configuration>
```

6. Using the IIS ASP.NET configuration editor, add a setting named *BackgroundColor*. Give
it a value of #00FF00. This will expose a setting that administrators can use to change
the background color of Default.aspx (after support for changing the background color
is built into the code).

7. Now add a property to the Default page (Default.aspx.cs) to retrieve the background
color. It should be available from the *ConfigurationManager.AppSettings* collection.

```
public partial class _Default : System.Web.UI.Page
{
    protected string BackgroundColor   {
        get { return
          ConfigurationManager.AppSettings["BackgroundColor"]; }
    }

    protected void Page_Load(object sender, EventArgs e)
    {
    }
}
```

8. Open the Default.aspx page to the Source view and update the body tag to retrieve
the background color from the application settings. Use the <% and %> braces to mark
executable code. Also add a line to the ASPX file to display background color value.

```
<%@ Page Language="C#" AutoEventWireup="true"
CodeFile="Default.aspx.cs" Inherits="_Default" %>
<!DOCTYPE html PUBLIC
..." >
<head runat="server">
    <title>Untitled Page</title>
</head>
<body style="background-color: <%=BackgroundColor%>" >
```

```
Body background color: <%=BackgroundColor%>
<form id="form1" runat="server">
<div>
</div>
</form>
</body>
</html>
```

9. Compile the program and run the page. The value #00FF00 translates to a bright green, so the background for your page should now appear bright green.

10. Browse through some of the other icons in the ASP.NET Configuration Settings featured in IIS. We'll encounter many of these settings as we go through ASP.NET in the coming chapters.

    ❑ The Authentication page is for setting up users and assigning them roles within your application.

    ❑ The .NET Globalization page manages localization issues.

    ❑ The Session State management feature is for managing session state. You can tell ASP.NET to store session state in any of a number of places, including in process on the host machine, out of process using a dedicated state server, or on a dedicated *SQLServer* database.

    ❑ The Pages and Controls page allows you to manage UI aspects of your application such as Themes and Master Pages.

The configuration story doesn't end here. ASP.NET relies on web.config for almost all of its settings. Although we touched on only a couple of settings in this chapter, we'll see most of them as well as many others throughout the next chapters. We'll revisit configuration when covering features such as security, session state, error messages, and HttpHandlers/HttpModules.

Summary

In this chapter, we saw how to manage configuration for a specific ASP.NET application. The configuration defaults are found within machine.config and web.config (as stored in the main .NET Framework directory). When it comes time for the ASP.NET runtime to apply configuration settings to a specific application, ASP.NET looks for overridden configuration settings within the XML-based web.config.

The web.config file that configures a specific application lives in that application's directory (as well as in the application's subdirectories—if any). If you're happy with the way Microsoft established the Web application settings within the primary web.config file, you don't need to change anything in your application's local web.config file. However, the default settings (using defaults such as *InProc* for your application's session state management, or using

Windows authentication to log users in) aren't generally useful for a Web site in a production environment.

To change these settings, you may edit the web.config file directly (as you had to do in the days of ASP.NET 1.x). However, ASP.NET 2.0 and later versions include new configuration tools that make configuring your site a very straightforward proposition.

We'll encounter ASP.NET configuration many more times in forthcoming chapters. In fact, we'll visit configuration heavily in the next chapter on ASP.NET security.

Chapter 9 Quick Reference

To	Do This
View global configuration files	Look in the Windows directory under Microsoft.NET\Framework\vxxxxx\config, where "vxxxxx" is the version of .NET your ASP.NET site is using.
Change configuration settings in a specific ASP.NET application	Place a web.config file in the application's directory and modify the settings.
Change configuration settings for a specific subdirectory underneath a virtual directory	Place a separate web.config file in the subdirectory OR Use the *location* element in the virtual directory's web.config file.
Modify a Web application's settings using the Web Site Administration Tool (WSAT)	Select **Web Site**, **ASP.NET Configuration** from the main menu in Visual Studio.
Modify a Web application's settings using the IIS ASP.NET Configuration tool	Open the IIS control panel. Highlight the virtual directory for your Web application. From the Features page for the virtual directory, double-click on the icon that represents the settings you want to view/modify.
Retrieve settings from the configuration file	Use the ASP.NET *ConfigurationManager* class.

Chapter 10
Logging In

After completing this chapter, you will be able to

- Manage Web-based security

- Implement Forms Authentication

- Work with Forms Authentication in the raw

- Work with ASP.NET login controls to make writing login pages painless

- Work with ASP.NET role-based authorization

This chapter covers managing access to your ASP.NET application. Web site security is a major concern for most enterprises. Without any means of securing a site, the Web site can expose areas of your enterprise that you may not want exposed to the general public. We'll take a quick look at what security means when it comes to Web applications. Then we'll look at various services available within ASP.NET for authenticating and authorizing users.

 Note "Authenticating users" means determining a user really is who he or she says they are (verifying the identity of a user). This is often done using a shared secret such as a password. "Authorizing users" means granting or restricting access to a specific user who has identified himself or herself based on specific permissions or "roles" granted to them. For example, clients in an administrative role are often granted more access than clients in a role as simple users.

Finally, we'll look at the new login controls, which greatly reduce the amount of development effort you might otherwise put into securing your site.

Web-Based Security

Software security is a prevalent topic these days, especially with ever increasing public awareness of security issues such as privacy. When a Web application runs on the Microsoft platform, several security issues arise immediately. They include (1) the security context of Internet Information Services (IIS), (2) being sure your clients are who they say they are, and (3) specifying what those clients may and may not do with your application.

Managing Web-based security is similar to managing normal network security in that you still need to manage the authentication and authorization of users. However, Web-based security involves managing clients running different platforms in an open system. That is, programming for a Web-based platform involves servicing requests from a client browser over which you have much less control in a closed network (like a Windows-based office network).

Although not quite a trivial problem, Windows security is at least a solved problem. Anyone who's configured a Windows network knows there are myriad issues involved in getting all the users of a network set up appropriately. But a Windows network is a closed system, and everyone on the network is connected and has a baseline level of trust between them (that is, they're all on the network). When you log on to a Windows network, you prove who you are (you *authenticate*) by providing your user name and password. If the security subsystem believes you are who you say you are, it issues a security token to your Windows session, and every application you start runs with that security token.

The resources (files, folders, drives, applications, etc.) on your computer and on your network are associated with Discretionary Access Control Lists (DACLs). If the security context under which your application runs belongs to a resource's DACL, then you may use it. Otherwise, the system will prevent you from using the resource. This is known as *authorization*.

In a closed system such as a Windows network, an administrator can effectively survey the whole system and assign users access to various resources. Because it's a closed system, the system can determine very easily whether or not a user belongs in the system and what that user may do.

Contrast this with a Web application. When considering a Web application, you realize first that the range of users of your application is quite wide. They are not necessarily part of your local network. That means you need another way (outside of the Windows infrastructure) to authenticate and authorize the users of your Web application. Or, put another way, Windows authentication doesn't scale well to the general Internet.

Securing IIS

The first security issue you encounter in programming Web applications on the Windows platform is understanding the security context for IIS. Virtually all access to your Web site will be directed through IIS. As with all Windows applications, IIS runs under a specific context. When you install IIS on your machine, the install process creates a separate security identity specifically for IIS.

You can see the identity under which your version of IIS runs by starting IIS from the control panel, selecting a virtual directory, viewing the features pane, clicking on the Authentication icon to open the Authentication page, and then clicking the right mouse button on the Anonymous Authentication and selecting Edit. On my computer, the name of the user is IUSR as you can see in Figure 10-1.

By default, IIS runs the virtual directories using Anonymous Authentication. When this mode is specified, IIS uses the principle identified in the *Specific User* field as its security principle. That is, IIS runs with access to the resources as being available for IUSR.

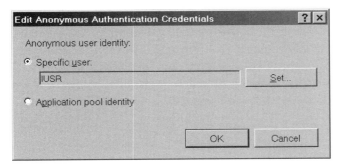

FIGURE 10-1 Managing IIS's authentication settings

IIS supports other forms of authentication, including applying Windows authentication to your Web application. In this case, you'd need to give all the potential clients a Windows user name and password. This only works when the clients are running on Windows-based platforms. Users logging on to your site are *challenged* (meaning they'll be asked to authenticate themselves). They'll see a Windows login dialog box when they log on to your Web site (perhaps you've run into this type of site before). This method of authentication does work well if you're writing an enterprise-wide site and you can count on your audience running Windows-based browsers. However, for a Web site with a wider audience using operating systems other than Windows, you'll want to use other means of authentication. This is because the underlying security mechanism available to Windows users is not present in other operating systems, so those users could not authenticate.

Fortunately, ASP.NET includes *Forms Authentication,* a straightforward means of authenticating clients. The Forms Authentication subsystem in ASP.NET 1.0 and 1.1 was a huge improvement from having to write your own authentication subsystem. Later versions of ASP.NET include and improve on the Forms Authentication model by adding an Authorization subsystem as well.

Let's start by taking a look at Forms Authentication in the raw.

Basic Forms Authentication

ASP.NET 1.0 and 1.1 introduced a straightforward means of authenticating users. Forms Authentication is driven by an application's web.config file. In addition to controlling such aspects as session state, tracing and debugging, and application key-value pairs, web.config includes authentication and authorization nodes.

To require users of your site to authenticate, you simply need to place some instructions into your web.config file. (You may edit the file directly, or you may use a tool such as the Web Site Administration Tool available through Visual Studio, which we examined in some detail in the previous chapter.)

Web.config has a section for specifying how your site should deal with authentication and authorization. In the absence of the authentication and authorization elements, ASP.NET allows unrestricted access to your site. However, once you add these elements to your web.config file, ASP.NET will force a redirect to a URI dedicated to authentication. Most of the time, the file will be some sort of login page in your Web application where users must do something such as type in a user name and password.

Before looking at the code, take a look at Figure 10-2, which illustrates how control flows on your Web site when you turn on Forms Authentication using web.config.

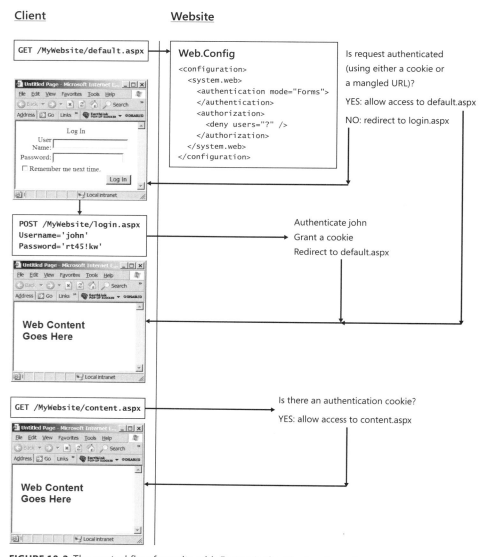

FIGURE 10-2 The control flow for a site with Forms Authentication turned on

The CD that comes with this book includes this login page. To see an example of the most basic authentication you can use in your application, take a look at the files Login.aspx and Web.ConfigFormsAuthentication. The web.config file includes the *Authentication* and *Authorization* elements to support Forms Authentication for the site. Listing 10-1 shows the web.config settings necessary to force authentication.

LISTING 10-1 A Basic Web.Config File Requiring Authentication

```
<configuration>
  <system.web>
    <authentication mode="Forms">
      <forms loginUrl="login.aspx" />
    </authentication>

    <authorization>
      <deny users="?" />
    </authorization>
  </system.web>
</configuration>
```

The login page that goes with it is shown in Listing 10-2.

LISTING 10-2 A Basic ASP.NET Login Page

```
<%@ Page language=C# %>
<html>
  <script runat=server>

  protected bool AuthenticateUser(String strUserName,
                                  String strPassword) {
    if (strUserName == "Gary") {
      if(strPassword== "K4T-YYY") {
        return true;
      }
    }
    else if(strUserName == "Jay") {
      if(strPassword== "RTY!333") {
        return true;
      }
    }
    else if(strUserName == "Susan") {
      if(strPassword== "erw3#54d") {
        return true;
      }
    }
    return false;
  }

  public void OnLogin(Object src, EventArgs e) {
    if (AuthenticateUser(m_textboxUserName.Text,
                         m_textboxPassword.Text)) {
```

```
        FormsAuthentication.RedirectFromLoginPage(
            m_textboxUserName.Text, m_bPersistCookie.Checked);
    } else {
        Response.Write("Invalid login: You don't belong here...");
    }
}
</script>

<body>
    <form runat=server>
        <h2>A most basic login page</h2>
        User name:
        <asp:TextBox id="m_textboxUserName" runat=server/><br>
        Password:
        <asp:TextBox id="m_textboxPassword"
            TextMode="password" runat=server/>
        <br/>
        Remember password and weaken security?:
        <asp:CheckBox id=m_bPersistCookie runat="server"/>
        <br/>
        <asp:Button text="Login" OnClick="OnLogin"
                    runat=server/>
        <br/>
    </form>
</body>
</html>
```

This is a simple login page that keeps track of three users—Gary, Jay, and Susan.

In this scenario, even if users try to surf to any page in the virtual directory, ASP.NET will stop them dead in their tracks and force them to pass the login page shown in Figure 10-3.

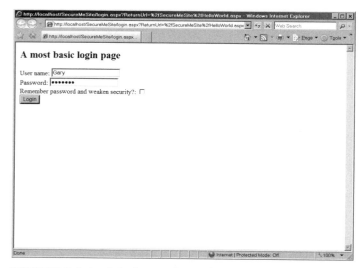

FIGURE 10-3 A simple login page for getting a user name and password from a client

This simple login page authenticates the user (out of a group of three possible users). In a real Web site, the authentication algorithm would probably use a database lookup to see if the user identifying himself or herself is in the database and whether the password matches. Later in this chapter, we'll see the ASP.NET authentication services. The login page then issues an authentication cookie using the *FormsAuthentication* utility class.

Figure 10-4 shows what the Web page looks like in the browser with tracing turned on. Here you can see the value of the authentication cookie in the (request) cookies collection.

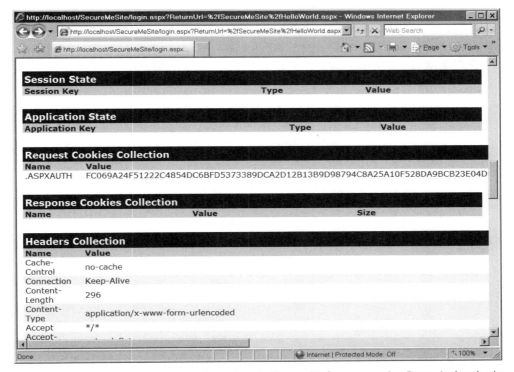

FIGURE 10-4 Tracing turned on reveals the authentication cookie for a page using Forms Authentication.

Run the Forms Authentication example

This example shows how to employ Forms Authentication on your site.

1. To run the Forms Authentication example, create a virtual directory to hold the site. Add an HTML file to the directory that simply displays a banner text "Hello World." Name the file *Default.htm.* You need to have a target file to surf to for Forms Authentication to work. Alternatively, you can use an already existing site and employ Forms Authentication there.

2. Copy the Login.aspx page from the Chapter 10 examples on the CD with this book into the virtual directory for which you want to apply Forms Authentication.

3. Copy the Web.ConfigForceAuthentication file from the Chapter 10 examples on the CD with this book into the virtual directory for which you want to apply Forms Authentication. Make sure to rename the configuration file *web.config* after you copy it.

4. Try to surf to a page in that virtual directory. ASP.NET should force you to complete the Login.aspx page before moving on.

5. Type in a valid user name and password. Subsequent access to that virtual directory should work just fine because now there's an Authentication ticket associated with the request and response.

Although you may build your own authentication algorithms, ASP.NET includes a number of new features that make authenticating users a straightforward and standard proposition. We'll look at those in a moment.

Briefly, ASP.NET allows two other types of authentication: Passport authentication and Windows authentication. There's not much talk about Passport anymore. Passport authentication has evolved into the Windows Live ID and requires a centralized authentication service provided by Microsoft. If you've ever used Hotmail.com, you've used Windows Live ID. The advantage of Windows Live ID authentication is that it centralizes login and personalization information at one source. While this is not a free service, your users can use a single user ID to log into many Web sites, providing convenience and easing your own development needs as you don't need to manage user authentication yourself.

The other type of authentication supported by ASP.NET is Windows authentication. If you specify Windows authentication, ASP.NET relies on IIS and Windows authentication to manage users. Any user making his or her way through IIS authentication (using basic, digest, or Integrated Windows Authentication as configured in IIS) will be authenticated for the Web site. These other forms of authentication are available when configuring IIS. However, for most ASP.NET Web sites, you'll be bypassing IIS authentication in favor of ASP.NET authentication even if only for scalability reasons. ASP.NET will use the authenticated identity to manage authorization.

ASP.NET Authentication Services

ASP.NET includes a great deal of support for authenticating users (outside of IIS's support). Most of it comes from the *FormsAuthentication* class.

The *FormsAuthentication* Class

Many of ASP.NET's authentication services center around the *FormsAuthentication* class. The examples shown in Listings 10-1 and 10-2 show how the rudimentary authentication works by installing an authentication cookie in the response and redirecting the processing back to the originally requested page. This is the primary purpose of *FormsAuthentication .RedirectFromLoginPage*. There are some other interesting methods in the *FormsAuthentication* class that allow for finer-grained control over the authentication process. For example, you can authenticate users manually (without forcing a redirect). That's useful for creating optional login pages that vary their content based on the authentication level of the client.

FormsAuthentication includes a number of other services as well. Table 10-1 shows some of the useful members of the *FormsAuthentication* class.

TABLE 10-1 Useful *FormsAuthentication* Class Members

FormsAuthentication Method	Description
CookiesSupported	Property indicating whether cookies are supported for authentication
FormsCookieName	Property representing the forms authentication cookie name
FormsCookiePath	Property representing the forms authentication cookie path
LoginUrl	Redirects URL for logging in
RequireSSL	Property representing whether secure sockets layer is required
SlidingExpiration	Property indicating whether sliding expiration is set
Authenticate	Authenticates the user
Encrypt	Generates an encrypted string representing a forms-authentication ticket suitable for use in an HTTP cookie
Decrypt	Creates a *FormsAuthenticationTicket* from an encrypted forms-authentication ticket
GetAuthCookie	Creates an authentication cookie for a specific user
GetRedirectUrl	Gets the original URL to which the client was surfing
HashPasswordForStoringInConfigFile	Creates a hashed password suitable for storing in a credential store
RedirectFromLoginPage	Authenticates the user and redirects to the originally requested page
SignOut	Invalidates the authentication ticket

An Optional Login Page

The code accompanying this book also includes an example showing how to authenticate separately. The page in Listing 10-3 uses the same authentication algorithm (three users—Gary, Jay, and Susan—with hard-coded passwords). However, the page authenticates users and then redirects them back to the same page (OptionalLogin.aspx).

LISTING 10-3 OptionalLogin.aspx

```
<%@ Page language=C# trace="false"%>
<html>
  <script runat=server>

  protected bool AuthenticateUser(String strUserName,
                                  String strPassword)
  {
    if (strUserName == "Gary")
    {
      if(strPassword== "K4T-YYY")
      {
        return true;
      }
    }
    else if(strUserName == "Jay")
    {
      if(strPassword== "RTY!333")
      {
        return true;
      }
    }
    else if(strUserName == "Susan")
    {
      if(strPassword== "erw3#54d")
      {
        return true;
      }
    }
    return false;
  }

  public void OnLogin(Object src, EventArgs e)  {
    if (AuthenticateUser(m_textboxUserName.Text,
                         m_textboxPassword.Text))
    {
     FormsAuthentication.SetAuthCookie(
               m_textboxUserName.Text,
      m_bPersistCookie.Checked);
          Response.Redirect("optionallogin.aspx");
    } else {
      Response.Write("Invalid login: You don't belong here...");
    }
  }

  protected void ShowContent()
  {
    if(Request.IsAuthenticated)
    {
      Response.Write("Hi, you are authenticated. <br>" );
      Response.Write("You get special content...<br>" );
    } else
```

```
        {
            Response.Write("You're anonymous. Nothing special for you... ");
        }
    }
    </script>
    <body><form runat=server>

        <h2>Optional Login Page</h2>

        User name:
        <asp:TextBox id="m_textboxUserName" runat=server/><br>
        Password:
        <asp:TextBox id="m_textboxPassword"
            TextMode="password" runat=server/>
        <br/>
        Remember password and weaken security?:
        <asp:CheckBox id=m_bPersistCookie runat="server"/>
        <br/>
        <asp:Button text="Login" OnClick="OnLogin"
                    runat=server/>

        <br/>

        <%ShowContent(); %>
    </form></body>
</html>
```

Notice that the page sets the authentication cookie manually by calling *FormsAuthentication*
.SetAuthCookie and then redirects the processing back to the page. Each time the page
shows, it calls the *ShowContent* method, which checks the authentication property in the
page to decide whether or not to display content specialized for an authenticated user.
Because the page redirects manually after authenticating, the web.config file needs to look a
bit different. To make it work, the authentication node should remain, but the authorization
node that denies anonymous users needs to be removed. That way, any user can log in to the
OptionLogin.aspx page (they won't be denied) but they may proceed after they're authenticated. Here's the new web.config file, shown in Listing 10-4. The file on the CD is named
Web.ConfigForOptionalLogin. To make it apply to the application, copy the file and name it
as *web.config*.

LISTING 10-4 A Web.Config File Supporting Optional Login

```
<configuration>
  <system.web>
    <authentication mode="Forms">
    </authentication>
  </system.web>
</configuration>
```

Figure 10-5 shows how the optional login page appears before the user has been authenticated.

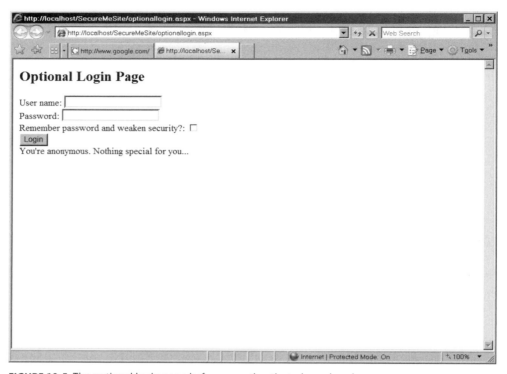

FIGURE 10-5 The optional login page before an authenticated user logs in

Run the optional login page

This example shows how to run the optional login page.

1. To run the optional login page, create a virtual directory to hold the site. Alternatively, you can use an already existing site and try the optional login page from there.

2. Copy the OptionalLogin.aspx page from the Chapter 10 examples on the CD with this book into the virtual directory.

3. Copy the Web.ConfigOptionalLogin from the Chapter 10 examples on the CD with this book into the virtual directory. Be sure to rename the configuration file *web.config* so ASP.NET loads the appropriate configuration settings.

4. Try to surf to a page in that virtual directory. ASP.NET should allow you to see the page, but as an unauthenticated user.

5. Type in a valid user name and password. You should see the content tailored for authenticated users. Subsequent requests/responses to and from the site will include an authentication token, so you would always see the special authenticated content.

After the user has been authenticated, the optional login page shows the content tailored to the specific authenticated user. Figure 10-6 shows the page after an authenticated user logs in.

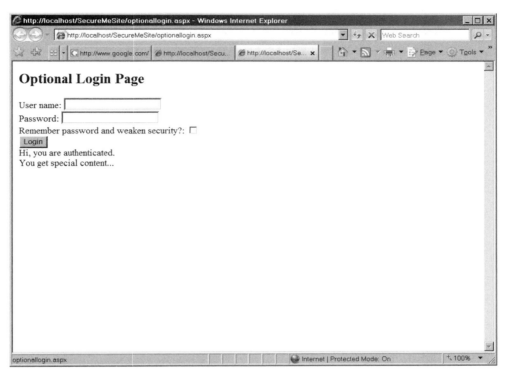

FIGURE 10-6 An authenticated user has logged in

Managing Users

So far, you can see that the fundamentals behind employing Forms Authentication are easy to manage. In the previous examples, the pages are inaccessible until you prove your identity. The example above shows raw authentication with the users and passwords hard-coded into the ASPX file. This is useful for illustration. However, in a production application you'll undoubtedly want to assign identities to the authorized users visiting your site.

ASP.NET and Visual Studio include facilities for both managing user identities and managing roles. The following exercise shows how to set up a secure site in which users are allowed access only after they identify themselves correctly.

Managing user access

1. Create a new Web site named *SecureSite*.

2. Add a label to the Default.aspx page with the text "Congratulations. You made it in." That way, when you get to the default page after logging in, you'll know which page it is in the browser.

3. Open the ASP.NET Web Site Administration Tool by selecting **Web Site**, **ASP.NET Configuration** from the main menu. Go to the **Provider** tab. Select the **Select A Single Provider For All Site Management Data** link. You can click the **Test** link to test the provider to make sure the connection is working.

 Tip As you recall from Chapter 9, IIS includes ASP.NET configuration facilities as well. If your site has a virtual directory, you can get to the facilities by opening IIS, selecting the virtual directory of interest, and navigating among the Features icons.

4. Run the program aspnet_regsql.exe to create a a data store to hold membership information. You'll find aspnet_regsql.exe in C:\Windows\Microsoft.NET\Framework\v2.0.50727>.

5. Go to the **Security** tab. You'll see the page shown in the following graphic. Click the **Select Authentication Type** link.

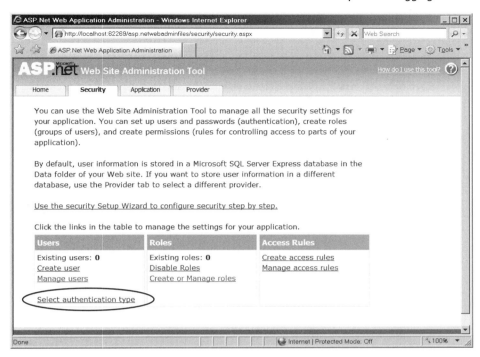

6. Select **From The Internet** as the access method. Then click the **Done** button. This will cause the site to use Forms Authentication.

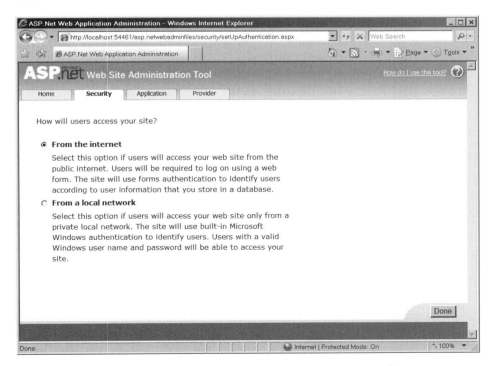

7. Select **Enable Roles** and then select **Create Or Manage Roles**. Add some roles to the site. The example here includes three roles: Administrator, JoeUser, and PowerUser. Add these roles now. We'll assign real users to them shortly.

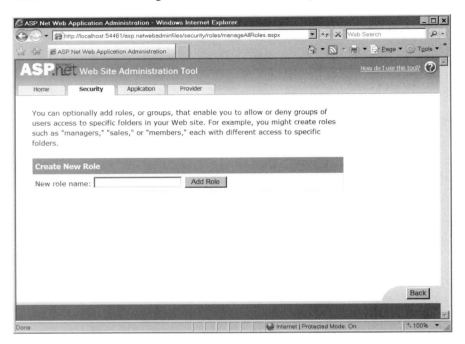

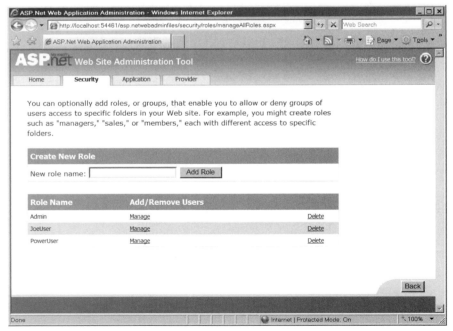

8. Now add some users and assign some roles. From the main security page, select the **Create User** link. Add some users. You may assign them to roles now if you wish.

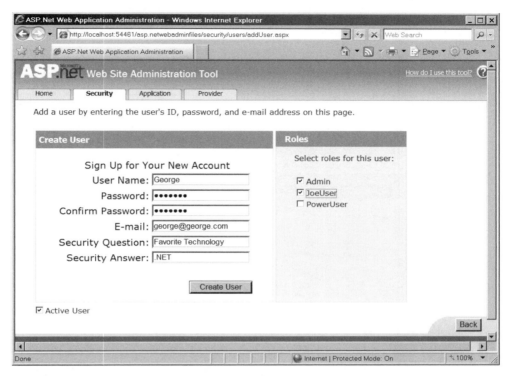

After you've added some users and assigned roles to them, web.config should look something like this:

```
<?xml version="1.0"?>
<configuration >
   <system.web>
    <authorization>
        <deny users="?" />
    </authorization>
    <authentication mode="Forms" />
    <roleManager enabled="true"/>
    <compilation debug="true"/></system.web>
</configuration>
```

9. At this point, you may authenticate users to your site. However, you would probably like to control what parts of your site they may access. To do that, create some access rules. Select the **Create Access Rules** (on the **Security** tab) link to manage authorization. Deny anonymous users, as shown in the following graphic:

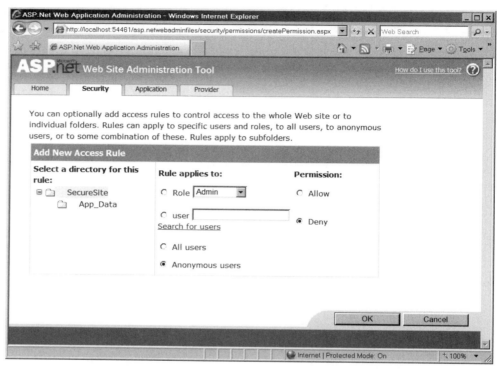

Denying access to anonymous users causes the following changes in web.config. Notice the *authorization* and the *roleManager* elements.

```xml
<?xml version="1.0" encoding="utf-8"?>
<configuration
>
  <system.web>
    <authorization>
      <deny users="?" />
    </authorization>
    <roleManager enabled="true"
      defaultProvider="AspNetSqlRoleProvider" />
    <authentication mode="Forms" />
  </system.web>
</configuration>
```

10. Now try running the site. ASP.NET should deny you access to the site, as shown here:

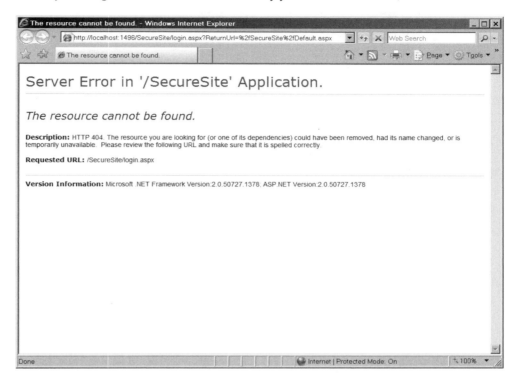

ASP.NET is looking for a way to authenticate the user. However, the site doesn't have one yet. The Forms Authentication setting is set to *true* and anonymous users are denied access, but there's no instruction to ASP.NET about what to do. There's no login redirect and no login page yet, so ASP.NET simply stops you in your tracks. Let's provide a login page using the ASP.NET login controls.

ASP.NET Login Controls

Earlier in this chapter, we handcrafted a couple of different login pages. During the heyday of ASP.NET 1.1, that's what you had to do to get Forms Authentication working. Modern ASP.NET improves things by adding a number of login controls that perform the most common login scenarios you might need for your site.

These controls include the *Login, LoginView, PasswordRecovery, LoginStatus, LoginName, ChangePassword, and CreateUserWizard* controls. Here's a summary of what each control does:

- **Login**   The *Login* control is the simplest login control and supports the most common login scenario—signing in using a user name and password. The control includes user name and password text boxes and a check box for users who want to compromise password security by saving their passwords on the machine. The control exposes properties through which you can change the text and appearance of the control. You may also add links to manage registration or password recovery. The *Login* control interacts with the ASP.NET membership component for authentication by default. If you want to manage authentication yourself, you may do so by handling the control's *Authenticate* event.

- **LoginView**   The *LoginView* control is very similar to the optional login page mentioned earlier. It's useful for managing the content you display for authenticated versus nonauthenticated users. The *LoginView* displays the login status via the display templates *AnonymousTemplate* and *LoggedInTemplate*. The control renders a different template depending on the status of the user. The *LoginView* also lets you manage text and links within each template.

- **PasswordRecovery**   The *PasswordRecovery* control supports Web sites that send user passwords to clients when they forget their passwords. The control collects the user's account name and then follows up with a security question (provided that functionality is set up correctly). The control either e-mails the current password to the user or creates a new one.

- **LoginStatus**   The *LoginStatus* control displays whether or not the current user is logged on. Nonlogged-in users are prompted to log in, whereas logged-in users are prompted to log out.

- **LoginName**   The *LoginName* control displays the user's login name.

- **ChangePassword**   The *ChangePassword* control gives users a chance to change their passwords. An authenticated user may change his or her password by supplying the original password and a new password (along with a confirmation of the new password).

- **CreateUserWizard**   The *CreateUserWizard* control collects information from users so it can set up an ASP.NET membership account for each user. Out of the box, the control gathers a user name, a password, an e-mail address, a security question, and a security answer. The *CreateUserWizard* will collect different information from users, depending on the membership provider used by your application.

The following exercise illustrates how to write a login page using the login controls.

Write a login page

1. Create a Login page. ASP.NET wants to see a login page for the SecureSite application called *Login.aspx*. Add a regular Web form to your application. Name the form *Login.aspx*. Grab a *Login* control from the toolbox and drag it onto the form, like so:

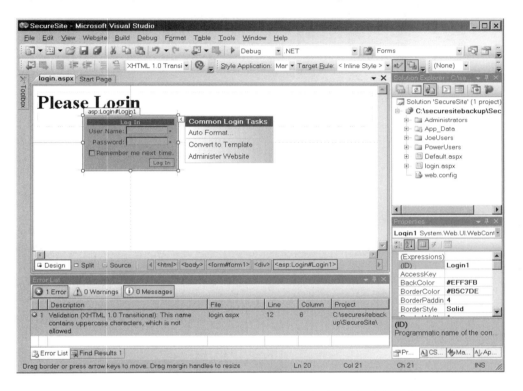

2. By selecting Internet access through the ASP.NET Web Site Administration Tool, ASP.NET understands to use Forms Authentication. The default login URL is Login.aspx.

Now try to surf to the default page. ASP.NET will confront you with the login page, like so:

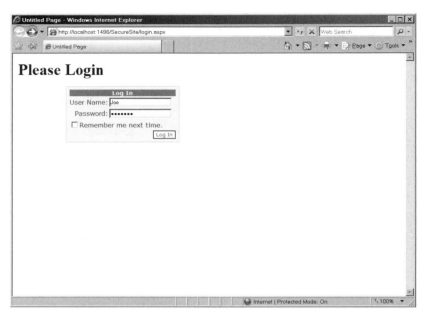

You'll see the default page (provided you logged in successfully):

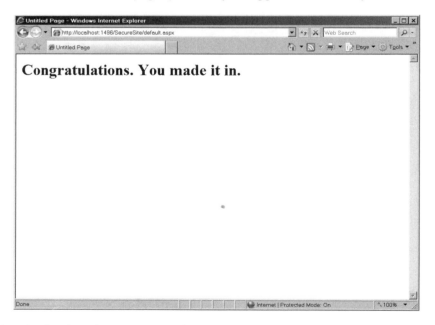

Authentication is an important step in managing the security of your site. The second half is managing access to your site once users have authenticated themselves. This is known as *authorization*.

Authorizing Users

Once you have authenticated a user, you have established his or her identity. Although that information is sometimes useful by itself, a system becomes more secure when authentication is combined with authorization. Authentication establishes identity, whereas authorization establishes what users can do when they're signed onto your site.

In the previous example, we added a couple of roles to the site. The following example illustrates how to limit access to certain areas of your site based on the user's identity.

Managing authorization

1. Add a folder for Administrators to access. Name the folder *Administrators*. Add a Web form to the folder with a label that says "Administrators Only." Make a JoeUsers folder (and a Web form for JoeUsers). Also make a PowerUsers folder. Add a single default file to each of these directories so that you will have something to surf to in each directory. Put labels on each of the pages with text to distinguish each page.

2. Now set up associations between the roles you've defined and these new resources. Go to the Web Site Administration Tool again. Add some more users, each with various roles assigned. For example, this site includes a user named George assigned to the Administrator role, a user named Joe assigned to the JoeUser role, and a user named Frodo assigned to the PowerUser role.

3. After adding the new users, set up some new access roles. You may do this by selecting the **Manage Access Rules** link and then selecting the **Add New Access Rule** link. You may selectively allow or deny various users or classes of users, as shown here:

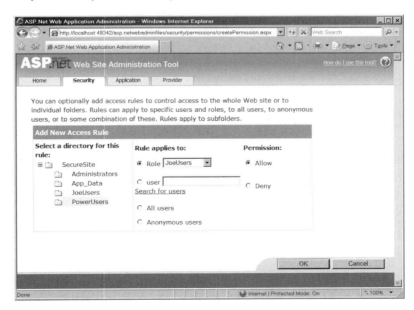

4. Add some hyperlinks to the default page so that clients can try to navigate to the various restricted pages. Drag three *Hyperlink* controls onto the default page—one for the Administrator page, one for the JoeUser page, and one for the PowerUsers page that you created in Step 1. Set the *Text* property of each *Hyperlink* to be meaningful (for example, the *Text* property for the Administrator.aspx file could be "Go to Administrator Page." Use the **Property** dialog box to set the *NavigationUrl* for each *Hyperlink* to the appropriate page.

5. Run the page. After logging in, you should see the default page, which says "Congratulations. You made it in." and has three *Hyperlinks*. Depending on your identity, ASP.NET will allow or disallow you to view the pages in the subdirectories.

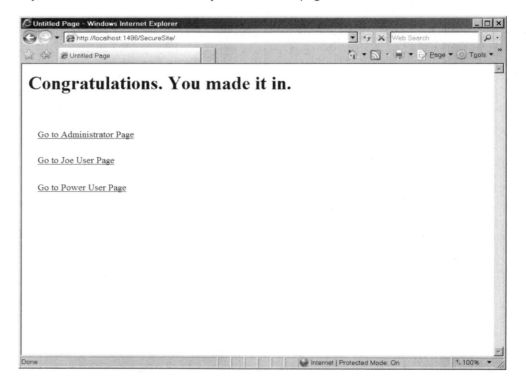

If you logged in successfully as a user in the JoeUser role, ASP.NET will let you view the pages in that subdirectory, like so:

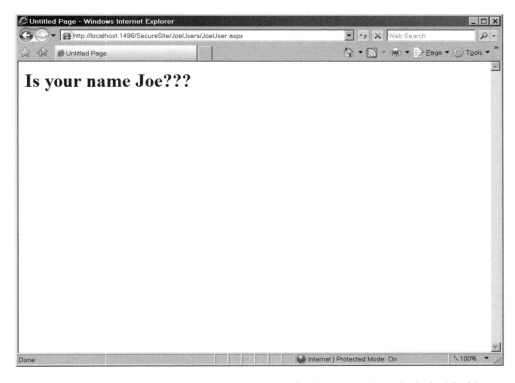

Table 10-2 shows the users' names and their passwords for the example included with this chapter.

TABLE 10-2 User Names and Passwords for the Example Code Available for this Book

User Name	Password
George	abc!123
Joe	abc!123
Frodo	abc!123

This touches on the utility provided by the login controls. For even more robust login scenarios (including password recovery and optional logins), try some of the other login controls.

Summary

In this chapter, we saw the ASP.NET security model. Although IIS does have its own security model, leveraging it for Web site security often amounts to giving users of your site a Windows user identity. Perhaps that's okay for a small, confined Web site. However, for a site that will be available to potentially the entire globe, that's not such a good thing.

If you decide to let ASP.NET handle authentication, then you have more control over how the authentication happens while at the same time leaving your set of Windows user identities unadulterated. To let a request get past IIS, allow anonymous access to your virtual directory.

Once a request gets past IIS, it's up to ASP.NET to figure out who the user is and how to dole out access. ASP.NET includes an authentication model named *Forms Authentication*. You turn on Forms Authentication through the web.config file. Either use the typing Wizard (that is, type the *<authentication>* element by hand) or use the Web Site Administration Tool (or the IIS ASP.NET tab) to turn on Forms Authentication.

The Web Site Administration Tool is useful for adding users, adding roles, and assigning users to roles. It's the most convenient way to manage users and roles. (If you want to, you may set up your own authentication scheme and database, bypassing the ASP.NET support, but this is very advanced and well beyond the scope of this book.)

By using ASP.NET authentication and authorization support, the login controls work automatically. The login controls supply login functionality for the majority of use cases. (As always, you may bypass the support for an authentication and authorization scheme of your own choosing.)

Chapter 10 Quick Reference

To	Do This
Use Forms Authentication in your application	1. Use the ASP.NET Web Site Administration tool (select **Web Site**, **ASP.NET Configuration**). 2. Use the ASP.NET tab in IIS.
Configure the security aspects of your Web site	1. Use the ASP.NET Web Site Administration Tool (select **Web Site**, **ASP.NET Configuration**). 2. Use the ASP.NET tab in IIS.
Authenticate a request by hand	Use the *FormsAuthentication* class's Set Auth cookie.
Invalidate an authentication cookie	Call the *FormsAuthentication* class's *SignOut* method.
Verify presence of the authentication cookie	Turn on tracing.

Chapter 11
Data Binding

After completing this chapter, you will be able to

- Represent collections using data-bound controls
- Talk to database providers in ASP.NET
- Customize data-bound controls

This chapter covers one of ASP.NET's most useful features: data binding. A number of controls within ASP.NET have the capability to understand the form and content of a collection and to render the correct tags to represent such user elements as list boxes, radio button lists, and combo boxes. Here we'll examine how these controls work and how to use them on a Web page.

Representing Collections without Data Binding

One of the most common problems encountered in building any software (and Web sites in particular) is representing collections as user interface (UI) elements. Think about some of the sites you have recently visited. If you ordered something from a commercial site, you no doubt hit a page that asked you to enter your address. What happened when you reached the *State* field? Most Web sites display a drop-down list box from which you may choose a state abbreviation.

How was that drop-down list filled? In HTML, the *<select>* tag nests several *<option>* tags that represent the elements to be listed. The state abbreviations probably came from a database or some other well-established source. Somewhere (most likely at the server), some piece of code had to go through the collection of states and render *<select>* and *<option>* tags for this hypothetical state selection control.

ASP.NET server-side controls, such as the *ListBox* and the *DropDownList*, include *Items* collections. For example, one way to render a collection as a drop-down list is to declare a drop-down list on your ASP.NET page and add the items individually via the *Items.Add* method like so (of course this assumes this object's *ToString* method returns something meaningful—not the type but the contents of the object):

```
protected void BuildDropDownList(IList techList)
{
    for(int i = 0; i < techList.Count; i++)
    {
        this.DropDownList2.Items.Add(techList[i]);
    }
}
```

Because representing collections as UI elements is such a prevalent programming task, it makes a lot of sense to push that down into the framework if possible. ASP.NET includes a number of data-bound controls that are capable of taking collections and rendering the correct tags for you. Let's see how this works.

Representing Collections with Data Binding

Each of the data-bound controls within ASP.NET includes properties to attach it to a data source. For simple data binding, these controls include a *DataSource* property to which you may attach any collection that implements the *IEnumerable* interface (as well as the *DataSet* and *DataTable* classes that we'll see shortly). After attaching the collection to the control, you call *DataBind* on the page (or the control) to instruct the control to iterate through the collection.

For more complex data binding, some controls include a property named *DataSourceID*. This new style of data binding is named *declarative data binding*. Instead of simply iterating through a collection, the declarative data binding classes use a separate *DataSource* control to manage data for the data-bound control. You can think of the *DataSource* controls as preconfigured database commands. Instead of littering your code with database commands and queries, the *DataSource* controls perform the commands on your behalf. These data managers support the data-bound controls in implementing standard functionality such as sorting, paging, and editing. Declarative binding greatly simplifies the process of rendering collections. They work by referencing the ID of a *DataSource* control on the page. .NET includes several of these *DataSource* controls—including one for Access databases, one for SQL Server, one for wrapping ad hoc collections (the *ObjectDataSource*), one for supporting Language Integrated Query (*LinqDataSource*), and one for supporting XML data access (the *XmlDataSource*). We'll look at the *SiteMapDataSource* in Chapter 12. With declarative data binding, calling *DataBind* is optional. The control will call *DataBind* during the *PreRendering* event.

ASP.NET includes a number of controls that support at least simple data binding, whereas others support declarative data binding as well. These controls include those based on the *ListControl*, the *CheckBoxList*, the *RadioButtonList*, the *DropDownList*, and the *ListBox*. In addition, the more advanced controls include the *TreeView*, the *Menu*, the *GridView*, the *DataGrid*, the *Repeater*, the *FormView*, and the *DetailsView*.

Here's a rundown of how each control works.

ListControl-Based Controls

The most common data-bound controls are those based on the *ListControl* base class. These controls include the *ListBox*, the *BulletedList*, the *RadioButtonList*, the *CheckBoxList*, and the *DropDownList*. We'll see these controls in detail in a moment. The names are self-explanatory for the most part. They all have direct analogs in Windows desktop programming as well as standard HTML control tags. The *ListBox* displays a list of strings. The *DropDownList* is similar to a *ComboBox*. The *RadioButtonList* displays a group of mutually exclusive radio buttons. The *CheckBoxList* displays a column of check box controls.

TreeView

We saw an example of the *TreeView* in Chapter 6. The *TreeView* control represents hierarchical data. It's perfect for matching up with XML data sources. The *TreeView* features collapsible nodes that allow users to drill down from abstract data elements into more detailed ones. The *TreeView* supports declarative data binding.

Menu

The *Menu* control also handles hierarchical data binding. The *Menu* control gives users the ability to navigate the site in much the same way that menus for desktop applications do. The *Menu* supports declarative data binding.

FormView

The *FormView* control supports free-form layout for individual controls (such as a *TextBox* or a *ListBox*) that render data from a data source. The *FormView* also supports editing of data in the data source through the controls. The *FormView* supports declarative data binding.

GridView

Whereas ASP.NET 1.x supported only the *DataGrid* control, later versions of ASP.NET support a *DataGrid* on steroids—the *GridView*. The *GridView* control is what it says it is—it renders collections via a grid with individual columns and rows. Each row in the grid represents an individual record in a collection. Each column within that row represents an individual field within the record. Moreover, the original *DataGrid* required you as a developer to manage paging and sorting of data. The *GridView* control, on the other hand, supports automatic paging and sorting. The *GridView* also supports editing (something that requires hand coding in the *DataGrid*). The *GridView* supports declarative data binding.

DetailsView

If the *GridView* gives you the whole gestalt of a data source, then the *DetailsView* control is for drilling down to display one record at a time. The *DetailsView* is often paired with controls such as the *ListBox*, the *DropDownList*, or the *GridView*. Users select the row using one of these controls and the *DetailsView* shows the associated data. The *DetailsView* supports declarative data binding.

DataList

The *DataGrid* and the *GridView* display the data in a data source using regular rows and columns, and that is that. However, if you want a little more control over the final rendered format, the *DataList* control displays the records in a data source in a format you determine using template controls.

Repeater

The *Repeater* control also displays data from a data source in a format you determine (rather than forcing it into rows and columns). The *Repeater* control uses both raw HTML and server-side controls to display the rows. The *Repeater* control repeats the format you define for each row.

Simple Data Binding

The simplest data binding entails attaching a simple collection to one of the *ListControl*-based control's *DataSource* property. If you have a collection, you can simply set the *DataSource* property of one of these controls and it will render the correct tags automatically.

The following example shows how to use some of the data-bound controls by hooking up a *List* to several of the *ListControl*-based controls.

Data binding with a collection

1. Start a new Web site named *DataBindORama*.

2. From the WebSite menu, select **Add New Item...** and add a class named *TechnologyDescriptor*. If Visual Studio asks if you want the file supporting this class to be placed in the *App_Code* folder, say yes (that is, click **OK**). Add two implicit string properties named *TechnologyName* and *Description*. This class will represent a technology name and an accompanying description.

> **Tip** Prior to .NET 3.5 you would have had to create private or protected fields to store the string-based information and then created public properties to expose the string values for public consumption. .NET 3.5 simplifies this by allowing you to use *implicit properties*. Implicit properties are really nothing more than a shortcut, saving time and unnecessary lines of code when your property is doing nothing more than providing access to private (or protected) fields.

Important Exposing the member variables as properties is important so the controls will work correctly with data binding. When a control binds to a collection composed of classes, it will look for the fields to expose via their property names. Using the data-binding controls, you may specify a "display name" (that is, the value that will appear in the control), and you may specify a second "hidden" value to be associated with the item that was selected. In the case of rendering collections of managed objects, the binding architecture depends on these fields being exposed as properties.

Listing 11-1 shows the *TechnologyDescriptor* that exposes a technology name and description as properties. The class also has a static method that creates a collection of *TechnologyDescriptors*.

LISTING 11-1 Code for the *TechnologyDescriptor*

```
public class TechnologyDescriptor
{
    public string TechnologyName { get; set; }
    public string Description { get; set; }

    public TechnologyDescriptor(string strTechnologyName,
             string strDescription)
    {
       this. TechnologyName = strTechnologyName;
       this. Description = strDescription;
    }

    public static List<TechnologyDescriptor> CreateTechnologyList()
    {

       List<TechnologyDescriptor> lTechnologies =
         new List<TechnologyDescriptor>();

       TechnologyDescriptor technologyDescriptor;

       technologyDescriptor =
         new TechnologyDescriptor("ASP.NET",
         "Handle HTTP Requests");
       lTechnologies.Add(technologyDescriptor);

       technologyDescriptor =
         new TechnologyDescriptor("Windows Forms",
         "Local Client UI technology");
       lTechnologies.Add(technologyDescriptor);

       technologyDescriptor =
         new TechnologyDescriptor("ADO.NET",
         "Talk to the database");
       lTechnologies.Add(technologyDescriptor);

       technologyDescriptor =
         new TechnologyDescriptor(".NET CLR",
         "Modern runtime environment for manage code");
       lTechnologies.Add(technologyDescriptor);
```

```
technologyDescriptor =
  new TechnologyDescriptor(".NET IL",
  "Intermediary representation for .NET applications");
lTechnologies.Add(technologyDescriptor);

technologyDescriptor =
  new TechnologyDescriptor(".NET Compact Framework",
  "Modern runtime environment for small devices");
lTechnologies.Add(technologyDescriptor);

return lTechnologies;
  }
}
```

3. After developing the *TechnologyDescriptor* class, add four data-bound controls to the default page: a *ListBox*, a *DropDownList*, a *RadioButtonList*, and a *CheckBoxList*.

4. Underneath each of these controls, place a *Label*. The label will be used to show the value associated with each selected item.

5. Set the *AutoPostBack* property for the *ListBox*, the *DropDownList*, the *RadioButtonList*, and the *CheckBoxList* to *true*. That way, selecting an item in each of the controls will cause a postback during which the selected item may be interrogated.

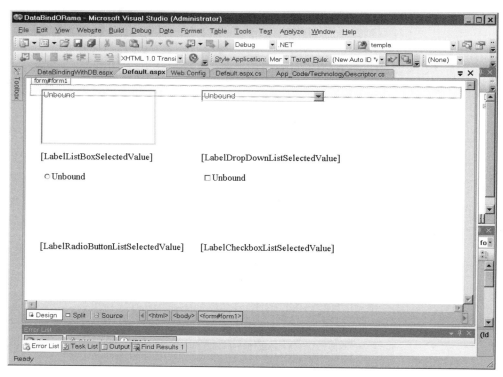

6. Now update the page to build a list of *TechnologyDescriptors* and to attach the collection of *TechnologyDescriptors* to each control. For each control, set the

DataTextField property to **TechnologyName** (to map it to the *TechnologyDescriptor*'s *TechnologyName* property). This will ensure that the technology name will appear in the control. Then set the *DataValueField* for each control to **Description** to map the *Description* property to be the associated value. Listing 11-2 shows creating a collection of *TechnologyDescriptors* and attaching the collection to each of the controls.

7. Add selection handlers for each of the controls (by double-clicking them). On receiving the selection events, interrogate the control for the selected item's value. Listing 11-2 also shows the handlers.

LISTING 11-2 Modifications to Default.aspx.cs to Support Data Binding and Control Events

```
using System.Collections.Generic;

protected void Page_Load(object sender, EventArgs e)
{

    if (!this.IsPostBack)
    {
        List<TechnologyDescriptor> techList =
          TechnologyDescriptor.CreateTechnologyList();
        this.ListBox1.DataSource = techList;
        this.ListBox1.DataTextField = "TechnologyName";

        this.DropDownList1.DataSource = techList;
        this.DropDownList1.DataTextField = "TechnologyName";

        this.RadioButtonList1.DataSource = techList;
        this.RadioButtonList1.DataTextField = "TechnologyName";

        this.CheckBoxList1.DataSource = techList;
        this.CheckBoxList1.DataTextField = "TechnologyName";

        this.DataBind();
    }
}
protected void ListBox1_SelectedIndexChanged(object sender, EventArgs e)
{
    this.LabelListBoxSelectedValue.Text = this.ListBox1.SelectedValue;
}
protected void DropDownList1_SelectedIndexChanged(object sender,
  EventArgs e)
{
    this.LabelDropDownListSelectedValue.Text =
      this.DropDownList1.SelectedValue;
}
protected void RadioButtonList1_SelectedIndexChanged(object sender,
  EventArgs e)
{
    this.LabelRadioButtonListSelectedValue.Text =
      this.RadioButtonList1.SelectedValue;
}
protected void CheckBoxList1_SelectedIndexChanged(object sender,
  EventArgs e)
```

```
       {
           this.LabelCheckboxListSelectedValue.Text =
               this.CheckBoxList1.SelectedValue;
       }
```

8. Compile the site and browse to the page.

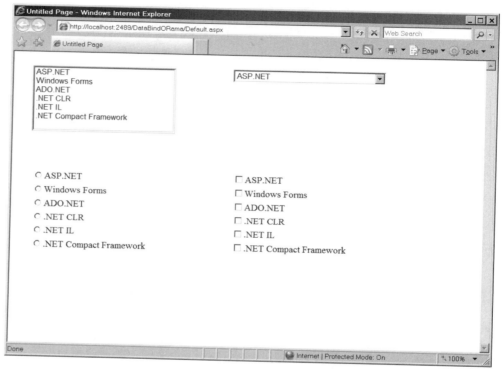

In the previous example, selecting one of the items within the data-bound controls will reveal the related value in the label beneath the control.

In certain programming situations, you may find yourself doing this kind of data binding. For example, simple collections such as states within the United States or short lists (perhaps of employee or contact names) work great with these *ListControl*-based controls. However, very often you'll find yourself dealing with data in a more complex format—beyond a simple standard collection. A number of controls can deal with more complex *DataSets*. However, we first need to look at ADO.NET because it provides the easiest way to reach these more complex data compositions.

Accessing Databases

The previous example shows how to attach in-memory collections (such as *ArrayLists* and *Lists*) to a server-side control and have it render the correct tags on the client. Although this is useful, the server-side controls are capable of working with other collections—including ones that come from databases. Before seeing how to render database queries using UI elements, let's take a quick look at the .NET database story.

The .NET Database Story

Just as .NET includes a library of classes for managing rich client UI (Windows Forms) and for handling HTTP requests (ASP.NET), .NET includes a library for connecting to a wide range of databases. That library is named *ADO.NET*.

ADO.NET is similar to Microsoft's previous database technology (named simply ADO). ADO stands for Active Data Objects. Although Microsoft has dropped "Active" from its marketing lexicon, it kept the name ADO and appended ".NET" to name the managed database technology (surely for brand name recognition). ADO represents a set of managed providers that is very similar in function and form to classic ADO. ADO.NET centers around three main units of functionality: connecting to a database, commanding the database, and using the results.

Connections

When you want to talk to a specific database, you usually need to *connect* to it. At the very least, most of the time this involves specifying the location of the database. For many scenarios, connecting also requires managing security (via user names and passwords). More advanced scenarios may also require dealing with such issues as connection pooling and transactions. These are all handled as part of the process of *connecting* to the database. The connection information is usually passed in via a string, the contents of which are used to set various connection parameters when the ADO.NET internals interpret the string.

ADO.NET has classes for making connections to a database. ADO.NET 1.x included only two: a connection for Microsoft SQL Server and another for connecting to OLEDB databases. Later versions of ADO.NET add classes specialized for more database types and include a new set of database services using the *provider pattern*.

Working with ADO.NET 1.x involved writing most of the data access code using the ADO interfaces (rather than directly instantiating the database classes). This allowed you to isolate the vendor-specific details in a single place in the code—in the spot where the connection is managed. After that, getting the other parts required for making queries (for example, getting the correct command object) was a matter of asking the connection for it. While you may still write code to connect to the database using ADO.NET 1.x–style code, there's now a better way—using the ADO.NET database provider factories.

The ADO.NET provider pattern offers an improvement in connecting to and using databases. By using the provider pattern, you limit exposing the kind of database you're using to a single call to a *provider factory*. You choose the kind of database in one place and the provider takes care of making sure the correct connection and command objects are used. This was less important in ADO 1.x, when ADO divided the database world into two kinds of databases: SQL Server and OLEDB databases. However, with its support of new database types, the provider pattern is a welcome addition.

If you look in machine.config, you'll see providers for the following database types:

- Odbc Data Provider

- OleDb Data Provider

- OracleClient Data Provider

- SqlClient Data Provider

- SQL Server CE Data Provider

Listing 11-3 shows a snippet from machine.config illustrating how the provider keys are mapped to provider factories.

LISTING 11-3 Default Provider Factories Defined in Machine.Config

```
<system.d<configuration>
 <system.data>
    <DbProviderFactories>
      <add name="Odbc Data Provider"
          invariant="System.Data.Odbc"
          type="System.Data.Odbc.OdbcFactory    " />
      <add name="OleDb Data Provider"
          invariant="System.Data.OleDb"
          type="System.Data.OleDb.OleDbFactory     "/>
      <add name="OracleClient Data Provider"
          invariant="System.Data.OracleClient"
          type="System.Data.OracleClient.OracleClientFactory    "/>
      <add name="SqlClient Data Provider"
          invariant="System.Data.SqlClient"
          "System.Data.SqlClient.SqlClientFactory" />
      <add name="Microsoft SQL Server Compact Data Provider"
          invariant="System.Data.SqlServerCe.3.5"
          type="Microsoft.SqlServerCe.Client.SqlCeClientFactory    " />
    </DbProviderFactories>
  </system.data>
</configuration>>
```

To get a connection to a database, you ask the runtime for a reference to the right factory and then get a connection from the factory, as shown in Listing 11-4. You use the name of the database type (*System.Data.SqlClient* or *System.Data.SqlServerCe.3.5*, for example). After getting the right kind of factory, you ask it to create a connection for you.

LISTING 11-4 Obtaining a Database Provider Factory

```
DbConnection GetConnectionUsingFactory()
{
  DbProviderFactory dbProviderFactory =
       DbProviderFactories.GetFactory("System.Data.SqlClient")
  return dbProviderFactory.CreateConnection();
}
```

Once you have a connection, you may use it to connect to the database. Given an SQL Server database named *AspDotNetStepByStep* available on your machine, you'd insert a connection string as shown in Listing 11-5 in your web.config. Listing 11-5 shows how this might appear in a web.config file.

LISTING 11-5 Example Web.Config Connection String Settings

```
<configuration>
  <connectionStrings>
    <add name="AspDotNetStepByStep"
      connectionString=
        "server=(local);integrated security=sspi;database=AspDotNetStepByStepDB "/>
  </connectionStrings>
</configuration>
```

Once you have a reference to the database connection, you may open the connection and start commanding the database.

Commands

Once connected, the database is waiting for you to send database commands. These commands usually include querying the database, updating existing data, inserting new data, and deleting data. Most databases support Structured Query Language (SQL) to manage these commands. (Some databases may support specialized variations of SQL, so the actual command text may differ from one implementation to the other.) Commanding the database usually entails writing SQL statements such as

```
SELECT * FROM DotNetReferences WHERE AuthorLastName = 'Petzold'
```

For example, to connect to an SQL database named *AspDotNetStepByStepDB* and query the *DotNetReferences* table for all the references by someone with the last name "Petzold," you'd use code as shown in Listing 11-6.

LISTING 11-6 Example Database Query Using a DataReader

```
class UseDBApp {
   static void Main()
   {
      DbProviderFactory dbProviderFactory =
        DbProviderFactories.GetFactory("System.Data.SqlClient");
      using(DbConnection conn = dbProviderFactory.CreateConnection())
      {
         string s =
           ConfigurationManager.ConnectionStrings["AspDotNetStepByStep"].ConnectionString;
         conn.ConnectionString = s;
         conn.Open();

         DbCommand cmd = conn.CreateCommand();
         cmd.CommandText =
           "SELECT * FROM DotNetReferences WHERE AuthorLastName='Petzold'";
```

```
            DbDataReader reader = cmd.ExecuteReader();
            // do something with the reader
        }
    }
}
```

Executing the command using *ExecuteReader* sends a query to the database. The results come back via an instance of the *IDataReader* interface. The code listed above stops short of using the results. Let's take a look at how that works.

Managing Results

Once you've connected to the database and issued a query, you probably need to sift through the data to use it. ADO.NET supports two broad approaches to managing result sets: the *IDataReader* interface and the *DataSet* class.

DataReader

The example above retrieves an *IDataReader* from the query operation. The *IDataReader* interface is useful for iterating through the results of the query. Listing 11-7 shows part of the *IDataReader* interface.

LISTING 11-7 Part of the *IDataReader* Interface

```
public interface IDataReader
{
    bool IsClosed {get;}
    int  RecordsAffected {get;}
    void Close();
    bool NextResult();
    bool Read();
    //...
}
```

When iterating through the results of a query, *Read* fetches the next row. *NextResult* will fetch the next result set.

Accessing data through *IDataReader* is often termed "fire hose mode" because you have to eat your way through the data one row at a time *going forward only*. There's no way to revert back to a previous row except by resetting the reader and starting again. The data rows the reader returns to you are also read-only. You can retrieve the data for whatever purpose you need them for, but you can't update the database (insert, update, or delete) using *IDataReader*. An alternative to accessing data through the *IDataReader* interface is to use a *DataSet*.

DataSet

In addition to the *IDataReader*, ADO.NET supports the notion of a disconnected record set—the *DataSet* class in ADO.NET. The ADO.NET is primarily designed to help you write large, highly scalable applications. One of the biggest hindrances to scalability is the limits of database connectivity. Databases usually have a limit on the number of active connections available at one time, and if all the connections are in use at any particular time, any piece of code wanting a database connection will need to wait. If the number of users of a system is about the same as the number of connections available, then perhaps that's not a problem. However, if the number of users of a system is greater than the number of database connections, the system performance will likely be impacted greatly.

To encourage scalability, ADO.NET includes a class named *DataSet* that's designed to give you an easily navigable snapshot of your application's database. The idea behind a database is to get in and get out quickly with a copy of the data. The really good news is that you can insert rows, update columns, and even delete rows using the *DataSet* and later have those changes propagated to the database.

The *DataSet* class is usually filled with data using a *DataAdapter*. A *DataSet* includes a *DataTable* array—one for each selection statement in the query. Once the *DataAdapter* comes back from fetching the data for the *DataSet*, you have the latest snapshot of the queried data in memory. The *DataSet* contains a *DataTable* collection and contains a *DataTable* element for each *SELECT* statement in the query. You may access the *Tables* collection using either ordinal or *String*-type indices. Once you get to a table, iterating through the rows and columns is a matter of indexing into the table using ordinal indices for the rows and ordinal or *String*-type indices for the columns. Listing 11-8 shows an example of using the *SqlDataAdapter* to get a *DataSet*.

LISTING 11-8 Example Database Query Using a *DataSet* and *DataAdapter*

```
class UseDBApp2
{
    static void Main()
    {
        DataSet ds = new DataSet();
        DbProviderFactory dbProviderFactory =
          DbProviderFactories.GetFactory("System.Data.SqlClient");
        using (DbConnection conn = dbProviderFactory.CreateConnection())
        {
            string s =
              ConfigurationManager.ConnectionStrings["AspDotNetStepByStep"].ConnectionString;
            conn.ConnectionString = s;
            conn.Open();

            DbCommand cmd = conn.CreateCommand();
            cmd.CommandText =
              "SELECT * FROM customer; SELECT * FROM country";

            DbDataAdapter adapter = dbProviderFactory.CreateDataAdapter();
            adapter.SelectCommand = cmd;
            adapter.Fill(ds);
        }
```

```
        foreach (DataTable t in ds.Tables)
        {
            Console.WriteLine("Table " + t.TableName + " is in dataset");
            Console.WriteLine("Row 0, column 1: " + t.Rows[0][1]);
            Console.WriteLine("Row 1, column 1: " + t.Rows[1][1]);
            Console.WriteLine("Row 2, column 1: " + t.Rows[2][1]);
        }
        ds.WriteXml("dataset.xml");
        ds.WriteXmlSchema("dataset.xsd");


        // Also- may bind to the tables here:
        ;
    }}
```

The code in Listing 11-8 illustrates using a *DataAdapter* and a *DataSet*. The code prints out the first two columns of the first three rows of each table in the *DataSet*. The example in Listing 11-8 indicates that a *DataTable* is valid as a *DataSource* for data-bound controls. The example also shows that the *DataSet* objects also serialize as XML. Both the table schema and the contents may be serialized this way—making it especially useful for transferring data between systems.

Here's one final note about items in the *DataSet* class: They're disconnected and are not restricted to the "fire hose mode" of data access. You have complete random access to any table, any column, and/or any row in the *DataSet*. In fact, objects in the *DataSet* class are also smart enough to keep track of any data you change inside of them. You may flush the data back to the physical database by using the *CommandBuilder* to prepare the *DataSet* for an *Update* through the *DataAdapter*. A *CommandBuilder* will construct SQL statements on your behalf. This is useful for simple commands and provides a quick and convenient approach for updating a database through a *DataAdapter*.

Given either an *IDataReader* or a *DataSet*, the data-bound controls will automatically render themselves appropriately to show the control on the browser. While you may always connect to the database and fetch the data manually through the standard connection/command architecture, ASP.NET and Visual Studio support an even easier-to-use way to render data—via declarative data binding.

ASP.NET Data Sources

After seeing how to access data in the raw using ADO.NET, let's look at an easier way. ASP.NET includes some new classes that hide the complexity of managing connections and of gathering data. They're the *DataSource* controls.

These *DataSource* controls abstract the entire connection and command mechanism so that all you need to do is decide on a data source, point the control to that data source, and provide an appropriate query. Visual Studio provides a wizard that guides you through this. Once you have a *DataSource*, you may attach it to a data-bound control that uses it.

Let's take a look at making a query and populating some controls with the results of the query.

Use a *DataSource* to populate controls using a *DataReader*

1. Add a new form to DataBindORama named *DataBindingWithDB*.

2. The example for this chapter (named *DataBindORama*), available on the CD that comes with this book, includes an Access database named *ASPNETStepByStep.mdb*. Set up an accessor for the database. Go to the *Data* controls in the toolbox. Drag an *AccessDataSource* onto the form. Select **Configure Data Source...** from the local menu displayed by Visual Studio. Click **Browse** in the **Configure Data Source** dialog box. You'll see a directory named App_Data in the list box on the left side. Highlight it. Then select ASPStepByStep.mdb from the list box on the right side. This will insert an Access database accessor into your project. Configure the data accessor to use the AspDotNetStepByStep database that comes with this book.

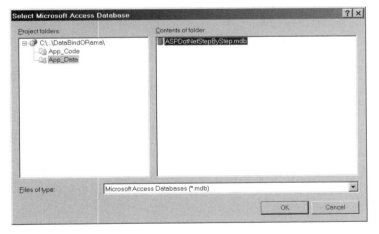

3. Select all the columns and all the rows from the *DotNetReferences* table when configuring the query (that is, choose "*" to query for all the columns). Click **Next**.

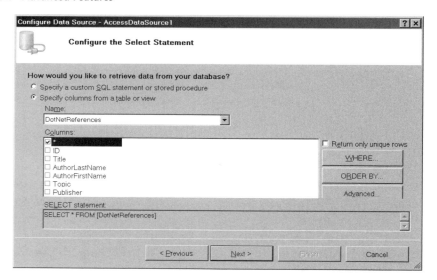

4. Test the query if you want to by clicking the **Test Query** button:

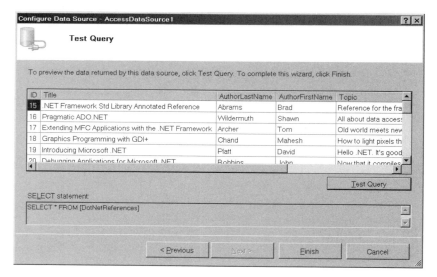

5. Set the *DataSourceMode* property to *DataReader*.

6. Now drag a *ListBox* onto the page. Set the *AutoPostBack* property to *true* by clicking the checkbox in the tasks window. You could, if you wanted, click *Choose Data Source* in the ListBox Tasks window. In practice, this is what you'd often do. However, let's add the code by hand to perform the data binding so that you see how it's done in code. In the code view, locate the *Page_Load* method and attach the *ListBox DataSource* property to *AccessDataSource1* like so:

```
protected void Page_Load(object sender, EventArgs e)
{
```

```
if (!this.IsPostBack)
{
    this.ListBox1.DataSource = this.AccessDataSource1;
    this.ListBox1.DataTextField = "AuthorLastName";
    this.ListBox1.DataValueField = "Title";
    this.ListBox1.DataBind();
}
```

}

7. Put a label near the bottom of the page. This label will hold the selected value from the *ListBox*.

8. Double-click on *ListBox1* to insert an item changed event handler into your code. In the event handler, set the *Label1* text property to the value field of the selected item.

```
protected void ListBox1_SelectedIndexChanged(object sender,
    EventArgs e)
{
    this.Label1.Text = this. ListBox1.SelectedItem.Value;
}
```

9. Now drag a *RadioButtonList* onto the form. When you finish dropping it on the form, Visual Studio will ask you if you want to configure the control. First, check the *Enable AutoPostBack* checkbox. Then, click **Choose Data Source...**.

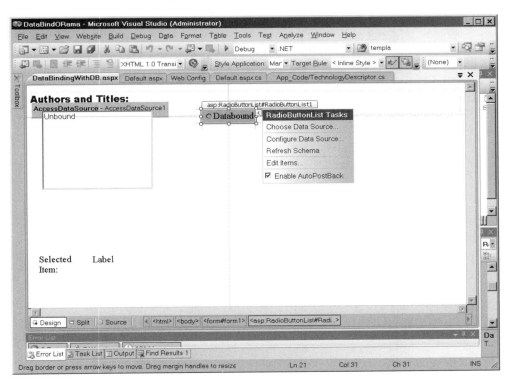

10. Configure the control to use *AccessDataSource1* that you just added.

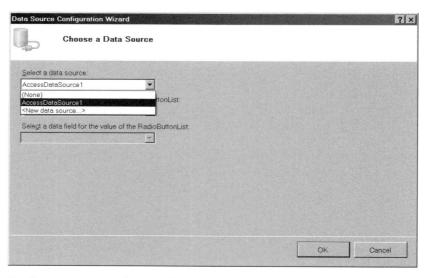

11. Configure the control to use the *AuthorLastName* column for the text field and the *Title* column for the value field. Click **OK**.

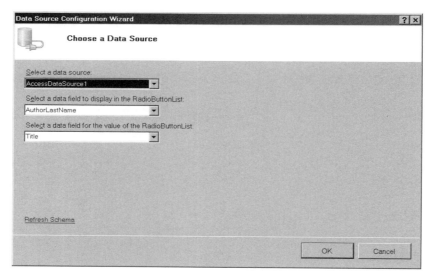

12. Double-click on the *RadioButtonList1* object on the form to create a handler for the radio button selection. Handle the selection by updating the *Label1* object with the value associated with the current radio button selection.

```
protected void RadioButtonList1_SelectedIndexChanged(object sender,
     EventArgs e)
{
   this.Label1.Text = this.RadioButtonList1.SelectedItem.Value;
}
```

13. Now run the program. The *ListBox* and the *RadioButton* list should show the *AuthorLastName* field. Selecting one name out of either list will cause a postback and show the title (the associated value) in the label near the bottom of the page.

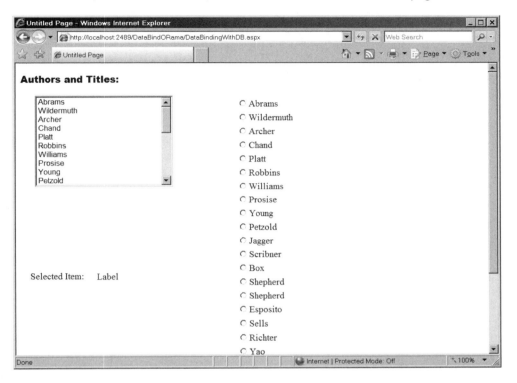

Now we've had a taste of how binding to the simple controls works. Although using these controls is common in many scenarios, the data-bound controls don't end there. ASP.NET includes other, more complex, controls that render data such as complex UI elements as grids and control combinations.

Other Data-bound Controls

In addition to the simple bound controls, ASP.NET includes several more complex controls. They work very much like the simple bound controls in that you attach a data source to them and they render automatically. However, these controls differ by displaying the data in more elaborate ways. These controls include the *GridView*, the *FormView*, the *DetailsView*, and the *DataList*.

The best way to understand the nature of these controls is to work through a couple of examples. Let's start with the *GridView*.

The *GridView*

1. Add a new Web form to the DataBindORama site. Name it *UseGridView*.

2. Pick up a *GridView* from the Toolbox (it's under the *Data* controls). Drop it on the form. Visual Studio will ask you to configure the *GridView*. Under the *Choose Data Source...* option, select **New Data Source....** Point Visual Studio to the ASPNetStepByStep.mdb under the *App_Data* directory. When specifying the query, select "*" to query for all the columns. Finally, enable *Paging*, *Sorting*, and *Selection* from the *GridView* Configuration menu. After configuring the *GridView*, Visual Studio will show you a representation of the format the query will use when it is rendered to the browser.

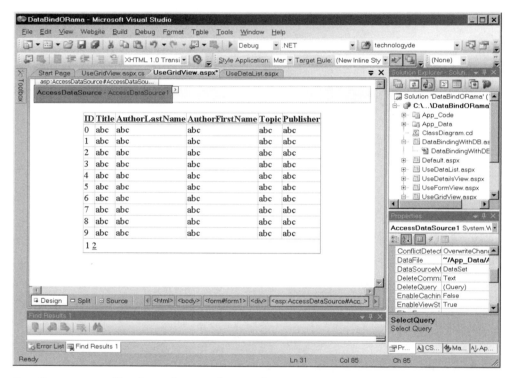

3. Run the program. Try the various options such as paging through the data and sorting to get a feel as to how the *GridView* works.

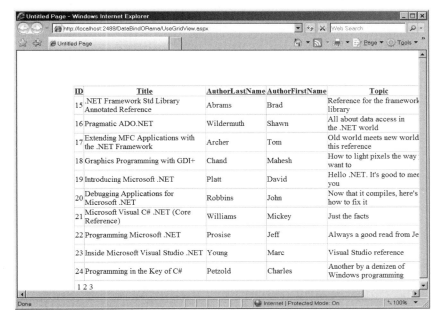

4. Go back to Visual Studio and try formatting the *GridView* to change its appearance. As with all the other ASP.NET controls, the *GridView* includes a number of configurable properties such as the foreground and background colors. Some of the other specialized properties within the *GridView* include the *AlternateRowStyle*, the *PagerSettings*, and the *PagerStyle*. The following graphic illustrates the UseGridView.aspx page with the *Classic* formatting style applied:

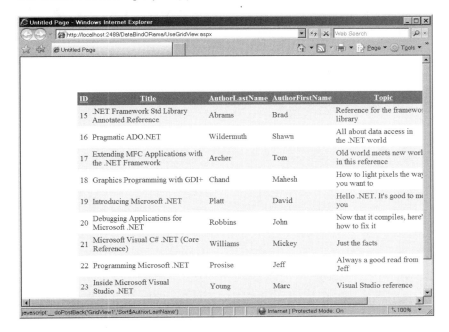

The *GridView* is useful for displaying tables in a format in which you can see all the rows and columns at once. While the classic *DataGrid* is still available, the *GridView* handles tasks such as selecting rows and sorting by column.

Here's a look at another complex control: the *FormView*.

The *FormView*

1. Add a new Web form to the DataBindORama site named *UseFormView*.

2. Pick up a *FormView* from the Toolbox (it's under the *Data* controls). Drop it on the form. Visual Studio will ask you to configure the *FormView*. Under the *Choose Data Source...* option, select **New Data Source....** Point Visual Studio to the ASPNetStepByStep.mdb under the *App_Data* directory. When specifying the query, select "*" to query for all the columns.

3. Select the *AutoFormat* option from the Configuration menu. Here you have the opportunity to apply a couple of canned styles to the *FormView*. The example accompanying this text uses the *Classic* formatting style.

4. Finally, enable paging from the *FormView* Configuration menu by selecting the **Enable Paging** check box. Set the *HeaderText* property (from the Visual Studio Properties window) to give the *FormView* a title (perhaps something like ".NET Reference Authors and Titles").

5. After configuring the *FormView*, Visual Studio will show you a representation of the format the query will use when it is rendered to the browser.

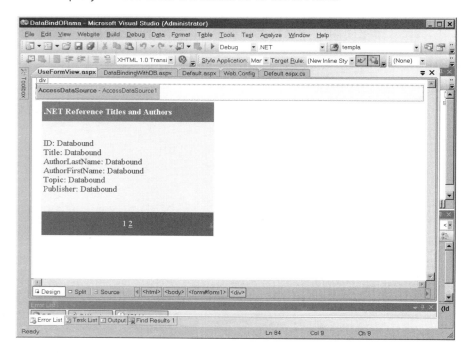

6. Run the program. Try the various options such as paging through the data to get a feel for how the *FormView* works.

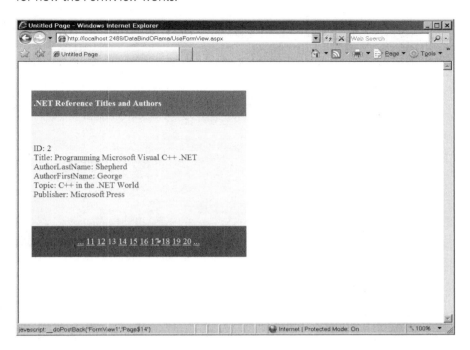

The *FormView* is useful for gathering the information for singular rows in one place. The user navigates between each row, but the focus is always on the current row.

The *DetailsView*

1. Add a new Web form to the DataBindORama site named *UseDetailsView*.

2. Pick up a *DetailView* from the Toolbox (it's under the *Data* controls). Drop it on the form. Visual Studio will ask you to configure the *DetailsView*. Under the *Choose Data Source...* option, select **New Data Source...**. Point Visual Studio to the ASPNetStepByStep.mdb under the *App_Data* directory. When specifying the query, select "***" to select all the columns.

3. Select the *AutoFormat* option from the Configuration menu. Here you have the opportunity to apply a couple of canned styles to the *DetailsView*. The example accompanying this text uses the *Classic* formatting style.

4. Select the **Edit Fields...** option from the *DetailsView Tasks* window. Check the **Auto-Generate Fields** check box on the dialog box if it isn't already checked.

5. Finally, enable paging from the *DetailsView Tasks* window. Set the *HeadingText* property (in the Visual Studio Properties window) to give the *DetailsView* a title (perhaps something like ".NET Reference Authors and Titles").

6. After configuring the *DetailsView*, Visual Studio will show you a representation of the format the query will use when it is rendered to the browser.

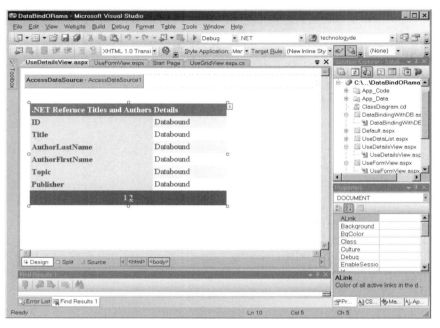

7. Run the program. Try the various options such as paging through the data to get a feel as to how the *DetailsView* works.

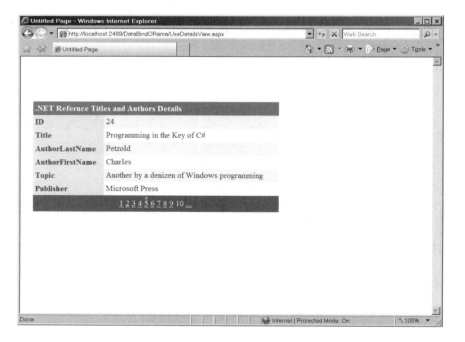

Now for the *DataList*. The *DataList* control was available in ASP.NET 1.x. It's been updated with later versions of ASP.NET to support declarative data binding. Here's a look at the *DataList*.

The *DataList*

1. Add a new Web form to the DataBindORama site named *UseDataList*.

2. Pick up a *DataList* from the toolbox (it's under the *Data* controls). Drop it on the form. Visual Studio will ask you to configure the *DataList*. Under the *Choose Data Source...* option, select **New Data Source...**. Point Visual Studio to the ASPNetStepByStep.mdb under the *App_Data* directory. When specifying the query, select "*" to query for all the columns.

3. Select the *AutoFormat* option from the *DataList Tasks* window. Here you have the opportunity to apply a couple of canned styles to the *DataList*. The example accompanying this text uses the *Slate* formatting style.

4. Select the *DataList* Properties dialog box from the *DataList Tasks* window by selecting **Property Builder**. If not already checked, make sure the **Show Header** and the **Show Footer** check boxes are selected.

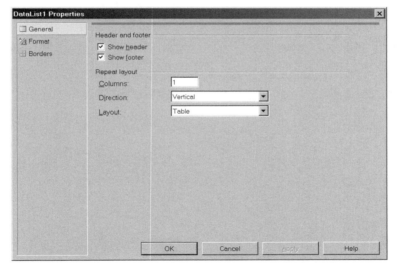

5. Set the *Caption* property to give the *DataList* a title (perhaps something like *.NET Reference Authors and Titles*).

6. After configuring the *DataList*, Visual Studio will show you a representation of the format the query will use when it is rendered to the browser.

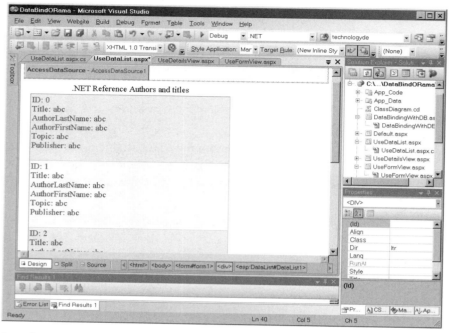

7. Run the program to see how the *DataList* renders itself.

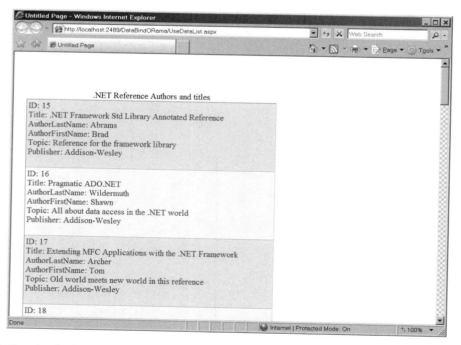

While the classic data access technologies are here to stay, .NET versions 3.0 and later bring a new way to access and manage data—Language Integrated Query. Let's take a look.

LINQ

New with .NET 3.0 is a database technology named Language Integrated Query (LINQ). LINQ is a set of extensions to the .NET Framework for performing data queries inline. LINQ extends the C# and Visual Basic syntaxes to enable inline queries in the native language syntax (versus SQL or XPath). LINQ doesn't replace existing data access technologies. Instead, LINQ augments existing data query technologies making it approachable to perform streamlined queries.

This new technology for making queries is called "language integrated" because you can build queries and use C# (or Visual Basic) language constructs to make selection statements. The following example shows how to develop some queries using LINQ.

Using LINQ

1. Add a new page to the DataBindORama site. Name the page *UseLinq*.

2. Drop a *GridView* onto the page. This will hold the information returned from the LINQ queries.

3. Update the *Page_Load* method to make a LINQ query. Use the *TechnologyDescriptor* collection mentioned earlier in the chapter as the data source for making the query. (Don't forget to add a using statement to include *System.Collections.Generic*!) Set the *DataGrid*'s *DataSource* property to the results of a LINQ query against the *TechnologyDescriptor* collection. The format of the LINQ statement should be *from* <variable of type held in collection> *in* <the collection> *where* <criteria> *orderby* <criteria> *select* <property from selected item>. Select *TechnologyDescriptors* that include ".NET" in the name and order them by length of the *TechnologyName* property. Here is the code that does just that:

```
public partial class UseLinq : System.Web.UI.Page
{
    protected void Page_Load(object sender, EventArgs e)
    {
        List<TechnologyDescriptor> techList =
            TechnologyDescriptor.CreateTechnologyList();

        GridView1.DataSource = from technologyDescriptor in techList

        where
        technologyDescriptor.TechnologyName.Contains(".NET") == true

        orderby technologyDescriptor.TechnologyName.Length

        select technologyDescriptor.TechnologyName.ToUpper();
        GridView1.DataBind();
    }
}
```

4. Run the UseLinq.aspx page to see how the query looks within the *GridView*.

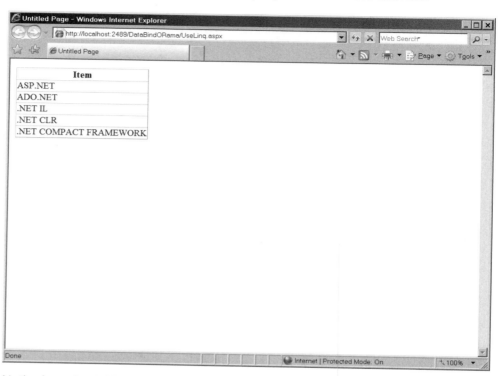

5. Notice how the *GridView* shows only the single property grabbed from each *TechnologyDescriptor*. Now update the query statement to include the whole *TechnologyDescriptor* structure. It should look like this:

```
public partial class UseLinq : System.Web.UI.Page
{
    protected void Page_Load(object sender, EventArgs e)
    {
        List<TechnologyDescriptor> techList =
            TechnologyDescriptor.CreateTechnologyList();

        GridView1.DataSource = from technologyDescriptor in techList

        where
        technologyDescriptor.TechnologyName.Contains(".NET") == true

        orderby technologyDescriptor.TechnologyName.Length

        select technologyDescriptor;
        GridView1.DataBind();
    }
}
```

6. Run the page and see how the *GridView* now shows the entire *TechnologyDescriptor*.

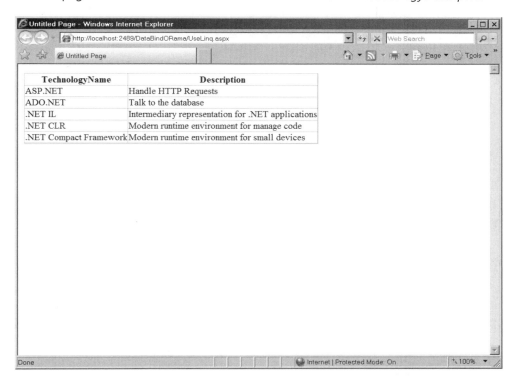

This example only scratches the surface of the power of LINQ. LINQ introduces a very streamlined way to make queries on demand from within your project using the language of your project (Visual Basic, C#, and so forth). The data coming back from the queries may be used in any context. In this case, the example shows using the results of a LINQ query within a *GridView*.

Summary

In this chapter, we looked at ASP.NET's support for data-bound controls. Although it's not rocket science to iterate through a collection and add the data to ASP.NET's server-side controls, it's a fairly common operation. That Microsoft pushed it down into the Framework classes is a good thing.

One of the advantages of these controls is that they don't care at all where their data comes from. The data might be as simple as an *ArrayList* composed of .NET types (with each element in the array representing a row and each property representing a column). On the other hand, the data bound to a control might be as complex as *IDataReader* or a *DataSet* acquired from a physical database.

Looking at data-bound controls invariably involves mentioning the ASP.NET database story: ADO.NET. The ADO.NET managed classes are for connecting to the database, commanding the database, and harvesting the results afterward. Although connecting to the database manually (via .NET 1.x-style code) is still supported, today .NET and Visual Studio offer an easier way to associate controls with data via the *DataSource* controls.

ASP.NET includes a number of data-bound controls that may be matched up with a collection or (in the case of certain *DataSource* controls) a data source. The controls then assume the burden of iterating through the data and rendering the correct tags to the client.

Chapter 11 Quick Reference

To	Do This
Bind a collection to a control	Set the control's *DataSource* property to the collection.
Choose a column to display in the control	Set the control's *TextTextField* property to the column name.
Choose a column to use programmatically (that's NOT displayed in the control)	Set the control's *TextValueField* property to the column name.
Display a *DataTable* as a grid	Use the *DataGrid* or the *GridView* controls.
Display a *DataTable* as a formatted, repeating list	Use the *DataList*
Make a class's member variables available as *DataTextFields* and *DataValueFields* within a control	Expose the members as properties.
Represent data using Master/Detail style presentations	Use the *FormView* control

Chapter 12
Web Site Navigation

After completing this chapter, you will be able to

- Understand ASP.NET's support for navigation and site maps
- Implement a site map using an XML data source
- Use the site map to power ASP.NET's navigation controls
- Capture and respond to site map navigation events

One of the major issues facing Web site users is figuring out how to get around the site effectively. Web sites are often hierarchical in nature, and pages are sometimes nested several layers deep. Users may often find themselves asking questions like "Where am I now?" and "Where can I go from here?" This chapter covers ASP.NET's support for addressing the issue of Web site navigation.

The art of Web site design has progressed far enough that some common navigation idioms are beginning to appear ubiquitously. If you browse a few Web sites hosted on various platforms, you'll notice that the sites support a number of different ways to navigate their content. For example, many Web sites include a menu bar across the top of the page with links to separate areas on the site. Certain sites include some sort of tree structure to navigate the site. Still others include a "breadcrumb" trail showing you where you are and how to get back. ASP.NET supports all these idioms.

ASP.NET's Navigation Support

ASP.NET's navigation support comes in three parts: the navigation controls, the site map data source, and the site map provider architecture. The *navigation controls* (the *Menu*, the *TreeView*, and the *SiteMapPath*) all have the capability to resolve human-readable display names to real URLs to which HTTP requests may be sent. The *site map data source* stores information about a site's hierarchical organization. The *site map provider* interprets physical data (often in the form of an XML file) and implements a kind of database cursor representing the current position within a site's hierarchy.

The Navigation Controls

ASP.NET includes three server-side controls devoted specifically to site navigation—the *SiteMapPath*, the *Menu*, and the *TreeView* control. The *Menu* and the *TreeView* both maintain collections of display name/URL mappings. These collections may be edited by hand. In addition, these controls can build hierarchical collections of display name/URL mappings based on information in a site map data source. The *SiteMapPath* builds its collection of display name/URL mappings solely through a site map data source. Table 12-1 summarizes the ASP.NET navigation controls.

TABLE 12-1 The ASP.NET Navigation Controls

Navigation Control	Description
Menu	Interprets the site navigational information contained in the sitemap XML file and presents it in a menu format. Top level XML nodes become top level menu items, with child XML nodes becoming child menu items.
TreeView	Interprets the site navigational information contained in the sitemap XML file and presents it in a tree format. The top level sitemap XML nodes in this case become higher-level branches in the tree, with child nodes represented as child tree nodes.
SiteMapPath	Interprets the site navigational information contained in the sitemap XML file and presents it in a "breadcrumb" format. In this case, only the current XML node's path is displayed (from the root node to the current child node).

All three controls are useful for navigation, but the *Menu* and the *TreeView* are useful outside the context of site navigation. *SiteMapPath* is designed strictly for navigating the Web site's sitemap XML file. The *Menu* control displays items hierarchically and fires events back to the server as the items are selected. The items in the *Menu* control may also be assigned navigation URLs. The *TreeView* is useful for displaying any hierarchical data source that implements either the *IHierarchicalDataSource* or the *IHierarchicalEnumerable* interface, and it also has the capability to cause redirects to other URLs (that is, it's useful for site navigation). And, as I mentioned, the *SiteMapPath* is meant specifically to be used for Web site navigation.

For shallow Web sites that will probably change very little over time, building a navigation infrastructure from scratch is not very difficult. However, as the complexity of a site increases, so does the difficulty in managing a navigation structure.

When you organize your site and determine the layout of your pages, it's easy to formalize the layout with a master page that includes a menu linking to other pages (just as in the master page chapter). The work involves creating the menu and adding the links (through the *NavigateUrl* property of the menu item). Implementing the navigation infrastructure by hand is easy enough the first time around. However, as your site grows and becomes more complex, having to update the navigation support repeatedly becomes a problem.

Enter ASP.NET's navigation and site map support. The main advantage of using ASP.NET's navigation support is that you can establish the layout of the site and then represent it using a hierarchical data structure (like an XML file or even a database table). The *Menu*, *TreeView*, and *SiteMapPath* controls may all point to a site map data source and use the data source to populate themselves. When you plug the site map data source into the navigation controls, the navigation controls use the data source to create the individual links.

After the site map has been established, updating the navigation links simply requires updating the site map. All controls using the site map data source will reflect the change automatically.

XML Site Maps

ASP.NET includes built-in support for navigation via XML files that describe the layout of the site. These are called *XML site maps*. ASP.NET's default site map support consists of an XML file describing the site layout and the *SiteMapProvider* that reads the XML file and generates *SiteMap* nodes to whatever components are listening (for example, a *Menu* or a *TreeView* control).

The *SiteMapProvider*

The *SiteMapProvider* establishes the base class used by the navigation controls. ASP.NET's default implementation is the *XmlSiteMapProvider*, which reads the XML file named (by default) *web.sitemap*.

While the default XML site map generally works very well, the ASP.NET navigation controls are perfectly happy using data sources generated from other places (rather than the XML data source). For example, you might decide to implement your own site map provider based on data in a database. The XML site map provides basic raw functionality for navigating a site. However, if you want to do something like manage the site map using a schema different from the default XML schema, that calls for designing a custom provider.

In this chapter, we'll look at the default XML site map provider—which is plenty powerful for most circumstances.

The *SiteMap* Class

The main rendezvous point for the ASP.NET navigation infrastructure is the *SiteMap* class. To support the navigation infrastructure, the *SiteMap* class has a set of static methods for managing site navigation. The *SiteMap* class serves as an in-memory representation of the navigation structure for a site, and its functionality is implemented by one or more site map providers. It's an abstract class so it must be inherited.

The *SiteMap* class performs several functions. First, it serves as the root node of the site navigation hierarchy. Second, it establishes the principal site map provider. Finally, it keeps track of all the provider objects that comprise the site map.

The *SiteMap* contains a hierarchical collection of *SiteMapNode* objects. Regardless of how the site map data are maintained, the *SiteMap* is the interface for accessing a site's navigation information.

The ASP.NET default configuration specifies a default site map. However, as with all things configurable in ASP.NET, you may easily override the default configuration to establish a different provider.

The *SiteMap* class offers only static members. By being static, they enhance performance. In addition, the site map functionality may be accessed at any time in a Web application from a page or even from within a server-side control.

Table 12-2 describes the properties and sole event the *SiteMap* class exhibits.

TABLE 12-2 SiteMap Events and Properties

Name	Type	Description
SiteMapResolve	Event	The *SiteMapResolve* event fires when the *CurrentNode* property is accessed. This enables you to implement custom logic when creating a *SiteMapNode* representation of the currently executing page without requiring a custom provider implementation.
CurrentNode	Property	A *SiteMapNode* instance that represents the currently requested page in the navigational hierarchy. If there is no node in the XML site map file, the returned value will be *null*.
Enabled	Property	Returns a Boolean value indicating if a site map provider is both specified and enabled in the web.config file.
Provider	Property	Returns the default *SiteMapProvider* for the current site map.
Providers	Property	Returns a read-only collection of named *SiteMapProvider* objects that are available to the *SiteMap* class as specified in the web.config file (since you can specify more than one if you wish). Note that only the default provider is used during initialization, however.
RootNode	Property	Returns the *SiteMapNode* that represents the top-level page of the navigation hierarchy for the site.

The *SiteMapNode*

The *SiteMapNode*s themselves represent the hierarchical elements of the site map, which is to say, each instance of a *SiteMapNode* represents a page in your Web site. Each node represents an individual page that is located somewhere in the overall Web site navigation hierarchy. When a Web application starts, the *SiteMap* loads the collection of *SiteMapNode*s based on the providers that have been configured in your web.config file for that site.

The *SiteMapNode* includes several useful properties: *ChildNodes*, *Description*, *HasChildNodes*, *Key*, *NextSibling*, *ParentNode*, *PreviousSibling*, *Provider*, *ReadOnly*, *ResourceKey*, *Roles*, *RootNode*, *Title*, and *Url*. It also includes several useful methods: *GetAllNodes*, *GetDataSourceView*, *GetHierarchicalDataSourceView*, *IsAccessibleToUsers*, and *IsDescendentOf*. We'll see some of these properties being used in later examples. For instance, we'll use many of these properties in the example for this chapter when we handle the *SiteMapResolve* event and modify the navigation functionality on the fly.

The Navigation Controls

When you run Visual Studio 2008 and look in the designer's Toolbox, you'll see that ASP.NET includes three controls categorized under the navigation category: the *Menu*, the *TreeView*, and the *SiteMapPath* control. Let's look at each in a bit more detail before diving into an example.

The *Menu* and *TreeView* Controls

The *Menu* and *TreeView* controls can bind to hierarchical data source implementing *IHierarchicalDataSource* or *IHierarchicalEnumerable*. Although they're tailor-made to support site maps, they work with other data sources. Figure 12-1 shows the *Menu* control in action, and Figure 12-2 shows the *TreeView* in action. Both are reading the data from the site map data source to populate themselves.

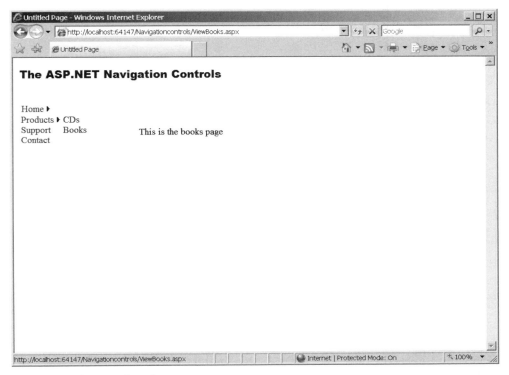

FIGURE 12-1 The *Menu* in action

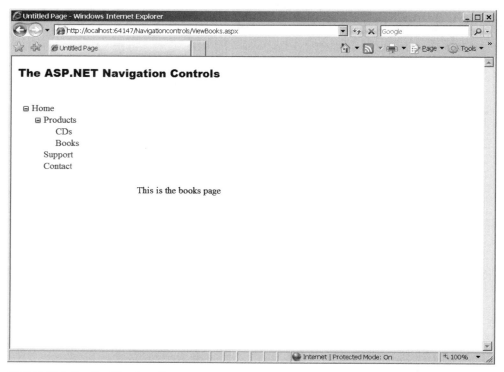

FIGURE 12-2 The *TreeView* in action

The *SiteMapPath* Control

You may have seen user interface (UI) elements similar to the *SiteMapPath* control on other sites—especially online forms that can go several layers deep. The *SiteMapPath* control shows a trail indicating where the user is within the Web page hierarchy and shows a path back to the top node (kind of like a trail of bread crumbs). The *SiteMapPath* is most useful within sites that maintain a very deep hierarchy for which a *Menu* or a *TreeView* control would be overwhelmed.

Although the *SiteMapPath* control is like the *Menu* and the *TreeView* (the *SiteMapPath* control reflects the state of the *SiteMap* object), it does deserve special attention. The *SiteMapPath* control and the site map data within the provider are tightly coupled. For example, if you leave a page out of your site map and the user somehow ends up on the page (perhaps through some other navigation method), the user will not see the *SiteMapPath* control on the page. Figure 12-3 shows the *SiteMapPath* control in action. The *Menu* shown in the figure is there so that the user can drill down into the page (the user would not be able to descend the hierarchy without a *Menu* or a *TreeView*).

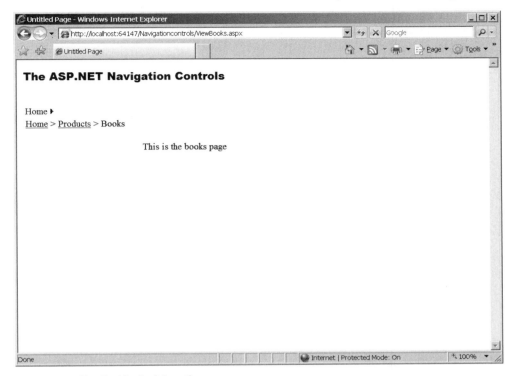

FIGURE 12-3 The *SiteMapPath* in action

Site Map Configuration

Setting up the XML site map happens through the configuration file. Adding a site map file
to the Web application automatically updates the web.config file to include the XML site map
provider. Listing 12-1 shows the configuration information that is added to web.config.

LISTING 12-1 Configuring the Site Map Data

```
<configuration><!-- default config -->
  <system.web>
    <siteMap defaultProvider="XmlSiteMapProvider">
      <providers>
        <add name="XmlSiteMapProvider"
          type="System.Web.XmlSiteMapProvider,
            System.Web, Version=2.0.3600.0,
            Culture=neutral,
            PublicKeyToken=b03f5f7f11d50a3a"
          siteMapFile="web.sitemap"/>
      </providers>
    </siteMap>
  </system.web>
</configuration>
```

In addition to adding the configuration information to web.config, Visual Studio 2008 adds a blank top-level node in the site map, as shown in Listing 12-2.

LISTING 12-2 The Default Site Map That Is Added by Visual Studio 2008

```xml
<?xml version="1.0" encoding="utf-8" ?>
<siteMap xmlns="http://schemas.microsoft.com/AspNet/SiteMap-File-1.0" >
    <siteMapNode url="" title=""  description="">
        <siteMapNode url="" title=""  description="" />
        <siteMapNode url="" title=""  description="" />
    </siteMapNode>
</siteMap>
```

Once the site map is added, it's easy to update—for example, to add a few new nodes to the site map, simply edit the file as (XML) text. Listing 12-3 shows an XML site map file with a few extra nodes added.

LISTING 12-3 Site Map Data in XML

```xml
<?xml version="1.0" encoding="utf-8" ?>
<siteMap xmlns="http://schemas.microsoft.com/AspNet/SiteMap-File-1.0" >
 <siteMapNode url=""
  title="Navigation Menu"  description="">
  <siteMapNode url="Default.aspx"
    title="Home"  description="" />
  <siteMapNode url="Products.aspx"
    title="Products"  description="" />
  <siteMapNode url="Support.aspx"
    title="Support" description="" />
  <siteMapNode url="Contact.aspx"
    title="Contacts"  description="" />
 </siteMapNode>
</siteMap>
```

Building a Navigable Web Site

Adding navigation support to a Web site is pretty straightforward. Once you establish the hierarchical layout of the site, use the site map XML file to describe the structure. Once that's done, just point any navigation controls you put on the page to the new XML site map file. The navigation controls will populate themselves and render a navigable Web site. The following example shows how to add navigation support to a Web site and use the ASP.NET navigation controls within the application.

Creating a site map

1. Start Visual Studio and create a new ASP.NET Web site project. Make it a file system–based Web site. The example here is called *NavigateMeSite*.

2. Remove the "Default" page from the application. In the next step you'll add a master page, and removing the "Default" page makes it easier to apply the master page to the

"Default" page. To remove the page, select it in Solution Explorer and press the **Delete** key. Visual Studio will ask if you really want to delete the page (as it will be deleted permanently). Click **Yes**.

3. Create a master page for the Web site. Click the right mouse button on the project node in the solution and select **Add New Item**. Choose **Master Page** from the templates.The default name will be fine. Click **Add**.

4. Add several pages based on the master page. The example here uses four—a Default page, a products page, a support page, and a contact page. For each page you add, click the right mouse button on the project and select **Add New Item**. Choose **Web Page** from the templates. Make sure the **Select Master Page** check box is checked as you select the template (so the master page will be applied automatically). Populate the pages with some content so you know what you're looking at when you run the site (simple text placed directly on the page will be fine).

5. Add a new site map to the project. Click the right mouse button on the project within the solution explorer. Select **Site Map** from the templates. Keep the name *Web.sitemap*. The following graphic shows the Visual Studio templates with the site navigation template highlighted:

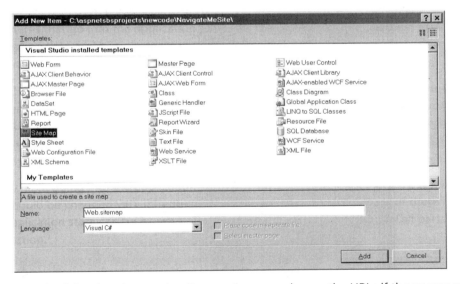

6. Add the following data to the site map (you can change the URLs if the names of the page files are different). Simply edit (or overwrite) the two blank nodes Visual Studio inserted for you:

```xml
<?xml version="1.0" encoding="utf-8" ?>
<siteMap xmlns="http://schemas.microsoft.com/AspNet/SiteMap-File-1.0" >
  <siteMapNode url="" title="Navigation Menu"  description="">
    <siteMapNode url="Default.aspx" title="Home"
        description="This is the home page" />
```

```
    <siteMapNode url="Products.aspx" title="Products"
        description="This is the products page" />
    <siteMapNode url="Support.aspx" title="Support"
        description="This is the support page" />
    <siteMapNode url="Contact.aspx" title="Contacts"
        description="This is the contacts page" />
  </siteMapNode>
</siteMap>
```

7. To see how the site map data work with the site, add some navigation controls to the master page. Start by adding a *Menu*. Go to the toolbox and pick up a *Menu* control and drop it onto the master page. When adding the *Menu*, one of the tasks you can perform is to set the data source. Select **New Data Source. . .** from the *Menu Tasks* window. Set the *Menu's* data source to the default site map file and click **OK**. The following graphic shows how to select a site map data source for the *Menu* control:

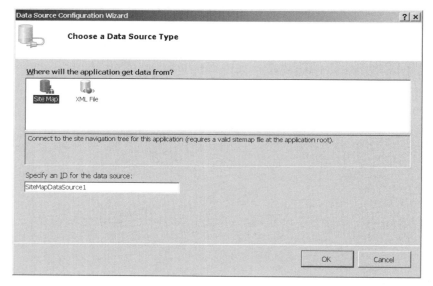

8. Run the site so that you can see the *Menu* in action. Select some pages from the *Menu* and notice that the selections navigate you to the correct places.

9. Next add a *TreeView* to the master page. Pick one up from the Toolbox and place it on the master page. Point the *TreeView* to the default site map data source. Run the application and see what happens.

10. Now add a *SiteMapPath* control to the master page. Apply the XML site map data source to the *DataSource* property of the *SiteMapPath* control.

11. Now add two more pages to the project in order to display two ways to contact the business running this site—perhaps one for displaying the physical address of

a business and the other for displaying other contact information such as e-mail addresses and phone numbers. First, create two new folders—one for each page. Name the folders *ContactAddress* and *ContactEmailPhone*. Add the new pages—one per folder. Name the pages *ContactAddress.aspx* and *ContactEmailPhone.aspx*. Be sure to have these pages use the master page. Add labels or text as before describing the page to each of these pages so you may identify them as the Web application runs.

12. Now add two more elements to the site map XML file (web.sitemap) to reflect these new pages. Nest them so their parent node is the **Contact** node.

```xml
<?xml version="1.0" encoding="utf-8" ?>
<siteMap xmlns="http://schemas.microsoft.com/AspNet/SiteMap-File-1.0" >
  <siteMapNode url="" title="Navigation Menu"  description="">
    <siteMapNode url="Default.aspx" title="Home"
        description="This is the home page" />
    <siteMapNode url="Products.aspx" title="Products"
        description="This is the products page" />
    <siteMapNode url="Support.aspx" title="Support"
        description="This is the support page"
        ImageURL="supportimage.jpg"/>
    <siteMapNode url="Contact.aspx" title="Contacts"
        description="This is the contacts page" >
      <siteMapNode url="~/ContactAddress/ContactAddress.aspx"
                    title="Contact using physical address"
                    description="This is the first contact page" />
      <siteMapNode url="!/ContactPhone/ContactEmailPhone.aspx"
                    title="Contact by email or phone"
                    description="This is the second contact page" />
    </siteMapNode>
  </siteMapNode>
</siteMap>
```

13. Now run the Web site and see what effect the changes have had. You should see new navigation options appear in the *Menu* and the *TreeView*, and the new pages should also be reflected in the *SiteMapPath* control.

14. Experiment with the *SiteMapDataSource* properties to see how the *Menu* and *TreeView* are affected. For example, *SiteMapDataSource.ShowStartingNode* turns off the root node (often the "home" page node). *SiteMapDataSource.StartFromCurrentNode* determines the hierarchical position at which the data source begins producing data.

15. Experiment with the *Menu* properties to see how the *Menu* is affected. For example, the *Menu.StaticDisplayLevels* and *MaximumDynamicDisplayLevels* determine how much of the data from *SiteMapDataSource* the *Menu* displays.

16. Notice how easy it is to add navigation capability to your Web site. By using the site map file (and underlying provider-based architecture), you limit the number of places you need to modify to update site navigation.

Trapping the *SiteMapResolve* Event

ASP.NET is full of extensibility points. They're all over the place—and the navigation architecture is no exception. ASP.NET's site map support includes an application-wide event that informs listeners (usually the application object) whenever the end user is navigating through the Web site using a control connected to the site map data. Here's an example that shows how to handle that event.

Handling *SiteMapResolve* event

1. You may add the *SiteMapResolve* handler anywhere you'd like to the project. In this example, it'll go in the global application object. Add a global application class to your project using **Add New Item**.

2. Add a *SiteMapResolve* event handler to the Global.asax file you just added. The handler can do whatever you want it to do. The example here clones the *SiteMapNode* object that's passed in via the event arguments (by cloning the node, the handler avoids modifying the underlying data structure). Then the handler modifies the node's *Title* field to add the phrase "(you are here)." (Note you'll see this only if the *Title* field is displayed by your navigation control. The *SiteMapPath* control displays it by default.) After finishing the handler, update *Application_Start* to connect the handler to the *SiteMapResolve* event within the *Application_Start* handler of Global.asax.

```
<%@ Application Language="C#" %>

<script runat="server">

    void Application_Start(object sender, EventArgs e)
    {
        SiteMap.SiteMapResolve +=
          new SiteMapResolveEventHandler(ResolveNode);
    }

    SiteMapNode ResolveNode(object sender,
                        SiteMapResolveEventArgs e)
    {
        SiteMapNode n = e.Provider.CurrentNode.Clone();
        n.Title = n.Title + " (you are here)";
        return n;
    }

    ...
</script>
```

3. Now run the site and navigate through the pages. You should see the title of each *SiteMapNode* change as you page through the site (reflected by the display name in

the *SiteMapPath* control). The following graphic shows the site map path control with the modified title:

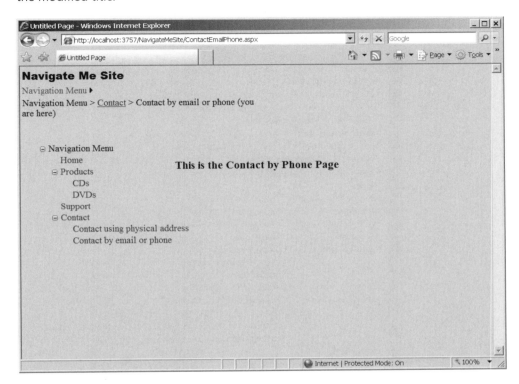

Custom Attributes for Each Node

Another way to extend your Web application's navigation includes the ability to define custom attributes for the site nodes in web.sitemap and retrieve them at run time. Imagine that you wanted to associate a specific image for each page in your site. How would you do this? To accomplish this, just create a new attribute and specify it in the *siteMapNode* element in the site map data. The following example shows how to add custom attributes to the site map nodes.

Adding custom attributes to the site map

ASP.NET's site map navigation support makes it very easy to add arbitrary attributes to each node. In this example, you'll add some JPEG URLs to the site map nodes. As each page is loaded, the master page will show the JPEG in an *Image* control.

1. Add six new JPEGs to the project—one to represent each kind of page (for example, produce separate JPEGs for the home page, the products page, the three contact pages, and the support page). Update the web.sitemap file to include an *ImageURL* property in each *siteMapNode* element, like so:

```xml
<?xml version="1.0" encoding="utf-8" ?>
<siteMap xmlns="http://schemas.microsoft.com/AspNet/SiteMap-File-1.0" >
  <siteMapNode url="" title="Navigation Menu"  description="">
    <siteMapNode url="Default.aspx" title="Home"
        description="This is the home page"
        ImageURL="homeimage.jpg"/>
    <siteMapNode url="Products.aspx" title="Products"
        description="This is the products page"
        ImageURL="productsimage.jpg" />
    <siteMapNode url="Support.aspx" title="Support"
        description="This is the support page"
        ImageURL="supportimage.jpg"/>
    <siteMapNode url="Contact.aspx" title="Contacts"
        description="This is the contacts page"
        ImageURL="contactimage.jpg">
      <siteMapNode url="ContactAddress.aspx"
                   title="Contact using physical address"
                   description="This is the first contact page"
                   ImageURL="contactPhysicalAddressimage.jpg"/>
      <siteMapNode url="ContactEmailPhone.aspx"
                   title="Contact by email or phone"
                   description="This is the second contact page"
                   ImageURL="contactPhoneimage.jpg" />
    </siteMapNode>
  </siteMapNode>
</siteMap>
```

2. Programmatically, the *ImageURL* custom attribute will show up as a property of the node when the nodes are accessed. There are many ways to use the new property. Probably the easiest way is to add an *Image* control to the master page and update the *Image* control's *ImageUrl* property with the value from the node in the master page's *Page_Load* method.

```csharp
public partial class MasterPage : System.Web.UI.MasterPage
{
    protected void Page_Load(object sender, EventArgs e)
    {
        SiteMapNode current = SiteMap.CurrentNode;
        string strImageURL = current["ImageURL"];
        if (strImageURL != null)
        {
            this.Image1.ImageUrl = strImageURL;
        }
    }
}
```

3. While setting an image during the master page's *Page_Load* method is pretty straightforward, it's not the only way to change the UI based on specific *SiteMapNode* information. For example, you might handle the *OnMenuItemDataBound* event and set any

custom properties there. The following two graphics illustrate how the master page plugs in a new image URL each time a postback is issued:

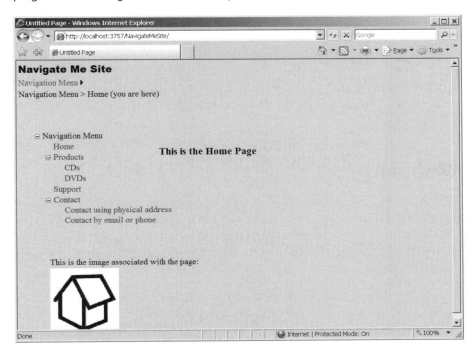

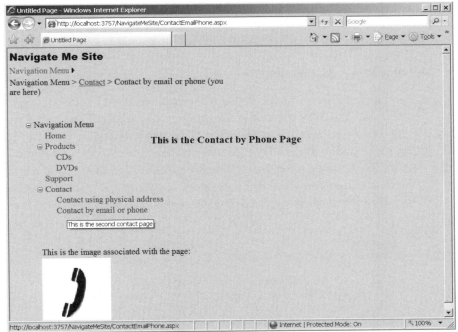

Security Trimming

ASP.NET's navigation support works with the authentication and authorization mechanisms to support *security trimming*. Security trimming means showing only part of the menu based on the role of the current user. Of course, this means that the Web site must somehow authenticate the user (see Chapter 10).

To make security trimming work, turn the *securityTrimmingEnabled* attribute on within web.config. The list of roles for which the navigation option is available is a property for each *SiteMapNode*.

URL Mapping

Finally, ASP.NET's navigation architecture supports URL mapping. URL mapping means mapping a virtual (or nonexistent) URL to existing ASPX file. This is done within the web.config file using the *urlMappings* element. Setting up URL mappings causes ASP.NET to read the requested URL and uses the handler for the mapped URL. This is done in *HttpApplication* using *HttpContext.RewritePath*.

For example, imagine your Web site contained a single products page containing both CDs and DVDs. However, your UI model requires you to build a menu structure that separates the CD products and the DVD products into two options appearing separately on the menu. URL mapping provides a way of handling this situation.

Here's an exercise showing how to use URL mapping to represent a single page as two separate menu items. In this case, the page's content is distinguished by a URL parameter.

Implementing URL mapping

1. Update the Products page so that it shows different content when the ID parameter is "1" or "2." This example divides the products into CDs and DVDs. The page will display different content based on the value of the ID parameter (whether it's "1" or "2" or something else). Place a *Label* control on the Products page and assign its ID property the value **LabelProductType**. Then, drop a *ListBox* on the page and assign its ID the value **ListBoxProducts**. The code-beside file then implements the URL mapping functionality within the *Page_Load* handler, as shown here.

```
public partial class Products : System.Web.UI.Page
{
    protected void AddCDsToListBox()
    {
        this.ListBoxProducts.Items.Add("CD- Snakes and Arrows");
        this.ListBoxProducts.Items.Add("CD- A Farewell To Kings");
        this.ListBoxProducts.Items.Add("CD- Moving Pictures");
        this.ListBoxProducts.Items.Add("CD- Hemispheres");
```

```
        this.ListBoxProducts.Items.Add("CD- Permanent Waves");
        this.ListBoxProducts.Items.Add("CD- Counterparts");
        this.ListBoxProducts.Items.Add("CD- Roll the Bones");
        this.ListBoxProducts.Items.Add("CD- Fly By Night");
        this.ListBoxProducts.Items.Add("CD- 2112");
    }

    protected void AddDVDsToListBox()
    {
        this.ListBoxProducts.Items.Add("DVD- A Show Of Hands");
        this.ListBoxProducts.Items.Add("DVD- Exit Stage Left");
        this.ListBoxProducts.Items.Add("DVD- Rush In Rio");
        this.ListBoxProducts.Items.Add("DVD- R30");
    }

    protected void Page_Load(object sender, EventArgs e)
    {
        if (this.Request.Params["ID"] == "1")
        {
            this.LabelProductType.Text = "CDs";
            AddCDsToListBox();
        }
        else if (this.Request.Params["ID"] == "2")
        {
            this.LabelProductType.Text = "DVDs";
            AddDVDsToListBox();
        }
        else
        {
            this.LabelProductType.Text = "All CDs and DVDs";
            AddCDsToListBox();
            AddDVDsToListBox();
        }
    }
}
```

2. Update the web.sitemap file to include the new menu items mapped to virtual files (for example, CDs.aspx and DVDs.aspx). Add this to the Web.site file:

```
<?xml version="1.0" encoding="utf-8" ?>
<siteMap xmlns=
  "http://schemas.microsoft.com/AspNet/SiteMap-File-1.0" >
    <siteMapNode url="" title="Navigation Menu"  description="">
      <siteMapNode url="Default.aspx" title="Home"
                   description="This is the home page"
                   ImageURL="homeimage.jpg"/>
      <siteMapNode url="Products.aspx" title="Products"
                   description="This is the products page"
                   ImageURL="productsimage.jpg">
        <siteMapNode url="CDs.aspx" title="CDs"
                   description="This is the CDs page"
                   ImageURL="productsimage.jpg"/>
        <siteMapNode url="DVDs.aspx" title="DVDs"
                   description="This is the DVDs page"
                   ImageURL="productsimage.jpg"/>
      </siteMapNode>
```

```
            <siteMapNode url="Support.aspx" title="Support"
                         description="This is the support page"
                         ImageURL="supportimage.jpg"/>
            <siteMapNode url="Contact.aspx" title="Contact"
                         description="This is the contacts page"
                         ImageURL="contactimage.jpg">
            <siteMapNode url="ContactAddress.aspx"
                            title="Contact using physical address"
                            description="This is the first contact page"
                            ImageURL="contactPhysicalAddressimage.jpg"/>
            <siteMapNode url="ContactEmailPhone.aspx"
                            title="Contact by email or phone"
                            description="This is the second contact page"
                            ImageURL="contactPhoneimage.jpg"/>
            </siteMapNode>
          </siteMapNode>
        </siteMap>
```

3. Add this to the web.config file:

```
<configuration>
  <system.web>
    <urlMappings>
      <add url="~/CDs.aspx" mappedUrl="~/Products.aspx?ID=1"/>
      <add url="~/DVDs.aspx" mappedUrl="~/Products.aspx?ID=2"/>
    </urlMappings>
  </system.web>
</configuration>
```

4. Run the page. Notice the menu has changed and now includes two new items under the Products menu. The site map points these two items to the CDs.aspx file and the DVDs.aspx file. Although the application does NOT include files with these names, the user still sees a page that works when they redirect using one of these menu items. The web.config file remaps the request back to the Products.aspx page, passing a URL parameter with a specific value. When the Products.aspx page is loaded and the ID parameter is "1" or "2," the page loads the list box with CD titles or DVD titles.

The following graphic shows the CDs "product page" being selected from the site map data:

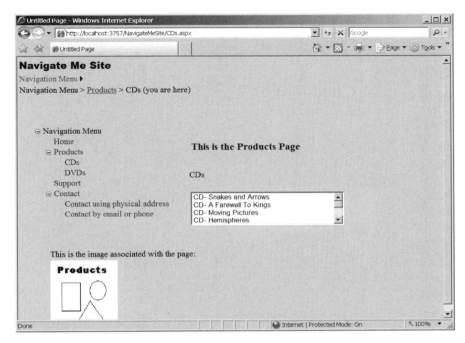

The following graphic shows the DVDs "product page" being selected from the site map data:

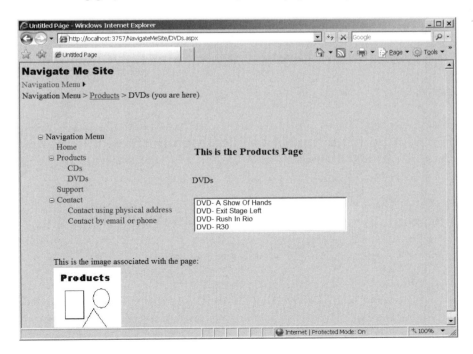

The following graphic shows the normal "product page" being selected from the site map data:

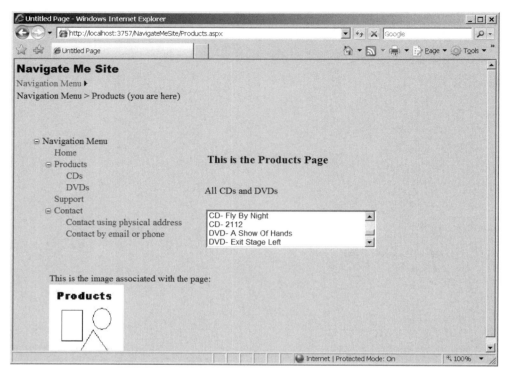

URL mapping is useful in all kinds of situations in which you need to represent pages within a navigation control, even though there may not be a physical page to support it.

Summary

Web applications have always been organized hierarchically; even the earliest sites containing simple HTML files and perhaps some image files (or other types of files) are typically hierarchical by nature. The fundamental architecture of any Web site is always considered hierarchical—whether the application is one or several layers deep.

Modern Web UIs have become sophisticated enough to need to represent a site's hierarchy. Very often you'll see a Web site's structure represented as a menu or some sort of tree. In addition, many sites now include a UI element representing the "path" along which the user is browsing (this is a common UI idiom with online forums).

ASP.NET includes an entire architecture designed to support Web site navigation. The standard involves using an XML file describing the site's hierarchy. The *SiteMap* object populates itself by reading the XML file and building an internal data structure representing the hierarchy. That data structure is made up of *SiteMapNodes*. You can always find the current node (representing the current page) within the Web site using the static *Current* property from the *SiteMap* object.

ASP.NET supports three controls for navigating a Web site: the *Menu*, the *TreeView*, and the *SiteMapPath* control. Each of these controls may be hooked up to the *SiteMap* data, and their contents will reflect the contents of the site map data. In addition to wiring the navigation controls up to the site map data source, ASP.NET supports hooking up an event handler for the *SiteMapResolve* event, which occurs every time the user navigates through a navigation control hooked up to the site map data. These controls are most useful when placed on a master page where they may be shared across all the pages on the site, giving the site a singular look to its layout. In addition, using the site map architecture makes updating the navigation scheme very straightforward. Simply update the site map information and it will be reflected by all the controls using it the next time the page renders.

Chapter 12 Quick Reference

To	Do This
Add an XML site map to the application	Click the right mouse button on the project name in Solution Explorer. Select **Add New Item** from the menu. Choose *Site Map* from the templates. This is useful for adding an XML-based site map to your site.
Add a navigation control to a page in your site	Open the Navigation controls node on the Toolbox. Select the *Menu*, the *TreeView*, or the *SiteMapPath* control and place it on the page.
	When you place the navigation control on the page, you'll see a small task window asking you to choose the data source. If you already have the appropriate data source on your page, select it. If you've created an XML-based site map for your page, choose *New Data Source. . .* and select "SiteMap" or "XML File"—depending on how your navigation data are packaged.
Intercept navigation requests as they occur	Write a handler for the *SiteMapResolve* event in the Global.asax file.
Map virtual nonexistent URLs to real URLs	Add a *urlMapping* section to web.config to map the virtual URLs. Add the virtual URLs to your site map data so that the user can more easily navigate to the given page.

Chapter 13
Personalization

After completing this chapter, you will be able to

- Use ASP.NET personalization
- Apply personalization to a Web site

This chapter covers ASP.NET's built-in personalization features. A major theme throughout ASP.NET is to provide frameworks and support for implementing features most Web sites need. For example, we saw the support ASP.NET provides for making a common look and feel throughout a site via Master Pages and Themes in Chapter 8. We saw the new login controls in Chapter 10. The new login controls are there so you don't have to hash out yet one more login control. Then there are authentication and authorization, site maps, and on and on. ASP.NET today is just packed with features to make your site development task easier and faster.

Personalizing Web sites is another feature that often makes for a great Web site. Until ASP.NET 2.0, it was up to you to provide any personalization support for your site. Now these features are rolled into ASP.NET.

Let's take a look at Web personalization.

Personalizing Web Visits

When the Internet and the Web first began coming into prominence, most of the sites you could surf to contained only static content. That is, they offered only text, graphics, and perhaps links to other pages. The early Web-surfing community consisted of only the few folks who knew about the Internet browsers peering into the contents of those early Web servers.

Until the Web began exploding with interactive sites, there was really no need for the Web site to care who was looking at it. However, any businessperson worth his or her salt will tell you that tailoring and targeting content toward specific individuals is good for business.

The next time you go online to shop or visit a subscription-type site, take note of how much the site knows about you. Very often (if you've provided login information) the site will greet you with your name. It may point you to information or products that might interest you. This demonstrates the notion of personalizing a Web site.

In the past, any personalization of your site resulted from code you wrote, such as code to manage user preferences in cookies or code to store personal information in databases. In addition to simply storing and managing the personal information, you had to integrate the personal information management with whatever authentication and authorization scheme you decided to use. That is, once you authenticated the user, you then could tailor your pages according to his or her personal information.

ASP.NET now includes services for personalizing a Web site to suit a particular client's taste. There's no reason you couldn't write your own database and services to provide this functionality. However, as with all these services provided by ASP.NET, they bring with them some consistency and prevent you from having to write all the code yourself.

Personalization in ASP.NET

While it may not be surprising to find that ASP.NET's personalization services follow the same provider pattern as authentication and site mapping, defining a Web site's personalization facilities begins by defining user profiles. We'll start there.

User Profiles

The heart of the new ASP.NET personalization service is the *user profile*. A user profile defines what kind of personal information your Web site needs. For example, you may want to know personal data about users of your Web site, such as name, gender, number of visits to the site, and so forth. User profiles are also handy for storing user preferences for your site. For example, you might include a Theme as part of a personal profile so that users can tailor the pages to their particular tastes.

Once the personalization properties are defined in web.config, a component within ASP.NET has to be able to read it and use it. That job is handled by ASP.NET personalization providers.

Personalization Providers

In Chapter 10, we saw that .NET includes a provider pattern. Providers hide the infrastructural code necessary to support the service, yet they allow you to choose different underlying storage media with little impact to your site. Maybe you start your site using XML files for storing data but later move to SQL Server or you have legacy authentication databases you want to connect to your ASP.NET site. ASP.NET personalization is no different. In fact, ASP .NET includes two personalization providers out of the box: a profile provider for custom user data and a personalization provider for Web Parts (as you recall, we looked at Web Parts themselves in Chapter 7).

ASP.NET defines the fundamental provider capabilities in an abstract class named *PersonalizationProvider*. Those capabilities include loading and saving personalization properties and managing their relationship to any Web Parts used within a site. ASP.NET provides a default implementation of these capabilities in a concrete class named *SqlPersonalizationProvider*, which is derived from *PersonalizationProvider*.

Using Personalization

Using personalization is pretty straightforward. You basically define personalization properties in web.config. ASP.NET will synthesize a class you may use to manage personalization settings. At that point, profile information is available in much the same way as session state is available.

Defining Profiles in Web.Config

Your site's profile schema is defined within web.config as name/type pairs. Imagine that in the course of designing your site, you decided you'd like to track the following information about a particular user:

- User name (a string)
- Gender (a Boolean value)
- Visit count (an integer)
- Birthday (a date)

Defining these properties is a matter of specifying them in web.config. A definition for the properties I just mentioned might look like the following when identified in web.config:

```
<system.web>
   <profile automaticSaveEnabled="true" >
      <properties>
         <add name="NumVisits" type="System.Int32"/>
         <add name="UserName" type="System.String"/>
         <add name="Gender" type="System.Boolean">
         <add name="Birthday" type="System.DateTime">
      </properties>
   </profile>
</system.web
```

Once defined in the web.config file, the profile may be used in the site through the *Profile* property found in the current *HttpContext* (and also via the *Page* base class).

Using Profile Information

To use the profile in your Web site, you access it in much the same way you might access session state. We'll see how session state works in Chapter 14—right now it's enough to say that you may access data tied to a specific session by accessing the page's *Session* member. The *Session* member is a name-value dictionary holding arbitrary information tied to a particular session. However, instead of being represented by name/value pairs accessed by enumerating a collection of stored state information, the ASP.NET compiler will synthesize a profile object based on the schema defined in the web.config file.

For example, given the schema I just mentioned, ASP.NET will synthesize a class named *ProfileCommon*, based on the *ProfileBase* class. The synthesized class will reflect the values written into the web.config by inserting actual class properties, shown here in bold:

```
public class ProfileCommon : ProfileBase
{
    public  virtual  HttpProfile GetProfile(string username);
    public  object GetPropertyValue(string propertyName);
    public  void SetPropertyValue(string propertyName,
             object propertyValue);
    public  HttpProfileGroupBase GetProfileGroup(String groupName);
    public  void Initialize(String username,Boolean isAuthenticated);
    public  virtual void Save();
    public  void Initialize(SettingsContext context,
             SettingsPropertyCollection properties,
             SettingsProviderCollection providers);
    public string UserName{get; set;};
    public int NumVisits{get; set;};
    public bool Gender(get; set; );
    public DateTime Birthdate{get; set; };
}
```

To access the profile properties, simply use the *Profile* property within the page. The *Profile* property is an instance of the *ProfileCommon* class synthesized by ASP.NET. Just access the members of the *Profile*, like so:

```
protected void Page_Load(object sender, EventArgs e)
{
    if (Profile.Name != null)
    {
        Response.Write("Hello " + Profile.Name);
        Response.Write("Your birthday is " +
            Profile.Birthdate);
    }
}
```

Saving Profile Changes

The preceding code snippet assumes there's already personalization information associated with the user. To insert profile data for a particular user, simply set the properties of the *Profile* object. For example, imagine a page that includes a handler for saving the profile. It might look something like this:

```
protected void ProfileSaveClicked(object sender, EventArgs e)
{
    Profile.Name = this.TextBox1.Text;
    Profile.Birthdate = this.Calendar1.SelectedDate;
}
```

The easiest way to ensure that the personalization properties persist is to set the *automaticSaveEnabled* to *true*. Personal profile data will be saved automatically by the provider.

Alternatively, you may call *Profile.Save* as necessary to save the personalization properties manually. In addition to saving and loading profiles, you may also delete the profile for a specific user by calling *Profile.DeleteProfile*.

Profiles and Users

Profile information is associated with the current user based on the identity of the user. By default, ASP.NET uses the *User.Identity.Name* within the current *HttpContext* as the key to store data. Because of this, profiles are generally available only for authenticated users.

However, ASP.NET supports anonymous profiles as well. As you might expect, this is also configured within web.config. The default tracking mechanism for anonymous profiles is to use cookies. However, you may tell ASP.NET to use a mangled URL. A mangled URL is one in which a key identifying the particular client is embedded in the URL used to post requests back to the server.

The following exercise illustrates using personalization profiles based on the user's login ID.

Using profiles

1. Before starting this project, add the profile tables to your installation of SQL Server. Run aspnet_regsql.exe to add the profile tables. Go to the directory \windows\microsoft.net\ framework\v2.0.50727 (that's the current version as of this writing). Microsoft provides a default SqlProfileProvider instance named *AspNetSqlProfileProvider*. This provider connects to your local SQL server. ASP.NET profile feature uses this instance of the provider by default.

2. Create a new project. Name the project *MakeItPersonal*.

3. Add a web.config file to the project if one isn't created for you (earlier versions of Visual Studio did not include the web.config file). Update web.config to include some profile properties. The example here includes a user name, a Theme, and a birthdate. The following example shows that you may group and nest profile structures using the *group* element. The *<group>* element allows you to nest data structures within a profile declaration.

```
<system.web>

  <profile>
    <properties >
      <add name="Theme" type="System.String"/>
      <add name="Name" type="System.String"/>
      <add name="Birthdate" type="System.DateTime"/>
      <group name="Address">
          <add name="StreetAddress" type="System.String"/>
          <add name="City" type="System.String"/>
          <add name="State" type="System.String"/>
```

```
                    <add name="ZipCode" type="System.String"/>
                 </group>
              </properties>
           </profile>

        </system.web>
```

> **Note** *Supporting Anonymous Personalization:* This example uses the authenticated user name as the key for locating personalization information. However, ASP.NET supports "anonymous" per-sonalization. That is, ASP.NET supports personalization information for anonymous users—but tracks the users via a cookie. You may add support for anonymous personalization tracking by turning the *anonymousIdentification* element to "true" and specifying cookie parameters like this:
>
> ```
> <anonymousIdentification enabled="true"
>     cookieName=".ASPXANONYMOUSUSER"
>     cookieTimeout="120000"
>     cookiePath="/"
>     cookieRequireSSL="false"
>     cookieSlidingExpiration="true"
>     cookieProtection="Encryption"
>     cookieless="UseDeviceProfile" />
> ```
>
> In addition to setting anonymous access up in web.config, you need to set the *[allowAnonymous]* attribute for the properties.
>
> By configuring the site this way and adding the *allowAnonymous* attribute to properties in the profile information, ASP.NET will store the personalization settings based on a cookie it gener-ates when a user first hits the site.

4. Borrow the Default and SeeingRed Themes from the MasterPageSite project (Chapter 8). This will let the user pick the Theme. First add Default and SeeingRed folders to the application's Themes directory. Then click the right mouse button on each of the theme folders and select **Add Existing Item...** from the local menu. Use the file navigation dialog box to navigate to the Chapter 8 directory and select the theme files. You can do the same for the master page file.

5. Borrow the UseThemes.aspx and .cs files from the MasterPageSite project.`

6. Now update the Default.aspx page. This will be where users type profile information.

   Add text boxes for the name, address, city, state, and zip code.

   Add a drop-down list box populated with Default and SeeingRed items. This will be used for selecting the Theme.

   Also add a calendar control to pick the birthdate.

7. Add a button that the user may click to submit profile information. Add a handler to input these values into the profile. Double-click on the button to add the handler.

The input screen should look something like this:

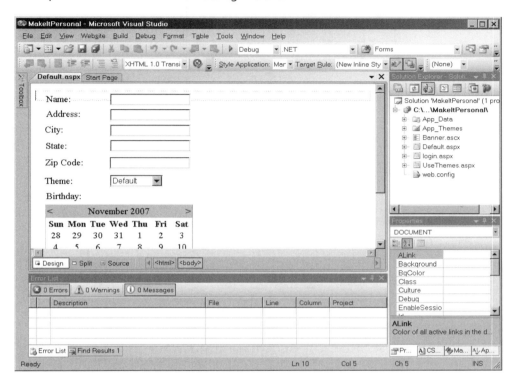

Note *Adding Users to Authenticate:* This example uses the authenticated user name as the key for storing personalization values. Use the ASP.NET Configuration Utility to apply Forms Authentication to this application (as described in Chapter 10). Also add at least one user so that you have one to personalize. Add a Login.aspx screen to the site and modify the site's access rules to enforce authentication. Then you will be able to see the personalization information being stored and retrieved. Add some users for this site using the Web configuration manager.

8. Update *Page_Load* to display profile information (if it's there). Grab the profile object and set each of the text boxes and the calendar control.

```
public partial class _Default : System.Web.UI.Page
{
    protected void Page_Load(object sender, EventArgs e)
    {
      if (!this.IsPostBack)

      {

          ProfileCommon pc = this.Profile.GetProfile(Profile.UserName);
          if (pc != null)
```

```
            {
                this.TextBoxName.Text = pc.Name;
                this.TextBoxAddress.Text = pc.Address.StreetAddress;
                this.TextBoxCity.Text = pc.Address.City;
                this.TextBoxState.Text = pc.Address.State;
                this.TextBoxZipCode.Text = pc.Address.ZipCode;
                this.DropDownList1.SelectedValue = pc.Theme;
                this.Calendar1.SelectedDate = pc.Birthdate;
            }
        }
    }
    // ...
}
```

9. Update the profile submission handler to store the profile information.

```
protected void ButtonSubmitProfile_Click(object sender, EventArgs e)
{
    ProfileCommon pc = this.Profile.GetProfile(Profile.UserName);

    if (pc != null)
    {
        pc.Name = this.TextBoxName.Text;
        pc.Address.StreetAddress = this.TextBoxAddress.Text;
        pc.Address.City = this.TextBoxCity.Text;
        pc.Address.State = this.TextBoxState.Text;
        pc.Address.ZipCode = this.TextBoxZipCode.Text;
        pc.Theme = this.DropDownList1.SelectedValue;
        pc.Birthdate = this.Calendar1.SelectedDate;

        pc.Save();
    }
}
```

10. Finally, update the UseThemes.aspx page to use the Theme. Override the page's *OnPreInit* method. Have the code apply the Theme as specified by the profile.

```
protected override void OnPreInit(EventArgs e)
{
    ProfileCommon pc = this.Profile.GetProfile(Profile.UserName);
        if (pc != null)
        {
            String strTheme = pc.Theme.ToString();
            if (strTheme != null &&
                strTheme.Length > 0)
            {
                this.Theme = strTheme;
            }
        }
    base.OnPreInit(e);
}
```

11. Add a *Hyperlink* control to the Default.aspx page. Set the *Text* property to *View Themes* and set the *NavigateURL* property to point to the UseThemes.aspx page. When you surf to the page, you should be able to enter the profile information and submit it. Following your initial visit, the profile will be available whenever you hit the site.

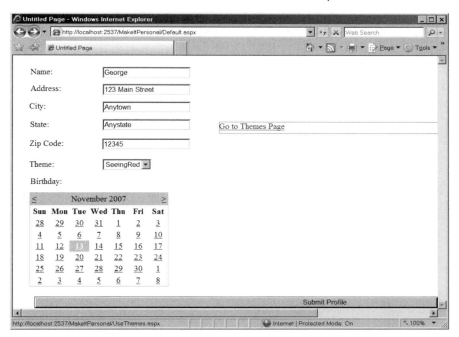

12. When you go to the UseThemes.aspx page, the page should use the theme that's been selected via the profile. The following graphic shows the UseThemes.aspx page using the *SeeingRed* theme pulled from the profile:

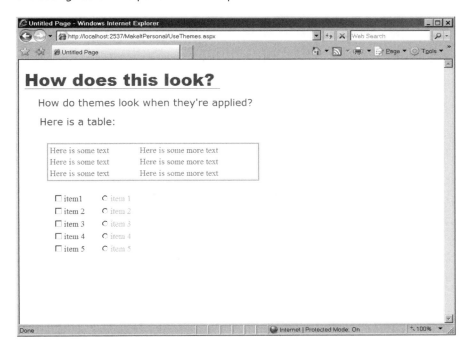

Summary

Profiles represent an effective way to add personalization to your site. The profile schema you create in your web.config file defines the profiles available to the application. ASP.NET will synthesize a *ProfileCommon* class that includes support for the properties defined in web.config. To access the properties, grab the *Profile* object from the *Page* or from the current *HttpContext*. ASP.NET will take care of the details of serializing the property data and tracking them either anonymously or by using the identity of the logged-in user.

Chapter 13 Quick Reference

To	Do This
Define personalization profile settings	Use the *<profile>* element in web.config. Define name/type pairs to create the profile schema.
Access the profile properties	Profile properties are available through the *Page* base class and through the current *HttpContext*.
Track anonymous profiles with cookies	Enable *anonymousIdentification* in web.config and add the *allowAnonymous* attribute to the profile properties.

Part III
Caching and State Management

Chapter 14
Session State

After completing this chapter, you will be able to

- Understand the importance of managing session state in a Web application

- Use the session state manager (the *Session* object)

- Configure session state

- Be aware of the different possibilities for storing session state with ASP.NET

This chapter covers managing session state within your ASP.NET application. Programming Web applications requires you to be very mindful of how the state of your application is distributed at any moment. One of the most important types of state in a Web application is session state—the state associated with a single particular session. Because Web applications are distributed by nature, and because the nature of the HTTP protocol is stateless, keeping track of any single client has to be done deliberately.

ASP.NET session state support is extensive, reliable, and flexible—offering many advantages over the session state support available in other Web platforms such as classic ASP. For starters, ASP.NET session state is handled by the *Session* object—an object dictionary that's automatically created with each new session (if you have session state enabled). The *Session* object is easily accessible through the *HttpContext* object, which you can reference at any point during the request. The process of associating user state with a particular user's session is handled automatically by ASP.NET. Whenever you want to access session state, you just grab it from the context (it's also mapped into a member variable living on the page). You may choose how ASP.NET tracks session state, and you may even tell ASP.NET where to store session state.

Let's begin with a look at how various pieces of state are managed by ASP.NET, and the gap filled by the session state manager.

Why Session State?

After working with ASP.NET during the previous chapters, one theme should be emerging. Web-based programming distinguishes itself as a programming idiom in which you're trying to manage an application serving multiple users distributed over a wide area. What's more, you're doing it over a disconnected (and stateless) protocol.

For example, imagine you're writing some sort of shopping portal. Certain types of the application data can be kept in a central database—things like inventory and supplier lists.

We've seen that *System.Web.UI.Page* and server-side controls themselves manage view state. However, when you think about the nature of data in a user's shopping cart, you see the data clearly belong elsewhere.

You don't really want to store those data in the page's *ViewState*. Although it's possible for simple applications, storing large chunks of data in view state will bog down your users' experience of the site (it'll be much slower) and it poses a security risk by having items travel back and forth with each request. In addition, only serializable types may be stored in view state. Finally, you will lose the view state if you redirect to another page.

Unfortunately, a single user's session data don't really belong in the application database either. Perhaps if you expected only one user over the lifetime of your application, that might work. However, remember the nature of a Web application is to make your application available to as many clients as possible. Suddenly, it becomes clear that you want to be able to carve out a small data-holding area that persists for the lifetime of a single user's session. This type of data is known as *session state*.

ASP.NET and Session State

Since its inception, ASP.NET has supported session state. When session state is turned on, ASP.NET creates a new *Session* object for each new request. The *Session* object becomes part of the context (and is available through the page). ASP.NET stamps the *Session* object with an identifier (more on that later), and the *Session* object is reconstituted when a request comes through containing a valid session identifier. The *Session* object follows the page around and becomes a convenient repository for storing information that has to survive throughout the session (and not simply for the duration of the page).

The *Session* object is a dictionary of name-value pairs. You can associate any Common Language Runtime (CLR)-based object with a key of your choosing and place it in the *Session* object so it will be there when the next request belonging to that session comes through. Then you may access that piece of data using the key under which it was stored. For example, if you wanted to store some information provided by the user in the *Session* object, you'd write code like this:

```
void StoreInfoInSession()
{
    String strFromUser = TextBox1.Text;
    Session["strFromUser"] = strFromUser;
}
```

To retrieve the string during the next request, you'd use code like this:

```
void GetInfoFromSession()
{
    String strFromUser = Session["strFromUser"] ; // NOTE: may be null
    TextBox1.Text = strFromUser;
}
```

The square braces on the *Session* object indicate an *indexer*. The indexer is a convenient syntax for expressing keys—both when inserting data into and retrieving data from the *Session* object. Do note, however, that if the key you provide doesn't map to a piece of data in the session dictionary, the *Session* object will return null. In production code it's always wise to check for a null value and react accordingly.

Managing session state in ASP.NET is extraordinarily convenient. In ASP.NET, session state may live in a number of places, including (1) "in proc"—in the ASP.NET worker process, (2) on a separate state server running a Windows Service process, and (3) in a SQL Server database. Because session management follows the provider pattern you've seen in earlier chapters, you can relatively easily replace ASP.NET's built-in session state management with an implementation of your own.

Let's start by getting a taste of using session state right now.

Introduction to Session State

To understand how session state works, here's an exercise that involves creating a Web site whose page stores a value as a member variable in the page and as an element of session state. It will illustrate the difference between page state during a request and session data that persist beyond a request.

Trying session state

1. Create a new Web site. Name it *SessionState*. Make it a File System site.

2. In the default page (Default.aspx), drag a text box (and a label to identify the *TextBox* if you want) onto the form. Then drag two buttons and another label onto the form like so:

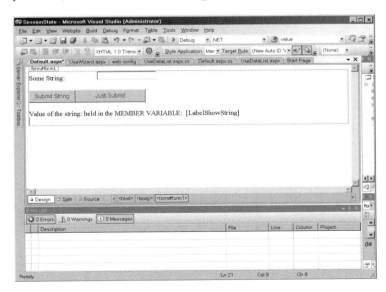

3. Set the *Text* property of the first button to *Submit String*. Then give the button the same value as an ID. That is, set the ID to **SubmitString**. Doing so will help you distinguish the buttons later on. It doesn't matter what you name the second button. The first button will submit the string to the form, and the other button will just perform a postback. That way, you'll be able to see the ephemeral nature of page member variables. Drop a *Label* on the page. Name the label *LabelShowString*. We'll use it to display the value of the string.

4. Add a *String* variable member to the page named *_str*. In the *Page_Load* handler, set the text box on the page to the value of the string. Then add a handler for the *SubmitString* button. Have the handler take the *Text* property from the *TextBox1* and store it in the page member variable. Then set the *LabelShowString* label text to the value of the string like so:

```
public partial class _Default : System.Web.UI.Page
{

    string _str = String.Empty;

    protected void Page_Load(object sender, EventArgs e)
    {

      this.LabelShowString.Text = this._str;
     }
    protected void SubmitString_Click(object sender, EventArgs e)
    {
      this._str = this.TextBox1.Text;
      this.LabelShowString.Text = this._str;
    }
}
```

5. Now run the program. Type a string into the text box and click **Submit String**. When the post goes to the page, the page will show the string in the label.

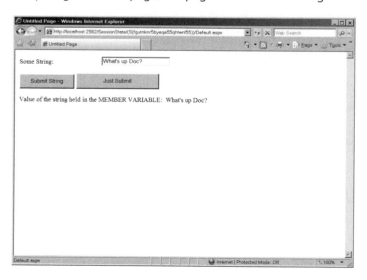

6. Now click **Just Submit**. What happens? Remember, *Page_Load* simply looks at the value of the *_str* member variable and stuffs it into the label. Pages (and HTTP handlers in general) are very short-lived objects. They live for the duration of the request and then are destroyed—along with all the data they hold. The *_str* member variable evaporated as soon as the last request finished. A new *_str* member variable (which was empty) was instantiated as soon as the page was re-created.

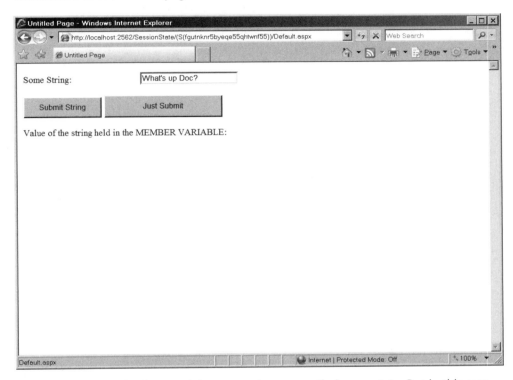

To sum up, we saw in Chapter 4 that controls manage their own state. But in this case, we're taking the data from the text box and storing them in a member variable in the *Page* class. The lifetime of the page is very short. The page lives long enough to generate a response, and then it disappears. Any state you've stored as data members in the page disappears too. That's why, when you click the **Just Submit** button, you don't see the string displayed. You *do* see the string when **Submit String** is clicked because the member variable survives long enough to support the button's *Click* event handler.

7. Using session state is a way to solve this issue. To show this, add a new label to the page. This one will show the data as retrieved from the *Session* object:

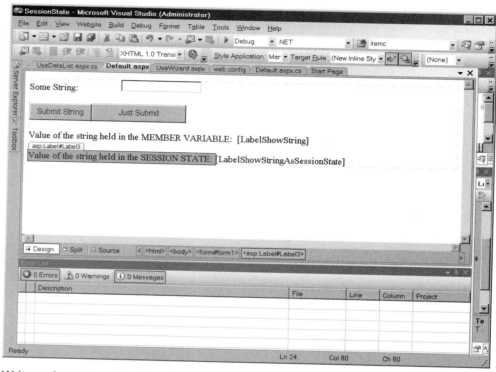

8. Write code to store the string in session state. Have the *SubmitString* take the text from the *TextBox1* and store it into the *Session* object. Then update the *Page_Load* method to display the value as it came from session state as shown below:

```
public partial class _Default : System.Web.UI.Page
{

    string _str = String.Empty;

    protected void Page_Load(object sender, EventArgs e)
    {
        this.LabelShowString.Text = this._str;

        this.LabelShowStringAsSessionState.Text =
            (String)this.Session["str"];
    }
```

```
protected void SubmitString_Click(object sender, EventArgs e)
{
    this._str = this.TextBox1.Text;
    this.Session["str"] = this.TextBox1.Text;
    this.LabelShowString.Text = this._str;

    this.LabelShowStringAsSessionState.Text =
        (String)this.Session["str"];
}
}
```

9. Run the program. Type in a string and click the **Submit String** button. Both labels should contain data. The *LabelShowString* label will hold data because the *SubmitString* handler made the member variable assignment. The *LabelShowStringAsSessionState* label also shows data because the handler stored that text in session state.

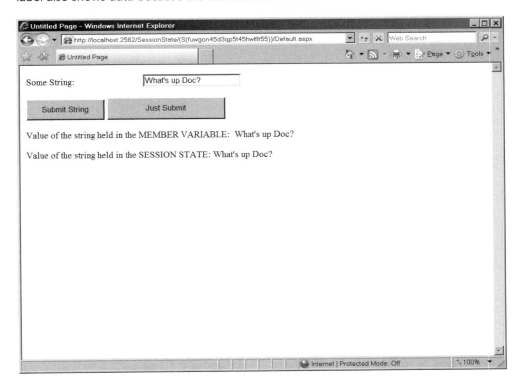

10. Now click the **Just Submit** button and see what happens:

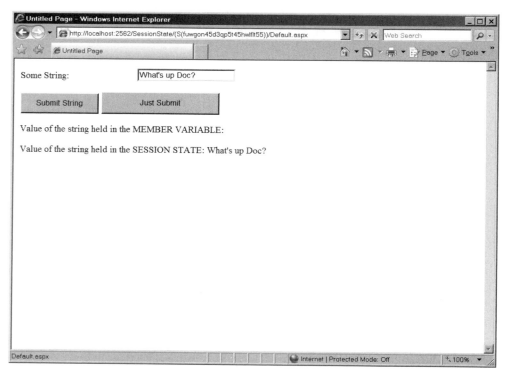

In this case, the page was simply submitted, causing only the *Page_Load* to be executed. *Page_Load* displays both the *_str* member variable (which is empty because it lives and dies with the page) and the data from the *Session* object (which lives independently of the page).

As you can see, session state is pretty convenient. However, we wouldn't get very far if all we could do was store simple strings and scalars. Fortunately, the session dictionary stores all manner of CLR objects.

Session State and More Complex Data

ASP.NET's *Session* object will store any (serializable) object running within the CLR. That goes for larger data—not just small strings or other scalar types. One of the most common uses for the *Session* object is for implementing features like shopping carts (or any other data that has to go with a particular client). For example, if you're developing a commerce-oriented site for customers to purchase products, you'd probably implement a central database representing your inventory. Then, as users sign on, they will have the opportunity to select items from your inventory and place them in a temporary holding area associated with the session they're running. In ASP.NET, that holding area is typically the *Session* object.

A number of different collections are useful for managing shopping cart-like scenarios. Probably the easiest to use is the good ol' *ArrayList*—an automatically sizing array that supports both random access and the *IList* interface. However, for other scenarios you might use a *DataTable*, a *DataSet*, or some other more complex type.

We took a quick look at ADO and data access in Chapter 11. The next example revisits data-bound controls (the *DataList* and the *GridView*). We'll also work with the *DataTable* in depth.

Session state, ADO.NET objects, and data-bound controls

This example illustrates using ADO.NET objects, data-bound controls, and session state to transfer items from an inventory (represented as a *DataList*) to a collection of selected items (represented using a *GridView*).

1. Create a new page on the SessionState site named *UseDataList.aspx*.

   Add *DataList* to the page by copying the following code between the <div> tags on the generated page. The *DataList* will display the elements in the .NET References table from the Access database we saw in Chapter 11.

```
<asp:DataList ID="DataList1"
    runat="server" BackColor="White" BorderColor="#E7E7FF"
    BorderStyle="None" BorderWidth="1px" CellPadding="3"
    GridLines="Horizontal"
    Style="z-index: 100; left: 8px; position: absolute; top: 16px"
    OnItemCommand="DataList1_ItemCommand" Caption="Items in Inventory" >
<FooterStyle BackColor="#B5C7DE" ForeColor="#4A3C8C" />
<SelectedItemStyle BackColor="#738A9C"
    Font-Bold="True" ForeColor="#F7F7F7" />
<AlternatingItemStyle BackColor="#F7F7F7" />
<ItemStyle BackColor="#E7E7FF" ForeColor="#4A3C8C" />
    <ItemTemplate>
    ID:
    <asp:Label ID="IDLabel"
    runat="server" Text='<%# Eval("ID") %>'></asp:Label><br />
    Title:
    <asp:Label ID="TitleLabel"
    runat="server" Text='<%# Eval("Title") %>'></asp:Label><br />
    AuthorLastName:
    <asp:Label ID="AuthorLastNameLabel"
    runat="server" Text='<%# Eval("AuthorLastName")
    %>'></asp:Label><br />
    AuthorFirstName:
    <asp:Label ID="AuthorFirstNameLabel"
    runat="server" Text='<%# Eval("AuthorFirstName")
    %>'></asp:Label><br />
    Topic:
    <asp:Label ID="TopicLabel" runat="server"
    Text='<%# Eval("Topic") %>'></asp:Label><br />
    Publisher:
    <asp:Label ID="PublisherLabel"
    runat="server"
```

```
          Text='<%# Eval("Publisher") %>'></asp:Label><br />
          <br />

   <asp:Button ID="SelectItem"

     runat="server" Text="Select Item" />

         
        </ItemTemplate>
          <HeaderStyle BackColor="#4A3C8C" Font-Bold="True"
             ForeColor="#F7F7F7" />
</asp:DataList>
```

The Visual Studio designer should appear like this when done.

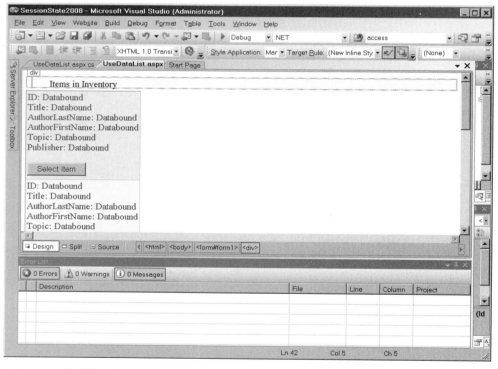

2. Stub out a shell for the **SelectItem** button on *Click* handler. Select *DataList1* on the
   page. In the **Properties** dialog box within Visual Studio, click the lightning bolt button
   to get the events. In the edit box next to the *ItemCommand* event, type **SelectItem**.
   The button handler should be named *DataList1_ItemCommand* to match the identifier
   in the *DataList1*. We'll use it shortly to move items from the inventory to the selected
   items table.

```
public partial class UseDataList : System.Web.UI.Page
{

    protected void DataList1_ItemCommand(object source,
            DataListCommandEventArgs e)
    {
    }

}
```

3. Go back to the code for the page and add some code to open a database and populate the *DataList*. Name the function *GetInventory*. The examples that come with this book include a database named *ASPDotNetStepByStep.mdb* that will work. Add the database from Chapter 11's example to the App_Data folder of this project. You can use the connection string listed below to connect to the database. Make sure the database path points to the file correctly using your directory structure.

```
public partial class UseDataList : System.Web.UI.Page
{

    protected DataTable GetInventory()
    {
        string strConnection =
        @"Provider=Microsoft.Jet.OLEDB.4.0; Data
        Source=|DataDirectory|ASPDotNetStepByStep.mdb";

        DbProviderFactory f =
            DbProviderFactories.GetFactory("System.Data.OleDb");

        DataTable dt = new DataTable();
        using (DbConnection connection = f.CreateConnection())
        {           connection.ConnectionString = strConnection;

            connection.Open();

            DbCommand command = f.CreateCommand();
            command.CommandText = "Select * from DotNetReferences";
            command.Connection = connection;

            IDataReader reader = command.ExecuteReader();

            dt.Load(reader);
            reader.Close();
            connection.Close();
        }

        return dt;
    }

    protected DataTable BindToinventory()
    {
        DataTable dt;
        dt = this.GetInventory();
        this.DataList1.DataSource = dt;
```

```
        this.DataBind();
        return dt;
    }

    // More goes here...
}
```

4. Now add a method named *CreateSelectedItemsData*. This will be a table into which selected items will be placed. The method will take a *DataTable* object that will describe the schema of the data in the live database (we'll see how to get that soon). You can create an empty *DataTable* by constructing it and then adding *Columns* to the column collection. The schema coming from the database will have the column name and the data type.

```
public partial class UseDataList : System.Web.UI.Page
{

    protected DataTable CreateSelectedItemsTable(DataTable tableSchema)
    {

        DataTable tableSelectedItemsData = new DataTable();

        foreach(DataColumn dc in tableSchema.Columns)
        {
            tableSelectedItemsData.Columns.Add(dc.ColumnName,
                dc.DataType);
        }
        return tableSelectedItemsData;

    }
}
```

5. Add code to the *Page_Load* handler. When the initial request to a page is made (that is, if the request is *not* a postback), *Page_Load* should call *BindToInventory* (which returns the *DataTable* snapshot of the *DotNetReferences* table). Use the *DataTable* as the schema on which to base the selected items table. That is, declare an instance of a *DataTable* and assign it the result of *CreateSelectedItemsTable*. Then store the (now empty) table in the *Session* object using the key *tableSelectedItems*.

```
public partial class UseDataList : System.Web.UI.Page
{
    protected void Page_Load(object sender, EventArgs e)
    {
        if (!IsPostBack)
        {
            DataTable dt = BindToinventory();
            DataTable tableSelectedItems =
                this.CreateSelectedItemsTable(dt);
            Session["tableSelectedItems"] = tableSelectedItems;
        }
    }
}
```

Browse to the Web site to make sure that the database connects. It should look something like this:

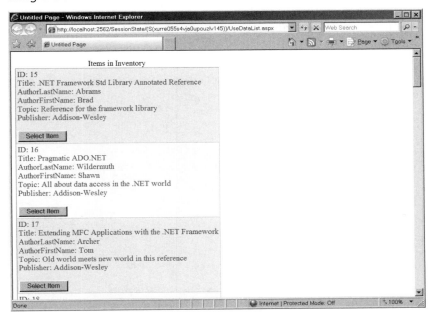

6. Now add a *GridView* to the page. Don't bother to give it a data source. It represents the table of selected items held in session state. We'll add that shortly. Make sure the *AutoGenerateColumns* property is set to *true*.

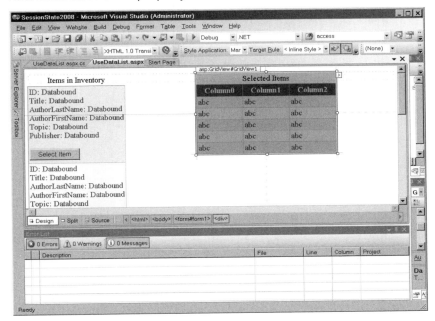

7. Finally, add a handler for the *SelectItem* button. This method should move items from the inventory to the selected items table. You can get the selected item index from the *DataListCommandEventArgs* coming into the handler. Calling *BindToInventory* will set up the *DataList* data source so you can fetch the selected item. You may access the columns within the selected row using ordinal indices. From the values in each column, construct a new *DataRow* and add it to the selected items table. Store the modified table back in session state. Finally, apply the new selected items table to the *DataSource* in the *GridView1* and bind the *GridView1*.

```csharp
public partial class UseDataList : System.Web.UI.Page
{
    protected void DataList1_ItemCommand(object source,
        DataListCommandEventArgs e)
    {
        int nItemIndex = e.Item.ItemIndex;
        this.DataList1.SelectedIndex = nItemIndex;

        BindToinventory();

        // Order of the columns is:
        // ID, Title, FirstName, LastName, Topic, Publisher

        DataTable dt = (DataTable)DataList1.DataSource;
        String strID = (dt.Rows[nItemIndex][0]).ToString();
        String strTitle = (dt.Rows[nItemIndex][1]).ToString();
        String strAuthorLastName = (dt.Rows[nItemIndex][2]).ToString();
        String strAuthorFirstName = (dt.Rows[nItemIndex][3]).ToString();
        String strTopic = (dt.Rows[nItemIndex][4]).ToString();
        String strPublisher = (dt.Rows[nItemIndex][5]).ToString();

        DataTable tableSelectedItems;
        tableSelectedItems = (DataTable)Session["tableSelectedItems"];

        DataRow dr = tableSelectedItems.NewRow();
        dr[0] = strID;
        dr[1] = strTitle;
        dr[2] = strAuthorLastName;
        dr[3] = strAuthorFirstName;
        dr[4] = strTopic;
        dr[3] = strPublisher;

        tableSelectedItems.Rows.Add(dr);

        Session["tableSelectedItems"] = tableSelectedItems;

        this.GridView1.DataSource = tableSelectedItems;
        this.GridView1.DataBind();
    }
}
```

8. Run the site. When the page first comes up, you should see only the inventory list on the left side of the page. Click the **Select Item** button on some of the items. You should see your browser post back to the server and render the *DataList* and the *GridView* with the newly added selected item.

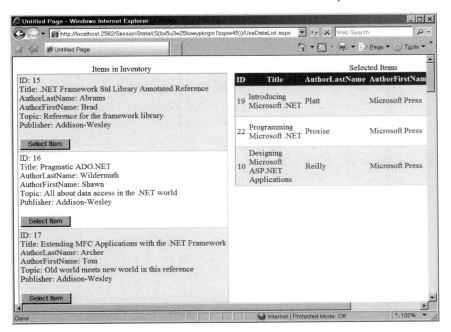

Now that you have a working application that uses session state, let's take a look at the different ways in which you may configure ASP.NET session state.

Configuring Session State

ASP.NET gives you several choices for managing session state. You can turn it off completely, you may run session state in the ASP.NET worker process, you may run it on a separate state server, or you may run it from a SQL Server database. Here's a rundown of the options available:

- **Don't use it at all.**   By disabling session state, your application performance will increase because the page doesn't need to load the session when starting, nor does it need to store session state when it's going away. On the other hand, you won't be able to associate any data with a particular user between page invocations.

- **Store session state "in proc."**   This is how session state is handled by default. In this case, the session dictionaries (the *Session* objects) are managed in the same process as the page and handler code. The advantage of using session state in process is that it's very fast and convenient. However, it's not durable. For example, if you restart IIS or somehow knock the server down, all session state is lost. In some cases, this may not be a big deal. However, if your shopping cart represents a shopping cart containing sizable orders, losing that might be a big deal. In addition, the in-process Session manager is confined to a single machine, meaning you can't use it in a Web farm. (A *Web farm* is a group of servers tied together to serve Web pages as a single application.)

- **Store session state in a state server.**   This option tells the ASP.NET runtime to direct all session management activities to a separate Windows Service process running on a particular machine. This option gives you the advantage of running your server in a Web farm. The ASP.NET Session State facilities support Web farms explicitly. To run in a Web farm, you would direct all your applications to go to the same place to retrieve session information. The downside to this approach is that it does impede performance somewhat—applications need to make a network round-trip to the state server when loading or saving session information.

- **Store session state in a database.**   Configuring your application to use a SQL Server database for state management causes ASP.NET to store session information within a SQL Server database somewhere on your network. Use this option when you want to run your server from within a Web farm when you want session state to be durable and safe.

When configuring ASP.NET session state during development, you may edit the configuration file directly. Once your site is deployed, you may prefer to configure session state through the session state configuration page in IIS.

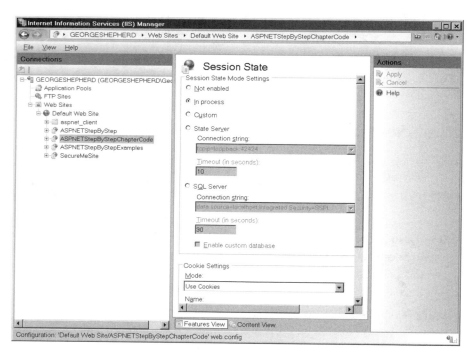

Turning Off Session State

The ASP.NET session state configuration tool available through IIS will touch your Web site's web.config file and insert the right configuration strings to enforce the settings you choose. To turn off session state completely, select Off from the session state mode control.

Storing Session State *InProc*

To store session state in the ASP.NET worker process, select *InProc* from the session state mode control. Your application will retrieve and store session information very quickly, but it will be available only to your application on the particular server the session information was originally stored within (that is, the session information will not be available to other servers that might be working together on a Web farm).

Storing Session State in a State Server

To have ASP.NET store session state on another server on your network, select *StateServer* from the *SessionState* mode control. When you select this item, the dialog box will enable the *Connection String* text box and the network *Timeout* text box. Insert the protocol, Internet Protocol (IP) address, and port for the state server in the *Connection String* text box. For example, the string

```
tcpip=loopback:42424
```

will store the session state on the local machine over port 42424. If you want to store the session state on a machine other than your local server, change the IP address. Before session state is stored on a machine, you need to make sure the ASP.NET state service is running on that machine. You may get to it via the Services panel under the control panel and the administration tools.

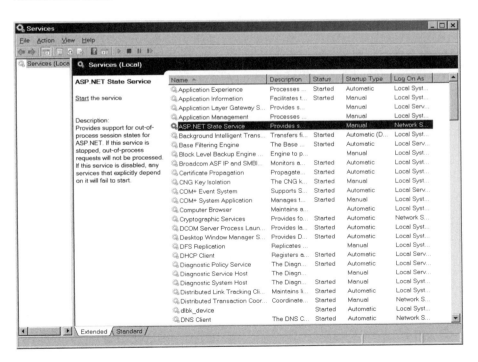

Storing Session State in a Database

The final option for storing session state is to use a SQL Server database. Select *SQLServer* from the ASP.NET session state mode combo box. You'll be asked to enter the connection string to the SQL Server state database. Here's the string provided by default:

```
data source=localhost;Integrated Security=SSPI
```

You may configure ASP.NET so it references a database on another machine. Of course, you need to have SQL Server installed on the target machine to make this work. In addition, you'll find some SQL scripts to create the state databases in your .NET system directory (C:\ WINDOWS\Microsoft.NET\Framework\v2.0.50727 on this machine at the time of this writing). The aspnet_regsql.exe tool will set up the databases for you.

Tracking Session State

Because Web-based applications rely on HTTP to connect browsers to servers and HTML to represent the state of the application, ASP.NET is essentially a disconnected architecture. When an application needs to use session state, the runtime needs a way of tracking the origin of the requests it receives so that it may associate data with a particular client. ASP.NET offers three options for tracking the session ID—via cookies, the URL, or device profiles.

Tracking Session State with Cookies

This is the default option for an ASP.NET Web site. In this scenario, ASP.NET generates a hard-to-guess identifier and uses it to store a new *Session* object. You can see the session identifier come through the cookie collection if you have tracing turned on. Notice how ASP.NET stores the session ID in a request cookie. The tracing information also reveals the names and the values of the session variables.

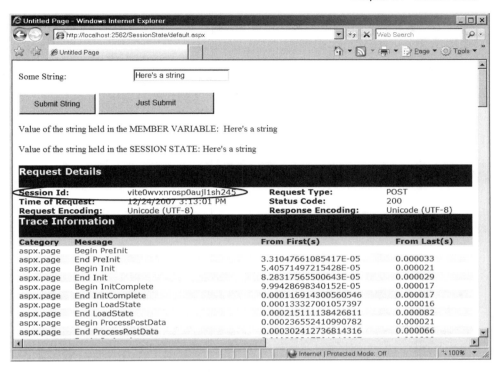

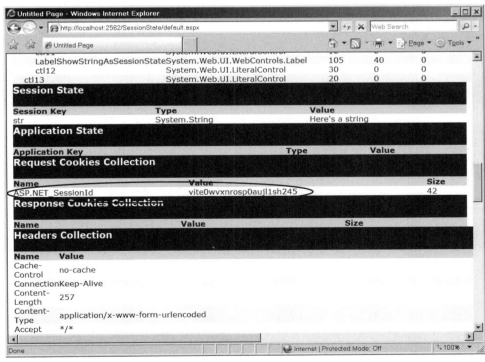

Tracking Session State with the URL

The other main option is to track session state by embedding the session ID as part of the request string. This is useful if you think your clients will turn off cookies (thereby disabling cookie-based session state tracking). Notice that the navigation URL has the session ID embedded within it.

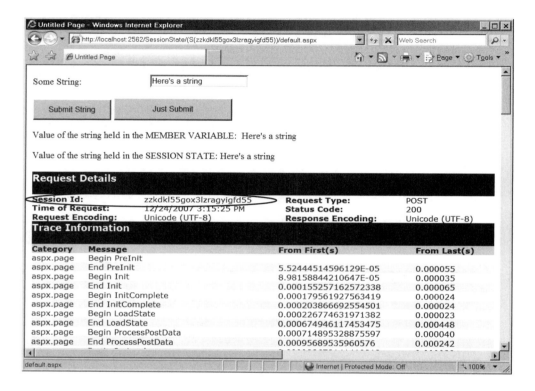

Using AutoDetect

By selecting *AutoDetect*, the ASP.NET runtime will determine if the client browser has cookies turned on. If cookies are turned on, then the session identifier is passed around as a cookie. If not, the session identifier will be stored in the URL.

Applying Device Profiles

The *UseDeviceProfile* option tells ASP.NET to determine if the browser supports cookies based on the *SupportsRedirectWithCookie* property of the *HttpBrowserCapabilities* object set up for the request. Requests that flip this bit to *true* cause session identifier values to be passed as cookies. Requests that flip this bit to *false* cause session identifiers to be passed in the URL.

Session State Timeouts

The *timeout* configuration setting manages the lifetime of the session. The lifetime of the session is the length of time in minutes a session may remain idle before ASP.NET abandons it and makes the session ID invalid. The maximum value is 525,601 minutes (one year), and the default is 20.

Other Session Configuration Settings

ASP.NET supports some other configuration settings not available through the IIS configuration utility. These are values you need to type into the web.config file directly.

If you don't like the rather obvious name of the session ID cookie made up by ASP.NET (the default is SessionID), you may change it. The *cookieName* setting lets you change that name. You might want to rename the cookie as a security measure to hamper hackers in their attempts to hijack a session ID key.

If you want to replace an expired session ID with a new one, setting the *regenerateExpiredSessionId* setting to *true* will perform that task. This is only for cookieless sessions.

If you don't like the SQL Server database already provided by ASP.NET to support session state, you may use your own database. The *allowCustomSqlDatabase* setting turns this feature on.

When using SQL Server to store session data, ASP.NET has to act as a client of SQL Server. Normally, the ASP.NET process identity is impersonated. You may instruct ASP.NET to use the user credentials supplied to the *identity* configuration element within web.config by setting the *mode* attribute to *Custom*. By setting the *mode* attribute to *SQLServer*, you tell ASP.NET to use a trusted connection.

The *stateNetworkTimeout* is for setting the number of seconds for the idle time limits of the TCP/IP network connection between the Web server and the state server, or between the SQL Server and the Web server. The default is 10.

Finally, you may instruct ASP.NET to use a custom provider by setting the name of the provider in the *custom* element. For this to work, the provider must be specified elsewhere in web.config (specifically in the *providers* element).

The *Wizard* Control: Alternative to Session State

One of the most common uses for session state is to keep track of information coming from a user even though the information is posted back via several pages. For example, scenarios such as collecting mailing addresses, applying for security credentials, or purchasing something on a Web site introduce this issue.

Sometimes gathering information is minimal and may be done through only one page. However, when collecting data from users requires several pages of forms, you need to keep track of that information between posts. For example, most commercial Web sites employ a multistage checkout process. After placing a bunch of items into your shopping cart, you click *Check Out* and the site redirects you to a checkout page. From there, you are usually required to perform several distinct steps—setting up a payment method, confirming your order, and getting an order confirmation.

While you could code something like this in ASP.NET 1.x, ASP.NET includes a *Wizard* control to deal with this sort of multistage data collection.

If you were to develop a multistage input sequence, you'd need to build in the navigation logic and keep track of the state of the transaction. The *Wizard* control provides a template that performs the basic tasks of navigating though multiple input pages while you provide the specifics. The *Wizard* control logic is built around specific steps and includes facilities for managing these steps. The *Wizard* control supports both linear and nonlinear navigation.

Using the *Wizard* control

This example shows how to use the *Wizard* control to gather several different pieces of information from the client: a name and address, what kinds of software he or she uses, and the kind of hardware he or she uses. For example, this might be used to qualify users for entry into a certain part of the Web site or perhaps to qualify them for a subscription.

1. Create a new page in the SessionState project named *UseWizard.aspx*.

2. Drop a *WizardControl* from the Toolbox onto the page.

3. When the *Wizard Tasks* window appears in the designer, click on the small arrow near the top right corner of the *Wizard*. Select **Auto Format** to style the Wizard. The example here uses the *Professional* style.

   The example here also uses a *StartNavigationTemplate* and a *SidebarTemplate* allowing you greater control over the look of these aspects of the *Wizard*. While they're not used explicitly in the example, they're shown here to illustrate how they fit into the *Wizard* control. Using these templates, you can define how these parts of the *Wizard* look by introducing controls to them. To convert these areas to templates, click on the small arrow on the upper right corner of the *Wizard* and choose **Convert To StartNavigationTemplate**. Then access the *Wizard*'s local menu again and choose **Convert To SideBarTemplate**.

Then click on the arrow again and select **Add/Remove Wizard Steps...** to show this dialog box (remove the two steps that Visual Studio inserts as default):

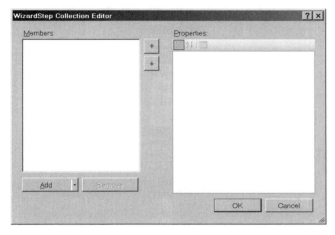

4. Add an Intro step, a Name and Address step, a Software step, a Hardware step, and a Submit information step. That is, click the **Add** button to bring up the dialog box for entering steps. "Name," "Address," "Software," "Hardware," and "Submit Information" are the *Titles* for these pages. Make sure Intro uses *StepType* of **Start**.

5. Make sure the Submit information step has its *StepType* set to **Finish**. With all of the steps in place, click **OK**.

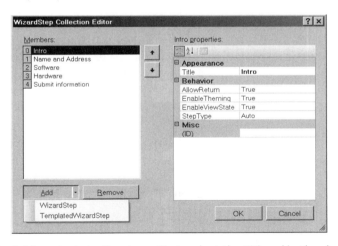

6. Add controls to the steps. First, select the *Wizard* in the designer and then choose **Set Position** from the **Format** menu. Choose **Absolute**. Now you can resize the *Wizard*. Set the *Height* to 240px and the *Width* to 650px. Now navigate to the step by selecting

the small arrow that appears on the upper right corner of the *Wizard* control. Select the *Intro* step. The *Intro* step gets a label that describes what the user is entering:

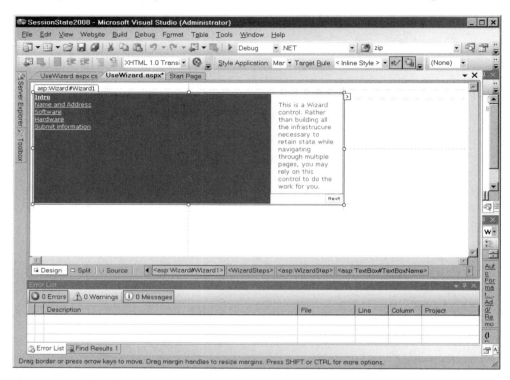

7. The *Name and Address* step should include labels and text boxes to get personal information. As you add these controls, select *Absolute* positioning for each one by selecting *Set Position* from the *Format* menu. This will let you move the elements around. Drop the name *Label* onto the pane on the right side of the *Wizard*. Below that, add the name *TextBox*. Below that, drop the address *Label* on the pane followed below by the address *TextBox*. Underneath that, add the city *Label* followed by the city *TextBox*. Drop the state and postal code *Label*s next, followed by the state and postal code *TextBox*es on that line. Be sure to give usable IDs to the text boxes. The name *TextBox* should have the ID **TextBoxName**. The address *TextBox* should have the ID **TextBoxAddress**. The city *TextBox* should have the ID **TextBoxCity**. The state *TextBox* should have the ID

TextBoxState, and the postal code *TextBox* should have the ID **TextBoxPostalCode**. You'll need them during the submission step:

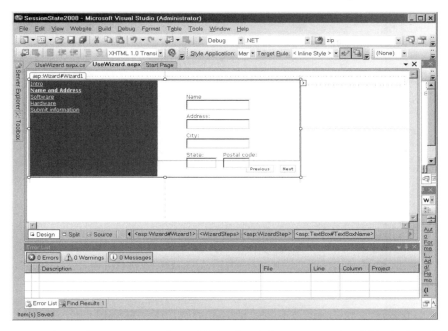

8. Select the *Software* step and modify it. The Software step should include a list of check boxes listing common software types. Add a *CheckBoxList* with the ID **CheckBoxListSoftware** and fill it with the values you see here:

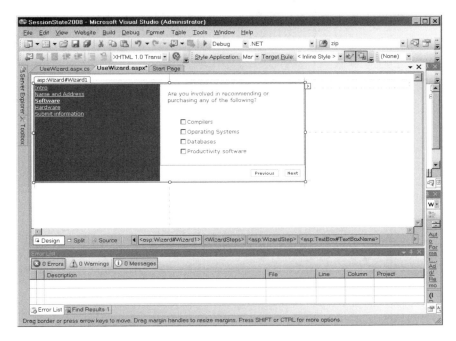

9. The *Hardware* step should include a list of check boxes listing common hardware types. Add a *CheckBoxList* with the ID **CheckBoxListHardware** and fill it with the values you see here:

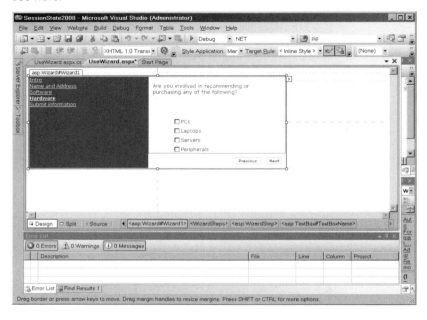

10. The *Submit Information* step (which you may use to show information before submitting) should include a multiline *TextBox* that will summarize the information collected. Give the TextBox the ID **TextBoxSummary** so you can use it to display the summary.

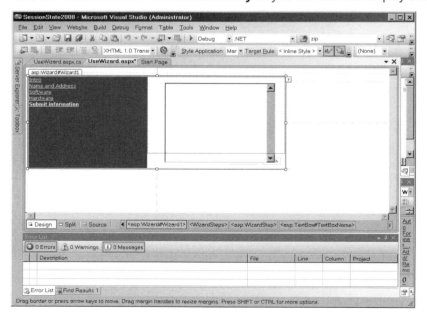

11. Finally, edit the *Page_Load* method to collect the information from each of the controls in the *Wizard*. The controls are actually available as member variables on the page. This information will be loaded every time the page is loaded. However, it will be hidden from view until the user selects the step. Double-clicking on the *Wizard* control will add a handler for the *Finish* button that you may use to harvest the information gathered via the wizard.

```
protected void Page_Load(object sender, EventArgs e)
{
    StringBuilder sb = new StringBuilder();
    sb.Append("You are about to submit. \n");

    sb.Append(" Personal: \n");
    sb.AppendFormat("  {0}\n", this.TextBoxName.Text);
    sb.AppendFormat("  {0}\n", this.TextBoxAddress.Text);
    sb.AppendFormat("  {0}\n", this.TextBoxCity.Text);
    sb.AppendFormat("  {0}\n", this.TextBoxState.Text);
    sb.AppendFormat("  {0}\n", this.TextBoxPostalCode.Text);
    sb.Append("\n Software: \n");
     foreach (ListItem listItem in CheckBoxListSoftware.Items)
     {
         if (listItem.Selected)
         {
             sb.AppendFormat("  {0}\n", listItem.Text);
         }
     }

        sb.Append("\n Hardware: \n");
    foreach (ListItem listItem in CheckBoxListHardware.Items)
    {
        if (listItem.Selected)
        {
            sb.AppendFormat("  {0}\n", listItem.Text);
        }
    }
    this.TextBoxSummary.Text = sb.ToString();}
}
protected void Wizard1_FinishButtonClick(object sender,
    WizardNavigationEventArgs e)
{
    // Do something with the data here
}
```

12. Now run the page and go through the steps. You'll see each step along the way and then finally a summary of the information collected. If the wizard on your page doesn't start with the first step (*Intro*), it's probably because you're running the page in the debugger and a wizard step other than *Intro* is selected in the designer. Simply select Intro in the designer and re-run the page.

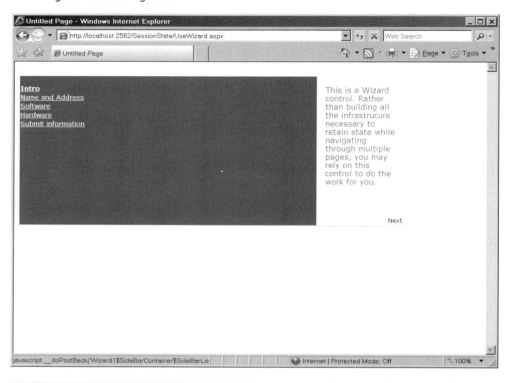

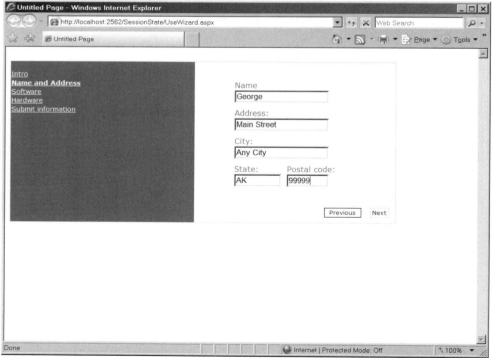

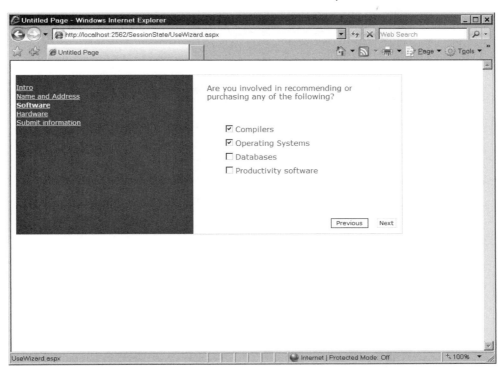

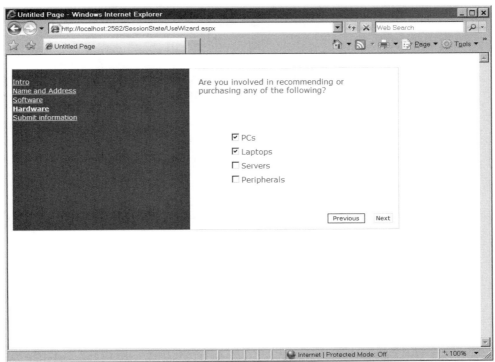

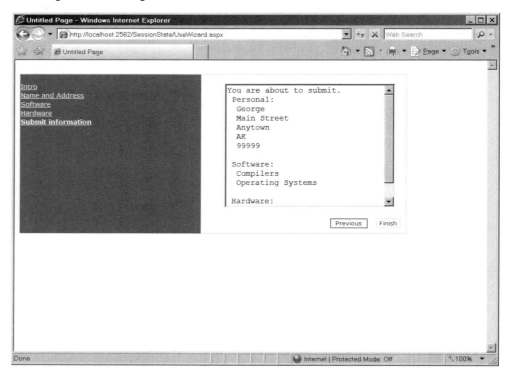

Summary

If anything distinguishes Web-based programming from other types of programming, it's probably the issue of tracking the state of any particular user. Because Web development inherently involves distributing and managing that state, it needs to be done deliberately.

Session state is one of the most important pieces of state in any application because it is associated with the particular client making the request. This is most important for applications in which you want to have the state associated with a single user available (as in the case of a shopping cart, for example).

Session state is always available through the *Page* (and through the *HttpContext*) via the *Session* object. It's a name value dictionary that holds any kind of (serializable) CLR object. Adding and retrieving information is accomplished most easily via indexers. In addition, session state may be configured in its storage location, in how it's tracked, and in how long it lasts. ASP.NET supports a number of other more advanced settings, too.

In this chapter, we also looked at the *Wizard* control as a way to retain information between several postbacks without resorting to session state. This is most useful when several kinds of related data need to be collected at once.

Chapter 14 Quick Reference

To	Do This
Access the current client's session state	Use the *Page.Session* property. Use the current context's *HttpContext.Session* property.
Access a specific value in the current client's session state	Session state is a set of key-value pairs. Access the data with the string-based key originally used to insert the data in the cache.
Store session state in proc	Edit the *sessionState* attributes in web.config. Set *mode* to *InProc*.
Store session state in a state server	Edit the *sessionState* attributes in web.config. Set *mode* to *StateServer*. Be sure to include a *stateConnectionString*.
Store session state in SQL Server	Set the *sessionState* attributes in web.config. Set *mode* to *SQLServer*. Be sure to include a *sqlConnectionString*.
Disable session state	Set the *sessionState* attributes in web.config. Set *mode* to *Off*.
Use cookies to track session state	Set the *sessionState* attributes in web.config. Set *cookieless* to *false*.
Use URL to track session state	Set the *sessionState* attributes in web.config. Set *cookieless* to *true*.
Set session state timeout	Set the *sessionState* attributes in web.config. Set *timeout* to a value (representing minutes).

Chapter 15
Application Data Caching

After completing this chapter, you will be able to

- Improve the performance of your application by using the application data cache

- Avoid unnecessary round-trips to the database

- Manage items in the application data cache

This chapter covers ASP.NET's built-in data-caching features. Caching is a long-standing means of improving the performance of any software system. The idea is to place frequently used data in quickly accessed media. Even though access times for mass storage continue to improve, accessing data from a standard hard disk is *much* slower than accessing it in memory. By taking often-used data and making it available quickly, you can improve the performance of your application dramatically.

The ASP.NET runtime includes a dictionary (key-value map) of Common Language Runtime (CLR) objects. The *Cache* lives with the application and is available via the *HttpContext* and *System.Web.UI.Page*. Using the cache is very much like using the *Session* object. You may access items in the cache using an indexer. In addition, you may control the lifetime of objects in the cache and even set up links between the cached objects and their physical data sources. Let's start by examining a case in which using the cache is justified.

Making an application that benefits from caching

1. Create a new site. Call it *UseDataCaching*. (If you prefer, you may use the project from Chapter 14 because this project uses the same database.)

2. Borrow the *UseDataList* code from the example in Chapter 14. To bring it into your new project, click the right mouse button on the project in Solution Explorer. Choose **Add Existing Item**. Navigate to the location of the code from Chapter 14. Grab the UseDataList.aspx and UseDataList.aspx.cs files from Chapter 14. Click **Add** to copy them into this new project.

   The code you imported refers to the database in the *SessionState* example. That's okay. If you want to, you can change it to the database in this application's *App_Data* directory, but it's not strictly necessary as long as the path points to an available database somewhere on your system.

3. Examine in particular the *GetInventory*, the *BindToInventory*, and the *Page_Load* methods. Listing 15-1 shows the code.

LISTING 15-1 Inventory Binding Code

```
protected DataTable CreateSelectedItemsTable(DataTable tableSchema)
{
    DataTable tableSelectedItemsData = new DataTable();

    foreach (DataColumn dc in tableSchema.Columns)
    {
        tableSelectedItemsData.Columns.Add(dc.ColumnName,
            dc.DataType);
    }
    return tableSelectedItemsData;
}

protected DataTable GetInventory()
{
    String strConnection =
    @"Provider=Microsoft.Jet.OLEDB.4.0;
    Data Source=|DataDirectory|ASPDotNetStepByStep.mdb";
    DbProviderFactory f =
        DbProviderFactories.GetFactory("System.Data.OleDb");
    DataTable dt = new DataTable();
    using (DbConnection connection = f.CreateConnection())
    {
        connection.ConnectionString = strConnection;

        connection.Open();

        DbCommand command = f.CreateCommand();
        command.CommandText = "Select * from DotNetReferences";
        command.Connection = connection;

        IDataReader reader = command.ExecuteReader();

        dt.Load(reader);
        reader.Close();
        connection.Close();
    }

    return dt;
}
protected DataTable BindToInventory()
{
    DataTable dt;
    dt = this.GetInventory();
    this.DataList1.DataSource = dt;
    this.DataBind();
    return dt;
}
protected void Page_Load(object sender, EventArgs e)
{   if (!IsPostBack)
```

```
        {
          DataTable dt = BindToInventory();
          DataTable tableSelectedItems =
             this.CreateSelectedItemsTable(dt);
             Session["tableSelectedItems"] = tableSelectedItems;
          }
      }
```

4. Run the application to make sure it works. That is, it should connect to the *DotNetReferences* table and bind the *DataList* to the table from the database.

The *GetInventory* and *BindToInventory* methods are called by the *Page_Load* method. How often is *Page_Load* called? Every time a new page is created—which happens for every single HTTP request destined for the UseDataList page. In the case of running this application on a single computer with one client (in a testing situation), perhaps connecting to the database for every request isn't a big deal. However, for applications that are expected to serve thousands of users making frequent requests, repeated database access actually becomes a very big deal. Accessing a database is actually a very expensive operation. As we'll see shortly, it may take up to a half second to simply connect to this access database and read the mere 25 rows contained in the *DotNetReferences* table. Data access can only get more expensive as the size of the tables in the database grows. A half second in the computer processing time scale is eons to the program.

Now think about the nature of the inventory table. Does it change often? Of course, not in the case of this simple application. However, think about how this might work in a real application. The items carried within an inventory may not change as often as other data sets might (and such changes might occur at regular, predictable intervals). If that's the case, why does the application need to hit the database each time a page is loaded? Doing so is certainly overkill. If you could take those data elements and store them in a medium that offers quicker access than the database (for example, the computer's internal memory), your site could potentially serve many more requests than if it had to make a round-trip to the database every time it loads a page. This is a perfect opportunity to cache the data. (The caveat here is that if the inventory data set begins fluctuating quickly, it will become a poor candidate for caching.)

Using the Data Cache

Using the data cache in the simplest and most naive way supported by ASP.NET is very much like accessing the *Session* object. Remember, accessing the *Session* object involves using an indexer (the square bracket syntax) and a consistent index to store and retrieve data. The data cache works in exactly the same way (although it has some other features for managing items in the cache).

The strategy for caching a piece of data usually involves these steps:

1. Look in the cache for the data element.

2. If it's there, use it (bypassing the expensive database round-trip).

3. If the data element is unavailable in the cache, make a round-trip to the database to fetch it.

4. If you had to fetch the data, cache the data element so it's available next time around.

The next example modifies the UseDataList page so that it stores the data item in the cache after acquiring it for the first time. Although the first time *Page_Load* is called, it may take a while (on a computer's time scale), subsequent calls are much faster.

Using the cache

1. Open the UseDataList.aspx.cs file and go to the *GetInventory* method.

2. Modifying the method to use the cache is fairly straightforward. The following listing highlights the changes. First, check to see if the item is in the cache. If searching the cache for the *DataSet* turns up a valid object reference, then you may bypass the database lookup code and return the referenced *DataSet*. If searching the cache turns up a null object reference, go ahead and make the round-trip to the database. When the database lookup finishes, you'll have a good *DataSet* (provided the query succeeds). Cache it before returning the reference to the caller. If you include the *Trace* statements, you'll be able to see exactly how big an impact caching can make. The changes you need to make are shown in bold:

```
protected DataTable GetInventory()
{
    DataTable dt = null;

    Trace.Warn("Page_Load", "looking in cache");
    dt = (DataTable)Cache["InventoryDataTable"];
    Trace.Warn("Page_Load", "done looking in cache");

    if (dt == null)
    {

        Trace.Warn("Page_Load", "Performing DB lookup");

        dt = new DataTable();

        String strConnection =
          @"Provider=Microsoft.Jet.OLEDB.4.0;
          Data Source=|DataDirectory|ASPDotNetStepByStep.mdb";

        DbProviderFactory f =
          DbProviderFactories.GetFactory("System.Data.OleDb");

        using (DbConnection connection = f.CreateConnection())
```

```
        {
            connection.ConnectionString = strConnection;

            connection.Open();

            DbCommand command = f.CreateCommand();
            command.CommandText = "Select * from DotNetReferences";
            command.Connection = connection;

            IDataReader reader = command.ExecuteReader();

            dt.Load(reader);
            reader.Close();
            connection.Close();
        }
        Cache["InventoryDataTable"] = dt;
        Trace.Warn("Page_Load", "Done performing DB lookup");

    }
    return dt;
}
```

This code reduces the cost of loading the page significantly (after the data are loaded in the cache, of course). Next time the page is loaded, it'll use the cached version—available through *Cache* at a tremendously reduced cost. How much is the cost savings? It's huge—as you can see looking at the trace pages for the application. Let's take a peek.

Impact of Caching

If you included the *Trace* statements in the *GetInventory* method, then you can surf to the trace page to see the effect of caching. The UseDataCaching application included here has the *Trace* attribute turned off in the page but has *application tracing* turned on. That is, the web.config includes the following section:

```
<configuration>
   <system.web>
   <trace enabled="true" />
   <system.web>
</configuration>
```

You can see the trace information by surfing to the virtual directory with a file name of *Trace.axd*. Instead of surfing to the UseDataList.aspx file, surf to the Trace.axd file in the same directory.

Figure 15-1 shows the trace statements produced by accessing the page for the first time. The column farthest to the right indicates the time elapsed since the previous trace statement. The trace statement shows that more than half a second has elapsed during the page loading time.

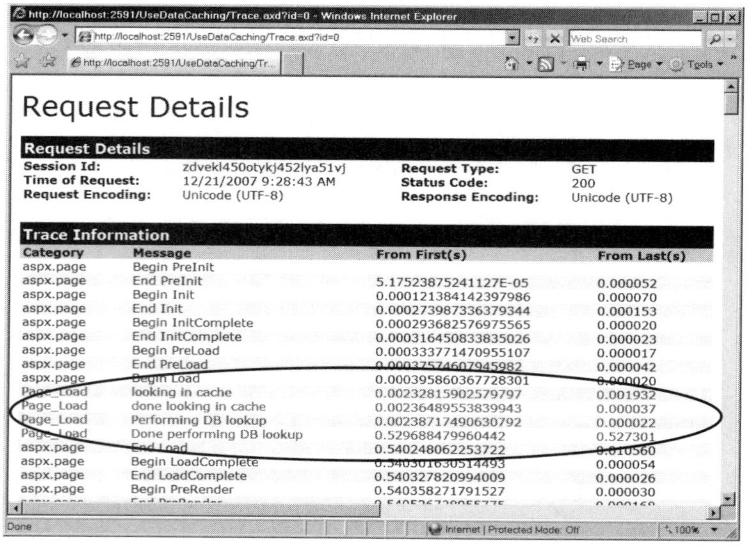

FIGURE 15-1 Hitting the database takes more than half a second in this scenario.

Make a few more posts to the page (for example, add some items from the inventory to the selected items grid). Then go back and look at the tracing information for the subsequent postbacks. Figure 15-2 shows some examples of trace statements. Fetching from the *Cache* is dramatically faster than hitting the database—by several orders of magnitude! Again, you may not notice the difference with just one client surfing the page every once in a while. However, when multiple clients are surfing to the same page simultaneously, they'll get their responses much more quickly than if the page had to make a round-trip to the database.

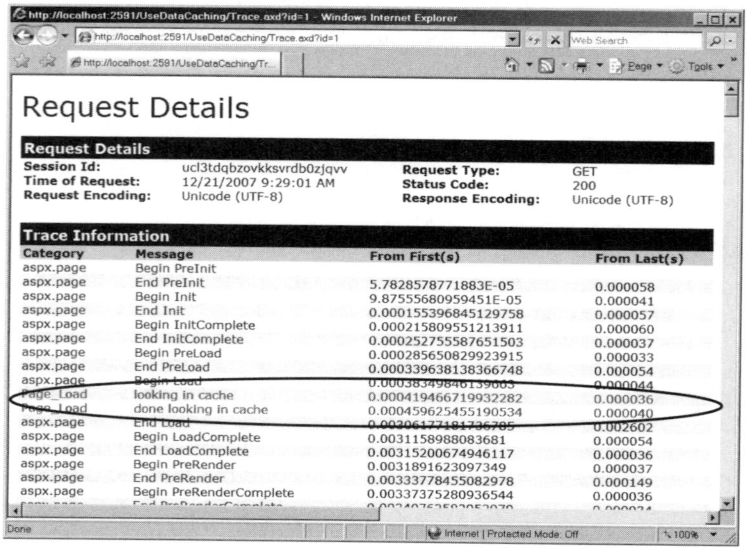

FIGURE 15-2 Fetching data from the cache takes 0.000040 seconds.

Managing the Cache

The last example cached items in the most naive way possible. They were simply placed in the cache and given an index. However, at times you may need a bit more control over the items in the cache. For example, what if the physical source backing one of the items you cache changes? If getting accurate information out to your users is important, you may want to know about the change so you can handle it (perhaps by reloading the new information into the cache). As another example, what if you knew that the data in your cache would become invalid after a certain period of time or on a certain date? You'd want to make sure that the data in the cache are invalidated and the cache is appropriately refreshed with new data.

In addition to placing items in the cache using the indexer, the *Cache* object implements a parameterized method named *Insert* that allows you control over many aspects of the cached item. The ways in which you may control cache entries include the following:

- Setting up an absolute expiration time

- Setting up a sliding expiration time

- Setting up dependencies between cached items and their backing sources (for example, database, file, or directory dependencies, or even dependencies on other cache entries)

- Managing a relative invalidation priority of cached items

- Setting up callback functions to be called when items are removed

The *Cache*'s insert method includes four overloads. Table 15-1 enumerates them.

TABLE 15-1 Overloads for the *Cache.Insert* Method

Insert Overload	Description
Insert (String, Object)	Directly corresponds to the indexer version. Blindly places the object in the Cache using the string key in the first parameter.
Insert (String, Object, CacheDependency)	Inserts an object into the Cache and associates it with a dependency.
Insert (String, Object, CacheDependency, DateTime, TimeSpan)	Inserts an object into the Cache, associating it with a dependency and an expiration policy.
Insert (String, Object, CacheDependency, DateTime, TimeSpan, CacheItemPriority, CacheItemRemovedCallback)	Inserts an object into the Cache. Associates a dependency and expiration and priority policies. Also associates the Cache entry with a delegate for a callback to notify the application when the item is removed from the cache.

The following example illustrates some of these settings and how they work. In addition, the forthcoming examples illustrate another way to get *DataTables* and *DataSets*. You may actually create them programmatically. The next few examples use a *DataTable* that is created in memory rather than being fetched from a database. Although the impact of caching isn't quite as dramatic when using the in-memory *DataTable*, it is still appreciable—and you can see this other approach to managing data. We'll also see how the *DataTable* serializes as XML as well (which will be useful for examining cached items with file dependencies).

DataSets in Memory

In Chapter 11, we looked at making a round-trip to the database to gather data suitable to bind to a control. In the previous chapter we looked at maintaining data between requests by using the *Session* object. The *Session* object holds any serializable .NET CLR object—even a *DataReader*. However, it's not a good idea to hold on to a *DataReader* for long periods of time because that means holding a connection open. Having too many open connections will ultimately slow your site to a crawl. A better approach is to make single round-trips to the database and hold on to a *DataTable* or a *DataSet*.

In addition to fetching them from databases, a *DataTable* may be synthesized program-matically (as we saw in Chapter 12). Doing so involves constructing a *DataTable* and adding *DataRows* to describe the schema. After constructing a *DataTable*, you may use it to create columns with the correct "shape," populate them, and then add them to the table's columns collection. Listing 15-2 shows an example of creating a *DataTable* in memory (note you also saw basic table creation in Listing 15-1 and in the previous chapter, but I didn't call your attention to it at the time so I could save the discussion for this section). The table is a collection of famous quotes and their originators that will be useful in the next examples.

LISTING 15-2 The *QuotesCollection* Object

```
public class QuotesCollection : DataTable
{
    public QuotesCollection()
    {

        //
        // TODO: Add constructor logic here
        //
    }

    public void Synthesize()
    {
        // Be sure to give a name so that it will serialize as XML
        this.TableName = "Quotations";
        DataRow dr;

        Columns.Add(new DataColumn("Quote", typeof(string)));
        Columns.Add(new DataColumn("OriginatorLastName",
            typeof(string)));
        Columns.Add(new DataColumn("OriginatorFirstName",
            typeof(string)));
```

```
dr = this.NewRow();
dr[0] = "Imagination is more important than knowledge.";
dr[1] = "Einstein";
dr[2] = "Albert";
Rows.Add(dr);

dr = this.NewRow();
dr[0] = "Assume a virtue, if you have it not";
dr[1] = "Shakespeare";
dr[2] = "William";
this.Rows.Add(dr);

dr = this.NewRow();
dr[0] = @"A banker is a fellow who lends you his umbrella
      when the sun is shining, but wants it back the
      minute it begins to rain.";
dr[1] = "Twain";
dr[2] = "Mark";
this.Rows.Add(dr);

dr = this.NewRow();
dr[0] = @"A man cannot be comfortable without his own
      approval.";
dr[1] = "Twain";
dr[2] = "Mark";
this.Rows.Add(dr);

dr = this.NewRow();
dr[0] = "Beware the young doctor and the old barber";
dr[1] = "Franklin";
dr[2] = "Benjamin";
this.Rows.Add(dr);

dr = this.NewRow();
dr[0] = @"Reality is merely an illusion, albeit a
          very persistent one.";
dr[1] = "Einstein";
dr[2] = "Albert";
this.Rows.Add(dr);

dr = this.NewRow();
dr[0] = "Beer has food value, but food has no beer value";
dr[1] = "Sticker";
dr[2] = "Bumper";
this.Rows.Add(dr);

dr = this.NewRow();
dr[0] = @"Research is what I'm doing when I don't know
            what I'm doing";
dr[1] = "Von Braun";
dr[2] = "Wernher";
this.Rows.Add(dr);
```

```
          dr = this.NewRow();
          dr[0] = "Whatever is begun in anger ends in shame";
          dr[1] = "Franklin";
          dr[2] = "Benjamin";
          this.Rows.Add(dr);

          dr = this.NewRow();
          dr[0] = "We think in generalities, but we live in details";
          dr[1] = "Whitehead";
          dr[2] = "Alfred North";
          this.Rows.Add(dr);

          dr = this.NewRow();
          dr[0] = "Every really new idea looks crazy at first.";
          dr[1] = "Whitehead";
          dr[2] = "Alfred North";
          this.Rows.Add(dr);

          dr = this.NewRow();
          dr[0] = @"The illiterate of the 21st century will not be
              those who cannot read and write, but
              those who cannot learn,
              unlearn, and relearn.";
          dr[1] = "Whitehead";
          dr[2] = "Alfred North";
          this.Rows.Add(dr);

      }
  }
```

Building a *DataTable* in memory is straightforward—it's mostly a matter of defining the column schema and adding rows to the table. This class is available on the CD accompanying this book, so you don't need to type the whole thing. You may just import it into the next examples.

Now let's take a look at managing items within the cache.

Cache Expirations

The first way to manage cached items is to give them expiration thresholds. In some cases, you may be aware of certain aspects of your cached data that allow you to place expiration times on it. The *Cache* supports both absolute expirations and sliding expirations.

Absolute expiration

1. To try out absolute expirations, add a new page to the UseDataCaching site named *CacheExpirations.aspx*.

2. Use the **Website**, **Add Existing Item** to bring the QuoteCollection.cs file from the CD accompanying this book and make it part of this project.

3. Drag a *GridView* onto the CacheExpirations page. Don't bind it to a data source yet. We'll handle that in the *Page_Load* method.

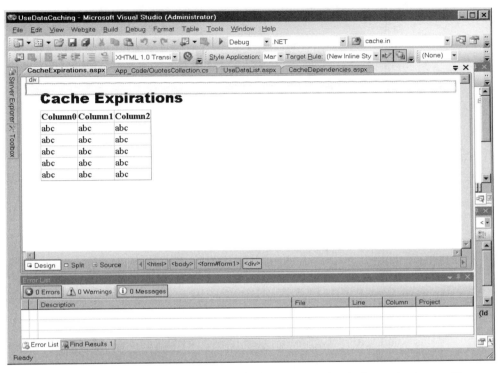

4. In the *Page_Load* method of the CacheExpirations page, check the cache to see if there's already an instance of the *QuoteCollections* object (just as in the previous example). If the data set is not available from the cache, create an instance of the *QuoteCollections* class and call the *Synthesize* method to populate the table. Finally, add it to the cache using the overloaded *Insert* method. You can use the *DataTime* class to generate an absolute expiration. Bind the *QuotesCollection* object to the *GridView*. The caching policy should be *Cache.NoSlidingExpiration*. Set up some trace statements so you may see how the expiration times affect the lifetime of the cached object.

```
protected void Page_Load(object sender, EventArgs e)
{

    QuotesCollection quotesCollection;

    DateTime dtCurrent = DateTime.Now;
    Trace.Warn("Page_Load",
      "Testing cache at: " +
      dtCurrent.ToString());
    quotesCollection = (QuotesCollection)Cache["QuotesCollection"];

    if (quotesCollection == null)
    {
```

```
            quotesCollection = new QuotesCollection();
            quotesCollection.Synthesize();

            DateTime dtExpires = new DateTime(2008, 5, 31, 23, 59, 59);
            dtCurrent = DateTime.Now;

            Trace.Warn("Page_Load",
              "Caching at: " +
              dtCurrent.ToString());
            Trace.Warn("Page_Load",
              "This entry will expire at: " +
               dtExpires);
            Cache.Insert("QuotesCollection",
                    quotesCollection,
                    null,
                    dtExpires,
                    System.Web.Caching.Cache.NoSlidingExpiration,
                    System.Web.Caching.CacheItemPriority.Default,
                    null);
        }

        this.GridView1.DataSource = quotesCollection;
        this.DataBind();

    }
```

5. Experiment with changing the dates and times to see how setting the expiration time forces a reload of the cache.

An absolute expiration time applied to the cached item tells ASP.NET to flush the item from the cache at a certain time. Now let's try using a different kind of expiration technique—the *sliding expiration*. Using a sliding expiration tells ASP.NET to keep the data in the cache as long as it has been accessed within a certain period of time. Items that have not been accessed within that time frame are subject to expiration.

Sliding expirations

1. Now try setting a sliding expiration for the cached data. Modify the *Page_Load* method in the CacheExpirations page. Getting a sliding expiration to work is simply a matter of changing the parameters of the *Insert* method. Make up a time span after which you want the cached items to expire. Pass *DateTime.MaxValue* as the absolute expiration date and the *timespan* as the final parameter like so:

```
protected void Page_Load(object sender, EventArgs e)
{
    QuotesCollection quotesCollection;

    DateTime dtCurrent = DateTime.Now;
    Trace.Warn("Page_Load",
        "Testing cache: " + dtCurrent.ToString());
```

```
    quotesCollection =
        (QuotesCollection)Cache["QuotesCollection"];

if (quotesCollection == null)
{
    quotesCollection = new QuotesCollection();
    quotesCollection.Synthesize();

    TimeSpan tsExpires = new TimeSpan(0, 0, 15);
    dtCurrent = DateTime.Now;

    Trace.Warn("Page_Load",
        "Caching at: " + dtCurrent.ToString());
    Trace.Warn("Page_Load",
        "This entry will expire in: " +
        tsExpires.ToString());
    Cache.Insert("QuotesCollection",
        quotesCollection,
            null,
            DateTime.MaxValue,
            tsExpires);
}

this.GridView1.DataSource = quotesCollection;
this.DataBind();
}
```

2. Surf to the page. You should see the cache reloading if you haven't accessed the cached item within the designated time frame.

Cache dependencies represent another way to manage cached items. Let's take a look at how they work.

Cache Dependencies

In addition to allowing objects in the cache to expire by duration, you may set up dependencies for the cached items. For example, imagine our program loads some data from a file and places them into the cache. The backing file (that is, the source of the cached information) may change, making the data in the cache invalid. ASP.NET supports setting up a dependency between the cached item and the file so that changing the file invalidates the cached item. The conditions under which the cached items may be flushed include when a file changes, a directory changes, another cache entry is removed, or data in a table in a SQL Server change (this is an often requested feature available since ASP.NET 2.0).

Here's an example that illustrates setting up cache dependencies.

Setting up cache dependencies

1. Add a new page to the UseDataCache site. Name it *CacheDependencies.aspx*.

2. Place a button on the page that you may use to post a request to the page to generate an XML file from the *QuotationsCollection*. Also, drag a *GridView* onto the page like so:

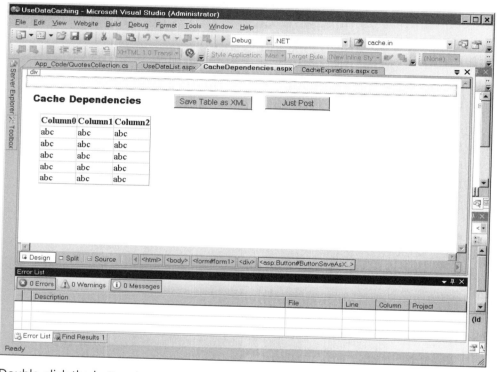

3. Double-click the button to generate a handler for the button that will save the XML Schema and the XML from the *DataTable* to .XML and .XSD files in the *App_Data* directory.

4. Within the handler, instantiate a *QuotesCollection* object and call *Synthesize* to generate the data. Within the page, you have a reference to the *Server* object. Call the *MapPath* method in the *Server* object to get the physical path for saving the file. Then use that path to create an XML file and a schema file. The *DataTable* will do this for you automatically by calling the *WriteXmlSchema* and *WriteXml* methods, respectively.

```
protected void ButtonSaveAsXML_Click(object sender, EventArgs e)
{
    QuotesCollection quotesCollection = new QuotesCollection();
    quotesCollection.Synthesize();
    String strFilePathXml =
```

```
Server.MapPath(Request.ApplicationPath +
"\\App_Data\\QuotesCollection.xml");
String strFilePathSchema =
Server.MapPath(Request.ApplicationPath +
"\\App_Data\\QuotesCollection.xsd");
quotesCollection.WriteXmlSchema(strFilePathSchema);
quotesCollection.WriteXml(strFilePathXml);
}
```

5. Now write a method to load the XML into the *QuotationsCollection* object and cache the
   data. You can use the file path to the XML file to create a dependency on the file. When
   it changes, ASP.NET will empty the cache. Turn off the absolute expiration and the sliding expiration by passing in *Cache.NoAbsoluteExpiration* and *Cache.NoSlidingExpiration*.
   If you put trace statements in, you can see the effect of updating the file after it's been
   loaded in the cache. Finally, make sure to bind the *GridView* to the *QuotationCollection*.

```
protected void CacheWithFileDependency()
{
    QuotesCollection quotesCollection;

    Trace.Warn("Page_Load", "Testing cache ");
    quotesCollection = (QuotesCollection)Cache["QuotesCollection"];

    if (quotesCollection == null)
    {
        Trace.Warn("Page_Load", "Not found in cache");
        quotesCollection = new QuotesCollection();

        String strFilePathXml =
            Server.MapPath(Request.ApplicationPath +
            "\\App_Data\\QuotesCollection.xml");
        String strFilePathSchema =
            Server.MapPath(Request.ApplicationPath +
            "\\App_Data\\QuotesCollection.xsd");

        quotesCollection.ReadXmlSchema(strFilePathSchema);
        quotesCollection.ReadXml(strFilePathXml);

        System.Web.Caching.CacheDependency cacheDependency =
                new System.Web.Caching.CacheDependency(strFilePathXml);

        Cache.Insert("QuotesCollection",
                        quotesCollection,
                        System.Web.Caching.cacheDependency,
                        System.Web.Caching.Cache.NoAbsoluteExpiration,
                        System.Web.Caching.Cache.NoSlidingExpiration,
                        CacheItemPriority.Default,
                            null);
    }

    this.GridView1.DataSource = quotesCollection;
    this.DataBind();
}
```

6. Call the *CacheWithFileDependency()* within the Page_Load method.

```
protected void Page_Load(object sender, EventArgs e)
{
    if (!IsPostBack)
    {
        ButtonSaveAsXML_Click(null, null);
    }
    CacheWithFileDependency();
}
```

7. Now run the page. It should load the XML and schema into the *QuotesCollection*, save the *QuotesCollection* in the cache, and then show the data in the grid. Clicking the **Save Table as XML** button will refresh the XML file (on which a cache dependency was made). Because the file on the disk changes, ASP.NET will flush the cache. Next time you load the page, the cache will need to be reloaded.

Now let's look at the final cache dependency: the SQL Server dependency.

The SQL Server Dependency

ASP.NET 1.0 had a huge gap in its cache dependency functionality. The most useful type of dependency was completely missing—that is, a dependency between a cached item coming from SQL Server and the physical database. Because so many sites use data provided by SQL Server to back their *DataGrids* and other controls, establishing this dependency is definitely a most useful way to manage cached data.

For the SQL Server dependency to work, you first configure SQL Server using the program aspnet_regsql.exe. The dependency is described in the configuration file, whose name is passed into the *SqlCacheDependency* constructor. The *SqlCacheDependency* class monitors the table. When something causes the table to change, ASP.NET will remove the item from the *Cache*.

Listing 15-3 shows a configuration file with a dependency on SQL Server. Listing 15-4 shows an ASP.NET page that loads the data from the SQL Server database and establishes a dependency between the database and the cached item.

LISTING 15-3 Configuration Settings for SQL Server Cache Dependency

```
<caching>
 <sqlCacheDependency enabled="true" >
   <databases >
      <add name="DBName" pollTime="500"
          connectionStringName="connectionString"/>
   </databases>
 </sqlCacheDependency>
</caching>
```

LISTING 15-4 Page Using *SqlCacheDependency*

```csharp
<%@ Page Language="C#" %>
<script runat="server">
    protected void Page_Load(Object sender, EventArgs e)
    {
        DataSet ds = null;
        ds = (DataSet)Cache["SomeData"];
        if (ds == null)
        {
            string cconnectionString =
                ConfigurationSettings.ConnectionStrings["connectionString"].
                    ConnectionString;
            SqlDataAdapter da =
                new SqlDataAdapter("select * from DBName.tableName",
                connectionString);
            ds = new DataSet();
            da.Fill(ds);
            SqlCacheDependency sqlCacheDependency =
                new SqlCacheDependency("DBName", "tableName");
            Cache.Insert("SomeData",
                            ds,
                            sqlCacheDependency);
        }
        GridView1.DataSource = ds;
        DataBind();
    }
</script>
<html><body>
    <form id="form1" runat="server">
        <asp:GridView ID="GridView1" Runat="server">
        </asp:GridView>
    </form>
</body></html>
```

Once items are in the cache and their lifetimes are established through expirations and cached item dependencies, one other cache administrative task remains—reacting when items are removed.

Clearing the Cache

As you can see from the previous examples, ASP.NET clears the cache on several occasions, including:

- removing items explicitly by calling *Cache.Remove*
- removing low-priority items due to memory consumption
- removing items that have expired

One of the parameters to one of the *Insert* overloaded methods is a callback delegate so that ASP.NET can tell you that something's been removed from the cache. To receive callbacks, you simply need to implement a method that matches the signature, wrap it in a delegate, and then pass it when calling the *Insert* method. When the object is removed, ASP.NET will call the method you supply.

The next example illustrates setting up a removal callback function.

Removal callback

1. One of the main tricks to getting the removal callback to work is finding an appropriate place to put the callback. What happens if you make the callback a normal instance member of your *Page* class? It won't work. The callback will become disconnected after the first page has come and gone. The callback has to live in a place that sticks around. (You could make the callback a static method, however.) The perfect class for establishing the callback is in the global application class. We'll see the application class and its services in more detail in Chapter 18. For now, add a global application class to your application. Select **Website**, **Add New Item**. Select the *Global Application Class* template and click **Add** to insert it into the project. Visual Studio will add a new file named *Global.asax* to your application.

2. Global.asax will include a server-side script block. Write a method to handle the callback within the Global.asax file. In this case, the response will be to set a flag indicating the cache is dirty. Then the code will simply place the data back into the cache during the *Application_BeginRequest* handler. The code for doing so will look very much like the code in the *CacheWithFileDependency* method shown earlier. You can get a reference to the cache through the current *HttpContext*.

```
<%@ Application Language="C#" %>

<script runat="server">

    bool  _bReloadQuotations = false;

    public void OnRemoveQuotesCollection(string key, object val,
        CacheItemRemovedReason r)
    {
        // Do something about the dependency Change
        if (r == CacheItemRemovedReason.DependencyChanged)
        {
            _bReloadQuotations = true;
        }
    }

    protected void Application_BeginRequest(object sender, EventArgs e)
    {
        if (_bReloadQuotations == true)
        {
            ReloadQuotations();
            _bReloadQuotations = false;
        }
    }
```

```
     protected void ReloadQuotations()
     {
         QuotesCollection quotesCollection = new QuotesCollection();

         String strFilePathXml =
             Server.MapPath(HttpContext.Current.Request.ApplicationPath +
             "\\App_Data\\QuotesCollection.xml");
         String strFilePathSchema =
             Server.MapPath(HttpContext.Current.Request.ApplicationPath +
             "\\App_Data\\QuotesCollection.xsd");

         quotesCollection.ReadXmlSchema(strFilePathSchema);
         quotesCollection.ReadXml(strFilePathXml);

         System.Web.Caching.CacheDependency
             cacheDependency =
             new System.Web.Caching.CacheDependency(strFilePathXml);

         HttpContext.Current.Cache.Insert("QuotesCollection",
             quotesCollection,
             cacheDependency,
             System.Web.Caching.Cache.NoAbsoluteExpiration,
             System.Web.Caching.Cache.NoSlidingExpiration,
             System.Web.Caching.CacheItemPriority.Default,

             this.OnRemoveQuotesCollection);
     }

</script>
```

3. Update the *CacheWithFileDependency* method to use the callback method when establishing the *QuotesServer* in the cache. You may access the callback method through the page's *Application* member.

```
protected void CacheWithFileDependency()
{
   QuotesCollection quotesCollection;

   Trace.Warn("Page_Load", "Testing cache ");
   quotesCollection = (QuotesCollection)Cache["QuotesCollection"];

   if (quotesCollection == null)
   {
      Trace.Warn("Page_Load", "Not found in cache");
      quotesCollection = new QuotesCollection();

      String strFilePathXml =
            Server.MapPath(Request.ApplicationPath +
            "\\App_Data\\QuotesCollection.xml");
      String strFilePathSchema =
            Server.MapPath(Request.ApplicationPath +
            "\\App_Data\\QuotesCollection.xsd");

      quotesCollection.ReadXmlSchema(strFilePathSchema);
      quotesCollection.ReadXml(strFilePathXml);
```

```
            System.Web.Caching.CacheDependency cacheDependency =
                new System.Web.Caching.CacheDependency(strFilePathXml);

        Cache.Insert("QuotesCollection",
            quotesCollection,
            cacheDependency,
            System.Web.Caching.Cache.NoAbsoluteExpiration,
            System.Web.Caching.Cache.NoSlidingExpiration,
            System.Web.Caching.CacheItemPriority.Default,
            this.ApplicationInstance.OnRemoveQuotesCollection);
    }

    this.GridView1.DataSource = quotesCollection;
    this.DataBind();
}
```

When you surf to the page, you should never see the *Page_Load* method refreshing the cache. That's because when the XML file is overwritten, ASP.NET immediately calls the *ReloadQuotations* method—which loads the cache again.

Summary

Caching is one of the easiest and most well-understood ways of wringing better performance out of an application. ASP.NET implements an easy-to-use application data cache. The application data cache stores any serializable CLR object and is available at any time while processing a request. You can dig it out of the current context (the *HttpContext*), and it's also available as a member variable of *System.Web.UI.Page*.

Probably the most common way to use the cache is to store database query results to avoid round-trips to a database. Accessing memory is often orders of magnitude faster than hitting the database. In addition, you sidestep issues such as limited connection resources and database contention.

Although you can effectively improve the performance of your application by simply putting items in the cache, ASP.NET's caching mechanism provides facilities for putting limits on the amount of time items remain cached. You may also set up dependencies between cached items and their physical data sources so that you may be alerted when items need to be reloaded into the cache.

Chapter 15 Quick Reference

To	Do This
Access the data cache	The data cache is available as ■ the *Cache* property in the page ■ the *Cache* property in the current *HttpContext*.
Insert an item in the cache	Use the indexer notation to add an object and a value to the cache.
Insert an item in the cache with a dependency	Create a *CacheDependency* object and add the object to the cache using the overloaded *Cache.Insert* method.
Insert an item in the cache with an expiration time	Create a *DateTime* object and add the object to the cache using the overloaded *Cache.Insert* method.
Delete an item from the cache	Call the cache's *Cache.Remove* method.
Be notified that an item is being removed from the cache	Include a callback delegate when inserting an item in the cache.

Chapter 16
Caching Output

After completing this chapter, you will be able to

- Cache page content
- Improve the performance of Web applications by using output caching
- Manage the cached content through the *OutputCache* directive
- Manage the cached content through the *HttpCachePolicy* class

This chapter covers ASP.NET's support for caching output. In Chapter 15, we saw what an impact data caching could make on your application. By avoiding round-trips to the database, you can make parts of your Web site run much faster than they otherwise would. In addition to data caching, however, ASP.NET supports *output caching*.

After spending a bit of time watching the entire page-rendering process, you now know it can be pretty involved. A lot happens between the time a page loads and the time when the final closing tag is sent to the browser. For example, the page may require database access. It may have a number of controls declared on it. Furthermore, perhaps some of those controls are the more complex controls like the *DataList* or the *GridView* whose rendering process is expensive. All of these things usually take time to process.

Just as you can bypass recurring round-trips to a database by caching data in memory, you may configure ASP.NET to bypass the entire page-rendering process and send back content that's already been rendered once. This is called *output caching*.

Caching Page Content

As you surf the Web, you see all manner of pages. Some sites churn their content very quickly, whereas others change much more slowly. Some pages have portions that change while other portions of the page remain static. If you have a page whose content changes infrequently, you may cache the output instead of regenerating it every time a request comes in.

At the outset, turning on output caching is easy. To set up caching, place the *OutputCache* directive on the page. It's a separate directive, like the *Page* directive. The *OutputCache* directive enables caching and provides certain control over its behavior. The following exercise introduces caching output.

Create a cacheable page

1. Create a new Web site named *OutputCaching*.

2. Open the Default.aspx file and insert the *OutputCache* directive near the top, immediately after the *Page* directive. For now, set the *Trace* attribute to false (we'll turn it on later when we look at caching User controls). At the very least, the *OutputCache* directive needs two things: (1) the *Duration* attribute to be set and (2) the *VaryByParam* attribute set to *none*. We'll see more about these attributes shortly. The *Duration* attribute specifies how long the content should be cached. The *VaryByParam* attribute is for managing the caching multiple versions of the page. The following code shows the syntax of the *OutputCache* directive. This example caches the page's content for 15 seconds. The code following the output directive was generated by Visual Studio.

```
<%@ Page Language="C#" AutoEventWireup="true"
CodeFile="Default.aspx.cs" Inherits="_Default" trace="false"%>
<%@ OutputCache Duration="15" VaryByParam="none" %>

<!DOCTYPE html PUBLIC
"...">

<html xmlns="http://www.w3.org/1999/xhtml" >
<head runat="server">
    <title>Untitled Page</title>
</head>
<body>
    <form id="form1" runat="server">
    <div>
    </div>
    </form>
</body>
</html>
```

3. Update the *Page_Load* method to print the date and time that this page was generated, like so:

```
public partial class _Default : System.Web.UI.Page
{
    protected void Page_Load(object sender, EventArgs e)
    {
        Response.Write("This page was generated and cached at: " +
            DateTime.Now.ToString());
    }
}
```

The first time the content is produced, the *Page_Load* method runs and produces the following output:

No matter now many times you refresh the browser (you may do this by pressing **F5** while running Internet Explorer within 15 seconds of first accessing the page), ASP.NET will grab the cached content and display that. As soon as 15 seconds has expired, ASP.NET runs the page in the normal way, calling *Page_Load*, regenerating the content, and caching it again. The following graphic illustrates the new page accessed just moments (no later than 15 seconds) following the first hit. The date and time are the same as the previous page, even though it's a completely new request (I promise these are two separate requests):

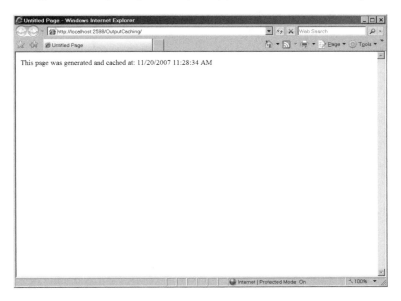

4. To get an idea as to how caching content might improve performance, add a small amount of code to the *Page_Load* method to put the executing thread to sleep for perhaps 10 seconds (this is to simulate an expensive content-generating routine). You'll need to use the *System.Threading* namespace to access the threading functions.

```
using System;
using System.Data;
using System.Configuration;
using System.Web;
using System.Web.Security;
using System.Web.UI;
using System.Web.UI.WebControls;
using System.Web.UI.WebControls.WebParts;
using System.Web.UI.HtmlControls;
using System.Threading;

public partial class _Default : System.Web.UI.Page
{
    protected void Page_Load(object sender, EventArgs e)
    {
      Thread.Sleep(10000);
      Response.Write("This page was generated and cached at: " +
          DateTime.Now.ToString());
    }
}
```

5. Now surf to the page. Notice how long the page took to load (about 10 seconds). Immediately refresh the page. Notice the browser displays the content right away—without the long wait time. Most pages don't take quite as long to load, but you get the idea of how caching content might improve the performance of your Web application. For pages that are expensive to generate and that don't change very often, caching the content represents an enormous performance boost for your Web site—especially as the number of clients increases.

Managing Cached Content

In some cases, it's enough to blindly cache the content of certain pages by simply putting the *OutputCache* directive in the page. However, sometimes you need a bit more control over what's happening in the output cache. ASP.NET supports a number of parameters you may use to manage the way the cache functions. You may control the output caching behavior by either changing the parameters in the *OutputCache* directive or tweaking the *HttpCachePolicy* property available through the *Response* object.

Modifying the *OutputCache* Directive

It's often very useful to be able to govern output caching. For example, some pages present exactly the same content to all the users who access the page. In that case, caching a single version of the content is just fine. However, there are other circumstances in which sending the same content to everyone is inappropriate. The easiest way to control the behavior of output caching is to modify the *OutputCache* directive.

One obvious case in which controlling the cache is important is while caching different versions of content for different browsers making requests. Different browsers often have different capabilities. If you send content that requires a feature not supported by all browsers, some browsers making requests will get a response that they're unable to adequately handle. The *VaryByCustom* parameter within the *OutputCache* directive allows you to cache different content based on different browsers.

Controlling the output caching is also important when your page renders content based on the parameters that are sent within the query string. For example, imagine you have a page through which a user has identified him- or herself by typing a name in a text box. The browser will insert that name inside a parameter inside the query list. You may instruct the output cache to cache different versions based on parameters in the query string. For example, users who identify themselves as "John Doe" can get a different version of cached content than users who identify themselves as "Jane Smith." The *VaryByParam* attribute controls this behavior.

Table 16-1 shows a summary of these parameters.

TABLE 16-1 Summary of *OutputCache* Parameters

Attribute	Option	Description
CacheProfile	A *string*	Name of a profile (found in web.config) to control output cache settings. Default is empty string.
Duration	number	Number of seconds the page or control is cached (required)
NoStore	*true* *false*	Specifies that the "no store" cache control header is sent (or not). Not available to User controls. Default value is *false*.
Location	*Any* *Client* *Downstream* *Server* *None*	Manages which header and metatags are sent to clients to support caching; here are their meanings: *Any*—page may be cached anywhere (default) *Client*—cached content remains at browser *Downstream*—cached content stored both downstream and on the client *Server*—content cached on the server only *None*—disables caching

Continued

TABLE 16-1   Continued

Attribute	Option	Description
Shared	*true* *false*	Determines whether User control output can be shared with multiple pages.
SqlDependency	A string representing a database/table name pair	Identifies a set of database and table name pairs on which a page or control's output cache depends
VaryByContentEncoding	encodings	Specifies a list of encoding strings separated by commas used to vary the output cache
VaryByCustom	browser custom string	Tells ASP.NET to vary the output cache by browser name and version, or by a custom string; must be handled by an override of *GetVaryByCustomString* in Global.asax.
VaryByHeader	* header names	A semicolon-delimited list of strings specifying headers that might be submitted by a client. Not available to User controls. Default value is empty string (no headers).
VaryByParam	*None* * param name	A semicolon-delimited list of strings specifies query string values in a GET request or variables in a POST request (required).

The following exercise illustrates creating separate versions of cached content based on how the user identifies himself or herself.

Varying cached content by query string parameters

1. Returning to the OutputCache Web application, add a *TextBox* and a *Button* to the default.aspx page. Give the *TextBox* an ID of **TextBoxName** and the *Button* an ID of **ButtonSubmitName**. This will hold the client's name and will serve as the parameter controlling the number of cached versions of the page.

2. Double-click on the button to add a *Click* event handler. In the handler, respond to the user's request by displaying a greeting using the contents of the text box. Also, modify the processing time of the page loading by reducing the amount of time the current thread sleeps (or by removing that line completely):

```
public partial class _Default : System.Web.UI.Page
{
    protected void Page_Load(object sender, EventArgs e)
    {
        Thread.Sleep(0);
        Response.Write("This page was generated and cached at: " +
            DateTime.Now.ToString());
```

```
    }
    protected void ButtonSubmitName_Click(object sender, EventArgs e)
    {
        Response.Write("<br><br>");
        Response.Write("<h2> Hello there, " +
        this.TextBoxName.Text + "</h2>");
    }
}
```

3. Increase the time that the content will be cached (this example uses 1 minute). That will give you time to change the contents of the *TextBox* to view the effects of caching. Also, include *TextBoxName* as the parameter by which to vary the content within the *OutputCache* directive.

```
<%@ Page Language="C#" AutoEventWireup="true"
CodeFile="Default.aspx.cs" Inherits="_Default"
trace="false"%>

<%@ OutputCache Duration="60" VaryByParam="TextBoxName" %>
```

4. Add a *Substitution* control to the page following the *TextBox* and the *Button*. You can just drag one from the Toolbox and drop it onto the page. You'll use the *Substitution* control to display the time of the request to compare it with the time displayed by the cached page. *Substitution* controls call back to a method on the code-beside that displays arbitrary strings. Write a method in the code-beside class to handle the substitution.

```
public partial class _Default : System.Web.UI.Page
{
    // Existing code...
    protected static string SubstituteDateAndTime(HttpContext c)
    {
        return "Request occurred at :" + DateTime.Now;
    }
}
```

5. Set the *MethodName* attribute of the *Substitution* control to the *SubstituteDateAndTime* method within the aspx file, like this:

```
<asp:Substitution MethodName="SubstituteDateAndTime"
  runat="server" />
```

6. Surf to the page and type in a name. Click the button to submit the form and note the time stamp of the page. Type a second name into the *TextBox* and click the button to submit the form. Note the time stamp. Then type the same name you typed the first time. Click the button to submit the form. If you do all this within the 60-second window, you should see the cached versions of the page, which you can discern using the time stamp displayed as part of each page. The following three graphics illustrate the caching varying by the value of the *TextBoxName* parameter. The first graphic shows the original request using a particular name in the *TextBox*. Notice that the request time shown by the *Substitution* and the time shown by the *Page_Load* method are the same.

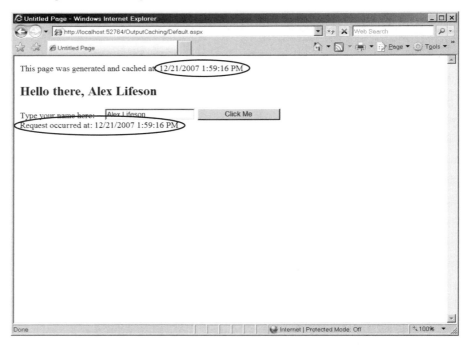

The second graphic shows a request with a new value for the *TextBoxName* parameter. Notice that the request time shown by the *Substitution* and the time shown by the *Page_Load* method are the same this time, as well.

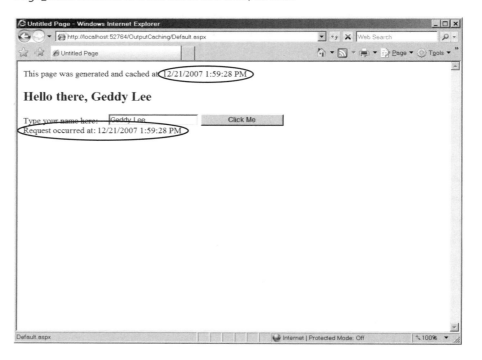

The third graphic shows making a request to the page using the same name as the original request. Notice that the request time shown by the *Substitution* and the time shown by the *Page_Load* method are different. The request time is earlier than the time shown during the *Page_Load* method, meaning the page content was cached.

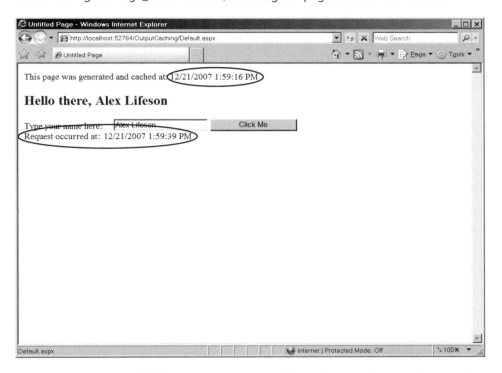

There are other ways to modify the *VaryByParam* attribute. One way is to use the word "none," which means ASP.NET will cache only one version of the page for each type of request (for example, GET, POST, and HEAD). Using an asterisk for *VaryByParam* ("*") tells ASP.NET to cache as many different versions of the page as there are query string or POST body requests. The previous example caches as many different versions of the page as there are unique names typed by users into the name text box.

Using *VaryByHeader* in the *OutputCache* directive tells ASP.NET to generate a separate cache entry for each new header string that comes down (for example, *UserAgent* and *UserLanguage* represent HTTP headers that may be sent by the client).

We'll cache a User control shortly. The *VaryByControl* attribute lets you cache separate content versions for each page that has a User control with unique properties.

Finally, *VaryByCustom* tells ASP.NET to manage separate cache entries dependent on a couple of factors. The first factor is the browser types and versions. Alternatively, you may provide a custom *GetVaryByCustomString* method in Global.asax that tells ASP.NET to create separate cached versions of a page based on a custom defined string.

The *HttpCachePolicy*

The second way to manage the output cache is through the *HttpCachePolicy*, which is available from the *Response* class. Table 16-2 shows a portion of the *HttpCachePolicy* class.

TABLE 16-2 The *HttpCachePolicy* Class

Member	Description
AppendCacheExtension	Appends specified text to the Cache-Control HTTP header
SetCacheability	Sets the Cache-Control HTTP header which controls how documents are to be cached on the network
SetETag	Sets the ETag HTTP header to the specified string
SetExpires	Sets the Expires HTTP header to an absolute date and time
SetLastModified	Sets the Last-Modified HTTP header to a specific date and time
SetMaxAge	Sets the Cache-Control: max-age HTTP header to a specific duration
SetRevalidation	Sets the Cache-Control HTTP header to either the must-revalidate or the proxy-revalidate directives
SetValidUntilExpires	Determines whether the ASP.NET cache should ignore HTTP Cache-Control headers sent by the client for invalidating the cache.
SetVaryByCustom	Specifies a custom text string for managing varying cached output responses
VaryByHeaders	Parameter list of all HTTP headers that will be used to vary cache output.
VaryByParam	Parameter list received by a GET (query string) or POST (in the body of the HTTP request) that affect caching

When you set up an *OutputCache* directive, you tell ASP.NET to populate this class during the *Page* class's *InitOutputCache* method. The *Response* object makes the *HttpCachePolicy* available through its *Cache* property. The name *Cache* is unfortunate because you might easily confuse it with the application data cache. Perhaps *CachePolicy* would have been a better name for the property to avoid such confusion. In any case, you can use the *HttpCachePolicy* class to control the behavior of the server-side output caching as well as the headers used for content caching. The *OutputCache* directive may also be used to control some of the same aspects as the *HttpCachePolicy* class. However, some features, such as sliding the expiration date or changing the "last modified" stamp for a page, are available only through the *HttpCachePolicy* class.

For example, Listing 16-1 shows a page fragment ensuring that all origin-server caching for the current response is stopped. It also sets the last modified date to the current date and time.

LISTING 16-1 Manipulating the Output Cache Policy

```
public partial class _Default : System.Web.UI.Page
{
    protected void Page_Load(object sender, EventArgs e)
```

```
    {
      Thread.Sleep(0);
      Response.Write("This page was generated and cached at: " +
          DateTime.Now.ToString());

      Response.Cache.SetNoServerCaching();
      Response.Cache.SetLastModified(DateTime.Now);
    }
  }
```

Caching Locations

In addition to varying the number of cached versions of a page, you may tell ASP.NET where to cache the content. This is controlled through either the *Location* attribute in the *OutputCache* directive or by using the *HttpCachePolicy* class's *SetCacheability* method.

ASP.NET supports several output caching locations for which you can specify using the *OutputCache* directive:

- **Any**   Page can be cached by the browser, a downstream server, or on the server
- **Client**   Page should be cached on the client browser only
- **Downstream**   Page should be cached on a downstream server and the client
- **Server**   Page will be cached on the server only
- **None**   Disable caching

The *HttpCachePolicy* also allows you to determine the location of the cached content programmatically. This is done through the *HttpCachePolicy.SetCacheability* method (or the *HttpResponse.CacheControl* property), which takes a parameter of the *HttpCacheability* enumeration. The enumeration is a bit easier to read than the attributes used in the *OutputCache* directive. They include:

- **NoCache**   Disable caching
- **Private**   Only cache on the client
- **Public**   Cache on the client *and* the shared proxy
- **Server**   Cache on the server
- **ServerAndNoCache**   Specify that the content is cached at the server but all others are explicitly denied the ability to cache the response
- **ServerAndPrivate**   Specify that the response is cached at the server and at the client but nowhere else; proxy servers are not allowed to cache the response

Output Cache Dependencies

We saw how ASP.NET supports data caching in Chapter 15. The contents of the application data cache in ASP.NET may be flushed due to various dependencies. The same is true of ASP.NET output caching. The response object has a number of methods for setting up dependencies based on cached content. For example, you may want to set up a page that renders data from a text file. You can set up a *CacheDependency* on that text file so that when the text file is changed, the cached output is invalidated and reloaded.

Caching Profiles

One of the problems associated with using the *OutputCache* directive directly is that the values become hard-coded. Changing the caching behavior means going in and changing the source code of the page. A feature added to ASP.NET 2.0 and later versions is the ability to add caching profiles. That way, setting the caching behavior variables is offloaded to the configuration file, and output caching becomes an administration issue and not a programming issue (as it should be).

The web.config file may include an *outputCacheSettings* section that may contain a list of *outputCacheProfiles*. The *outputCacheProfiles* are simply key-value pairs whose keys are the output caching variables (such as *Duration*). When you mention the profile name in the *OutputCache* directive, ASP.NET will simply read the values out of the configuration file and apply them to the *OutputCache* directive.

The following exercise illustrates setting up a cache profile instead of hard-coding the values into the page.

Set up a cache profile

1. Add a cache profile to the site's web.config file. If web.config isn't already there, go ahead and add one to the project. Then add a cache profile to web.config nested between the system.web opening and closing tags. Name the cache profile *profile*.

```
<configuration>
  <system.web>
    <caching>
      <outputCacheSettings>
        <outputCacheProfiles>
          <add name="profile"
            duration="60"
            varyByParam="TextBoxName" />
        </outputCacheProfiles>
      </outputCacheSettings>
    </caching>
  </system.web>
</configuration>
```

2. Change the *OutputCache* directive in the Default.aspx page to use the new profile:

```
<%@ Page Language="C#" AutoEventWireup="true"
CodeFile="Default.aspx.cs" Inherits="_Default"
trace="false"%>

<%@ OutputCache CacheProfile="profile" %>
```

3. Surf to the page. It should work exactly as it did before when the caching values were hard-coded. That is, run the page, type a name, and note the date and time stamp. Type a new name and note the date and time stamp. Type the original name, submit it, and you should see the original cached page appear (as long as you complete the post within the specified time window).

Caching User Controls

Just as whole pages may be cached, ASP.NET supports caching User controls as well. Imagine your job is to create a sizable Web site that allows users to navigate through information via various navigation controls (menus, hyperlinks, and so forth). For example, imagine a part of your page shows links or other navigation controls that lead users to the most recent news, summary information, and other places. The actual content may change, but the links probably don't. If the links don't change very often and the cost of generating that section of the page is expensive, it makes sense to move the functionality into a User control and apply the *OutputCache* directive to the User control. Doing so will cause ASP.NET to cache the portion of the page represented by the control.

The *OutputDirective* may be applied to the ASCX file that comprises a User control. The *OutputDirective* for a User control may also use the *Shared* property to tell ASP.NET to cache one version of the control for all pages that use it, resulting in potentially even higher performance over the span of many hits (the default is *false*).

The following exercise illustrates caching the output of a User control.

User controls and output caching

1. Create a simple User control for the OutputCaching project. Navigation controls are perfect for caching, so create a control that has a menu. Name the control *SiteMenu.ascx*. Drag a *Menu* control onto the User control, as shown here:

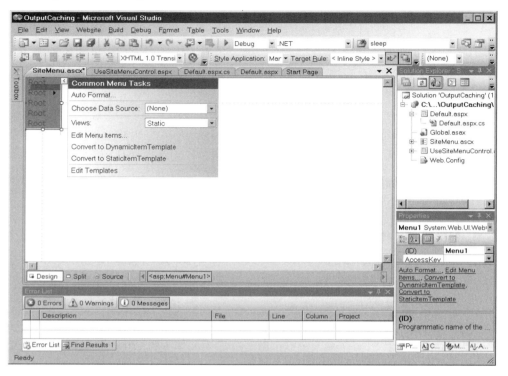

Add some menu items, as shown in this graphic:

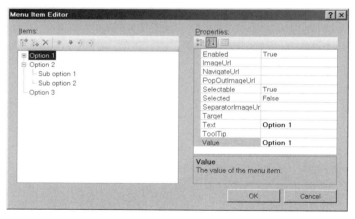

2. Add the *OutputCache* directive with the following parameters in the control source, like so:

```
<%@ Control Language="C#" AutoEventWireup="true"
CodeFile="SiteMenu.ascx.cs" Inherits="SiteMenu" %>
<%@ OutputCache Duration="60" VaryByParam="none" %>
```

3. Create a new page in the project. Name it *UseSiteMenuControl.aspx*.

4. Drag the *SiteMenu* User control onto the UseSiteMenuControl page. When ASP.NET loads and runs your Web page, ASP.NET will cache the User control because the User control mentions the *OutputDirective*.

5. Make sure tracing is turned on in the UseSiteMenuControl.aspx file. (That is, set the *Trace="true"* attribute in the *Page* directive.) Surf to the page. The first time you surf to the page, you'll see the following information in the control tree section of the *Trace* output:

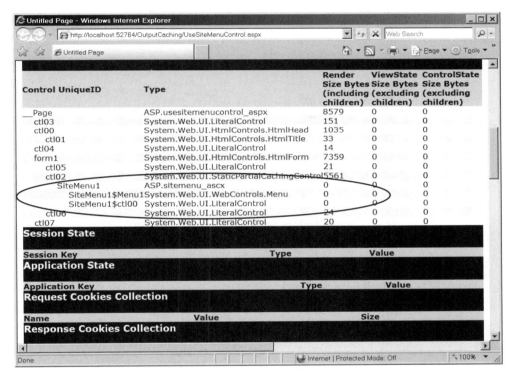

Notice the entire control tree was rendered. Push the refresh key (**F5** in Internet Explorer) while looking at UseSiteMenuControl.aspx. Examine the control tree portion of the *Trace* output again. Notice that ASP.NET uses the cached control instead of re-rendering the entire *SiteMenu* control.

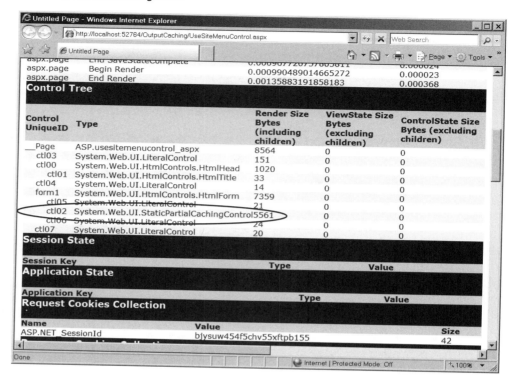

When Output Caching Makes Sense

As with other caching techniques, one of the most effective strategies is to turn on output caching for those pages that are accessed frequently but yet are expensive to generate. Also, be sure to cache only those pages that don't change frequently (otherwise, you may be better off simply *not* using output caching).

For example, pages full of controls that render a great deal of HTML are probably expensive. Imagine a page including a *DataGrid* displaying an employee directory. This is a perfect candidate for caching for several reasons. First, a database access (or even an in-memory cache hit) is required. Second, a *DataGrid* is pretty expensive to render—especially if it needs to figure out the schema of the employee directory table on the fly. Finally, an employee directory probably doesn't change very often. By caching it once, you can avoid spending a great deal of unnecessary cycles.

A related issue here is to be careful when typing asterisks into the output caching parameters such as *VaryByParam*. Using *VaryByParam=** tells ASP.NET to generate a new page for every single request in which *any* query string parameter has changed. That's almost the same as *not* caching altogether—with the added cost of the memory consumed by the output cache. However, this may make sense for Web sites with limited audiences where the parameter variance between requests remains limited.

In addition, be wary of how caching might affect the appearance of your page on different browsers. Much of the time, content will appear the same regardless of the browser. However, if you cache some content that depends on a specific browser feature (such as Dynamic HTML), clients whose browsers don't understand the feature may see some very weird behavior in the browser.

Tuning the behavior of the output cache is also important. Effective caching is always a matter of balance. Although you can potentially speed up your site by employing output caching, the cost is memory consumption. Using instrumentation tools can help you balance performance against cost.

Finally, User controls often represent a prime output caching opportunity—especially if they don't change frequently. Wrapping the portion of a page that *doesn't* change in an output-cached User control will usually enhance the perceived performance of your application at a minimal cost because only the User control content is cached.

Summary

Caching is a tried and true way to improve the performance of almost any system. By making frequently used content available quickly through the output cache, you can often speed up the perceived performance of your application by a wide margin.

Turning on output caching in ASP.NET is a matter of including the correct directive at the top of your page. Naive use of the cache involves simply placing it on the page code and setting the *Duration* to some number and the *VaryByParam* attribute to *none*. However, you may also control various behaviors of the output cache by setting variables within the *OutputCache* directive. You may also control output caching behaviors through the *HttpCachePolicy* class, available through the *Cache* property of the *Response* object. Later versions of ASP.NET support cache profiles so you don't have to hard-code the caching parameters into the *OutputDirective*.

User controls often represent a prime output caching opportunity—especially if they're navigation controls or some other control that doesn't change very often. By applying the *OutputCache* directive to the User control, ASP.NET caches that part of the page on which it was placed.

Chapter 16 Quick Reference

To	Do This
Cache a page's output	Add the *OutputCache* directive to the page.
Store multiple versions of a page based on varying query string parameters	Use the *VaryByParam* attribute of the *OutputCache* directive.
Store multiple versions of a page based on varying headers	Use the *VaryByHeader* attribute of the *OutputCache* directive.
Store multiple versions of a page based on varying browsers	Use the *VaryByCustom* attribute of the *OutputCache* directive, selecting *browser* as the value.
Specify the location of the cached content	Specify the *Location* attribute in the *OutputCache* directive.
Access caching attributes programmatically	Use the *Cache* property of the *Response* object, which is an instance of the *HttpCachePolicy* class.
Offload output caching configuration to the web.config file	Add *outputCacheProfile* elements to your web.config file. Use them as necessary.
Cache a User control	Apply the *OutputCache* directive to the control's ASCX file.

Part IV
Diagnostics and Plumbing

Chapter 17
Diagnostics and Debugging

After completing this chapter, you will be able to

- Turn on page tracing
- Insert custom trace messages into the page trace
- Turn tracing on for the entire application
- Manage custom error pages
- Manage exceptions within your application

Even with all the software architecture methodologies and development practices available these days, software is still very much a craft. Software libraries such as ASP.NET and Windows Forms go a long way toward making development more standardized and predictable (good things in software practice). However, there are still almost inevitable times when you need to figure out what's wrong with an application that decides to behave differently than you expected it to.

This chapter covers the support provided by ASP.NET for figuring out what's wrong with your ASP.NET application. As you can imagine, debugging Web applications introduces a whole new set of challenges. Remember, HTTP is basically connectionless, and the only thing the client really gets to see is a snapshot of the application. This chapter shows you how to watch your application as it runs and how to trace the state of any particular request. We'll also cover managing error pages and trapping application exceptions within ASP.NET.

Page Tracing

The first place to start with debugging is to examine ASP.NET page tracing. The *Page* class has a property named *Trace*. When *Trace* is turned on, it tells the ASP.NET runtime to insert a rendering of the entire context of the request and response at the end of the HTML sent to the client.

We've already seen page tracing to some extent. When we looked at the ASP.NET server-side control architecture, the page trace was invaluable in understanding the structure of the page. Remember, a rendered page is composed of a number of server-side controls collected as a hierarchical tree. A *Page* nests several controls, and the controls themselves may nest other controls (they may be nested several levels deep, as a matter of fact). The page trace includes a section displaying the composition of the page in terms of server-side controls.

Turning on Tracing

Turning on tracing is easy. Simply set the *Trace* property of the page to *true*. You may turn on tracing either by modifying the ASPX code directly or by setting the *Trace* property using the designer. Here's the *Trace* property being turned on directly within the ASPX code as part of the page directive.

```
<%@ Page Language="C#" AutoEventWireup="true" CodeFile="TraceMe.aspx.cs"
Inherits="TraceMe" Trace="true" %>
```

As soon as you turn tracing on and surf to the page, you'll see tracing information appear at the end of the HTML stream. Listing 17-1 shows some code from the DebugORama example that came with the CD accompanying this book. The TraceMe.aspx page builds a table of strings as they're entered on the site. The list of strings is kept in session state and refreshes the table every time a new string is submitted.

LISTING 17-1 Code That Builds a Table on Loading

```
public partial class TraceMe : System.Web.UI.Page
{
    ArrayList alTableEntries = null;

    protected void Page_Load(object sender, EventArgs e)
    {
        alTableEntries = (ArrayList)this.Session["TableEntries"];
        if (alTableEntries == null)
        {
            alTableEntries = new ArrayList();
        }
        AssembleTable();
    }

    protected void AssembleTable()
    {
        this.Table1.Rows.Clear();
        foreach (string s in alTableEntries)
        {
            TableRow row = new TableRow();
            TableCell cell = new TableCell();
            cell.Text = s;
            row.Cells.Add(cell);
            this.Table1.Rows.Add(row);
        }
    }

    protected void Button1_Click(object sender, EventArgs e)
    {
        alTableEntries.Add(this.TextBox1.Text);
        this.Session["TableEntries"] = alTableEntries;
        AssembleTable();
    }
}
```

Figure 17-1 shows how the page appears with tracing turned on.

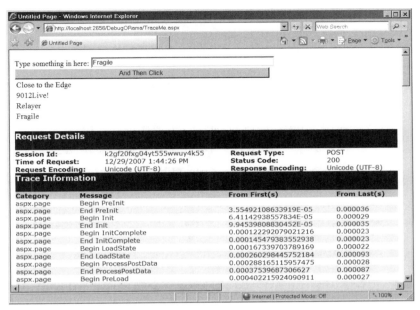

FIGURE 17-1 Tracing turned on for the application in Listing 17-1

A bit farther down the tracing output, you'll see the control tree (as we saw in several earlier chapters). The control tree for this page is shown in Figure 17-2.

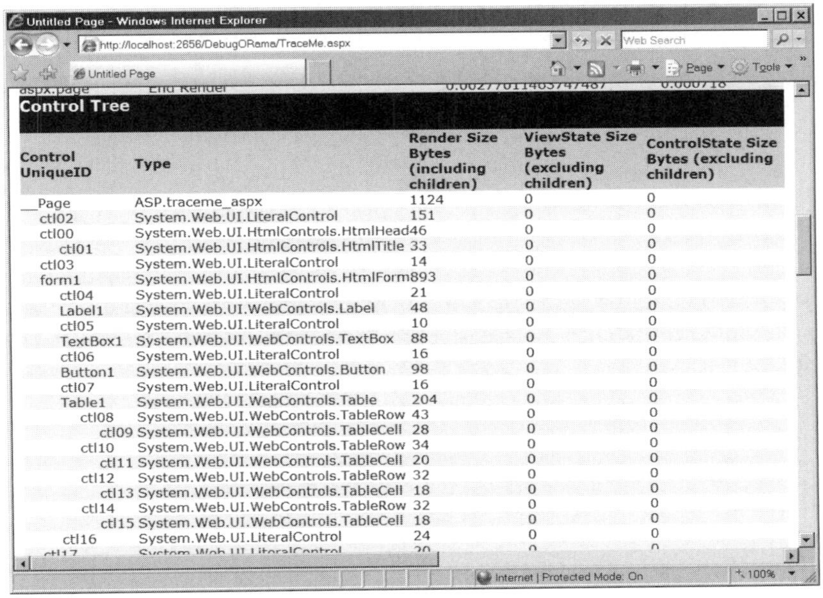

FIGURE 17-2 Tracing turned on for the application in Listing 17-1. Notice the control tree.

Finally, scroll down a bit more and you start seeing some of the context information associated with the request. Figures 17-3 and 17-4 show some of this context information. This application uses session state to save the array of strings. Notice that the session state tracing shows the contents of the session state dictionary. You also get to see other context information. For example, the tracing section shows the session ID and the URL used to surf to this page.

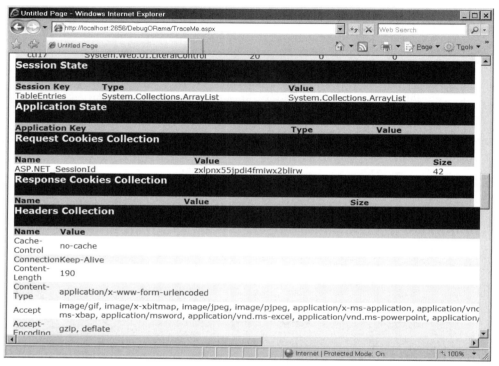

FIGURE 17-3 Tracing turned on for the application in Listing 17-1. Note the detailed information about the context of the request.

Of course, much of this information becomes more useful in cases in which there's a problem with your Web site. For example, the table might stop building itself because you somehow removed the session state item holding the list of strings. You could detect that by examining the page trace. If users begin to complain about layout issues with your site, you may look at the user agent coming down with the request and learn that the client is using a browser not accommodated by your application.

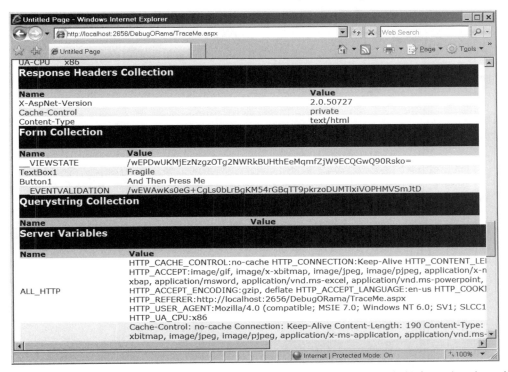

FIGURE 17-4 Tracing turned on for the application in Listing 17-1. Note the detailed information about the context of the request.

Trace Statements

In addition to all the request context information included with the HTML stream, the page trace also includes specific statements printed out during execution. If you scroll to the Trace Information block on the page, you can see these trace statements, shown in Figure 17-5.

The statements that appear in Figure 17-5 were produced by the ASP.NET framework. You can see the execution of the page progressing through the various events such as *PreInit*, *Init*, *LoadState*, and so forth.

Not only do you get tracing information from ASP.NET itself, but you may also insert your own tracing information. The *Page* class's *Trace* object provides a means of tracing page execution. Here's an exercise that shows you how to do this.

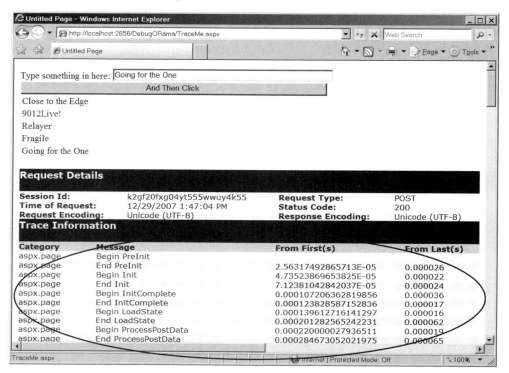

FIGURE 17-5 Tracing turned on for the application in Listing 17-1. These Trace statements track the execution of the page.

Adding tracing statements

1. Create a new Web site called *DebugORama* (it can be a File System–based Web site). Add a new page called *TraceMe.aspx*.

2. Open the TraceMe.aspx page and add the *Label* (which says "Type something in here:"), the *TextBox*, the *Button*, and the *Table* as they appear in the previous figures. Double-click on the *Button* to add a handler for the *Click* event. Add the code from Listing 17-1 (the code that builds the table during the *Page*'s *Load* event). Enable tracing by including *Trace="true"* in the *Page* directive. Run the page to ensure that page tracing is occurring.

3. Add tracing statements in strategic places through the page's *Trace* object. For example, you might want to monitor the table as it's being built. Do this by calling either *Trace.Write* or *Trace.Warn* within the page. *Trace.Write* renders the string in black, whereas *Trace.Warn* renders the tracing string in red. The first parameter is a category string you may use to help distinguish the statements you write when they finally render. You may add whatever you want to the category string.

```
public partial class TraceMe : System.Web.UI.Page
{
    ArrayList alTableEntries = null;

    protected void Page_Load(object sender, EventArgs e)
    {
        alTableEntries = (ArrayList)this.Session["TableEntries"];
        if (alTableEntries == null)
        {
            Trace.Warn("Page_Load", "alTableEntries is null");
            alTableEntries = new ArrayList();
        }
        AssembleTable();
    }

    protected void AssembleTable()
    {
        this.Table1.Rows.Clear();

        foreach (String s in alTableEntries)
        {
            Trace.Write("AssembleTable", "String found: " + s);
            TableRow row = new TableRow();
            TableCell cell = new TableCell();
            cell.Text = s;
            row.Cells.Add(cell);
            this.Table1.Rows.Add(row);
        }
    }

    protected void Button1_Click(object sender, EventArgs e)
    {
        Trace.Write("Button1_Click", "Adding string: " + this.TextBox1.Text);
        alTableEntries.Add(this.TextBox1.Text);
        this.Session["TableEntries"] = alTableEntries;
        AssembleTable();
    }
}
```

4. Compile the program and run the Web site. You should see your trace statements appearing in the output (as long as tracing is turned on). The tracing will appear red on your computer screen—although it appears as gray on the following graphics.

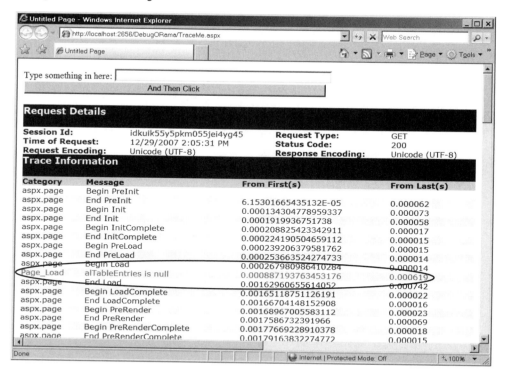

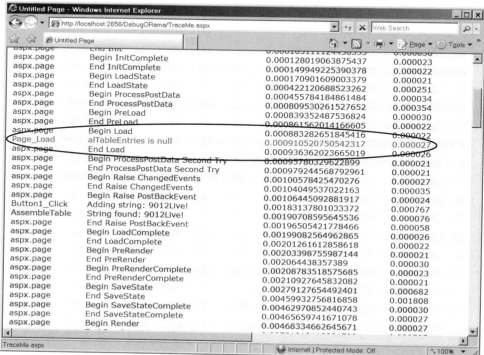

Application Tracing

Although single page tracing is useful (especially for quick spot checks for problems), it has a major downside in that it litters the page with lots of garbage at the end. You can use application tracing to get around that. Application tracing shows you exactly the same details as page tracing, except they're held in memory and made available rendered as a different page and through a special handler.

To turn on tracing, you need to enable tracing in web.config like so:

```
<configuration>
  <system.web>
    <trace enabled="true"/>
  </system.web>
</configuration>
```

This simply turns on tracing. You can actually control several aspects of page tracing. For example, you could have tracing available on the host machine (in case you don't want clients getting to your trace information). You might also want to control the number of responses that are held in memory.

Table 17-1 shows the possible values that may go in the configuration file to support tracing.

TABLE 17-1 Web.Config Settings Supporting Tracing

Key	Possible Values	Meaning
enabled	true false	Enable or disable application-level tracing
localOnly	true false	Specify whether to show trace output only on local host or everywhere
mostRecent	true false	Specify whether to recycle traces once requestLimit is met or to keep the first *N* (up to the *requestLimit* threshold)
pageOutput	true false	Specify whether to display trace output on individual pages in addition to caching application-level traces
requestLimit	Decimal number	Specify how many traces to store in memory before removing earlier traces (default is 10)
writeToDiagnosticsTrace	true false	Specify whether the trace data are also piped to *System.Diagnostics.Trace*

The following exercise demonstrates how application-level tracing works and how to navigate around the results.

Application-level tracing

1. Open the DebugORama project. Open the TraceMe.aspx page. Turn off tracing in the page by ensuring the *Page* class's *Trace* property is *false*.

2. Ensure that application-level tracing is turned on in web.config. That is, open web.config and add a *trace* element, as shown above. If the application doesn't yet have a configuration file, you may add one by selecting **Add New Item** from the local project menu.

3. Surf to the page a few times.

4. In the URL that appears in the navigation bar, make the endpoint *Trace.axd*. Using this name in the URL redirects request processing through a special handler that will render the tracing results being kept in memory.

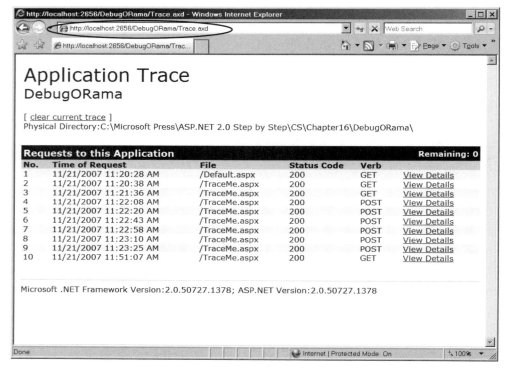

5. You should be able to see a list of requests. To see individual requests, get the request details by clicking on the *View Details* link.

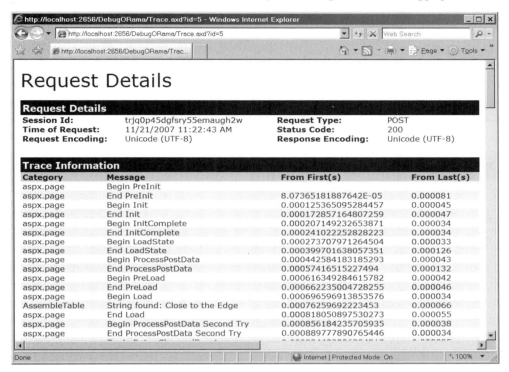

Notice how the output is exactly the same as the output on the earlier page tracing example. However, now the tracing information stands alone without cluttering up the Web page.

Enabling Tracing Programmatically

Although much of the time you'll find yourself enabling tracing via the designer, there are times when it's useful to manage tracing during run time (programmatically). For example, you might have regular clients receive normal content; however, when someone with specific credentials appears, you might want to enable tracing for that individual. You might also decide to modify tracing when a certain parameter comes through the request.

The DebugORama site includes a page named *EnableTracing.aspx* that illustrates how to control the tracing programmatically. If the user types the correct password, the tracing is turned on. The page also shows how to enable and disable tracing programmatically.

```
public partial class EnableTracing : System.Web.UI.Page
{
    protected void Page_Load(object sender, EventArgs e)
    {
    }
    protected void Button1_Click(object sender, EventArgs e)
    {
```

```
        if (this.TextBoxSecretCode.Text == "password")
        {
            this.Trace.IsEnabled = true;
        }
    }
    protected void Button2_Click(object sender, EventArgs e)
    {
        this.Trace.IsEnabled = false;
    }
}
```

The *TraceFinished* Event

The tracing context includes an interesting event named *TraceFinished* that gives you a last chance opportunity to log the tracing information or deal with it in some other way. The *TraceFinished* event is raised by the *Trace* object after all request information is gathered.

To subscribe to the event, simply set up the handler during the *Page_Load* event. The DebugORama example includes a page named *TraceFinished.aspx* that shows gathering the trace information and writing it to the debug console using *System.Diagnostics.Debug*.

```
public partial class TraceFinished : System.Web.UI.Page
{
    protected void Page_Load(object sender, EventArgs e)
    {
      Trace.TraceFinished +=
          new TraceContextEventHandler(TracingFinished);
    }
    void TracingFinished(object sender, TraceContextEventArgs e)
    {
      foreach (TraceContextRecord traceContextRecord in e.TraceRecords)
      {
          System.Diagnostics.Debug.WriteLine(traceContextRecord.Message);
      }
    }
}
```

Piping Other Trace Messages

In the last example, tracing messages were logged manually to the debug console by setting up the *TraceFinished* event handler in the *Trace* context. *System.Diagnostics.Debug* is a standard .NET type that's helpful for managing tracing and debugging information. Since version 2.0, ASP.NET has had the ability to plug in the *WebPageTraceListener* type so that calls to *System.Diagnostics.Trace* are also inserted into the ASP.NET trace. Setting it up is simply a matter of inserting a line into web.config (note the *writeToDiagnosticsTrace* option in Table 17-1). A case in which this is useful is when logging compiler output. To do this, set the *writeToDiagnosticsTrace* option to *true* and then turn on compiler tracing. Compiler tracing is another setting you can set in web.config, but notice this lies outside the normal *System.web* section of web.config.

```
<system.codedom>
    <compilers>
        <compiler compilerOptions="/d:TRACE" />
    </compilers>
</system.codedom>
```

Debugging with Visual Studio

The tracing support built into ASP.NET works really well and is a great way to debug your application—especially once it's deployed. However, when you're in development mode, having to plant tracing messages into your page and then run it to see what happened is old school and sometimes not the most efficient way of debugging. Visual Studio provides excellent debugging support through the environment, and you may use it to watch your code execute and to step through the code one line at a time. In fact, you have access to all of Visual Studio's debugging facilities, even though you're developing Web applications.

Remember, ASP.NET and Visual Studio work in concert to make it feel like you're doing desktop application development, even though it's a Web application. That goes for the debugger as well. The following exercise will familiarize you with the Visual Studio debugging environment.

Debug an application

1. Open the DebugORama Web site. To support debugging, web.config needs to include the right settings. You may type the debugger setting in by hand if you wish; however, Visual Studio will insert it for you once you start debugging.

    ```
    <system.web>
        <compilation debug="true"/>
    </system.web>
    ```

2. Open the TraceMe.aspx page and insert breakpoints in *Page_Load*, *AssembleTable*, and *Button1_Click*. You may insert breakpoints by highlighting a line in the editor window and pressing the **F9** key. You may also select **Debug**, **Toggle Breakpoint** from the main menu or simply click on the light gray ribbon to the left of the text in the code editor (where the breakpoints are indicated). Visual Studio will show a big red dot to the left of the breakpoint lines.

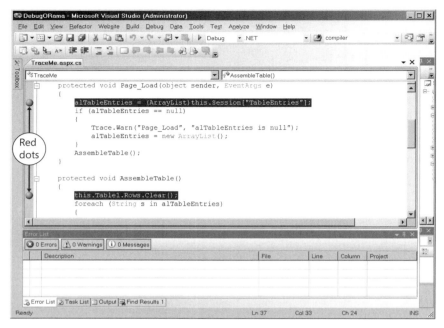

3. Start debugging by pressing the **F5** key. You may also debug by selecting **Debug**, **Start Debugging** from the main menu. If debugging is *not* turned on in the web.config file, Visual Studio will ask you before it sets the debugging attribute. Visual Studio will start running the site. When it comes to your breakpoints, Visual Studio will stop execution and highlight the current line in yellow in the window:

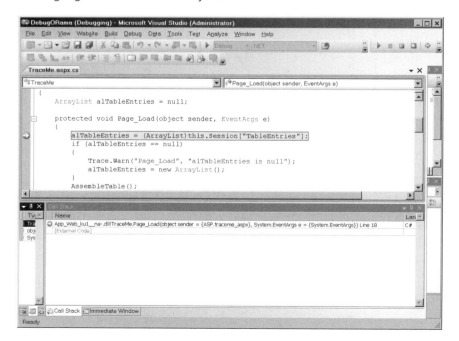

4. In this example, *Page_Load* is the first breakpoint Visual Studio encounters. At this point, you may start stepping through the code. **F10** steps over methods, whereas **F11** steps *into* methods. Alternatively, you may use **Debug**, **Step Over** and **Debug**, **Step Into** from the main menu.

5. Hover your mouse cursor over any variables you see. Notice how Visual Studio displays the value of the variable in a ToolTip.

6. Press **F5** to resume the program. Visual Studio will run until it hits another breakpoint. Run through all the breakpoints.

7. Next, post back to the server using the button. Notice the breakpoints are hit again. Also notice that first the *Page_Load* is hit and then the *Button_Click* handler. This highlights the ephemeral nature of a Web page. A new page is being created for each request that comes in.

8. Finally, try out a couple of the debug windows. You can monitor various aspects of your program by selecting **Debug**, **Window** from the main menu and choosing the window. Here's the *Locals* window, showing those variables within local scope:

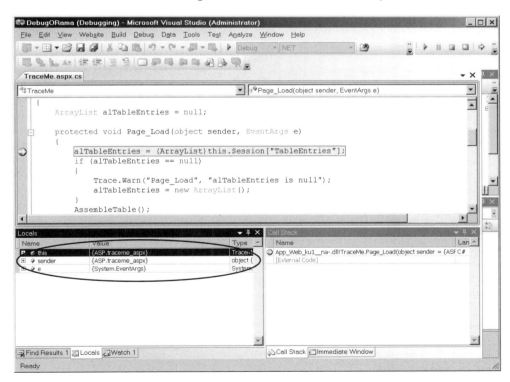

9. The *Call Stack* window shows how execution finally arrived at this spot. You may trace through and follow the entire program execution up to this point.

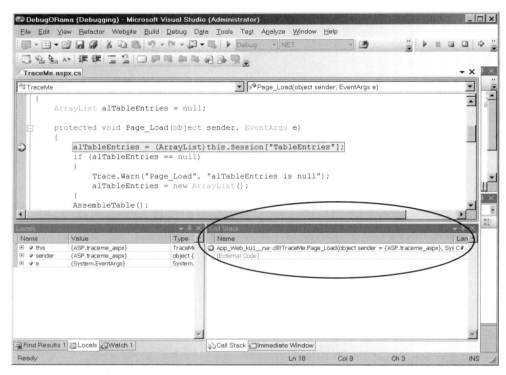

Other notable windows include the *Watch* window that lets you examine any variable you want. In addition, the *Threads* window will let you see how many threads are running, what their thread IDs are, and so forth.

Error Pages

As we've seen throughout the tour of ASP.NET, one of the main goals has always been to incorporate as much of the management of Web development as possible into ASP.NET. At this point, Internet Information Services (IIS) is really only a middle manager in the scheme of things. Many facilities previously handled exclusively by IIS are now handled by ASP.NET (although IIS brings many ASP.NET features under its auspices with version 7.0 running in Integrated mode). One of those facilities is managing custom error pages. In ASP.NET, you may introduce custom error pages (instead of the client being bombarded with ASP.NET error messages).

To tell ASP.NET to display a particular page on encountering errors anywhere within your application, just tweak the web.config file. Table 17-2 shows the custom error attributes for web.config.

TABLE 17-2 Web.Config Values for Setting Error Pages

Attribute	Description
defaultRedirect	Direct users here in the event of an exception
on/off	on = display custom pages off = display ASP.NET error pages
remoteOnly	Display custom errors to client, display ASP.NET errors locally

The following example illustrates how to work with custom error pages.

Work with error pages

In this example, you'll add some error pages to your application and see what conditions cause them to appear.

1. Open the DebugORama project.

2. Add a new Web Form named *ThrowErrors.aspx* to the DebugORama application.

3. Add two buttons: one to throw 404 errors (the nearly ubiquitous "object not found" error) and one to throw other exceptions. Set the 404 button's ID to **ButtonThrow404** and set the other button's ID to **ButtonThrowOther**.

4. Add two HTML pages to your application to act as custom error pages. Name one page *404Error.htm* and the other *SomethingBadHappened.htm*. (This example uses straight HTML pages, although you can use ASPX files here.)

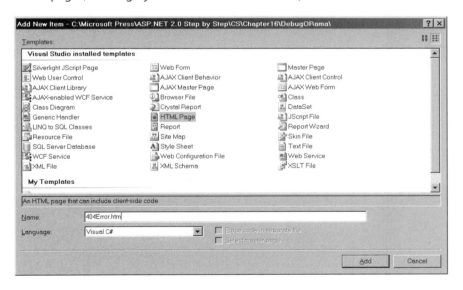

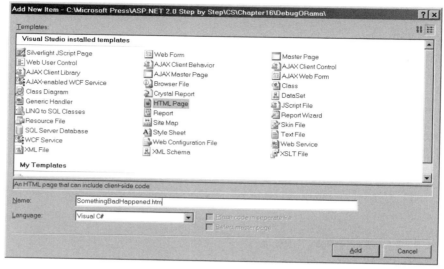

5. Add some content to the error pages. The 404 error handler here displays an error message in haiku. The other error page simply displays a label saying "Something bad happened."

6. Tell ASP.NET to use the error pages by adding the *customErrors* section to web.config, like so:

```
<configuration>
    <system.web>
        <customErrors
            defaultRedirect="SomethingBadHappened.htm" mode="On">
                <error statusCode="404"
                    redirect="404Error.htm"/>
        </customErrors>
    </system.web>
</configuration>
```

This tells ASP.NET to show the 404Error.htm page when a file isn't found. ASP.NET will show SomethingBadHappened.htm for any other error.

7. Now add handlers to generate the errors. Handle the 404 error button by directing the client to a nonexistent page (in this example, there is no page named *NonExistent* .aspx, so redirecting to it will cause a 404 error). Handle the second error generator by throwing a random exception.

```
public partial class ThrowErrors : System.Web.UI.Page
{
    protected void Page_Load(object sender, EventArgs e)
    {
    }
    protected void ButtonThrow404_Click(object sender, EventArgs e)
    {
        this.Response.Redirect("NonExistent.aspx");
    }
    protected void ButtonThrowOther_Click(object sender, EventArgs e)
```

```
    {
        throw new Exception();
    }
}
```

When you try to redirect to a nonexistent file, the "object not found" error page shows.

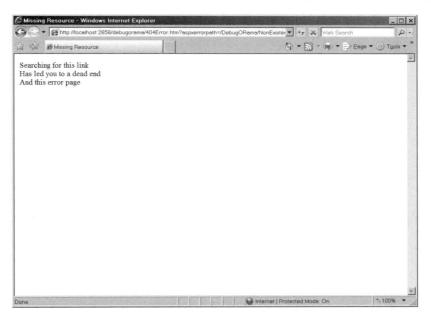

Throwing a generic exception will cause the other page to show.

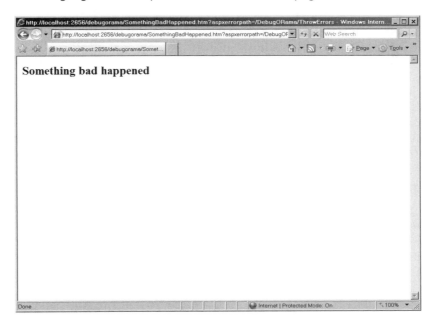

If you're running the example in the debugger, the debugger will break as soon as an exception is encountered. To continue, and show the error page after Visual Studio reports the exception, hit **F5**.

In this example, the error pages I've shown don't really help the end user because there's no detailed information about the exception. Your own error pages should provide a bit more information, perhaps a way to contact someone for assistance. Before leaving debugging and diagnostics, let's take a look at trapping exceptions in a more graceful way.

Unhandled Exceptions

In the last example page that threw an exception, ASP.NET responded by redirecting to the default error page. ASP.NET also lets you trap exceptions by setting up a handler for *Error* events fired by *HttpApplication* so that you may handle them more appropriately.

The easiest way to accomplish this is to define a handler in your *HttpApplication*-derived class within Global.asax. With the handler connected to the event, your application will receive notifications whenever something bad happens, and you can deal with it gracefully. For example, you might log the error or show it on the debug console before redirecting the user to an error page. The following example redirects the exception to an error page.

```
<script runat="server">

    void Application_Start(Object sender, EventArgs e) {
     }

    void Application_End(Object sender, EventArgs e) {
     }

    void Application_Error(Object sender, EventArgs e) {
      Exception ex = Server.GetLastError();

      // display the exception before redirecting
      System.Diagnostics.Debug.WriteLine("Error in app: " + ex);

      if (ex is HttpUnhandledException)
      {
          Context.ClearError(); // clear error
          Server.Transfer("somethingbadhappened.htm");
      }
    }

    void Session_Start(Object sender, EventArgs e) {

    }

    void Session_End(Object sender, EventArgs e) {
    }

</script>
```

The code above traps the exception before the redirection happens. This gives you the opportunity to log the exception (or, as in the example above, to show it in the *System.Diagnostics.Debug* context).

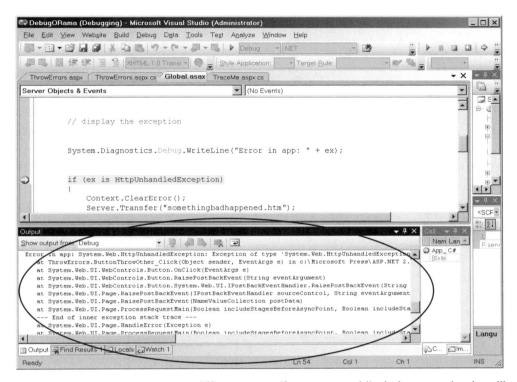

You may also redirect users to a different page, if you want to hijack the exception handling before ASP.NET redirects to the page specified in web.config. Be sure to call *Context.ClearError* first to clear the error so ASP.NET won't generate its standard error page.

Summary

Web development is difficult because an application's state can be all over the place. For example, the application holds some of the state, the browser holds some of the state, and some of the state is stuck in a session database. In addition, the executing portions of an application happen in multiple places—both on the server and on the client. That calls for debugging techniques different from what you'd require with a desktop application.

ASP.NET supports page-level tracing and application-level tracing. In both cases, ASP.NET displays the entire context of a request and response, including tracing statements. Visual Studio also supports debugging ASP.NET applications as though they were desktop applications. You simply set up breakpoints, fire up the debugger, and watch the fireworks.

Debugging ASP.NET applications is very much like debugging desktop applications, thanks to Visual Studio. Moreover, the debugging works over a network, even the Internet.

Finally, ASP.NET takes over the custom error page handling process (which used to be managed by IIS in classic ASP). You may direct users to new pages depending on the error that occurs. Finally, you can trap exceptions before they redirect and perform additional processing.

Chapter 17 Quick Reference

To	Do This
Prepare a Web site for debugging	Include the following in web.config: ``` <system.web> <compilation debug="true"/> </system.web> ```
Enable tracing for an entire application	Include the following in web.config: ``` <system.web> <trace enabled="true"/> </system.web> ```
Enable tracing for your page	Set the *Page* class's *trace* attribute to *true* by either using the property page in Visual Studio or declaring *Trace="true"* in the page directive.
Debug a Web application in Visual Studio	Ensure that the debug attribute is turned on in web.config. Start the program running in debug mode by 1. Selecting **Debug**, **Start Debugging** from the main menu OR 2. Pressing the **F5** key
Set up breakpoints in an application in Visual Studio	Place the cursor on the line at which you'd like to stop execution and 1. Select **Debug**, **Toggle Breakpoint** OR 2. Press the **F9** key OR 3. Toggle the breakpoint by clicking the mouse in the gray ribbon to the left of the text in the code editor
Execute a line of source code in the Visual Studio debugger	While the debugger is running and execution has stopped at the line you'd like to execute 1. Select **Debug**, **Step Over** from the main menu OR 2. Press the **F10** key

To	Do This
Step into a line of source code in the Visual Studio debugger	While the debugger is running and execution has stopped at the line you'd like to execute 1. Select **Debug**, **Step Into** from the main menu OR 2. Press the **F11** key
Instruct ASP.NET to show a particular page when a specific HTTP error occurs	Assign the error-handling page to the specific error in the *<customErrors>* section of web.config.
Trap specific .NET exceptions or deal with general unhandled exceptions in ASP.NET	Handle exceptions, including otherwise uncaught exceptions, within the *Application_Error* handler in Global.asax. Usually, you'd then redirect to a specific page. (Note that specific errors will be assigned as the *InnerException* of the *HttpUnhandledException*!)

Chapter 18
The *HttpApplication* Class and HTTP Modules

After completing this chapter, you will be able to

- Use *HttpApplication* as a rendezvous point for your application
- Manage data within the *HttpApplication* object
- Manage events within the *HttpApplication* object
- Work with HTTP Modules

This chapter covers working with *application state* and *applicationwide events* within your ASP.NET application. In normal desktop applications, the notion of a global meeting place for various parts of an application is well understood. For example, MFC, a C++ class library supporting low-level Windows development, includes a class named *CWinApp* that holds state useful throughout the program. This state includes such items as a handle to the current instance of the application, a handle to the main window, and the parameters that were passed in when the application started. The *CWinApp* class also runs the message loop—something that can be done only within the global scope of a Windows application. A running Windows application contains one and only one instance of the *CWinApp* class, and it's universally available from anywhere within the application.

Windows Forms—the .NET library that supports Windows forms—has a similar class named *Application*. It includes the same sort of state (command line parameters, a top-level window, other state required by the program). The Windows Forms *Application* class also runs the message loop.

Web development also requires the same sort of "global space" that a desktop application requires. Having a global space within a Web application makes implementing features such as caching data and session state possible. Let's take a look at how ASP.NET implements a global space for Web applications.

The Application: A Rendezvous Point

As we've seen so far, one of the most distinctive aspects of Web-based development is the requirement to be very mindful of the state of your application. By itself, raw Web application development includes no support for dealing with state. After all, Web requests are made over a disconnected protocol and the state of a request evaporates as soon as it hits an endpoint.

In Chapter 4, we took a look at the notion of view state within an ASP.NET application. ASP.NET server-side controls have the option of supporting view state. View state is embedded within the data going back and forth between the browser and the server and is used (most of the time) to keep the user interface (UI) appearing as though the browser and the server are connected continually. For example, without view state (or some special coding within the server application), UI elements such as drop-down lists lose their state between posts, causing the first item in the list to always show as the selected item—even if it wasn't really the item selected.

In Chapter 14, we looked at *session state*—or the data accompanying a specific session. Session state is useful for items such as shopping carts, for which the application has to associate data with a client.

Finally, in Chapter 15, we took a look at caching state so as to avoid unnecessary round-trips to a data source. Loading data from memory is usually much faster than loading it from a database or regenerating it. When it comes to storing data that all parts of your application can access, the data must be stored somewhere else besides view state and session state. We saw that the cache is available from virtually anywhere in the application via the *HttpContext* object. The *HttpContext* includes a reference to an instance of the *HttpApplication* object. In addition to being a holding place for the cache, the application object has its own dictionary that serves as a useful place to hold data. It works in very much the same way that the *Cache* does. However, there are some subtle yet important differences between the *Cache* and the dictionary held by *HttpApplication*.

Keeping a dictionary and a data cache available for the rest of the application isn't the only good reason to implement a central application object. The other reason is to have a mechanism for handling applicationwide events. We've seen that the *Page* class handles events for a request specifically. However, think about how the entire ASP.NET pipeline works. Some useful events aren't part of the page processing or request processing mechanism. Implementing those involves code working outside the normal page processing mechanism.

For example, we looked at session state in Chapter 14. When a request first comes through a site whose session state is enabled, when should the session object be set up? Certainly, you want it set up before the page-specific processing begins. In Chapter 10, we saw the ASP.NET security model. When should authentication and authorization be handled? You want those things to happen outside the context of the normal request processing, too. A final example is output caching, as we saw in Chapter 16. For output caching to work, ASP.NET needs to intercept the request when it first enters the pipeline so that it may bypass the whole page creation process and render the cached content instead.

ASP.NET's *HttpApplication* object can manage these sorts of things. When running, the *HttpApplication* object represents a rendezvous point for all the parts of your entire

Web application. If you're looking for software patterns to identify within ASP.NET, the *HttpApplication* most closely represents the *singleton* pattern. You treat it as a single instance of an object within your application. A reference to it is accessible at any point in time through the *HttpContext* class via the *Current* property.

Overriding *HttpApplication*

Overriding the *HttpApplication* to include your own state and event handling is a matter of adding a file named *Global.asax* to your application. In fact, you may use Visual Studio to add one to your application. Once you add a Global.asax file to your application, it is set up and ready to handle a few applicationwide events. Remember from examining ASPX files that *Page* files include the *Page* directive at the top of the file. The Global.asax file includes a similar directive. The *Application* directive tells the runtime compiling machinery that this file is meant to serve as the application object.

Listing 18-1 shows an example of the *HttpApplication* expressed within a file named *Global.asax*. The Global.asax provided by Visual Studio overrides the *Application_Start*, *Application_End*, *Application_Error*, *Session_Start*, and *Session_End* events.

LISTING 18-1 Global.asax File and Stubbed-out Application Event Handlers

```
<%@ Application Language="C#" %>

<script runat="server">

    void Application_Start(object sender, EventArgs e) {}
    void Application_End(object sender, EventArgs e) {}
    void Application_Error(object sender, EventArgs e) {}
    void Session_Start(object sender, EventArgs e) {}
    void Session_End(object sender, EventArgs e) {}

</script>
```

To get an idea as to how these events work, the following example illustrates placing a piece of data in the application's dictionary and retrieving it later when the page loads.

Managing application state

1. Start a new Web site named *UseApplication*.

2. Drag a *GridView* onto the default page. Don't assign a data source to it yet. You'll populate it with data that are stored with the application in later steps.

3. Add a Global.asax to the site. Click the right mouse button on the project in the Project Explorer (or select **Web Site**, **Add New Item** from the main menu). Choose the **Global Application Class** template, as shown here:

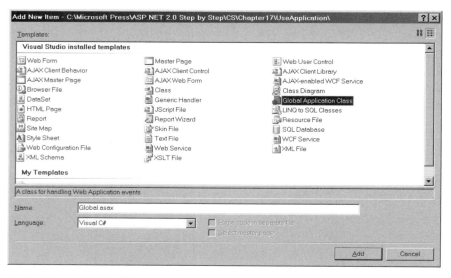

4. You've just added a file named *Global.asax* to your application. You can see that the *Application_Start* event is already handled (although it does nothing right now).

5. To have some data to store with the application object, import the *QuotesCollection* from Chapter 15. The project name is *UseDataCaching*. Select **Web Site, Add Existing Item** from the main menu and find the file *QuotesCollection.cs*. In addition to importing the QuotesCollection.cs file, grab the *QuotesCollection.xml* and *QuotesCollection.xsd* files from the UseDataCaching\App_Data directory.

6. Add some code to the *Application_Start* event to load the quotes data and place it in the application dictionary. *Server.MapPath* will give you the path from which the application is executing so you can load the XML and XSD files. Storing the data in the dictionary is very much like adding it to the cache.

```
void Application_Start(Object sender, EventArgs e) {
    QuotesCollection quotesCollection = new QuotesCollection();

    String strAppPath = Server.MapPath("");

    String strFilePathXml =
            strAppPath  + "\\app_data\\QuotesCollection.xml";
    String strFilePathSchema = strAppPath +
            "\\app_data\\QuotesCollection.xsd";
    quotesCollection.ReadXmlSchema(strFilePathSchema);
    quotesCollection.ReadXml(strFilePathXml);

    Application["quotesCollection"] = quotesCollection;
}
```

7. Update *Page_Load* method in the Default.aspx page to load the data from the application's dictionary. The application state is available through the page's reference to the *Application* object. Accessing data within the dictionary is a matter of indexing it correctly. After loading the data from the dictionary, apply it to the *DataSource* property in the *GridView* and bind the *DataGrid*.

```
protected void Page_Load(object sender, EventArgs e)
{
  QuotesCollection quotesCollection =
    (QuotesCollection)Application["quotesCollection"];

  GridView1.DataSource = quotesCollection;
  GridView1.DataBind();
}
```

Application State Caveats

As you can see, the application state and the application data cache seem to overlap in their functionality. Indeed, they're both available from similar scopes (from any point in the application), and getting the data in and out involves using the right indexer. However, the application state and the cache vary in a couple of significant ways.

First, items that go into the application state stay there until you remove them explicitly. The application data cache implements more flexibility in terms of setting expirations and other removal/refresh conditions.

In addition, putting many items into the application state dictionary will inhibit the scalability of your application. To make the application state thread safe, the *HttpApplicationState* class has a *Lock* method that you may use to make the global state thread safe. Although using the *Lock* method will ensure that the data are not corrupted, locking the application frequently will greatly reduce the number of requests it can handle.

Ideally, data going into the application state should be read only once when it is loaded—and should be changed very infrequently, if at all. As long as you're aware of these issues, the application state can be a useful place to store information required by all parts of your application.

Handling Events

The other useful aspect of the application object is its ability to handle applicationwide events. As we saw in the previous example, the Global.asax file is a handy place to insert event handlers. Visual Studio will insert a few for you when you simply add one to your application. Some events are handled only in Global.asax, whereas others may be handled outside Global.asax. The events for which Visual Studio generates stub handlers inside Global.asax include *Application_Start*, *Application_End*, *Application_Error*, *Session_Start*, and *Session_End*. A rundown of these events follows.

Application_Start

Application_Start happens when the application is first initialized—that is, when the first request comes through. Because *Application_Start* happens first (and only once) during the lifetime of an application, the most common response for the event is to load and initialize data at the start of the application (as with the previous example).

Application_End

The ASP.NET runtime raises *Application_End* as the application is shutting down. This is a useful place to clean up any resources requiring special attention for disposal.

Application_Error

Unfortunately, bad things sometimes happen inside Web applications. If something bad has happened in one of your existing applications, you may already have seen the standard pale yellow and red ASP.NET error page. Once you deploy your application, you probably don't want clients to see this sort of page. Intercept this event (*Application_Error*) to handle the error. Of course, the best place to handle exceptions is right when they occur. If an exception goes this far, that indicates a real problem. It's best to use this event as a last resort.

Session_Start

The *Session_Start* event occurs when a user makes an initial request to the application, which initializes a new session. This is a good place to initialize session variables (if you want to initialize them before the page loads).

Session_End

This event occurs when a session is released. Sessions end when they time out or when the *Abandon* method is called explicitly. This event happens only for applications whose session state is being held in-process.

HttpApplication Events

The events listed previously are implemented in Visual Studio's default Global.asax. The application object can fire a number of other events. Table 18-1 shows a summary of all the events pumped through the application object. Some of these events are handled only through Global.asax, whereas the others are handled within *HttpModules*.

TABLE 18-1 Applicationwide Events

Event	Reason	Order	Only in Global.asax
Application_Start	Application is spinning up.	Start of app	*
Application_End	Application is ending.	End of app	*
Session_Start	Session is starting.		*
Session_End	Session is ending.		*
BeginRequest	A new request has been received.	1	
AuthenticateRequest/ PostAuthenticateRequest	The user has been authenticated—that is, the security identity of the user has been established.	2	
AuthorizeRequest/ PostAuthorizeRequest	The user has been authorized to use the requests resource.	3	
ResolveRequestCache/ PostResolveRequestCache	Occurs between authorizing the user and invoking handler. This is where the output caching is handled. If content is cached, the application can bypass the entire page-rendering process.	4	
AcquireRequestState/ PostAcquireRequestState	Occurs when session state needs to be initialized.	5	
PreRequestHandlerExecute	Occurs immediately before request is sent to the handler. This is a last-minute chance to modify the output before it heads off to the client.	6	
PostRequestHandlerExecute	Occurs following the content being sent to the client.	7	
ReleaseRequestState/ PostReleaseRequestState	Occurs following request handling. This event occurs so the system may save state used if necessary.	8	
UpdateRequestCache/ PostUpdateRequestCache	Occurs following handler execution. This is used by caching modules to cache responses.	9	

Continued

TABLE 18-1 Continued

Event	Reason	Order	Only in Global.asax
EndRequest	Fires after request is processed.	10	
Disposed	Occurs before the application shuts down.	End of app	
Error	Fired when an unhandled application error occurs.	When an exception occurs	
PreSendRequestContent	Fired before content is sent to client.		
PreSendRequestHeaders	Fired before HTTP headers are sent to client.		

The following example shows how to time requests by intercepting the *BeginRequest* and the *EndRequest* events within Global.asax.

Timing requests

1. Open up Global.asax within the UseApplication Web site.

2. Add handlers for *BeginRequest* and *EndRequest*. While editing the Global.asax file, select **Application** from the drop-down list on the top left side of the window, and then select the events to add from the drop-down list on the top right side of the editing window as shown below:

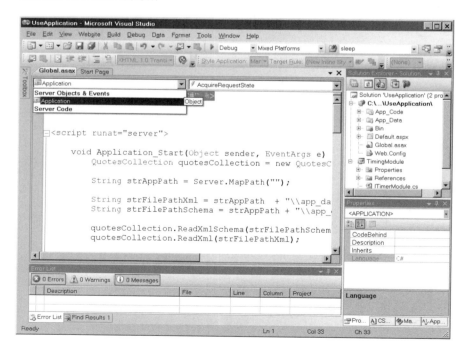

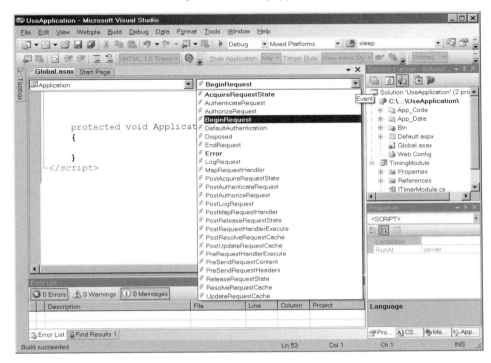

Visual Studio will insert the following stubs in Global.asax:

```
protected void Application_BeginRequest(object sender, EventArgs e)
{

}

protected void Application_EndRequest(object sender, EventArgs e)
{

}
```

3. Implement the *BeginRequest* handler by getting the current date and time and storing them within the *Items* property of the current *HttpContext*. The *Items* property is a name-value collection that you may index in the same way you index the cache, the session state, and the *HttpApplication* dictionary. Implement the *EndRequest* handler by comparing the time stamp obtained from the beginning of the request to the current date and time. Print out the amount of time taken to process the request using *Response.Write*.

```
protected void Application_BeginRequest(object sender, EventArgs e)
{
    DateTime dateTimeBeginRequest = DateTime.Now;

    HttpContext ctx = HttpContext.Current;
    ctx.Items["dateTimeBeginRequest"] = dateTimeBeginRequest;
}
```

```
protected void Application_EndRequest(object sender, EventArgs e)
{
    DateTime dateTimeEndRequest = DateTime.Now;

    HttpContext ctx = HttpContext.Current;
    DateTime dateTimeBeginRequest =
        (DateTime)ctx.Items["dateTimeBeginRequest"];

    TimeSpan duration = dateTimeEndRequest - dateTimeBeginRequest;

    Response.Write("<b>From Global.asax: This request took " +
        duration.ToString() + "</b></br>");
}
```

You should see the duration printed within the response returned to the browser.

HttpModules

Overriding Global.asax is a very convenient way to manage data and events within an application. Visual Studio generates a Global.asax and even stubs out the more important events for you. However, overriding Global.asax isn't the only way to store state and handle applicationwide events. The other way is to write an HTTP Module.

HTTP Modules serve very much the same role that ISAPI filters served for classic ASP—as a place to insert functionality into the request processing. HTTP Modules plug into the ASP.NET processing chain to handle applicationwide events in the same way that Global.asax handles applicationwide events. In fact, many ASP.NET features are implemented through HTTP Modules.

Existing Modules

ASP.NET employs HTTP Modules to enable features such as output caching and session state. To get an idea of what features are implemented via HTTP Modules, take a look at the master configuration file for your machine (that is, go to the Windows directory, look in the Microsoft.NET directory, and drill down to the configuration directory for the most current release). The master web.config file mentions several modules in the *httpModules* section of the configuration, as shown in Listing 18-2. For brevity, this list does not include entire strong names of the assemblies, but it gives you an idea as to what modules are already part of the ASP.NET pipeline.

LISTING 18-2 Excerpt from the Master Web.Config File Indicating Configured *HttpModules*

```
<httpModules>
 <add name="OutputCache"
  type="System.Web.Caching.OutputCacheModule" />
 <add name="Session"
  type="System.Web.SessionState.SessionStateModule" />
 <add name="WindowsAuthentication"
  type="System.Web.Security.WindowsAuthenticationModule" />
```

```
<add name="FormsAuthentication"
  type="System.Web.Security.FormsAuthenticationModule" />
 <add name="PassportAuthentication"
  type="System.Web.Security.PassportAuthenticationModule" />
<add name="RoleManager"
  type="System.Web.Security.RoleManagerModule" />
<add name="UrlAuthorization"
  type="System.Web.Security.UrlAuthorizationModule" />
<add name="FileAuthorization"
  type="System.Web.Security.FileAuthorizationModule" />
<add name="AnonymousIdentification"
  type="System.Web.Security.AnonymousIdentificationModule" />
<add name="Profile"
  type="System.Web.Profile.ProfileModule" />
<add name="ErrorHandlerModule"
type="System.Web.Mobile.ErrorHandlerModule" />
</httpModules>
```

The *httpModules* section mentions the name of a module, followed by a fully specified type that implements the feature. The following features are handled by modules:

- Output Caching

- Session State

- Windows Authentication

- Forms Authentication

- Passport Authentication

- Role Manager

- URL Authorization

- File Authorization

- Anonymous Identification

- Profile

Chapter 2, includes a short summary of the ASP.NET pipeline. The modules fit into the processing chain and take effect prior to being processed by the *HttpApplication* object. In fact, IIS 7.0 uses modules extensively—especially when running in integrated mode. Although the features themselves may require extensive code to implement (for example, imagine all the work that went into the session state manager), the basic formula for hooking a module into your application is pretty straightforward. Creating a module involves four steps:

1. Writing a class implementing *IHttpModule*

2. Writing handlers for the events you want handled

3. Subscribing to the events

4. Configuring the module in web.config

Implementing a Module

Here's an example illustrating how HTTP Modules work. The previous example in this chapter demonstrated how to time requests by handling events within Global.asax. The example showed time stamping the beginning of a request, storing the time stamp in the current *HttpContext*, and examining the time stamp as the request finished.

The following example performs the same functionality. However, the example uses an HTTP Module to handle the events.

A timing module

1. To implement a timing module, open the Web site solution file for this chapter—UseApplication. To work, the module needs to exist in an assembly. It's easiest to write a completely separate assembly for the module. Add a project to the solution by selecting **File, Add, New Project** from the main menu. Make the project a Class Library and name the project *TimingModule*.

2. Visual Studio will add a class to the library named *Class1*. (The name of the file generated by Visual Studio is *Class1.cs* and the name of the class generated by Visual Studio is *Class1*.) Change the name of the file to *Timer.cs* and the name of the class to *Timer*. Place the code into the *TimingModule* namespace.

3. The module as generated by Visual Studio doesn't understand the ASP.NET types. Add a reference to System.Web to make the ASP.NET types available.

4. Add handlers for the beginning and ending of the request. You may borrow the code from Global.asax if you want. The signatures for the event's handlers are such that the methods have the return type of *void* and accept two arguments: an *object* and *EventArgs*.

```
using System;
using System.Data;
using System.Configuration;
using System.Web;
/// <summary>
/// Summary description for Timer
/// </summary>

namespace TimingModule {
   public class Timer
   {
      public Timer()
      {
      }

      public void OnBeginRequest(object o, EventArgs ea)
      {
            DateTime dateTimeBeginRequest = DateTime.Now;
```

```
        HttpContext ctx;
        ctx = HttpContext.Current;
        ctx.Items["dateTimeBeginRequest"] = dateTimeBeginRequest;
    }

    public void OnEndRequest(object o, EventArgs ea)
    {
        DateTime dateTimeEndRequest = DateTime.Now;

        HttpContext ctx;
        ctx = HttpContext.Current;
        DateTime dateTimeBeginRequest =
            (DateTime)ctx.Items["dateTimeBeginRequest"];

        TimeSpan duration = dateTimeEndRequest - dateTimeBeginRequest;

        ctx.Response.Write("<b>From the TimingModule: This request took " +
            duration.ToString() + "</b></br>");
    }
  }
}
```

5. Add *IHttpModule* to the class's inheritance list. Add implementations for the methods *Init* and *Dispose*. The job performed by *Init* is to subscribe to events. The job performed by *Dispose* is to release any resources used by the module (*Dispose* doesn't need to do anything in this example).

```
public class Timer
        : IHttpModule
{
    public Timer()
    {
    }

    public void Init(HttpApplication httpApp)
    {
        httpApp.BeginRequest +=
            new EventHandler(this.OnBeginRequest);

        httpApp.EndRequest +=
            new EventHandler(this.OnEndRequest);
    }
    public void Dispose() { }

// ...
}
```

6. Add a project-level reference to the new module so you may call it from the page code. Click the right mouse button on the **UseApplication** node within Solution Explorer. Select **Add Reference** from the local menu. When the **Add Reference** dialog box appears, select the **Project** tab and choose the **TimingModule** from the list. The following shows the **Visual Studio** dialog box for adding references.

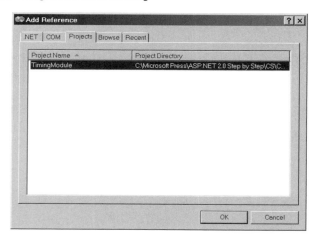

7. Finally, mention the *TimingModule* in the web.config file. It needs to appear within the *httpModules* section, nested within the *system.web* section, like so (notice that Visual Studio has already added a module to the configuration file).

```
<configuration>
 <system.web>
    <httpModules>
     <add name="TimingModule"
          type="TimingModule.Timer, TimingModule" />
     <add name="ScriptModule"
        type="System.Web.Handlers.ScriptModule,
          System.Web.Extensions, Version=3.5.0.0,
          Culture=neutral, PublicKeyToken=31BF3856AD364E35" /></httpModules>
    </httpModules>
 </system.web>
</configuration>
```

As long as the *TimingModule* assembly is available to your application (that is, it's in the *Bin* subdirectory of your virtual directory), it will be linked into the processing chain. When you run the page, you'll see the timing information coming from both the Global.asax file and the timing module.

See Active Modules

We previously saw that many ASP.NET features are implemented through modules. While you can see the modules listed within the master configuration file, you can also see the list of available modules at run time. They're available through the current application instance. The following exercise illustrates how to do this.

Listing the modules

1. Add a button to the Default.aspx page of the UseApplication solution. This button will list the attached modules, so set its *Text* property to **Show Modules**. Also add a list box to the page that will show the modules.

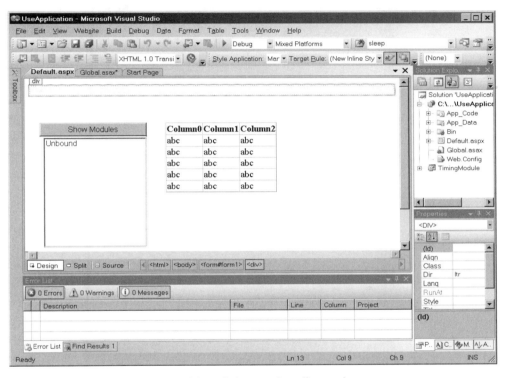

2. Double-click on the button to add a *Click* event handler to the page.

3. Handle the button event by grabbing the list of modules from the application instance. The list comes back as a collection that you can apply to the list box's *DataSource* property. Calling *DataBind* on the *ListBox* will put the names of all the modules in the *ListBox*.

```
protected void ButtonShowmodules_Click(object sender, EventArgs e)
{
    HttpApplication httpApp = HttpContext.Current.ApplicationInstance;
    HttpModuleCollection httpModuleColl = httpApp.Modules;

    Response.Write("<br>");
    String[] rgstrModuleNames;
    rgstrModuleNames = httpModuleColl.AllKeys;

    this.ListBox1.DataSource = rgstrModuleNames;
    this.ListBox1.DataBind();
}
```

Running the page and clicking the **Show Module** button will fill the list box with a list of modules plugged into the application (check out the *TimingModule* entry in the list).

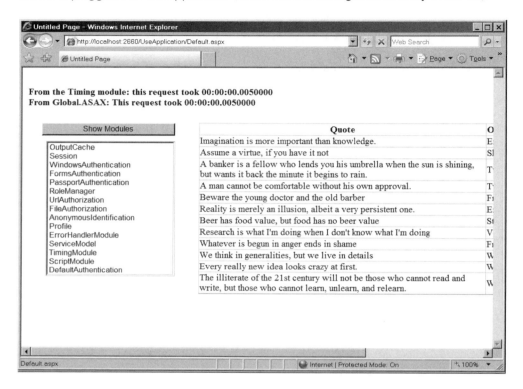

Storing State in Modules

HTTP Modules are also a very handy place to store global state for your application. The following example shows how to track the average request duration (which requires storing the duration of each request as part of application state).

Tracking average request duration

1. Before inserting the functionality into the module, let's think a bit about how to use the information about the average request duration. You might use it to profile and to find bottlenecks in your application. Although sending the information out to the client browser is always useful, there might be times when you want to use the information programmatically. To retrieve the information from the module, you'll need to add one or more methods (above and beyond the *Init* and *Dispose* methods) to the *TimingModule*. The best way to do that is to define an interface that has functions you can use to talk to the module. The following listing defines an interface for retrieving

the average request duration. Create a file named *ITimingModule.cs* and add it to the TimerModule subproject.

```
public interface ITimingModule
{
    TimeSpan GetAverageLengthOfRequest();
}
```

2. Implement the *ITimingModule* interface within the *Timer* class. Include an *ArrayList* in the *Timer* class to hold on to durations of the requests (you'll need to add the *System.Collections* namespace to the list of *using* directives). Store the duration of the request at the end of each request (in the *OnEndRequest* handler). Use clock ticks as the measurement to make it easier to compute the average duration. Finally, implement *GetAverageLengthOfRequest* (the method defined by the *ITimingModule* interface) by adding all the elements in the *ArrayList* and dividing that number by the size of the *ArrayList*. Create a *TimeSpan* using the result of the calculation and return that to the client.

```
public class Timer : IHttpModule,    ITimingModule
{
    public Timer()
    {
    }

    protected ArrayList _alRequestDurations = new ArrayList();
    public void Init(HttpApplication httpApp)
    {
        httpApp.BeginRequest +=
            new EventHandler(this.OnBeginRequest);
        httpApp.EndRequest +=
            new EventHandler(this.OnEndRequest);
    }
    public void Dispose() { }

    public void OnBeginRequest(object o, EventArgs ea)
    {
        DateTime dateTimeBeginRequest = DateTime.Now;

        HttpContext ctx;
        ctx = HttpContext.Current;
        ctx.Items["dateTimeBeginRequest"] = dateTimeBeginRequest;
    }

    public void OnEndRequest(object o, EventArgs ea)
    {
        DateTime dateTimeEndRequest = DateTime.Now;

        HttpContext ctx;
        ctx = HttpContext.Current;
        DateTime dateTimeBeginRequest =
            (DateTime)ctx.Items["dateTimeBeginRequest"];

        TimeSpan duration =
                dateTimeEndRequest - dateTimeBeginRequest;
```

```
    ctx.Response.Write("<b> From the TimingModule: this request took " +
    duration.Duration().ToString() + "</b></br>");
    _alRequestDurations.Add(duration);
  }
  public TimeSpan GetAverageLengthOfRequest()
  {
    long lTicks = 0;
    foreach (TimeSpan timespanDuration in this._alRequestDurations)
    {
        lTicks += timespanDuration.Ticks;
    }

    long lAverageTicks = lTicks / _alRequestDurations.Count;
    TimeSpan timespanAverageDuration = new TimeSpan(lAverageTicks);
    return timespanAverageDuration;
  }
}
```

3. Now add some code in the Default.aspx page to examine the average time taken to process each request. Add a button to fetch the average duration, and add a label to display the average duration. Give the button the *Text* value **Show Average Duration Of Requests** and the ID **ButtonShowAverageDurationOfRequests**. The label should have an empty *Text* value and the ID **LabelAverageDurationOfRequests**. You'll need to include a reference to the *TimingModule* in the Default.aspx page so the page code has access to the interface.

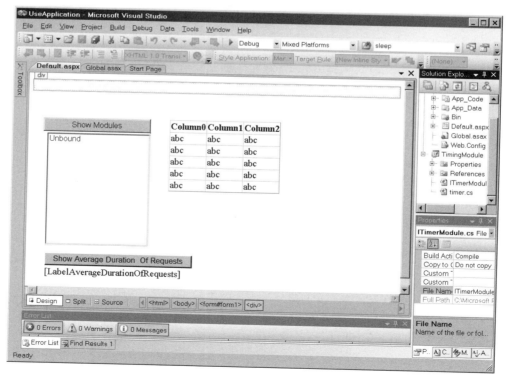

4. Double-click on the **Show Average Duration Of Requests** button within Visual Studio to add a *Click* event handler. Handle the event by fetching the *TimingModule* from the collection of Modules. You can fetch it by name because the collection is indexed by module name (as specified in web.config).

```
protected void
    ButtonShowAverageDurationOfRequests_Click(
        object sender,
        EventArgs e)
{
    HttpApplication httpApp =
        HttpContext.Current.ApplicationInstance;

    HttpModuleCollection httpModuleColl = httpApp.Modules;
    IHttpModule httpModule =
        httpModuleColl.Get("TimingModule");
    ITimingModule TimingModule =
        (ITimingModule)httpModule;

    TimeSpan timeSpanAverageDurationOfRequest =
        TimingModule.GetAverageLengthOfRequest();
    LabelAverageDurationOfRequests.Text =
        timeSpanAverageDurationOfRequest.ToString();
}
```

The object you get back by accessing the module collection is an *HttpModule*. To be able to talk to it using the *ITimingModule* interface, you need to cast the reference to the module. Once you do that, you may call *GetAverageLengthOfRequest* and display it in the label.

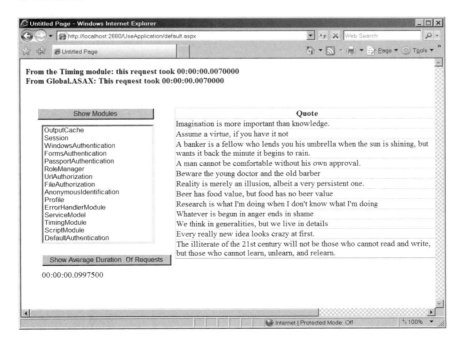

Global.asax versus *HttpModules*

Both the application object expressed through Global.asax and HTTP Modules offer a rendezvous point for your application. You can use both of them to store global state between requests as well as respond to applicationwide events. When choosing one over the other, remember that Global.asax really goes with your application. Global.asax is intended to manage state and events specific to your application. HTTP Modules exist as completely separate assemblies. They're not necessarily tied to a particular application, and they may even be signed and deployed in the Global Assembly Cache. That makes modules an ideal vehicle for implementing generic functionality that's useful between different applications.

Summary

In this chapter, we saw how the ASP.NET architecture includes a rendezvous point for all the requests passing through an application. This is especially important in Web applications composed of disparate components centered around a pipeline. Although there are certain obvious places where a request context can show up (most notably in the end handler), it's clear that there are other points in the request chain where you need to have something to hold on to.

ASP.NET offers two broad choices in implementing such a "global space." Global.asax is a convenient representation of the *HttpApplication* object. ASP.NET applications have a singular instance of the *HttpApplication* class. The application object includes a handy dictionary in which to store data that need to survive and be available from all points within the application. However, using the dictionary is widely discouraged. It is not thread safe, and locking it to make it thread safe can have very adverse effects on the performance of your application. In addition, Global.asax offers a place to intercept various applicationwide events.

HTTP Modules offer very much the same functionality, although in a different package. HTTP Modules implement the *IHttpModule* interface and are deployed with the application via the web.config file. When an application starts up, the ASP.NET runtime looks in the web.config file to see if any additional handlers need to be attached to the pipeline. (ASP.NET plugs in a number of modules already—they implement such features as authentication and session state.) When ASP.NET sees a new module within the web.config file, ASP.NET loads the module and calls the *Init* method. Modules usually initialize by setting up handlers for various applicationwide events.

Chapter 18 Quick Reference

To	Do This
Create a custom module assembly	Create a new class implementing *IHttpModule*.
	Implement *Init*.
	Implement *Dispose*.
Insert the module into the processing chain	Configure the module in the *httpModule* node of the application's web.config file.
Handle application events in the module	Write a handler (within the module) for every event you want to handle.
	During the *Init* method, subscribe to the events by attaching the event handlers to the events.
Override the application object in the Global.asax file	Select **Web site, Add New Item.**
	Select **Global Application Class** from the templates.
	Insert your own code for responding to the applicationwide events.
Use the application's dictionary	Access the application object (it's always available from the current *HttpContext*). Use the indexer notation to access the dictionary.

Chapter 19
Custom Handlers

After completing this chapter, you will be able to

- Recognize the role of custom handlers in ASP.NET
- Write custom handlers
- Write just-in-time compiled custom handlers
- Configure your site to include your custom handler

This chapter covers writing custom HTTP handlers. In Chapter 2, we saw the ASP.NET pipeline. Remember that the endpoint of all requests handled by ASP.NET is always an implementation of *IHttpHandler*.

ASP.NET includes several classes capable of handling requests in the most common ways. For example, the *Page* class handles requests by interpreting the query strings and returning meaningful user interface (UI)-oriented HTML. The *Service* class interprets incoming query strings as method calls and processes them accordingly. So far, we've been focusing on a single handler—*System.Web.UI.Page*. However, there are other times when it's appropriate to tweak the processing or even handle it in a completely different way. You may find yourself needing to handle a request in a way not already provided through the *System.Web.UI.Page* or the *System.Web.Services.Service* classes. What do you do then? ASP.NET supports custom HTTP handlers for just such occasions.

Handlers

So far, we've focused most attention on the *Page* class. The *Page* class is responsible primarily for managing the UI aspects of an application. Because UI processing is very involved (and much of it is boilerplate-type code), the *Page* class has a great deal of functionality built into it. The *Page* class will solve the majority of user interface needs that require UI processing.

Although we haven't come across Web services yet, the *WebService* class implements the details required to interpret HTTP requests as method calls. Clients call Web services by packaging method calls in an XML format formalized as SOAP. (Formerly the SOAP acronym stood for Simple Object Access Protocol, but as of SOAP 1.2 the acronym has been dropped to avoid some earlier confusion—SOAP isn't about objects and it isn't necessarily simple, at least to implement.) Clients call Web services in the same way they make HTTP requests for Web pages—via HTTP GET and POST requests. When the request reaches the server, it becomes the server's job to unpack the parameters, place them on a real or virtual call stack, and finally invoke the correct method. Most of the work required to make a method call via HTTP is well understood and consistent and may be pushed down into the *WebService* class.

As we saw in Chapter 2, the endpoint for all HTTP requests destined for ASP.NET is a class implementing *IHttpHandler*. *IHttpHandler* is a simple interface, including a mere two methods. However, any class implementing that interface qualifies to participate in the HTTP pipeline as an HTTP handler. We'll see the interface in detail shortly.

HTTP handlers are simply classes that implement *IHttpHandler* (just as HTTP modules are classes implementing *IHttpModule*). Handlers are listed inside web.config. As with the HTTP modules, ASP.NET comes out of the box with several HTTP handlers already (for implementing features such as tracing and preventing access to sensitive files on the site). ASP.NET comes with these HTTP handlers already registered in the master web.config configuration file (which resides alongside machine.config in the main configuration directory).

So far, ASPX, ASAX, and ASCX files have seemed to magically work within ASP.NET. For example, we saw earlier that simply surfing to an ASPX file causes ASP.NET to compile the file just in time and to synthesize a class based on *System.Web.UI.Page*. The reason the ASPX files work that way is that ASP.NET includes handlers for that functionality.

ASP.NET HTTP handlers are specified in web.config in much the same way as HTTP modules. The format of the handler elements includes four items. First, they include a file name and/or extension to which the handler applies. This is done through the *add* attribute. Remember, all HTTP requests come to the server as resource requests—the HTTP protocol is built around the idea that requests contain resource names. The second part of the handler specification, *verb*, is a list of verbs to which this handler applies. These verbs correspond to the HTTP specification. For example, you might want a handler to apply only to GET and not to POST requests. Or you may wish to have a handler apply to all requests. The third element, *type*, is the name of the .NET type assigned to handle the request. Finally, the last attribute, *validate*, specifies whether or not ASP.NET should load the class at startup immediately or wait until a matching request is received.

Listing 19-1 includes a smattering of the HTTP handlers already installed as part of ASP.NET's master web.config file.

LISTING 19-1 Excerpt from the Master Web.Config File

```
<httpHandlers>
   <add path="trace.axd" verb="*"
    type="System.Web.Handlers.TraceHandler" validate="True" />
   <add path="WebResource.axd" verb="GET"
    type="System.Web.Handlers.AssemblyResourceLoader" validate="True" />
   <add path="*.axd" verb="*"
    type="System.Web.HttpNotFoundHandler" validate="True" />
   <add path="*.aspx" verb="*"
    type="System.Web.UI.PageHandlerFactory" validate="True" />
```

```
   <add path="*.ashx" verb="*"
    type="System.Web.UI.SimpleHandlerFactory" validate="True" />
   <add path="*.asax" verb="*"
    type="System.Web.HttpForbiddenHandler" validate="True" />
   <add path="*.ascx" verb="*"
    type="System.Web.HttpForbiddenHandler" validate="True" />
   <add path="*.master" verb="*"
    type="System.Web.HttpForbiddenHandler" validate="True" />
   <add path="*.config" verb="*"
    type="System.Web.HttpForbiddenHandler" validate="True" />
   <add path="*.cs" verb="*"
    type="System.Web.HttpForbiddenHandler" validate="True" />
<!--More handlers follow... -->
</httpHandlers>
```

Let's take a look at a couple of specific handlers—the *Trace* handler and the *Forbidden* handler—to get a good idea as to how having a separate request handling facility (i.e., one that is not tied specifically to UI or to Web services) can be useful.

Built-in Handlers

One of the best examples of custom handling is the *Trace* handler that is built into ASP.NET. We looked at tracing in Chapter 17. You turn tracing on within the web.config file by inserting the trace element, *<trace enabled=true />*. This instructs the ASP.NET runtime to store summaries of the requests going through the site so they may be viewed for diagnostic purposes.

ASP.NET caches the tracing output in memory. To view the trace results, you surf to the virtual directory managing the site and ask for a specific resource: Trace.axd. Take a look at Listing 19-1 and you'll see the first entry among all the standard HTTP handlers is for a resource named *Trace.axd*. The tracing functionality behind ASP.NET falls outside of normal UI processing, so it makes sense that tracing is handled by a custom handler.

When you surf to the Trace.axd resource, the handler renders HTML that looks like the output shown in Figure 19-1. The processing for this handler is very specific—the handler's job is to render the results of the last few requests. As you can see in Figure 19-2, selecting the *View Details* link resubmits the request with a parameter *id=3* in the query string. This causes the handler to render the details of the third request. Figure 19-3 shows the Internet Information Services (IIS) file mapping for files with the .axd extension. Although you won't really see this aspect until deployment time, it's interesting to observe because it shows how ASP.NET is very versatile in the kinds of requests it can handle. IIS handles Trace.axd requests the same way as any other ASP.NET request. That means IIS will pass requests for resources with an extension of .axd on to ASP.NET. Once inside the ASP.NET pipeline, the web.config file tells ASP.NET to handle the request with the *Trace* handler.

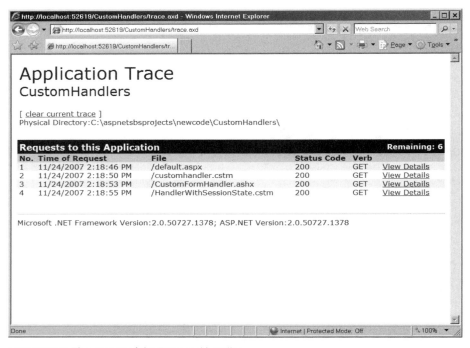

FIGURE 19-1 The output of the Trace.axd handler

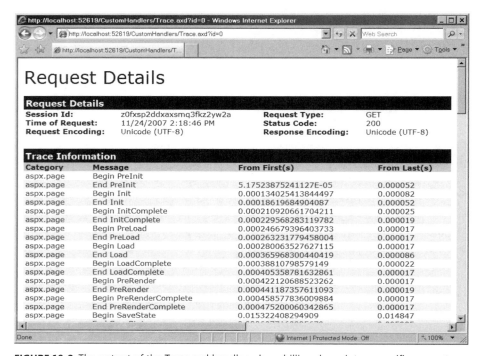

FIGURE 19-2 The output of the Trace.axd handler when drilling down into a specific request summary

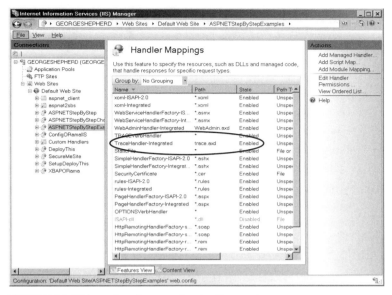

FIGURE 19-3 IIS has a handler mapping for Trace.axd.

If you look through the default web.config file a bit more, you'll see some other critical ASP.NET handlers. As you might expect, source code is banned explicitly from normal clients by default. Notice that files such as *.cs, *.config, and *.vb are handled by the *Forbidden* handler. If you try to look at source code via a Web browser, ASP.NET returns the page shown in Figure 19-4 by default.

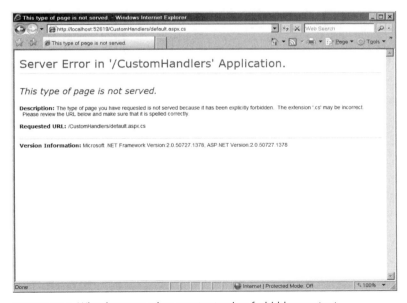

FIGURE 19-4 What happens when you try to view forbidden content

Remember that ASP.NET's configuration is very malleable and that you may choose to let clients see your source code by one of two means. You may remove the source code extension to ASP.NET mappings within IIS. Alternatively, you may write your own source code viewer handlers and declare them in your application's web.config file.

These handlers plug into the pipeline by implementing *IHttpHandler*. Let's take a look at this key interface.

IHttpHandler

Here it is. Shield your eyes while you look at Listing 19-2 (just kidding—it's not a very big interface).

LISTING 19-2 The *IHttpHandler* Interface

```
public interface IHttpHandler
{
  void ProcessRequest(HttpContext ctx);
  bool IsReusable {get;}
}
```

There's really not much to it, is there? The interface includes a method named *ProcessRequest* and a property named *IsReusable*. If the handler instance can be used multiple times, then *IsReusable* should return true. If the handler generally returns static content, it's probably reusable. If the content is dynamic, it's probably not reusable. The heart of the handler is the *ProcessRequest* method that includes a single parameter: the current *HttpContext*.

Once a request finally arrives at the handler (through the *ProcessRequest* method), *ProcessRequest* can literally do anything to respond to the request. The Trace.axd handler responds to a GET request by listing the requests being tracked by the runtime. The forbidden handler responds by tossing a roadblock in the processing pipeline so the client can't see the forbidden resource. A custom Web service might respond to the request by parsing the XML payload, constructing a call stack, and making a call to an internal method.

Implementing *IHttpHandler* is simple—at least from the architectural standpoint. The *ProcessRequest* method takes a single parameter—the current *HttpContext*. However, the code inside *ProcessRequest* is free to do just about anything, possibly making the internal processing quite complex! The following example illustrates taking over the entire form-rendering process to display a list of choices within a combo box, allowing the end client to select from the choices, and finally rendering the chosen item.

Writing a Custom Handler

1. Create a project named *CustomHandlers*.

2. Add a new class library subproject to the CustomHandlers Web site (just as you did when you created an HTTP module). Name the project *CustomFormHandlerLib*. The name of the class it generates for you is *Class1*. Rename the file *CustomFormHandler.cs* and the class *CustomFormHandler*.

3. The library generated by Visual Studio comes without any knowledge of the ASP.NET classes. Add a reference to the *System.Web* assembly.

4. To turn the *CustomFormHandler* class into an eligible handler, add the *IHttpHandler* interface to the inheritance list and implement *ProcessRequest*. Add a method named *ManageForm* that takes a parameter of type *HttpContext*. *ManageForm* should write out *<html>*, *<body>*, and *<form>* tags through *Response.Write*. Write the question "Hello there. What's cool about .NET?" followed by a line break. Next, write a *<select>* tag and set the *name* attribute to "Feature." Then write several .NET features surrounded by *<option>* tags. This will produce a drop-down list box on the client's browser. Write out an *<input>* tag. The tag's *type* attribute should be *submit*, its *name* attribute should be "Lookup," and its *value* attribute should be "Lookup." Next, look up the new value for the "Feature" selection tag within the *HttpContext*'s *Request.Params* collection. If the value is not *null*, then the end user selected something. Write the value provided by the "Feature" selection tag. Finally, write out closing tags. That is, *</form>*, *</body>*, and *</html>* tags.

Have the *ProcessRequest* method call the *ManageForm* method like so:

```
using System;
using System.Collections.Generic;
using System.Text;
using System.Web;
public class CustomFormHandler : IHttpHandler
{
    public void ProcessRequest(HttpContext ctx)
    {
        ManageForm(ctx);
    }

    public void ManageForm(HttpContext context)
    {
        context.Response.Write("<html><body><form>");

        context.Response.Write(
            "<h2>Hello there. What's cool about .NET?</h2>");

        context.Response.Write(
            "<select name='Feature'>");
        context.Response.Write(
            "<option> Strong typing</option>");
        context.Response.Write(
            "<option> Managed code</option>");
        context.Response.Write(
            "<option> Language agnosticism</option>");
```

```
            context.Response.Write(
                "<option> Better security model</option>");
            context.Response.Write(
                "<option> Threading and async delegates</option>");
            context.Response.Write(
                "<option> XCOPY deployment</option>");
            context.Response.Write(
                "<option> Reasonable HTTP handling framework</option>");
            context.Response.Write("</select>");
            context.Response.Write("</br>");

            context.Response.Write(
                "<input type=submit name='Lookup' value='Lookup'></input>");
            context.Response.Write("</br>");

            if (context.Request.Params["Feature"] != null)
            {
                context.Response.Write("Hi, you picked: ");
                context.Response.Write(
                    context.Request.Params["Feature"]);
                context.Response.Write(
                    " as your favorite feature.</br>");
            }

            context.Response.Write("</form></body></html>");
        }

        public bool IsReusable {
            get
            {
                return true;
            }
        }
    }
}
```

The code within the *ProcessRequest* will render a *form* element and a *select* element that renders a form that can be submitted by the browser. When the form is submitted back to the server, the parameter collection will contain a *Features* element. The code examines the parameter collection to see if it references a feature, and it displays the feature if it's been selected.

5. The class library you just created deposits its output in the project directory. In order for ASP.NET to use the page, the resulting executable needs to live in the application directory's *bin* subdirectory. You can do this by adding the CustomHandlerLib.dll as a project reference to the Web site. Click the right mouse button on the Web site project within the Solution Explorer and add a new project reference. Navigate to the *CustomFormHandlerLib* project's *bin* directory and choose the CustomFormHandlerLib.dll file.

6. Now update web.config so that it uses the handler when clients request the *CustomFormHandler* resource. If you don't already have a web.config in the project, add one. Then insert an *httpHandlers* section that points requests for the *CustomFormHandler* to the new *CustomFormHandler* class.

```
<configuration >
  <appSettings/>
  <connectionStrings/>
<system.web>
    <httpHandlers>

        <!-- There will be some other entries here... -->
        <add path="*.cstm" verb="*"
           type="CustomFormHandlerLib.CustomFormHandler, CustomFormHandlerLib"
           validate="true" />
    </httpHandlers>
</system.web>
</configuration>
```

Note If this site were running under IIS, you would need to tell IIS about the new file types to be handled by the *CustomFormHandler*. If you decide to run this application under IIS (instead of the Visual Studio Web server), you may configure IIS to run your handler by doing the following. Open IIS and drill down to the CustomHandler virtual directory. Open the Features View and locate the **Handler Mappings** icon.

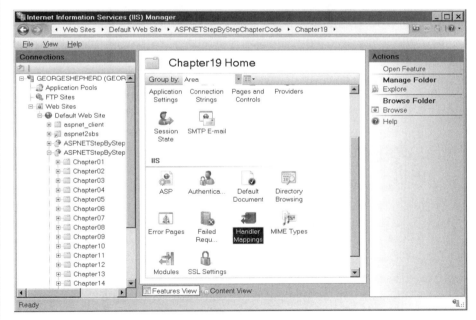

Double-click on the **Handler Mappings** icon to bring up the Handler Mappings page.

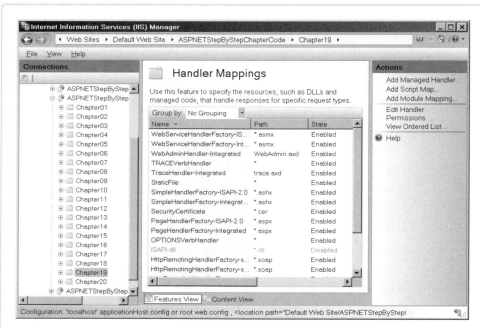

Click the right mouse button in the middle of the Handler Mappings page to bring up the local menu. Select **Add Managed Handler**. Type in an extension you'd like to have mapped to the custom handler. Then assign a handler. IIS will look at all the handlers available to your application (including the ones local to your application). Select the handler from the drop-down list, give the handler an alias, and you'll be able to surf to that file type to invoke the handler.

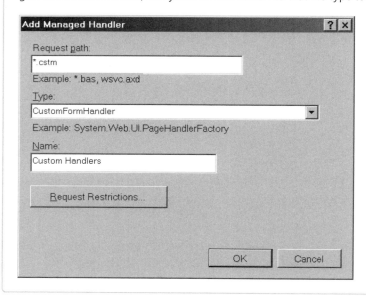

7. Finally, create a blank Text file named *CustomHandler.cstm* to your project. You can use the file with that extension to surf to the handler.

8. Surf to the customhandler.cstm resource and ASP.NET will invoke the custom handler you just created.

Of course, most of this processing could be handled more easily by setting up a Web form. However, this example shows the flexibility of the ASP.NET handler architecture. It should also give you more appreciation for the Web form and custom controls machinery within ASP.NET.

Handlers and Session State

In Chapter 14, we looked at session state. Session state works automatically within the context of *System.Web.UI.Page*. However, custom handlers need to turn on the ability to use session state deliberately.

The .NET architecture uses an interesting idiom known as *marker interfaces*. Marker interfaces are empty interfaces (without any methods or properties defined). Their sole purpose is to signal the runtime as to various aspects of the application. For example, ASP.NET runtime often uses them to turn on and off various features. When the runtime detects a marker interface as part of an object's class hierarchy, the runtime can bring into play certain features.

For a handler to use session state, it must have the *System.Web.SessionState.IRequiresSessionState* interface in its inheritance list. That way the runtime will know to load and store session state at the beginning and end of each request.

Listing 19-3 shows a handler with session state enabled.

LISTING 19-3 Example HTTP Handler That Accesses Session State

```
using System;
using System.Collections.Generic;
using System.Text;
using System.Web;
using System.Web.SessionState;

public class HandlerWithSessionState : IHttpHandler, IRequiresSessionState
{
    public void ProcessRequest(HttpContext ctx)
    {
        string strData = (string)ctx.Session["SomeSessionData"];

        if (String.IsNullOrEmpty(strData))
        {
            strData = "This goes in session state";
            ctx.Session["SomeSessionData"] = strData;
        }
        ctx.Response.Write("This was in session state: " + strData);
    }
```

```
public bool IsReusable {
  get
  {
    return true;
  }
}
}
```

Generic Handlers (ASHX Files)

Just as ASPX files can be compiled on the fly ("just in time"), so can handlers. Generic handlers have an extension of ASHX. They're equivalent to custom handlers written in C# or Visual Basic in that they contain classes that fully implement *IHttpHandler*. They're convenient in the same way ASPX files are convenient. You simply surf to them and they're compiled automatically.

The following example illustrates the *CustomFormHandler* implemented as a "generic handler."

Writing a generic handler

1. Add a "generic" handler to the Web site. Go to the Solution Explorer, click the right mouse button on the **CustomHandler Web site** node and select **Add New Item**. Select *Generic Handler* from the templates. Name the handler *CustomFormHandler.ashx*.

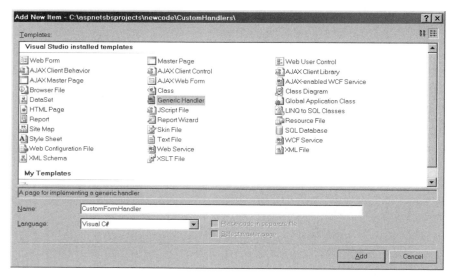

2. Visual Studio generates a handler that includes a stubbed-out *ProcessRequest* method and a completed *IsReusable* property. Write a function to emit the form-handling code (you can borrow it from the last exercise), and call the method from inside

ProcessRequest. Borrow the code from the earlier example to implement the handler. Replace the stubbed-out method and property with real implementations.

```
<%@ WebHandler Language="C#" Class="CustomFormHandler" %>
using System.Web;
public class CustomFormHandler : IHttpHandler {

    public void ProcessRequest (HttpContext context) {
        ManageForm(context);
    }

    public void ManageForm(HttpContext context)
    {
        context.Response.Write("<html><body><form>");

        context.Response.Write(
          "<h2>Hello there. What's cool about .NET?</h2>");
        context.Response.Write("<select name='Feature'>");
        context.Response.Write("<option> Strong typing</option>");
        context.Response.Write("<option> Managed code</option>");
        context.Response.Write("<option> Language agnosticism</option>");
        context.Response.Write("<option> Better security model</option>");
        context.Response.Write(
            "<option> Threading and async delegates</option>");
        context.Response.Write("<option> XCOPY deployment</option>");
        context.Response.Write(
            "<option> Reasonable HTTP handling framework</option>");
        context.Response.Write("</select>");
        context.Response.Write("</br>");
      context.Response.Write(
          "<input type=submit name='Lookup' value='Lookup'></input>");
        context.Response.Write("</br>");
        if (context.Request.Params["Feature"] != null)
        {
            context.Response.Write("Hi, you picked: ");
            context.Response.Write(context.Request.Params["Feature"]);
            context.Response.Write(" as your favorite feature.</br>");
        }

        context.Response.Write("</form></body></html>");
    }

    public bool IsReusable
    {
        get
        {
            return false;
        }
    }
}
```

3. Browse to the CustomFormHandler.ashx file. It should work in just the same way as the handler implemented in the *CustomFormHandler* class (that you wrote in the first example):

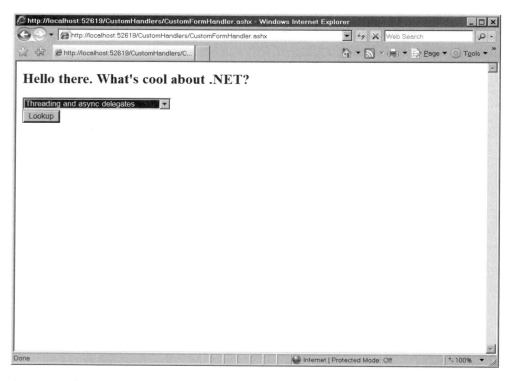

The advantage of using the generic handler is twofold. First, it's usually much more convenient to generate a simple handler than it is to create a whole new assembly to handle the request. Second, you don't need to configure either web.config or IIS (when it comes time to deploy). That is, ASP.NET and IIS already understand what to do when encountering resource requests with the extension of .ashx. Installing ASP.NET places those when mapping into IIS.

However, ASHX files have the same limitations as ASPX and ASCX files in terms of their place in an ASP.NET project. Simple generic handlers go with the project. That is, for the handler to work, it must accompany the whole project. Alternatively, custom handlers deployed as separate assemblies may be deployed and shared among the enterprise as Global assemblies (that is, strongly named assemblies placed in the Global Assembly Cache).

Summary

ASP.NET includes a number of built-in classes to handle most kinds of requests. For example, ASP.NET includes UI handlers (*System.Web.UI.Page* and *System.Web.UI.Control*). ASP.NET also includes a Web service handler (*System.Web.Services.WebService*). These classes will probably handle most of the requirements you might come across. However, for those fringe cases that require custom handling, ASP.NET supports the custom handler.

The endpoint for requests coming through ASP.NET is always a class implementing *IHttpHandler*. *IHttpHandler* has very little surface area. You simply override the *IsReusable* property and the *ProcessRequest* method. *ProcessRequest* can pretty much do anything you want it to do. The example in this book included a handler that manages rendering a form and handling input.

For a custom handler assembly to work, it must be mapped to a file path or extension in the application's web.config file. The extension must also be mapped within the IIS metabase if you intend to deploy it to IIS.

ASP.NET also supports handlers that may be compiled just in time. Simple handlers are easy to create and deploy because you don't need to modify the web.config file, nor do you need to modify the IIS metabase.

Chapter 19 Quick Reference

To	Do This
Create a custom handler assembly	Create a new class implementing *IHttpHandler*.
	Implement the *IsReusable* property.
	Implement *ProcessRequest*.
Assign a file mapping to the handler in ASP.NET	Configure the handler in the *httpHandler* segment of the application's web.config file.
Assign a file mapping to the handler in IIS	Click the right mouse button on the virtual directory.
	Select **Properties**.
	Click the **Configure** button.
	Click the **Add** button.
	Add a new extension and map it to aspnet_isapi.dll.
Create a simple handler	Select **Web site, Add New Item**.
	Select **Generic Handler** from the templates.
	Insert your own code for responding to the request.

Part V

Services, AJAX, Deployment, and Silverlight

Chapter 20
ASP.NET Web Services

After completing this chapter, you will be able to

- Understand the importance of Web services
- Use the technologies underlying Web services
- Write Web services using ASP.NET
- Consume Web services synchronously
- Consume Web services asynchronously

This chapter covers Web services from an ASP.NET perspective. During the past decade, "Web services" has emerged as a buzzword for enabling the next generation of computer connectivity. Although networking a bunch of computers isn't trivial, it's generally a solved problem these days. Most workplaces in the modern world depend on an internal network of computers to allow the people staffing the enterprise to communicate and work effectively. Even though Microsoft has recently released Windows Communication Foundation (which unifies the programming model for sockets, Web services, Microsoft Message Queue, and .NET Remoting), ASP.NET's ASMX framework is still part of the ASP.NET canon and remains a viable way to do remoting over the Internet.

High connectivity among computers has been a goal since personal computing began. Although only a pipe dream in the earliest years, the ability to connect computers is commonplace these days. With the rise of the internal company network comes the desire to tie machines together programmatically as well. That is, a program on one machine should be able to call program methods on another machine without human intervention. Many enterprises spent nearly the entire last decade of the twentieth century trying to get their computers to talk to one another programmatically. On the Microsoft platform, this was usually done with Distributed Component Object Model (DCOM) before .NET came along.

The next step in connecting computers is happening over the Internet. There's already a ubiquitous connection available (computers connected via HTTP, the HyperText Transfer Protocol) and a well-understood wire format (XML). Together, these two elements make up *XML Web Services*.

Remoting

The desire to call software methods "over there" from "over here" has been around ever since the advent of distributed computing networks. Beginning in the days of Remote Procedure Calls all the way through the latest version of DCOM, the promise of remoting has been to exercise a network of computers to solve computing problems rather than pinning the whole problem on a single computer.

Remoting involves several fundamental steps:

1. The caller flattens the local method call stack into a stream that may be sent over the wire. This process is known as *serialization*.

2. The caller sends the serialized call stack across the wire.

3. The endpoint receives the serialized call stack and turns it into a usable call stack on the server. This is known as *deserialization*.

4. The endpoint processes the method call.

5. The endpoint transmits the results back to the caller.

Figure 20-1 illustrates the basic connection underlying any remoting activity.

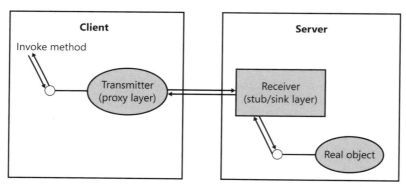

FIGURE 20-1 The general remoting architecture employed by most remoting systems

Several different network remoting technologies have emerged during the past decade, including DCOM and CORBA. (CORBA is an acronym for Common Object Request Broker Architecture—a remoting technology prevalent on other operating systems in the mid- to late 1990s.) It doesn't matter if the remoting framework is DCOM, CORBA, or even the .NET Remoting services—the fundamental steps of remoting remain the same. For example, in DCOM the client talks to a component called the *proxy*, whose job it is to flatten the call stack (serialization) and send it on its way. On the server side, a component called the *stub* receives the network packets and turns the incoming stream into a real call on the server (deserialization). If the framework is .NET Remoting, then the term for the proxy component is the *transparent proxy*. The transparent proxy talks to the real proxy, which sends the bytes across the network. Once at the server, a component called the *sink* unpacks the bytes and turns them into a real call.

XML Web Services work much the same way. The fundamental remoting steps are all there. However, this time around the wire format is an XML format formalized as SOAP and the connection protocol is, at least for ASP.NET, HTTP. Other systems might use other connection protocols, like the Simple Mail Transfer Protocol, or SMTP. ASP.NET, however, only supports HTTP.

Remoting over the Web

In the previous 19 chapters, we've looked primarily at how ASP.NET makes it easy to handle a wide variety of Web application scenarios. We've seen that ASP.NET handles HTTP GET and POST verbs, redirecting the request to a handler. Until now, the job of the handler has been to process the incoming query string and render some output generally intended for human consumption. Developing an XML Web Service is all about writing an application intended for consumption by another program.

XML Web Services are Internet endpoints available most commonly through HTTP and HTTPS (Hypertext Transfer Protocol Secure). The job of an XML Web Service is to consume HTTP requests containing XML payloads formatted as SOAP. The messages have a specific schema applied to them, which in effect may be thought of as a transportable type system. Web services are also responsible for providing metadata (Web Service Description Language) describing the messages they consume and produce.

SOAP

Although it seems obvious that the Web is an excellent medium for distributing a user interface–oriented application to the masses, it may not seem so obvious that the same technology might be used to make method calls. One of the main reasons Web services may exist now is because different enterprises can agree on what a method call looks like, and they can all access it over already existing HTTP connections.

XML Web Service method calls are encoded using XML. The format that callers and services agree on was originally named *Simple Object Access Protocol*. The full name has been dropped, but the moniker "SOAP" remains. The SOAP protocol is an XML formalization for message-based communication. SOAP defines how to format messages, how to bind messages over HTTP, and a standard error representation.

Transporting the Type System

The primary interoperability focus of XML Web Services is to widen the audience of an application so that as many clients as possible can invoke methods of the service. Because the connective medium involved is the Internet, any computer that can invoke HTTP requests becomes a potential client. Paired with the ability to connect over HTTP and to format calls as SOAP messages, a client can make calls to any of your Web service's methods.

With the focus on interoperability among as many platforms as possible, it becomes very important that the caller and the service agree on the data types being passed back and forth. When a client calls a method containing parameters, the two endpoints might each have their own way of interpreting the parameter types. For example, passing a character string between two .NET endpoints does *not* pose a major problem. However, passing a string between a client running a non-.NET platform and a service written using .NET *does* pose a problem because a character string type is almost certainly represented differently on each platform.

When calling methods between two computers using HTTP and XML, it's very important that a schema is provided on each end so that the parameter types are interpreted correctly. Fortunately, this detail has been pushed down into the Web service tools that are currently available.

Web Service Description Language

Given a connection protocol (HTTP) and wire format (XML + SOAP), the final ingredient that makes Web services a viable technology is the notion of a service description. Even though two endpoints agree on the connection protocol and the wire format, the client still has to know how to set up the call to a service.

Services advertise their capabilities via another XML formalization named *Web Service Description Language* (WSDL). WSDL specifies the target URL of the service, the format in which the service expects to see methods packaged, and how the messages will be encoded.

If You Couldn't Use ASP.NET...

Just as there's nothing stopping you from writing code to handle HTTP requests from scratch, you could handle Web service requests from handwritten code. You could write a Web service armed with only a decent XML parser and a socket library (for communicating over your server's communication ports). The work involved includes the following:

1. Listening to port 80 to receive method calls
2. Parsing the incoming XML stream, unpacking the parameters
3. Setting up the incoming parameters and performing the work
4. Packing a suitable XML SOAP response and sending it to the caller
5. Advertising the service's capabilities via WSDL

After the second or third time implementing a service by hand, you'd probably come to the following conclusion: Much of the work involved in making a Web service work is repetitive and might as well be pushed into a library. That's exactly what ASP.NET does. ASP.NET handles the details of making a Web service through the *System.Web.Services.WebService* class.

A Web Service in ASP.NET

ASP.NET handles Web services with a limited amount of programming effort. Remember how the ASP.NET pipeline architecture works. Requests coming from clients end up at the server's port 80. ASP.NET Web services live in a file type named with the extension .asmx. If the server is running ASP.NET, Internet Information Services (IIS) routes the request for files with the ASMX extension to ASP.NET, where they're handled like any other request.

ASP.NET includes an attribute named *WebMethod* that maps a SOAP request and its response to a real method in a class. To make the service work, you simply derive a class from *System .Web.Services.WebService* and expose methods using *WebMethod*. When the request comes through, the target class will be "bound" to the .asmx endpoint. As with normal page execution, the current *HttpContext* is always available. In addition, ASP.NET automates WSDL generation, and Microsoft provides tools to automate generating client-side proxies given WSDL input from an XML Web Service.

The following example illustrates an XML Web Service that retrieves quotes from the quotes collection we saw in Chapters 15 and 18. This example will expose the quotes collection via a set of methods expressed as an XML Web Service.

Write an ASP.NET Web service

1. Create a new Web site project. Name the project *QuoteService*. Make it a file system–based ASP.NET Web Service.

2. Rename the code file in *App_Code* from *Service.cs* to *QuoteService.cs*. Rename the ASMX file from *Service.asmx* to *QuoteService.asmx*. Use the Visual Studio refactoring facilities to change the name of the service class from *Service* to *QuoteService*. Open the QuoteService.cs file. Highlight the name of the *Service* class and click the right mouse button on it. From the local menu, select **Rename** from the **Refactor** menu. When prompted, type **QuoteService** for the new name of the class. This will change the name of the class in the C# code files. Then you'll need to change the reference to the service class in the .asmx file manually. This is the line at the top of the .asmx file:

   ```
   <%@ WebService Language="C#" CodeBehind="~/App_Code/QuoteService.cs" Class="Service" %>
   ```

   It should become

   ```
   <%@ WebService Language="C#" CodeBehind="~/App_Code/QuoteService.cs" Class="QuoteService" %>
   ```

3. After all this is done, your stubbed-out XML Web Service should look like this:

   ```
   using System;
   using System.Linq;
   using System.Web;
   using System.Web.Services;
   using System.Web.Services.Protocols;
   using System.Xml.Linq;
   ```

```
[WebService(Namespace = "http://tempuri.org/"")]
[WebServiceBinding(ConformsTo = WsiProfiles.BasicProfile1_1)]
// To allow this Web Service to be called from script,
// using ASP.NET AJAX, uncomment the following line.
// [System.Web.Script.Services.ScriptService]
public class QuoteService : System.Web.Services.WebService
{
    public QuoteService () {
        //Uncomment the following line if using designed components
        //InitializeComponent();
    }

    [WebMethod]
    public string HelloWorld() {
        return "Hello World";
    }
}
```

In addition to the C# file, you'll also get an ASMX file. The XML Web Service handler (named *ASMX*, with "M" standing for "method") works very much like the ASPX page handlers and the ASHX custom handlers. When clients surf to the ASMX page, the Web server directs the request to the appropriate handler (the ASMX handler factory). Once there, ASP.NET compiles the code associated with the ASMX file and runs it just as it would any other HTTP handler. Here's what the ASMX file looks like. There's not much here. Most of the code lies within the accompanying code file.

```
<%@ WebService Language="C#"
CodeBehind="~/App_Code/QuoteService.cs" Class="QuoteService" %>
```

4. Surf to the QuoteService.asmx file to see what a default HTTP GET renders.

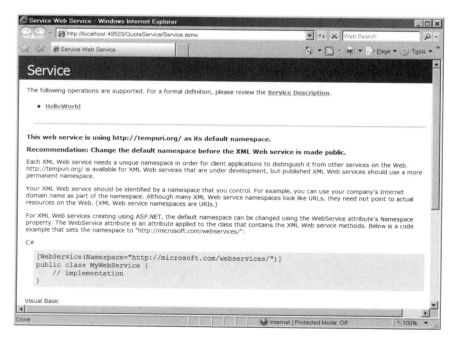

By default, ASP.NET renders the names of the available methods when you just GET the ASMX file. Notice that the *HelloWorld* method (provided by Visual Studio) is exposed. If you want to try running the *HelloWorld* method, click the *HelloWorld* link, which renders a new page with a button you can click to invoke the method. The site will respond with this page:

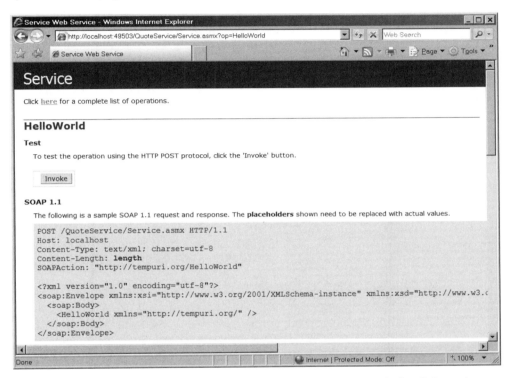

5. Examine the WSDL. Before adding any code, click the *Service Description* link on the first page displayed after surfing to the XML Web Service. The Web service will send back the WSDL for the site. You can page through it to see what WSDL looks like. The information contained in the WSDL is not meant for human consumption but, rather, for client proxy generators (which we'll examine soon).

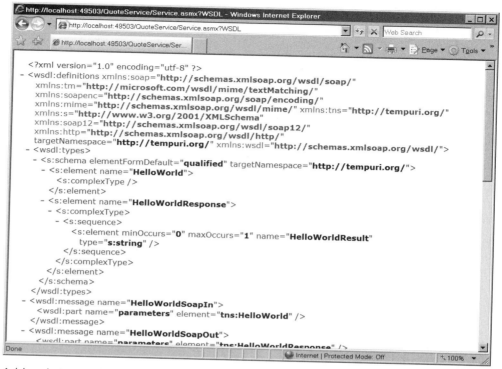

6. Add code to manage quotes. To have some quotes to expose as Web methods, import the *QuotesCollection* from Chapter 15. The project name is *UseDataCaching*. Highlight the *App_Code* node within the solution explorer. Select **Web Site**, **Add Existing Item** from the main menu and find the file QuotesCollection.cs. In addition to importing the QuotesCollection.cs file, grab the QuotesCollection.xml and QuotesCollection.xsd files from the *UseDataCaching\App_Data* directory and place them in the *App_Data* directory for this project.

7. Write a method to load the *QuotesCollection*. Put the code in the QuoteService.cs file. Check first to see if the *QuotesCollection* is in the cache. If not, create a *QuotesCollection* object and load it using the quotescollection.xml and quotescollection.xsd files. Load the quotes into the application cache during the construction of the *QuoteService* class. When you add the data to the cache, build a dependency on the quotescollection.xml file. One of the Web methods we'll add will modify the XML file, so we'll want to flush it from the cache when it's updated. The code from the data caching chapter loaded the XML data in the *Page_Load* handler. In this case, there's no page, so you need a separate method to load the quotes. Here's the code that does the trick. Also, notice the addition of the *System.Data* namespace.

```csharp
using System;
using System.Web;
using System.Data;
using System.Web.Services;
```

```
using System.Web.Services.Protocols;
using System.Web.Caching;

[WebService(Namespace = "http://tempuri.org/")]
[WebServiceBinding(ConformsTo = WsiProfiles.BasicProfile1_1)]
public class QuoteService : System.Web.Services.WebService
{

    QuotesCollection LoadQuotes()
    {
        QuotesCollection quotesCollection;

        HttpContext ctx = HttpContext.Current;
        quotesCollection = (QuotesCollection)ctx.Cache["quotesCollection"];
        if (quotesCollection == null)
        {
            quotesCollection = new QuotesCollection();
            String strAppPath = Server.MapPath("");

            String strFilePathXml =
                strAppPath +
                "\\App_Data\\QuotesCollection.xml";
            String strFilePathSchema =
                strAppPath +
                "\\App_Data\\QuotesCollection.xsd";

            quotesCollection.ReadXmlSchema(strFilePathSchema);
            quotesCollection.ReadXml(strFilePathXml);

            CacheDependency cacheDependency =
                new CacheDependency(strFilePathXml);

            ctx.Cache.Insert("quotesCollection",
                    quotesCollection,
                    cacheDependency,
                    Cache.NoAbsoluteExpiration,
                    Cache.NoSlidingExpiration,
                    CacheItemPriority.Default,
                    null);
        }
        return quotesCollection;
    }

    public QuoteService () {
    }

    [WebMethod]
    public string HelloWorld() {
        return "Hello World";
    }
}
```

8. Write a method that retrieves a random quote from the table and sends it back to the client. The *QuotesCollection* class derives from the *DataTable* class, which is a collection of *DataRows*. Unfortunately, returning a *DataRow* from a Web method doesn't work

because *DataRow* doesn't have a default constructor. So instead, add a new class to the Web service that wraps the quote data. That is, add a new class that contains strings for the quote, the originator's first name, and the originator's last name.

Delete the *HelloWorld* Web method and add a new Web method. Name the new Web method for fetching a quote *GetAQuote*. Have *GetAQuote* load the quotes using *LoadQuotes*. The *GetAQuote* method should generate a number between zero and the number of rows in the *QuotesCollection*, fetch that row from the table, wrap the data in a Quote class, and return it to the client. Be sure to adorn the *GetAQuote* method with the *WebMethod* attribute. To do all of this, add this code to the QuoteService.cs file.

```
using System;
using System.Web;
using System.Data;
using System.Web.Services;
using System.Web.Services.Protocols;
using System.Web.Caching;
using System.Data;

public class Quote
{
    private string _strQuote;
    private string _strOriginatorLastName;
    private string _strOriginatorFirstName;

    public string strQuote
    {
        get { return _strQuote; }
        set { _strQuote = value; }
    }

    public string strOriginatorLastName
    {
        get { return _strOriginatorLastName; }
        set { _strOriginatorLastName = value; }
    }

    public string strOriginatorFirstName
    {
        get { return _strOriginatorFirstName; }
        set { _strOriginatorFirstName = value; }
    }

    public Quote()
    {
    }

    public Quote(String strQuote,
                 String strOriginatorLastName,
                 String strOriginatorFirstName)
    {
        _strQuote = strQuote;
        _strOriginatorLastName = strOriginatorLastName;
        _strOriginatorFirstName = strOriginatorFirstName;
```

```
        }
    }

    [WebService(Namespace = "http://tempuri.org/")]
    [WebServiceBinding(ConformsTo = WsiProfiles.BasicProfile1_1)]
    public class QuoteService : System.Web.Services.WebService
    {

        // Other code here...

        // LoadQuotes goes here
        [WebMethod]
        public Quote GetAQuote()
        {
            QuotesCollection quotesCollection = this.LoadQuotes();
            int nNumQuotes = quotesCollection.Rows.Count;
            Random random = new Random();
            int nQuote = random.Next(nNumQuotes);
            DataRow dataRow = quotesCollection.Rows[nQuote];
            Quote quote = new Quote((String)dataRow["Quote"],
                          (String)dataRow["OriginatorLastName"],
                          (String)dataRow["OriginatorFirstName"]);
            return quote;
        }

    }
```

9. Finally, add two more methods: one to add a quote to the *QuotesCollection* and another to fetch all the quotes. Name the method for adding quotes *AddQuote*. *AddQuote* should take a *Quote* class as a parameter and use it to create a new row in the *QuotesCollection*. *AddQuote* should reserialize the XML and XSD files.

   GetAllQuotes should load the quotes from the cache, place the *QuotesCollection* in a *DataSet*, and return a *DataSet*. Use a *DataSet* because it is more easily deserialized by the client. Be sure to adorn the methods with the *WebMethod* attribute.

```
using System;
using System.Web;
using System.Web.Services;
using System.Web.Services.Protocols;
using System.Web.Caching;
using System.Data;

// Quote structure goes here...

[WebService(Namespace = "http://tempuri.org/")]
[WebServiceBinding(ConformsTo = WsiProfiles.BasicProfile1_1)]
public class QuoteService : System.Web.Services.WebService
{

    // LoadQuotes goes here

    // Other code here...
    [WebMethod]
    public void AddQuote(Quote quote)
```

```
        {
            QuotesCollection quotesCollection = this.LoadQuotes();

            DataRow dr = quotesCollection.NewRow();
            dr[0] = quote.strQuote;
            dr[1] = quote.strOriginatorLastName;
            dr[2] = quote.strOriginatorFirstName;
            quotesCollection.Rows.Add(dr);

            String strAppPath = Server.MapPath("");
            String strFilePathXml =
                strAppPath + "\\App_Data\\QuotesCollection.xml";
            String strFilePathSchema =
                strAppPath + "\\App_Data\\QuotesCollection.xsd";

            quotesCollection.WriteXmlSchema(strFilePathSchema);
            quotesCollection.WriteXml(strFilePathXml);
        }

        [WebMethod]
        public DataSet GetAllQuotes()
        {
            QuotesCollection quotesCollection = LoadQuotes();
            DataSet dataSet = new DataSet();
            dataSet.Tables.Add(quotesCollection);
            return dataSet;
        }

    }
```

You now have an XML Web Service that will deliver quotes to the client on request. You can surf to the ASMX page and try out the methods if you want to see them work (using the default page rendered by the ASMX file). However, the real power lies in writing clients against the XML Web Service so the client can consume the Web Service programmatically.

Consuming Web Services

Consuming a Web service is nearly as easy as writing one. The Microsoft .NET Framework and Visual Studio have handy utilities that automatically generate proxies for XML Web Services. Visual Studio is not the only way to consume XML Web Services, however. Many modern applications have ways to consume XML Web Services, including such applications as the Microsoft Office suite. XML Web Services are meant to be platform independent, and most modern computing platforms support consuming XML Web Services.

The following example illustrates consuming the QuoteService via a small command line program.

Use the QuoteService synchronously

1. Add a new subproject to the solution. Make the new project a console application by selecting the *Console Application* template. Name the project *ConsumeWebService*.

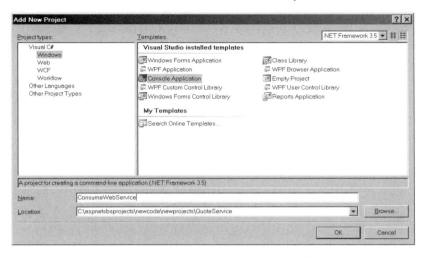

2. Create a Service Reference to the quote service. Highlight the ConsumeWebService project in the solution explorer and click the right mouse button. Select **Add Service Reference** from the local menu. You'll see this dialog box:

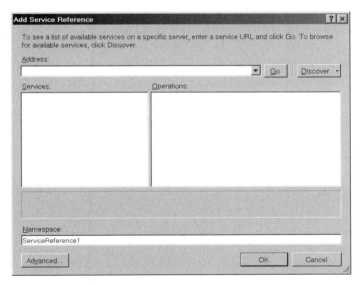

Click the **Discover** button to get a listing of available services. Expand the tree to show the *QuoteService*:

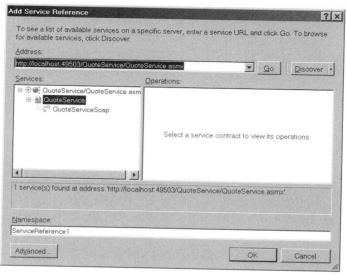

3. Click the **QuoteServiceSoap** tree node. You should see all the available services (in this case, there are three). Give the new reference the namespace *QuoteServer*, which is more meaningful.

4. Tell the proxy generator to build asynchronous methods, which you'll need for a later example. Click the **Advanced...** button of the **Add Service Reference** dialog box. You should see a dialog box like the following. Make sure the **Generate Asynchronous Operations** check box is checked.

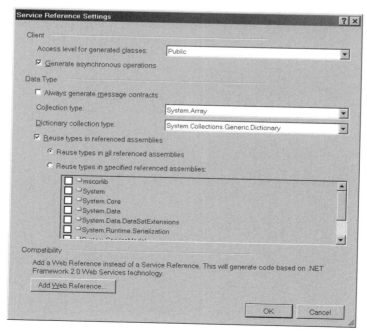

Click **OK**. Visual Studio will generate a proxy for you.

The proxy for the QuoteService is in a file named *Reference.cs*. The namespace in which the proxy lives is *QuoteServer*. You may view it by double-clicking on the **QuoteServer** node under the *ServiceReferences* in the Solution Explorer. This will bring up the Object Browser. Double-clicking on the elements within the service references will open up the Reference.cs file.

> **Tip** Another way to generate a proxy is to surf to the Web service, ask for the WSDL manually, and then run the WSDL code through a utility named *WSDL.exe*.
>
> For example, the following query string fetches the WSDL:
>
> *http://localhost:port/QuoteService/QuoteService.asmx?wsdl*
>
> Simply run this URL through the WSDL command line utility:
>
> `C:\>WSDL` *http://localhost:port/QuoteService/QuoteService.asmx?wsdl*
>
> This will generate a C# proxy file you may use in your application.

5. Call the XML Web Service through the proxy. The name of the QuoteService proxy is *QuoteServiceSoapClient*. You instantiate it like you would any other class. When you call methods, the proxy will wrap the call in a SOAP envelope and send the request to the destination specified within the proxy. Try making calls to *GetAQuote*, *AddQuote*, and *GetAllQuotes*, as shown here.

```
using System;
using System.Collections.Generic;
using System.Linq;
using System.Text;
using System.Data;
using ConsumeWebService.QuoteServer;

namespace ConsumeWebService
{
    class Program
    {
        static void Main(string[] args)
        {
            Quote quote = null;

            QuoteServiceSoapClient quoteService =
                new QuoteServiceSoapClient();

            for (int i = 0; i < 10; i++)
            {
                quote = quoteService.GetAQuote();

                StringBuilder sb = new StringBuilder();
                sb.AppendFormat("Quote: {0} \n Originator: {1} {2}",
                    quote.strQuote,
                    quote.strOriginatorFirstName,
                    quote.strOriginatorLastName);
```

```
                    System.Console.WriteLine(sb.ToString());
                    System.Console.WriteLine();
                }

            Quote quoteToAdd =
                new Quote();
            quoteToAdd.strQuote = "256K RAM should be enough for ANYONE";
            quoteToAdd.strOriginatorLastName = "Gates";
            quoteToAdd.strOriginatorFirstName = "Bill";

            System.Console.WriteLine("Adding quote: ");

            quoteService.AddQuote(quoteToAdd);

            System.Console.WriteLine("Added quote. Now display quotes: ");

            DataSet dataSetQuotes = quoteService.GetAllQuotes();

            DataTable tableQuotes = dataSetQuotes.Tables[0];
            foreach (DataRow dr in tableQuotes.Rows)
            {
                StringBuilder sb = new StringBuilder();
                sb.AppendFormat("{0} {1} {2}",
                    dr[0], dr[1], dr[2]);
                System.Console.WriteLine(sb.ToString());
            }
        }
    }
}
```

When you run the application, you should see some output like the following.

Remember, the beauty of XML Web Services is that they're not tied to a particular platform. The previous example shows how to consume the QuoteService (which is an ASP.NET

application). However, Visual Studio builds proxies for any XML Web Service. You could easily have searched for other sites that implement Web services for which Visual Studio will also build you a suitable proxy.

Asynchronous Execution

The major advantage of using Web services is that they expose functionality literally world-wide. Because the Internet is so far-reaching, you can call a method between a client located in the United States and a service located in some place such as Australia.

One of the downsides involved in making calls over such long distances is the latency. In addition to the expense of dropping everything locally to make a remote method invocation, the speed of information communication is finite. Bits having to travel far distances make for long waits during remote Web method calls. For that reason, the proxies generated by Visual Studio include an asynchronous calling mechanism complete with completion callbacks.

If you look at the proxy generated by Visual Studio (Visual Studio includes it in the source code set. You may get to it using the Object Browser, or you may look for the file in the Service References subdirectory of the project), you'll see multiple versions of the methods exposed by the XML Web Service. For example, there's a *GetAQuote* method and a *BeginGetAQuote* method. The former is the synchronous method, whereas the latter invokes the method asynchronously.

These asynchronous method calls use the standard .NET asynchronous delegate pattern. When you call them, you pass in a callback method using the same method signature as the *System.AsyncCallback* delegate. The callback delegate defined for notifying the client when the *BeginGetAQuote* method is finished is based on this delegate:

```
public delegate void AsyncCallback (IAsyncResult ar)
```

The callbacks include a single argument of type *IAsyncResult*. We'll soon see that we can use that to get the returned method results (in this case, a *Quote* class).

To make an asynchronous method call (and then be notified when it's complete), you simply need to provide a callback method that matches the corresponding delegate and pass the callback through the *BeginXXX* method call (*BeginGetAQuote*, *BeginGetAllQuotes*, or *BeginAddAQuote*). Let's work through an example to see how this works.

Using the QuoteService asynchronously

In this exercise, you'll see how to call Web methods asynchronously.

1. Add a callback for the *BeginGetAQuote* method. The asynchronous method calls require a callback as the first parameter. Define a static callback method named

OnGetAQuoteCallback and add it to the console application's *Program* class. The original caller—the *quoteService*—is passed through the *IAsynchResult* parameter as the *AsyncState* field. Cast the *AsyncState* field of *IAsyncResult* to an instance of the *QuoteServiceSoapClient*. Use the *quoteService* to call *EndGetAQuote*, which completes the asynchronous call and harvests the result as a return value. Cast the return value to a *Quote* class and display the quote on the screen.

```
namespace ConsumeWebService
{
    class Program
    {
      public static void OnGetAQuoteCompleted(IAsyncResult ar)
      {
            QuoteServiceSoapClient quoteService =
                ar.AsyncState as QuoteServiceSoapClient;
            Quote quote =
                quoteService.EndGetAQuote(ar) as Quote;
            System.Console.WriteLine();
            StringBuilder sb = new StringBuilder();
            sb.Append("This is the callback for GetAQuote");
            sb.AppendFormat("Quote: {0} \n Originator: {1} {2}",
                quote._strQuote,
                quote._strOriginatorFirstName,
                quote._strOriginatorLastName);
            System.Console.WriteLine(sb.ToString());
      }
     // Rest of program Main etc. is here...
    }
}
```

2. Now augment the application to call *GetAQuote* asynchronously. At the end of the program's *Main* method, make a call to *BeginGetAQuote*. Pass the *OnGetAQuoteComplete* method as the first parameter and a reference to the *quoteService* as the second parameter (this is how the *quoteService* will be passed to the callback as *AsyncState*). Put a call to *System.Console.ReadLine* immediately following the call to *BeginAddAQuote* so the program does not end prematurely (that is, before the *GetAQuoteCompleted* callback finishes.

```
using System;
using System.Collections.Generic;
using System.Linq;
using System.Text;
using System.Data;
using ConsumeWebService.QuoteServer;

namespace ConsumeWebService
{
    class Program
    {
        // OnGetAQuoteCompleted method here...

        static void Main(string[] args)
        {
```

```
            // other example code here

            System.Console.WriteLine();
            quoteService.BeginGetAQuote(OnGetAQuoteCompleted, quoteService);

            System.Console.WriteLine("Press Return to end the program");
            System.Console.ReadLine();
        }
    }
}
```

After running the asynchronous version, you should see output like this. The callback should display two randomly selected quotes—the result of calling the *GetAQuote* method twice:

The screen shots look a bit odd here because of the order in which the code runs. The program fetches 10 quotes synchronously. Then, it waits for the **Enter** key to be pressed (that's the "Press Return to end program" line you see). Remember that the last Web method call is running asynchronously, so we see the result of the asynchronous call even as the main thread is waiting for the Enter keypress.

The callback mechanism is especially useful for application environments that cannot afford to stall (for example, if the client is a Windows application).

Evolution of Web Services

So, it's pretty neat that you can call a method from one computer that is implemented on another. How is that useful? Web services represent the underpinnings of a whole new model for communicating between enterprises. Here are a couple of examples of how they are useful.

If you've ever received a package delivered to you via United Parcel Service (UPS), you almost invariably need to scrawl your name on the big, brown, bulky tablet handed to you by the guy in the brown shirt. When you sign the tablet, UPS knows that you received the package and it can record that information. Tracking packages in real time is very useful for UPS's business. Recipients always want to know where their packages are at any time, and using this technology helps UPS provide this information to end customers.

UPS undoubtedly spent a great deal of money on its package tracking system. UPS developed the technology in the early 1990s—long before even Al Gore knew what the Internet was. With the advent of a worldwide connected network (the Internet), small and manageable wireless devices to connect to the Internet, and a commonly understood wire format, enterprises can develop functionality similar to that used by UPS for a fraction of the cost. In addition, businesses may interact with each other on a much wider scale, which we'll see more and more as Service-Oriented Architecture (SOA) takes off.

A second way in which Web services are proving useful is in supply chain management. In the 1980s, Electronic Data Interchange (EDI) promised to allow companies to order supplies and services automatically with little or no human intervention. The idea was that different companies would subscribe to a data format and would be able to order supplies and services from other enterprises in a much more streamlined way.

Unfortunately, EDI turned out to be mostly a glorified e-mail system. The formats for data interchange were brittle and easily broken. Furthermore, when the format broke, it took a long time for the companies involved to reach another agreement on a new format.

Web services promise to help solve the problem of a brittle data interchange mechanism. Through more elaborate orchestration frameworks (like BizTalk from Microsoft), Web services promise to make automatic data interchange between enterprises much more doable and affordable than ever before.

Through these examples, I'm hoping to make a simple point. Web services are starting to form the underpinnings of SOAs, and companies large and small will someday use SOAs to bind their partners' business logic into their own, forming distributed business logic and processes. In the end, the goal is to reduce the cost of information transport and management while increasing robustness and security. Web services are the necessary communication conduit for businesses of tomorrow (and even today in some cases). In the not-too-distant future, the world will view the SOA in the same way it views the telephone and e-mail—as an essential part of daily commerce.

Other Features

ASP.NET also implements a number of other features for enhancing XML Web Services. For example, sometimes you want to include some metadata as part of a method call. If you want to ensure that only paying clients call your Web methods, you might issue them a token to prove they bought the service. The SOAP specification defines *SOAP headers* as a way to include such metadata in the method call.

In addition, it's sometimes useful to install pre- and postprocessing for Web methods. ASP.NET supports various SOAP extensions. For example, if you wanted to write your own encryption mechanism, you might write a client-side and a service-side extension that encrypts and decrypts messages interacting with your server. Describing both of these capabilies is beyond the scope of this chapter, but you can find many freely available examples on the Internet. Search for such terms as "SOAPHeader" and "SOAPExtension" and you'll find thousands of useful examples and descriptions.

Summary

Web services represent the next generation of computer connectivity. Instead of relying on a closed network protocol and wire format, Web services open the availability of an application to the entire world. Web services are built on an already existing network using a wire format that many enterprises agree on for making method calls.

ASP.NET automates the detailed work necessary to unpack a SOAP request and turn it into a local method call. ASMX files are handlers in the same way as ASPX and ASHX files. ASMX files implement *IHttpHandler* by parsing the incoming XML, calling a method in the code-beside class, and returning a result. Simply adorning the method with the *WebMethod* attribute inserts the necessary functionality.

Visual Studio is also useful for consuming Web services. By adding a service reference to your application, Visual Studio will consult the Web service for the WSDL code and use it to build a proxy. From there, you simply instantiate the proxy and call methods. The proxy takes care of preparing the SOAP payload and sending it. The proxies generated by Visual

Studio also support asynchronous method invocation so that the main calling thread doesn't block for too long.

Chapter 20 Quick Reference

To	Do This
Create a Web service	From an ASP.NET project, select **Web Site, Add New Item** from the main menu.
	Select the Web Service template.
Expose a class method as a Web method	Apply the *WebMethod* attribute immediately preceding the method signature.
Consume a Web service	From within Visual Studio, select the project in Solution Explorer.
	Click the right mouse button on the project name.
	Select **Add Service Reference.**
	Locate the service and configure any advanced settings (such as asynchronous method execution). Visual Studio will automatically ask for the WSDL and build a proxy for you.

Chapter 21
Windows Communication Foundation

After completing this chapter you will be able to

- Understand the motivation behind Windows Communication Foundation

- Understand the WCF architecture

- Implement a WCF-based server

- Build a client to use the WCF server

Distributed Computing Redux

The Windows Communication Foundation (WCF) represents one of three main pillars of .NET 3.x. These three specific highly leverageable technologies include Windows Workflow Foundation, Windows Presentation Foundation, and Windows Communication Foundation. Each of these technologies redefines programming within a certain idiom. Windows Workflow Foundation unifies the business work flow model. Windows Presentation Foundation redefines writing user interfaces, whether for Windows desktop applications or for the Web (using Silverlight). Finally, Windows Communication Foundation unifies the distributed programming model for the Microsoft platform. Clearly unifying these fragmented programming models is the main theme of .NET 3.5.

To get an idea of how fragmented the distributed computing solutions are, think back to the earliest ways to connect two computers together. At one point, the only thing you could program in any standard way was the old venerable RS232 serial connection or through a modem. Over the years, distributed computing on the Microsoft platform has grown to encompass many different protocols. For example, Windows NT supported a Remote Procedure Call mechanism that was eventually wrapped using the Distributed Component Object Model (DCOM). In addition, Windows also supports sockets programming. Near the turn of the century, Microsoft released Microsoft Message Queue (MSMQ) to support disconnected queuing-style distributed application. When it became apparent that DCOM was running into some dead ends, Microsoft introduced .NET remoting. (The "dead ends" that DCOM implemented are mainly its requirement to periodically contact client objects to remain assured of a connection, limiting scalability, its complex programming model, difficult configuration needs, and Internet-vicious security architecture.) Finally, to help supplement a wider reach available for distributed programming, Microsoft introduced an XML Web Service framework within ASP.NET (the ASMX files you looked at earlier in Chapter 20).

A Fragmented Communications API

Each of the older technologies mentioned previously has its own specific advantages—especially when you take into account the periods during computing history that they were introduced. However, having so many different means of writing distributed computing applications has led to a fragmented application programming interface (API). Making the decision as to which technology to use has always been an early decision. Earlier distributed technologies often tied your application to a specific transport protocol. If you made the wrong architectural decision or simply wanted to later migrate to a newer technology, it was often difficult if not nearly impossible to do so. Even if it could be done, it was usually an expensive proposition in terms of application redevelopment and end-user acceptance and deployment.

There are a number of programming and configuration issues involved when relying on these older technologies. The previous connection technologies coupled multiple auxiliary factors not required directly for communicating data with the communication process itself. For example, earlier distributed computing systems forced decisions such as how to format data into the early stages of design, as well as into the implementation of a distributed system. Referring back to DCOM, making DCOM remote procedure calls required an application to be tied to the DCOM connection protocol and wire format. This forced administrators to open port 135, the DCOM object discovery port, leading to immense security risks. .NET improved on things by allowing you the choice of transports and wire formats (out of the box you get a choice of using HTTP or TCP as the connection protocol, and you may use either SOAP or the .NET binary format as the wire format). However, even with those choices provided by .NET remoting, applications using classic .NET remoting are often fated to use a single connection protocol and wire format once the configuration is set. You can swap out connection protocols and wire formats, but it's not very easy.

In addition to tying wire formats and connection protocols to the implementation of a distributed system, there are many more issues cropping up when you try to connect two computers together. The minute you try to do something useful, you have to begin thinking about issues such as transactions, security, reliability, and serialization—and these issues inevitably become embedded in the application code (instead of being added later as necessary). In addition, previous communication technologies don't lend themselves to the currently in vogue Service-Oriented Architectures (SOA) where interoperability is key, although in practice interoperability is tricky to achieve.

WCF for Connected Systems

WCF's main job is to replace the previously fragmented Windows communication APIs under a single umbrella. At the same time, WCF aims to decouple the processing of communicating over a distributed system distinct from the applications themselves. When working with

WCF, you'll see that the distinctions between contracts, transports, and implementation are enforced, rather than just being a good idea. In addition, Microsoft has always been attuned to the needs of existing applications and therefore has designed WCF to accommodate partial or complete migrations from earlier communication technologies (.NET remoting or XML Web Services) to WCF-based computing.

SOA is becoming an important design influence within modern software. SOA is an architectural philosophy that encourages building large distributed systems from loosely coupled endpoints that expose their capabilities through well-known interfaces. WCF adheres to standard SOA principles, such as setting explicit boundaries between autonomous services, having services be contract and policy based (rather than being class based), having business processes be the focal point of the services (rather than services themselves), and accommodating fluctuating business models easily. WCF is designed for both high performance and maximum interoperability.

WCF represents a communication *layer*, and so introduces a level of indirection between a distributable application and the means by which the application is distributed. As an independent layer, WCF makes implementing and configuring a distributed application simpler by providing a consistent interface for managing such aspects as security, reliability, concurrency, transactions, throttling (throughput limitations for some or all callers or methods), serialization, error handling, and instance management.

While WCF is very at home when communicating via XML Web Services using SOAP (a standard for many existing Web services), it may also be configured and extended to communicate using messages based on non-SOAP formats, such as custom XML formats and RSS.

WCF is smart enough to know if both endpoints are WCF-based endpoints, in which case it will use optimized wire encoding. The structures of the messages are the same—they're just encoded in binary form. WCF includes other services often required by distributed systems. For example, WCF includes built-in queued messaging.

WCF Constituent Elements

WCF is composed of a few separate elements: endpoints, channels, messages, and behaviors. Whereas earlier communication technologies tended to couple these concepts together, WCF distinguishes them as truly separate entities. Here's a rundown of the elements of WCF.

WCF Endpoints

Endpoints define the originators and recipients of WCF communications. Microsoft has come up with a clever acronym for defining endpoints: *ABC*. That is, WCF endpoints are defined by an *address*, a *binding*, and a *contract*.

Address

The address identifies the network location of the endpoint. WCF endpoints use the addressing style of the transport moving the message. WCF addressing supports using both fully qualified addresses and relative addresses. For example, a fully qualified Internet protocol address looks like the following: *http://someserver/someapp/mathservice.svc/calculator.* WCF supports relative addressing by using a base address and then a relative address. Base addresses are registered with the service, and WCF can find services relative to the base address of the service. For example, an endpoint might comprise a whole address using a base address such as *http://someserver/someapp/mathservice.svc* and a relative address of calc.

Binding

WCF bindings specify *how* messages are transmitted. Rather than being identified simply by a transport and wire format coupled together (à la DCOM), WCF bindings are composed from a stack of binding elements which at a minimum include a protocol, a transport, and an encoder.

Contract

The final element defining an endpoint is the contract. The contract specifies the primary agreement between the client and the service as to what the service can do for the client. The contract specifies the information to be exchanged during a service call.

WCF expresses a Service Contract as a .NET interface adorned with the *[ServiceContract]* attribute. Methods within the WCF contract interface are annotated with the *[OperationContract]* attribute. WCF interfaces may pass data structures as well. Data members within the structures are exposed as properties and adorned with the *[DataMember]* attribute.

Channels

WCF channels represent the message transmission system. WCF defines *protocol channels* and *transport channels*. Protocol channels add services such as security and transactions independently of transport. Transport channels manage the physical movement of bytes between endpoints (for example, WCF uses protocols such as MSMQ, HTTP, P2P, TCP, or Named Pipes). WCF uses a factory pattern to make creating channels consistent.

Behaviors

In WFC, the service contract defines *what* the service will do. The service contract implementation specifies exactly *how* the service contract functionality works. However, one of the hallmarks of a distributed system is that it usually requires some add-on functionality that may not necessarily be tied to contract implementation. For example, when securing a Web service, authenticating and authorizing the client may be necessary, but it's usually not part of the service contract. WFC implements this kind of add-on functionality through *behaviors*. Behaviors implement the SOA higher-order notion of policy and are used to customize local execution.

Behaviors are governed by attributes—the main two of which are the *ServiceBehaviorAttribute* and the *OperationBehaviorAttribute*. The *ServiceBehaviorAttribute* and *OperationBehaviorAttribute* attributes control the following aspects of the service execution:

- Impersonation
- Concurrency and synchronization support
- Transaction behavior
- Address filtering and header processing
- Serialization behavior
- Configuration behavior
- Session lifetime
- Metadata transformation
- Instance lifetimes

Applying these attributes to modify the server execution is easy. Just adorn a service or operation implementation with the appropriate attribute and set the properties. For example, to require that callers of an operation support impersonation, adorn a service operation with the *OperationBehavior* attribute and set the *Impersonation* property to *ImpersonationOption.Require*.

Messages

The final element of WCF is the actual message. WCF messages are modeled on SOAP messages. They are composed of an envelope, a header, a body, and addressing information. Of course, messages also include the information being exchanged. WCF supports three Message Exchange Patterns: one-way, request-response, and duplex. One-way messages are passed from the transmitter to the receiver only. Messages passed using the request response pattern are sent from the transmitter to the receiver, and the receiver is expected to send a reply back to the originator. Messages using the request response pattern block until the receiver sends a response to the originator. When using the duplex messaging, services can call back to the client while executing a service requested by the client. The default Message Exchange Pattern is request-response.

How WCF Plays with ASP.NET

Although WCF applications may be hosted by manually written servers, ASP.NET makes a perfectly good host. You can either write your own Windows Service to act as a host, or you can take advantage of a readily available Windows Service, IIS, and consequently ASP.NET. WCF and ASP.NET may co-exist on a single machine in two different modes—side-by-side mode and ASP.NET compatibility mode. Here's a rundown of these two modes.

Side-by-Side Mode

When running in side-by-side mode, WCF services hosted by Internet Information Services (IIS) are co-located with ASP.NET applications composed of .ASPX files and ASMX files (and ASCX and ASHX files when necessary). ASP.NET files and WCF services reside inside a single, common Application Domain (AppDomain). When run this way, ASP.NET provides common infrastructure services such as AppDomain management and dynamic compilation for both WCF and the ASP.NET HTTP runtime. WCF runs in side-by-side mode with ASP.NET by default.

When running in side-by-side mode, the ASP.NET runtime manages only ASP.NET requests. Requests meant for a WCF service go straight to the WCR-based service. Although the ASP.NET runtime does not participate in processing the requests, there are some specific ramifications of running in side-by-side mode.

First, ASP.NET and WCF services can share AppDomain state. This includes such items as static variables and public events. Although it shares an AppDomain with ASP.NET, WCF runs independently—meaning some features you may count on when working with ASP.NET become unavailable. Probably the major restriction is that there's no such thing as a current *HttpContext* from within a WCF service (despite WCF's architectural similarity to ASP.NET's runtime pipeline). Architecturally speaking, WCF can communicate over many different protocols, including but not limited to HTTP, so an HTTP-specific context may not even make sense in many given scenarios. Second, authentication and authorization can get a bit tricky.

Even though WCF applications do not interfere with ASP.NET applications, WCF applications may access various parts of the ASP.NET infrastructure such as the application data cache. In fact, this chapter's example shows one approach to accessing the cache.

ASP.NET Compatibility Mode

WCF is designed primarily to unify the programming model over a number of transports and hosting environments. However, there are times when a uniform programming model with this much flexibility is not necessary and the application may desire or even require some of the services provided by the ASP.NET runtime. For those cases, WCF introduces the ASP.NET compatibility mode. WCF's ASP.NET compatibility mode lets you run your WCF application as a full-fledged ASP.NET citizen, complete with all the functionality and services available through ASP.NET.

WCF services that run using ASP.NET compatibility mode have complete access to the ASP.NET pipeline and execute through the entire ASP.NET HTTP request life cycle. WCF includes an implementation of *IHttpHandler* that wraps WCF services and fosters them through the pipeline when run in ASP.NET compatibility mode. In effect, a WCF service running in ASP.NET compatibility mode looks, tastes, and feels just like a standard ASP.NET Web service (that is, an ASMX file).

WCF applications running under the ASP.NET compatibility mode get a current *HttpContext* with all its contents—the session state, the *Server* object, the *Response* object, and the *Request* object. WCF applications running as ASP.NET compatible applications may secure themselves by associating Windows Access Control Lists (ACLs) to the service's .svc file. In this manner, only specific Windows users could use the WCF service. ASP.NET URL authorization also works for WCF applications running as ASP.NET compatible applications. The pipeline remains arbitrarily extensible for WCF applications running as ASP.NET applications because service requests are not intercepted as with the general purpose side-by-side mode—they're managed by ASP.NET for the entire request life cycle.

You can turn on WCF's ASP.NET compatibility mode at the application level through the application's web.config file. You can also apply ASP.NET compatibility to a specific WCF service implementation.

Writing a WCF Service

Here's an example of WCF service to help illustrate how WCF works. Recall the XML Web Service example application from Chapter 20, the QuoteService that doled out pithy quotes to any client wishing to invoke the service. The example here represents the same service—but using a WCF-based Web site instead of an ASMX-based Web service. This way, you'll see what it takes to write a WCF-based service and client, and you'll see some of the differences between WCF-based services and ASMX-based services (there are a couple of distinct differences).

QuotesService

1. Start by creating a WCF project. This example takes you through the nuts and bolts of developing a working WCF application that may be accessed from any client anywhere. Start Visual Studio 2008. Select **File**, **New**, **Web Site** and choose **WCF Service** from the

available templates. Name the site *WCFQuotesService*. The following graphic shows the **New Web Site** dialog box:

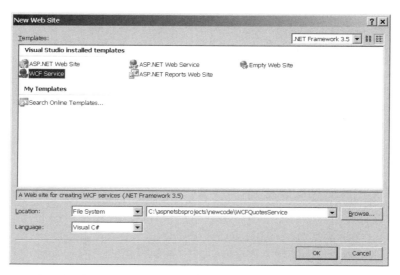

2. Examine the files created by Visual Studio. The *App_Code* directory includes two files: IService.cs and Service.cs. These two files are placeholders representing the WCF contract (as a .NET interface type) and a class implementing the contract.

3. Tweak the files produced by Visual Studio. Name the code files representing the service. *IService.cs* should become *IQuotesService.cs*, and *Service.cs* should become *QuotesService.cs*.

4. Change the service interface name from *IService* to *IQuotesService* and change the service class name from *Service* to *QuotesService*. Use Visual Studio's refactoring facilities to do this. That is, highlight the identifier you want to change, click the right mouse button in the text editor and select **Rename** from the Refactoring menu. Visual Studio will make sure the change is propagated through the entire project.

5. Borrow the *QuotesCollection* object from the Web Service chapter. Bring in the QuotesCollection.cs file from the QuotesService Web site. To do this, select the *App_Code* directory in the WCFQuotesService project. Click the right mouse button and select **Add Existing Item**. Go to the Web services project and pick up the *QuotesCollection* class by bringing in the file QuotesCollection.cs. The QuotesCollection.cs file will be copied into your WCF solution and added to the project.

6. Borrow the QuotesCollection.xml and QuotesCollection.xsd from the Web service example. Select the *App_Data* directory in the WCFQuotesService project. Click the right mouse click and select **Add Existing Item**. Go to the Web services project and pick up the XML and XSD files.

7. Develop a data contract. Now that the data and the data management code are in place, the service needs a way to expose itself. It's time to develop a contract for the service. First, create a structure for passing quotes back and forth. Open the file IQuotesService.cs to add the data and operation contracts. To do so, first delete the *CompositeType* class Visual Studio placed there for you as an example. In its place, type in the following code for the *Quote* structure. The *Quote* structure should contain three strings—one to represent the quote text and separate strings to represent the originator's first and last names. Expose the strings as properties adorned with the *[DataMember]* attribute.

```
[DataContract]
public struct Quote
{
    private String _strQuote;

    [DataMember]
    public String StrQuote
    {
        get { return _strQuote; }
        set { _strQuote = value; }
    }

    private String _strOriginatorLastName;

    [DataMember]
    public String StrOriginatorLastName
    {
        get { return _strOriginatorLastName; }
        set { _strOriginatorLastName = value; }
    }

    private String _strOriginatorFirstName;

    [DataMember]
    public String StrOriginatorFirstName
    {
        get { return _strOriginatorFirstName; }
        set { _strOriginatorFirstName = value; }
    }

    public Quote(String strQuote,
                 String strOriginatorLastName,
                 String strOriginatorFirstName)
    {
        _strQuote = strQuote;
        _strOriginatorLastName = strOriginatorLastName;
        _strOriginatorFirstName = strOriginatorFirstName;
    }
}
```

8. Next, develop a service contract for the service. In the IQuotesService.cs file, update the interface to include methods to get a single quote, add a quote, and get all the quotes.

```
using System.Data; // must be added to identify DataSet

[ServiceContract]
public interface IQuotesService
{
    [OperationContract]
    Quote GetAQuote();

    [OperationContract]
    void AddQuote(Quote quote);

    [OperationContract]
    DataSet GetAllQuotes();
}
```

9. Next, implement the service contract. Much of the work for this step is already done from the Web service chapter example. However, there are a couple of critical differences between the two implementations (those being the Web service implementation and the WCF implementation). Open the file QuotesService.cs to add the implementation. Start by implementing a method that loads the quotes into memory and stores the collection and the ASP.NET cache. Although this application is an ASP.NET application, ASP.NET handles WCF method calls earlier in the pipeline than normal ASP.NET requests, and because of that there's no such thing as a current *HttpContext* object. You can still get to the cache through the *HttpRuntime* object, which is available within the context of WCF. The *HttpRuntime.AppDomainAppPath* property includes the path to the application that's useful for setting up a cache dependency for the XML file containing the quotes.

```
using System.Web; // must be added to identify HttpRuntime
using System.Web.Caching; // must be added to identify Cache
using System.Data; // must be added to identify DataSet

public class QuotesService : IQuotesService
{
    QuotesCollection LoadQuotes()
    {
        QuotesCollection quotesCollection;
        quotesCollection =
            (QuotesCollection)
            HttpRuntime.Cache["quotesCollection"];
        if (quotesCollection == null)
        {
            quotesCollection = new QuotesCollection();

            String strAppPath;
            strAppPath = HttpRuntime.AppDomainAppPath;
```

```
        String strFilePathXml =
            String.Format("{0}\\App_Data\\QuotesCollection.xml", strAppPath);
        String strFilePathSchema =
            String.Format("{0}\\App_Data\\QuotesCollection.xsd", strAppPath);

        quotesCollection.ReadXmlSchema(strFilePathSchema);
        quotesCollection.ReadXml(strFilePathXml);

        CacheDependency cacheDependency =
            new CacheDependency(strFilePathXml);

        HttpRuntime.Cache.Insert("quotesCollection",
                    quotesCollection,
                    cacheDependency,
                    Cache.NoAbsoluteExpiration,
                    Cache.NoSlidingExpiration,
                    CacheItemPriority.Default,
                     null);
    }
    return quotesCollection;
}
// more code will go here...
}
```

10. Next, implement the *GetAQuote* operation. Call *LoadQuotes* to get the *QuotesCollection* object. Generate a random number between 0 and the number of quotes in the collection and use it to select a quote within the collection. Create an instance of the *Quote* structure and return it after populating it with the data from the stored quote.

```
public class QuotesService : IQuotesService
{
    // LoadQuotes here...

    public Quote GetAQuote()
    {
        QuotesCollection quotesCollection = this.LoadQuotes();
        int nNumQuotes = quotesCollection.Rows.Count;

        Random random = new Random();
        int nQuote = random.Next(nNumQuotes);
        DataRow dataRow = quotesCollection.Rows[nQuote];
        Quote quote = new Quote((String)dataRow["Quote"],
                            (String)dataRow["OriginatorLastName"],
                            (String)dataRow["OriginatorFirstName"]);
        return quote;
    }
    // more code will go here...
}
```

11. Implement *AddAQuote*. Call *LoadQuotes* to get the *QuotesCollection*. Create a new row in the *QuotesCollection* and populate it with information coming from the client (that is, the *Quote* parameter). Use the *HttpRuntime.AppDomainAppPath* to construct the path

to the QuotesCollection.XML file and use the *QuotesCollection*'s *WriteXml* method to re-serialize the XML file. *WriteXml* is available from the *QuotesCollection* class because *QuotesCollection* derives from *System.Data.DataTable*. Because it was loaded in the cache with a file dependency, the cache will be invalidated and the new quotes collection will be loaded the next time around.

```
public class QuotesService : IQuotesService
{
    // LoadQuotes here...
    // GetAQuote here

    public void AddQuote(Quote quote)
    {
        QuotesCollection quotesCollection = this.LoadQuotes();

        DataRow dr = quotesCollection.NewRow();
        dr[0] = quote.StrQuote;
        dr[1] = quote.StrOriginatorLastName;
        dr[2] = quote.StrOriginatorFirstName;
        quotesCollection.Rows.Add(dr);

        string strAppPath;
        strAppPath = HttpRuntime.AppDomainAppPath;

        String strFilePathXml =
            String.Format("{0}\\App_Data\\QuotesCollection.xml", strAppPath);
        String strFilePathSchema =
            String.Format("{0}\\App_Data\\QuotesCollection.xsd", strAppPath);

        quotesCollection.WriteXmlSchema(strFilePathSchema);
        quotesCollection.WriteXml(strFilePathXml);
    }
}
```

12. Finally, implement the *GetAllQuotes* operation. Create a new *DataSet*, load the quotes, and add the *QuotesCollection* to the data set as the first table. Then return the *DataSet*.

```
public class QuotesService : IQuotesService
{
    // LoadQuotes here
    // GetAQuote here
    // AddQuote here

    public DataSet GetAllQuotes()
    {
        QuotesCollection quotesCollection = LoadQuotes();
        DataSet dataSet = new DataSet();
        dataSet.Tables.Add(quotesCollection);
        return dataSet;
    }
}
```

13. Tweak the web.config file. Now that the service is implemented, the web.config file needs to be tweaked just slightly to expose the service. Visual Studio created this file and so exposes the service that it generated—the one named *Service*. However, you renamed the service to give it a more useful name in the code and the service needs to be exposed as *QuotesService* now. Update the web.config file to reflect the change. Change the *name* attribute in the service node to be *QuotesService*. Change the *contract* attribute in the endpoint node to be *IQuotesService* to match the interface name.

```
<system.serviceModel>
    <services>
        <service
            name="QuotesService"
            behaviorConfiguration="ServiceBehavior">
            <!-- Service Endpoints -->
            <endpoint address=""
                binding="wsHttpBinding"
                contract="IQuotesService"/>
            <endpoint address="mex"
                binding="mexHttpBinding"
                contract="IMetadataExchange"/>
        </service>
    </services>
    <behaviors>
        ...
    </behaviors>
</system.serviceModel>
```

That does it for building a WCF service hosted through ASP.NET that may be called from anywhere in the world (that has Internet service available, that is). In many ways, this is very similar to writing a classic ASP.NET Web service. However, because this service runs in ASP.NET side-by-side mode, there's no such thing as a current *HttpContext* (as is available in normal ASP.NET applications). In many cases, this may not be necessary. You can get to many of the critical ASP.NET runtime services (for example, the Cache) via the *HttpRuntime* object. If you need ASP.NET's full support (such as for session state if the WCF service you write depends on session data), WCF supports the ASP.NET Compatibility mode.

Building a WCF Client

A WCF service is useless without any clients around to employ it. This section illustrates how to build a client application that consumes the Quotes service. Here, you'll see how Visual Studio makes it very easy to create a reference to a service. You'll see how to make WCF service calls both synchronously and asynchronously.

Building the QuotesService client

1. Start Visual Studio 2008. Open the QuotesService solution and add a new project to it. Make it a console application named *ConsumeQuotesService*. The following graphic illustrates adding the Console project to the solution:

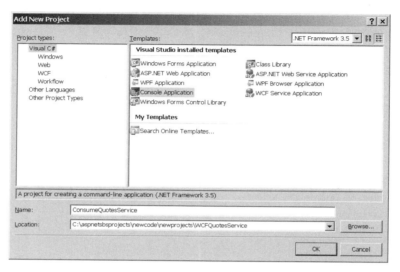

2. Create a reference to the QuotesService WCF application. Click the right mouse button on the **ConsumeQuotesService Project** tree node within the solution explorer. Select **Add Service Reference**. When the **Add Service Reference** dialog box shows, click the **Discover** button. Select the Service.svc file from this project and expand its associated tree node. After a minute, the dialog will display the service contracts that are available through the service. Expand the Services tree in the left pane to make sure you see the *IQuotesService* contract. Notice the namespace given by the dialog box—*ServiceReference1*. DON'T click **OK** yet. The following graphic shows adding the Service Reference:

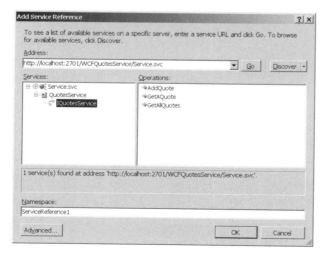

3. Click the **Advanced...** button. Click on the **Generate Asynchronous Operations** radio button so that Visual Studio generates the asynchronous versions of the proxy methods.

4. Click the **OK** button to add the service reference. Visual Studio will produce a new directory within the ConsumeQuotesService project directory named *ServiceReferences*. Visual Studio generates information about the service in the form of XML files, XSD files, and a WSDL file (among others). You'll also get source code for a proxy class that will call the service on your behalf (by default, the proxy lands in a file named *Reference.cs*).

5. Try calling the *GetAQuote* operation. Calling the proxy methods generated for the WCF service calls can be a bit verbose from time to time, but they are effective and it's much better than setting everything up manually by yourself. First, create an instance of the *QuotesServiceClient*, available from the *ServiceReference* you just created. Create an instance of the *ServiceReference1.Quote* structure to receive the results of calling *GetAQuote*. Call *GetAQuote* from the *QuotesServiceClient*, and print the result on the console.

```
using System;
using System.Collections.Generic;
using System.Linq;
using System.Text;

namespace ConsumeQuotesService
{
    class Program
    {
        static void Main(string[] args)
        {
            // Get a single random quote
            ServiceReference1.QuotesServiceClient quotesServiceClient =
                new ServiceReference1.QuotesServiceClient();

            ServiceReference1.Quote quote = quotesServiceClient.GetAQuote();

            Console.WriteLine("Getting a single quote: " + quote.StrQuote);
            Console.WriteLine();
        }
    }
}
```

6. Now try calling *AddAQuote*. This will be very much like calling *GetAQuote*. However, this time the request requires some parameters. Create an instance of the *Quote* (available from the *ServiceReference*). Find some pithy quote somewhere (or make one up) and plug it into the *Quote* object along with the first and last names of the originator. You can use the same instance of the *QuotesServiceClient* to call *AddAQuote*, passing the *Quote* object in. The next call to *GetAllQuotes* will reveal that the quote was added to the quotes collection (which we'll see in a minute).

```
using System;
using System.Collections.Generic;
using System.Linq;
using System.Text;
```

```
namespace ConsumeQuotesService
{
    class Program
    {
        static void Main(string[] args)
        {
            // Get a single random quote
            ...

            // Now add a quote
            ServiceReference1.Quote newQuote = new ServiceReference1.Quote();
            newQuote.StrQuote = "But to me nothing - the negative, the empty" +
                "- is exceedingly powerful.";
            newQuote.StrOriginatorFirstName = "Alan";
            newQuote.StrOriginatorLastName = "Watts";

            quotesServiceClient.AddQuote(newQuote);

            Console.WriteLine("Added a quote");
            Console.WriteLine();
        }
    }
}
```

7. Now try calling *GetAllQuotes*. By now you should know the pattern pretty well. Use the *QuotesServiceClient* to call *GetAllQuotes*. *GetAllQuotes* will return a *DataSet* object that will contain a collection of all the quotes, so declare one of those, too. Use the *QuotesServiceClient* object to call *GetAllQuotes*. When the call returns, use the *DataSet* object to print the quotes to the console. Be sure to include the *System.Data* namespace so the compiler understand the *DataSet*.

```
using System;
using System.Collections.Generic;
using System.Linq;
using System.Text;
using System.Data;

namespace ConsumeQuotesService
{
    class Program
    {
        static void Main(string[] args)
        {
            // Get a single random quote

            // Now add a quote

            // Now get all the quotes
            DataSet dataSet = quotesServiceClient.GetAllQuotes();
            DataTable tableQuotes = dataSet.Tables[0];
```

```
              foreach (DataRow dr in tableQuotes.Rows)
              {
                  System.Console.WriteLine(dr[0] + " " +
                  dr[1] + "  " + dr[2]);
              }
          }
      }
}
```

8. Try calling *GetAQuote* asynchronously. The proxy created by Visual Studio supports asynchronous invocation if you ask it to generate the asynchronous methods. To call *GetAQuote* asynchronously, you'll need to implement a callback method that WCF will call when the method is done executing. Add a static method named *GetAQuoteCallback* to your *Program* class. Have the method return void, and take *IAsyncResult* as a parameter. When WCF calls back into this method, the *IAsyncResult* parameter will be an instance of the class originating the call—an instance of *QuotesServiceClient*. Declare an instance of the *ServiceReference1.QuotesServiceClient* class and assign it by casting the *IAsyncResult* parameter's *AsyncState* property to the *ServiceReference1.QuotesServiceClient* type. Then declare an instance of the *Quote* class and harvest the quote by calling *QuotesServiceClient.EndGetAQuote*, passing the *AsyncResult* parameter. Finally, write the quote out to the console.

```
using System;
using System.Collections.Generic;
using System.Linq;
using System.Text;
using System.Data;

namespace ConsumeQuotesService
{
    class Program
    {
        static void Main(string[] args)
        {
            // Get a single random quote

            // Now add a quote

            // Now get all the quotes
        }

        static void GetAQuoteCallback(IAsyncResult asyncResult)
        {
            ServiceReference1.QuotesServiceClient quotesServiceClient =
                (ServiceReference1.QuotesServiceClient)
                asyncResult.AsyncState;
```

```
ServiceReference1.Quote quote =
    quotesServiceClient.EndGetAQuote(asyncResult);

Console.WriteLine(quote.StrQuote);
            }
        }
    }
```

9. Now make the asynchronous call to *GetAQuote*. This is easy—just call the *QuotesServiceClient*'s *BeginGetAQuote* method from the *Program* class's *Main* method. Pass in the *GetAQuoteCallback* method you just wrote as the first parameter, and the *QuotesServiceClient* object as the second parameter. Add a call to *System.Console .ReadLine* to pause the main thread so that the asynchronous call has time to execute.

```
using System;
using System.Collections.Generic;
using System.Linq;
using System.Text;
using System.Data;

namespace ConsumeQuotesService
{
    class Program
    {
        static void Main(string[] args)
        {
            // Get a single random quote

            // Now add a quote

            // Now get all the quotes

            // Now call GetAQuote asynchronously
            System.Console.WriteLine(
                "Now fetching a quote asynchronously");
            Console.WriteLine();

            quotesServiceClient.BeginGetAQuote(GetAQuoteCallback,
                quotesServiceClient);

            Console.WriteLine("Press enter to exit...");
            Console.ReadLine();
        }

        static void GetAQuoteCallback(IAsyncResult asyncResult)
        {
            // implementation removed for clarity
        }
    }
}
```

10. Run the program to watch the console application call the WCFQuotesService. You should see the following output:

Summary

Out of the box, The Windows Communication Foundation unifies the programming interface for the two modern .NET remoting technologies: standard .NET remoting and .NET XML Web Services (and will also accommodate MSMQ and sockets communication). Although effective at the time, the communication infrastructures of the late 1980s through the mid-2000s narrowed the design and implementation possibilities for a distributed system. WCF offers a single framework for creating a distributed system. WCF marks clear boundaries between the elements of a distributed system, making it much easier to design a distributed system independently of the communication mechanism it will use eventually. WCF doesn't hem you into specific communication infrastructure choices early on. In addition, WCF makes it very straightforward to add features such as security and transaction management.

Distributed WCF applications are composed of several different elements: endpoints, channels, messages, and behaviors. An endpoint is defined by an address, a binding, and a contract. Endpoints specify message originators and recipients. WCF channels represent the means by which messages are transmitted. WCF defines protocol channels and transport channels. Messages are the actual data sent between the endpoints, and behaviors specify how a WCF service operates at run time, allowing you to configure the runtime characteristics of the services, such as concurrency and security.

WCF applications are easily hosted by ASP.NET. The Visual Studio ASP.NET wizard provides a template for creating WCF applications. When hosting WCF applications via ASP.NET, you have two options: running in ASP.NET side-by-side mode and running in ASP.NET compatibility mode. When running in ASP.NET side-by-side mode, the WCF services may run in the same AppDomain and share state and event handlers exposed by other assemblies loaded in the AppDomain. However, normal ASP.NET features such as session state and the current request context are unavailable. You may get to certain ASP.NET features such as the application cache through the *HttpRuntime* class. When running under ASP.NET compatibility mode, calls to the WCF service are full-fledged ASP.NET requests. The WCF requests that run within an ASP.NET compatible service have full access to all of ASP.NET's features, including access to the current *HttpContext* and the session state.

Chapter 21 Quick Reference

To	Do This
Create a WCF-enabled Web site	In Visual Studio, choose **File**, **New**, **Web Site** and select **WCF Service** from the available templates. This will produce a WCF-enabled Web site for you and will stub out a default contract and implementation that you may change to fit your needs.
Create a service contract	Service contracts are defined as .NET interfaces. The entire interface should be adorned with the *[ServiceContract]* attribute. Interface members meant to be exposed as individual services are adorned with the *[OperationContract]* attribute. Data structures may be passed through the interface. Structure members meant to be visible through the interface are adorned with the *[DataContract]* attribute.
Implement the service contract	Create a class that derives from the interface defining the service contract and implement the members.
Expose the WCF service as an ASP.NET application	Make sure that the web.config file mentions the service contract and the implementation.
Create a client to consume the WCF service	Use the Add Service Reference menu item found in the project's context menu (exposed from Visual Studio's Solution Explorer) to discover and locate the service metadata. Alternatively, use the ServiceModel Metadata Utility Tool (packaged as an assembly named *Svcutil.exe*).
Customize the service's local execution, managing execution aspects such as security, instance lifetime, and threading	Apply the *ServiceBehaviorAttribute* and *OperationBehaviorAttribute* attributes as necessary to control the following aspects of the service execution: instance lifetimes, concurrency and synchronization support, configuration behavior, transaction behavior, serialization behavior, metadata transformation, session lifetime, address filtering and header processing, and impersonation.
Access the ASP.NET application cache from a standard WCF application (one not configured to run in ASP.NET compatibility mode)	Use the *HttpRuntime.Cache* property.

Chapter 22
AJAX

After completing this chapter, you will be able to

- Understand the problem AJAX solves

- Understand ASP.NET's support for AJAX

- Write AJAX-enabled Web sites

- Take advantage of AJAX as necessary to improve the user's experience

This chapter covers AJAX, possibly the most interesting feature added to ASP.NET recently. AJAX stands for "Asynchronous JavaScript and XML," and it promises to produce an entirely new look and feel for Web sites throughout the world.

Software evolution always seems to happen in this typical fashion: Once a technology is grounded firmly (meaning the connections between the parts work and the architecture is fundamentally sound), upgrading the end user's experience becomes a much higher priority. AJAX's primary reason for existence is to improve on the standard HTTP GET/POST idiom with which Web users are so familiar. That is, the standard Web protocol in which entire forms and pages are sent between the client and the server is getting a whole new addition.

Although standard HTTP is functional and well understood by Web developers, it does have certain drawbacks—the primary one being that the user is forced to wait for relatively long periods while pages refresh. AJAX introduces technology that shields end users from having to wait for a whole page to post. This has been a common problem within all event-driven interfaces (Microsoft Windows being one of the best examples).

Think back to the way HTTP normally works. When you make a request (using GET or POST, for example), the Web browser sends the request to the server, but you can do nothing until the request finishes. That is, you make the request and wait—watching the little thermometer on the browser fill up. Once the request returns to the browser, you may begin using the application again. The application is basically useless until the request returns. In some cases, the browser's window even goes completely blank. Web browsers have to wait for Web sites to finish an HTTP request—in much the same way that Windows programs have to wait for message handlers to complete their processing. (Actually, if the client browser uses a multithreaded user interface such as Microsoft Internet Explorer, you can usually cancel the request—but that's all you can really do.) You can easily demonstrate this problem for yourself by introducing a call to *System.Threading.Thread.Sleep* inside the *Page_Load* method. Putting the thread to sleep will force the end user to wait for the request to finish.

The solution to this problem is to introduce some way to handle the request asynchronously. What if there were a way to introduce asynchronous background processing into a Web site so that the browser would appear much more responsive to the user? What if (for certain applications) making an HTTP request didn't stall the entire browser for the duration of the request, but instead seemed to run the request in the background, leaving the foreground unhindered and changing only the necessary portion of the rendered page? The site would present a much more continuous and smooth look and feel to the user. As another example, what if ASP.NET included some controls that injected script into the rendered pages that modified the HTML Document Object Model, providing more interaction from the client's point of view? Well, that's exactly what ASP.NET's AJAX support was designed to do.

What Is AJAX?

AJAX formalizes a style of programming meant to improve the user interface (UI) responsiveness and visual appeal of Web sites. Many of AJAX's capabilities have been available for a while now. AJAX consolidates several good ideas and uses them to define a style of programming and extends the standard HTTP mechanism that is the backbone of the Internet. Like most Web application development environments, ASP.NET has leveraged HTTP in a very standard way. The browser usually initiates contact with the server using an HTTP GET request, followed by any number of POSTs. The high-level application flow is predicated upon sending a whole request and then waiting for an entire reply from the server. Although ASP .NET's server-side control architecture greatly improves back-end programming, users still get their information a whole page at a time. It's almost like the mainframe/terminal model popular during the 1970s and early 1980s. However, this time the terminal is one of many modern sophisticated browsers and the mainframe is replaced by a Web server (or Web Farm).

The standard HTTP round-trip has been a useful application strategy, and the Web grew up using it. While the Web was growing up in the late 1990s, browsers had widely varying degrees of functionality. For example, browsers ranged all the way from the very rudimentary America Online Browser (which had very limited capabilities) to cell phones and PDAs, to more sophisticated browsers such as Microsoft Internet Explorer and Netscape Navigator that were very rich in capability. For instance, Internet Explorer supports higher level features such as JavaScript and Dynamic HTML. This made striking a balance between usability of your site and the reach of your site very difficult prior to the advent of ASP.NET.

However, being able to run a decent browser that understands how to process client-side scripting is almost a given for the majority of modern computing platforms. These days, most computing platforms run a modern operating system (such as Microsoft Windows XP or Microsoft Vista, or even MAC OS X). These platforms run browsers fully capable of supporting XML and JavaScript. With so many Web client platforms supporting this functionality, it makes sense to take advantage of the capabilities. As we'll see in this chapter, AJAX makes good use of these modern browser features to improve the user's experience.

In addition to extending standard HTTP, AJAX is also a very clever way to use the Web service idiom. Web services are traditionally geared toward enterprise-to-enterprise business communications. However, Web services are also useful on a smaller scale for handling Web requests out of band. ("Out of band" simply means making HTTP requests using means other than the standard page posting mechanism.) AJAX uses Web services behind the scenes to make the client UI more responsive than when using traditional HTTP GETs and POSTs. We'll see how that works in this chapter—especially when we look at the ASP.NET AJAX Control Toolkit Extender controls.

AJAX Overview

One of the primary changes AJAX brings to Web programming is that it depends on the browser taking an even more active role in the process. Instead of the browser simply rendering streams of HTML and executing small custom-written script blocks, AJAX includes some new client-script libraries to facilitate the asynchronous calls back to the server. AJAX also includes some basic server-side components to support these new asynchronous calls coming from the client. There's even a community-supported AJAX Control Toolkit available for ASP.NET's AJAX implementation. Figure 22-1 shows the organization of ASP.NET's AJAX support.

Client Side

The AJAX Library

Components
Nonvisual components
Behaviors, Controls

Browser Compatibility
Support for browsers:
Microsoft Internet Explorer,
Mozilla Firefox, Apple Safari

Networking
Asynchronous requests,
XML and JSON Serialization,
Web and Application Services

Core Services
JavaScript, Base Client
Extensions, Type System,
Events, Serialization

Server Side

ASP.NET Extensions for AJAX

Scripting
Localization, Globalization,
Debugging, Tracing

Web Services
Proxy Generation,
Page Methods,
XML and JSON Serialization

Application Services
Authentication and
profile support

Server Controls
ScriptManager, Update Panel.
Update Progress, Timer

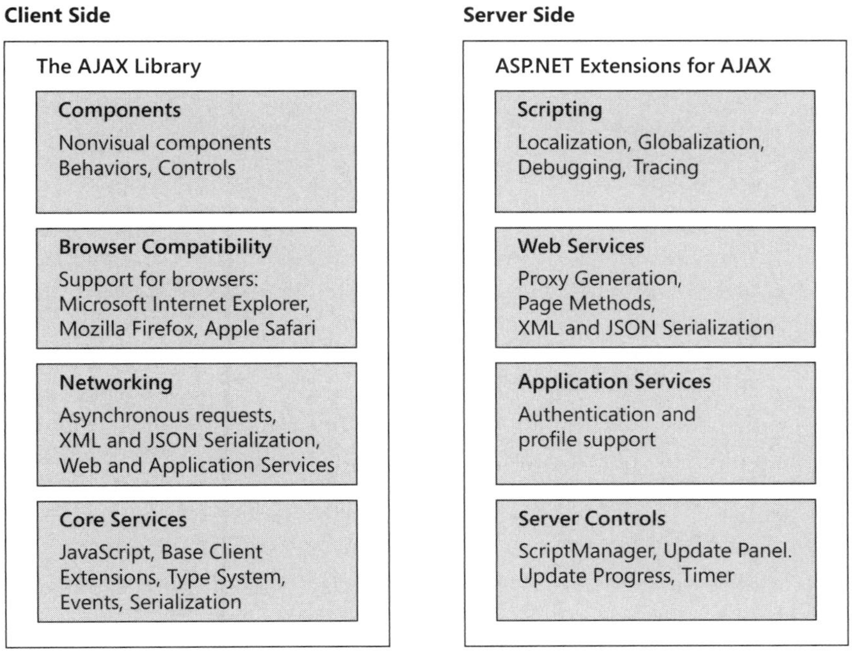

FIGURE 22-1 The conceptual organization of ASP.NET's AJAX support layers

Reasons to Use AJAX

If traditional ASP.NET development is so entrenched and well established, then why would you want to introduce AJAX? At first glance, AJAX seems to introduce some new complexities into the ASP.NET programming picture. In fact, it seems to re-introduce some programming idioms that ASP.NET was designed to deprecate (such as overuse of client-side script). However, AJAX promises to produce a richer experience for the user. Because ASP.NET's support for AJAX is nearly seamless, the added complexities are well mitigated. When building a Web site, there are a few reasons you might choose to AJAX-enable the site.

- AJAX improves the overall efficiency of your site by performing parts of a Web page's processing in the browser when appropriate. Instead of waiting for the entire HTTP protocol to get a response from the browser, pushing certain parts of the page processing to the client helps the client to react much more quickly. Of course, this type of functionality has always been available—as long as you're willing to write the code to make it happen. ASP.NET's AJAX support includes a number of scripts so that you can get a lot of browser-based efficiency by simply using a few server-side controls.

- AJAX introduces UI elements usually found in desktop applications to a Web site. These UI elements include such items as rectangle rounding, callouts, progress indicators, and pop-up windows that work for a wide range of browsers (more browser-side scripting—but most of it's been written for you).

- AJAX introduces partial-page updates. By refreshing only the parts of the Web page that have been updated, the user's wait time is reduced significantly. This brings Web-based applications much closer to desktop applications with regard to perceived UI performance.

- AJAX is supported by most popular browsers—not just Microsoft Internet Explorer. It works for Mozilla Firefox and Apple Safari, too. Although it still requires some effort to strike a balance between UI richness and the ability to reach a wider audience, the fact that AJAX depends on features available in most modern browsers makes this balance much easier to achieve.

- AJAX introduces a huge number of new capabilities. Whereas standard ASP.NET's control and page-rendering model provides great flexibility and extensibility for programming Web sites, AJAX brings in a new concept—the extender control. Extender controls attach to existing server-side controls (such as the *TextBox*, *ListBox*, and *DropDownList*) at run time and add new client-side appearances and behaviors to the controls. Sometimes extender controls can even call a predefined Web service to get data to populate list boxes and such (for example, the *AutoComplete* extender).

- AJAX improves on ASP.NET's forms authentication and profiles and personalization services. ASP.NET's support for authentication and personalization provided a great boon to Web developers—and AJAX just sweetens the pot.

Today when you browse different Web sites, you'll run into lots of examples of AJAX-style programming. Here are some examples:

- Colorado Geographic: *http://www.coloradogeographic.com/*
- Cyber Homes: *http://www.cyberhomes.com/default .aspx?AspxAutoDetectCookieSupport=1&bhcp=1*
- Component Art: *http://www.componentart.com/*

Real-World AJAX

Throughout the 1990s and into the mid-2000s, Web applications were nearly a throwback to 1970s mainframe and minicomputer architectures. However, instead of finding a single large computer serving dumb terminals, Web applications consist of a Web server (or a Web Farm) connected to smart browsers capable of fairly sophisticated rendering capabilities. Until recently, Web applications took their input via HTTP forms and presented output via HTML pages. The real trick in understanding standard Web applications is to see the disconnected and stateless nature of HTTP. Classic Web applications can only show a snapshot of the state of the application.

As we'll see in this chapter, Microsoft supports standard AJAX idioms and patterns within its ASP.NET framework. However, AJAX is more a style of Web programming involving out-of-band HTTP requests than any specific technology.

You've no doubt seen sites engaging the new interface features and stylings available through AJAX programming. Examples include Microsoft.com, Google.com, and Yahoo.com. Very often while browsing these sites, you'll see modern features such as automatic page up-dates without you having to generate a postback explicitly. Modal-type dialog boxes requiring your attention will pop up until you dismiss them. These are all features available through AJAX-style programming patterns, and ASP.NET has lots of new support for it.

If you're a long-time Microsoft-platform Web developer, you may be asking yourself whether AJAX is something really worthwhile or whether you might be able to get much of the same type of functionality using a tried and true technology like DHTML.

AJAX in Perspective

Any seasoned Web developer targeting Microsoft Internet Explorer as the browser is un-doubtedly familiar with Dynamic HTML (DHTML). DHTML is a technology running at the browser for enabling Windows desktop-style UI elements into the Web client environment. DHTML was a good start, and AJAX brings the promise of more desktop-like capabilities to Web applications.

AJAX makes available wider capabilities than simply using DHTML. DHTML is primarily about being able to change the style declarations of an HTML element through JavaScript. However, that's about as far as it goes. DHTML is very useful for implementing such UI features as having a menu drop down when the mouse is rolled over it. AJAX expands on this idea of client-based UI using JavaScript as well as out-of-band calls to the server. Because AJAX is based on out-of-band server requests (rather than relying *only* on a lot of client script code), AJAX has the potential for much more growth in terms of future capabilities than DHTML.

AJAX represents another level in client-side performance for Web application. Through AJAX, Web sites can now support features such as partial page updates, ToolTips and pop-up windows, and data-driven UI elements (that get their data from Web services).

ASP.NET Server-Side Support for AJAX

Much of ASP.NET's support for AJAX resides in a collection of server-side controls responsible for rendering AJAX-style output to the browser. Recall from Chapter 3 on the page rendering model that the entire page-rendering process of an ASP.NET application is broken down into little bite-sized chunks. Each individual bit of rendering is handled by a class derived from *System.Web.UI.Control*. The entire job of a server-side control is to render output that places HTML elements in the output stream so they appear correctly in the browser. For example, *ListBox* controls render a *<select/>* tag. *TextBox* controls render an *<input type="text" />* tag. ASP.NET's AJAX server-side controls render AJAX-style script along with HTML to the browser.

ASP.NET's AJAX support consists of these server-side controls along with client code scripts that integrate to produce AJAX-like behavior. Here's a description of the most frequently used official ASP.NET AJAX server controls: *ScriptManager*, *ScriptManagerProxy*, *UpdatePanel*, *UpdateProgress*, and *Timer*.

ScriptManager Control

The *ScriptManager* control manages script resources for the page. The *ScriptManager* control's primary action is to register the AJAX Library script with the page so the client script may use type system extensions. The *ScriptManager* also makes possible partial-page rendering and supports localization as well as custom user scripts. The *ScriptManager* assists with out-of-band calls back to the server. Any ASP.NET site wishing to use AJAX must include an instance of the *ScriptManager* control on any page using AJAX functionality.

ScriptManagerProxy Control

Scripts on a Web page often require a bit of special handling in terms of how the server renders them. Normally, the page uses a *ScriptManager* control to organize the scripts at the page level. Nested components such as content pages and User controls require the *ScriptManagerProxy* to manage script and service references to pages that already have a *ScriptManager* control.

This is most notable in the case of Master Pages. The Master Page typically houses the *ScriptManager* control. However, ASP.NET will throw an exception if a second instance of *ScriptManager* is found within a given page. So what would content pages do if they needed to access the *ScriptManager* control that the Master Page contains? The answer is that the content page should house the *ScriptManagerProxy* control and work with the true *ScriptManager* control via the proxy. Of course, as mentioned, this also applies to User controls as well.

UpdatePanel Control

The *UpdatePanel* control supports partial page updates by tying together specific server-side controls and events that cause them to render. The *UpdatePanel* control causes only selected parts of the page to be refreshed instead of refreshing the whole page (as happens during a normal HTTP postback).

UpdateProgress Control

The *UpdateProgress* control coordinates status information about partial-page updates as they occur within *UpdatePanel* controls. The *UpdateProgress* control supports intermediate feedback for long-running operations.

Timer Control

The *Timer* control will issue postbacks at defined intervals. Although the *Timer* control will perform a normal postback (posting the whole page), it is especially useful when coordinated with the *UpdatePanel* control to perform periodic partial-page updates.

AJAX Client Support

ASP.NET's AJAX client-side support is centered around a set of JavaScript libraries. The following layers are included in the ASP.NET AJAX script libraries:

- The browser compatibility layer for assisting in managing compatibility across the most frequently used browsers. Whereas ASP.NET by itself implements browser capabilities on the server end, this layer handles compatibility on the client end (the browsers supported include Internet Explorer, Mozilla Firefox, and Apple Safari).

- The ASP.NET AJAX core services layer extends the normal JavaScript environment by introducing classes, namespaces, event handling, data types, and object serialization that are useful in AJAX programming.

- The ASP.NET AJAX base class library for clients includes various components, such as components for string management and for extended error handling.

- The networking layer of the AJAX client-side support manages communication with Web-based services and applications. The networking layer also handles asynchronous remote method calls.

The piece de resistance of ASP.NET's AJAX support is the community-supported Control Toolkit. Although everything mentioned previously provides solid infrastructure for ASP.NET AJAX, AJAX isn't really compelling until you add a rich tool set.

ASP.NET AJAX Control Toolkit

The ASP.NET AJAX Control Toolkit is a collection of components (and samples showing how to use them) encapsulating AJAX's capabilities. When you browse through the samples, you can get an idea of the kind of user experiences available through the controls and extenders. The Control Toolkit also provides a powerful software development kit for creating custom controls and extenders. You can download the ASP.NET AJAX Control Toolkit from the ASP.NET AJAX Web site.

The AJAX Control Toolkit is a separate download and not automatically included with Visual Studio 2008. To use the controls in the toolkit, follow these steps:

1. Download the tool. There are two versions—2.0 and 3.5. Version 3.5 is the most up to date and requires .NET 3.5 on your development machine. (See *http://asp.net/ajax/ ajaxcontroltoolkit/* for details.)

2. After unzipping the Toolkit file, open the AjaxControlToolkit solution file in Visual Studio.

3. Build the AjaxControlKit project.

4. The compilation process will produce a file named *AjaxControlToolkit.dll* in the AjaxControlToolkit\bin directory.

5. Click the right mouse button on the Toolbox in Visual Studio, select **Choose Items...** from the menu. Browse to the AjaxControlToolkit.dll file in the AjaxControlToolkit\bin directory and include the DLL. This will bring all the new AJAX Controls from the toolkit into Visual Studio so you may drag and drop them onto forms in your applications.

Other ASP.NET AJAX Community-Supported Stuff

Although not quite officially part of AJAX, you'll find a wealth of AJAX-enabled server-side controls and client-side scripts available through a community-supported effort. The support includes ASP.NET AJAX community-supported controls (mentioned previously) as well as support for client declarative syntax (XML-script) and more.

AJAX Control Toolkit Potpourri

There are a number of other extenders and controls available through a community-supported effort. You can find a link to the AJAX Control Toolkit through *http://asp.net/ajax/*. We'll see a few of the controls available from the toolkit throughout this chapter. Table 22-1 lists the controls and extenders available through this toolkit.

TABLE 22-1 The ASP.NET Control Toolkit

Component	Description
Accordion	This extender is useful for displaying a group of panes one pane at a time. It's similar to using several *CollapsiblePanels* constrained to allow only one to be expanded at a time. The *Accordion* is composed of a group of *AccordionPane* controls.
AlwaysVisibleControl	This extender is useful for pinning a control to the page so its position remains constant while content behind it moves and scrolls.
Animation	This extender provides a clean interface for animating page content.
AutoComplete	This extender is designed to communicate with a Web service to list possible text entries based on what's already in the text box.
Calendar	This extender is targeted for the *TextBox* control providing client-side date-picking functionality in a customizable way.
CascadingDropDown	This extender is targeted toward the *DropDownList* control. It functions to populate a set of related *DropDownList* controls automatically.
CollapsiblePanel	This extender is targeted toward the *Panel* control for adding collapsible sections to a Web page.
ConfirmButton	This extender is targeted toward the *Button* control (and types derived from the *Button* control) useful for displaying messages to the user. The scenarios for which this extender is useful include those requiring confirmation from the user (for example, where linking to another page might cause your end user to lose state).
DragPanel	This is an extender targeted toward *Panel* controls for adding the capability for users to drag the *Panel* around the page.
DropDown	This extender implements a SharePoint-style drop-down menu.
DropShadow	This extender is targeted toward the *Panel* control that applies a drop shadow to the *Panel*.
DynamicPopulate	This extender uses an HTML string returned by a Web service or page method call.

Continued

TABLE 22-1 Continued

Component	Description
FilteredTextBox	This extender is used to ensure that an end user enters only valid characters into a text box.
HoverMenu	This extender is targeted for any *WebControl* that associates that control with a pop-up panel for displaying additional content. It's activated when the user hovers the mouse cursor over the targeted control.
ListSearch	This extender searches items in a designated *ListBox* or *DropDownList* based on keystrokes as they're typed by the user.
MaskedEdit	This extender is targeted toward *TextBox* controls to constrain the kind of text that the *TextBox* will accept by applying a mask.
ModalPopup	This extender mimics the standard Windows modal dialog box behavior. Using the *ModalPopup*, a page may display content of a pop-up window that focuses attention on itself until it is dismissed explicitly by the end user.
MutuallyExclusiveCheckBox	This extender is targeted toward the *CheckBox* control. The extender groups *Checkbox* controls using a key. When a number of *CheckBox* controls all share the same key, the extender ensures that only a single check box will appear checked at a time.
NoBot	This control attempts to provide CAPTCHA (Completely Automated Public Turing test to tell Computers and Humans Apart)-like bot/spam detection and prevention without requiring any user interaction. While using a noninteractive approach may be bypassed more easily than one requiring actual human interaction, this implementation is invisible.
NumericUpDown	This extender is targeted toward the *TextBox* control to create a control very similar to the standard Windows *Edit* control with the *Spin* button. The extender adds "up" and "down" buttons for incrementing and decrementing the value in the *TextBox*.
PagingBulletedList	This extender is targeted toward the *BulletedList* control. The extender enables sorted paging on the client side.
PasswordStrength	This extender is targeted toward the *TextBox* control to help when end users type passwords. While the normal *TextBox* only hides the actual text, the *PasswordStrength* extender also displays the strength of the password using visual cues.
PopupControl	This extender is targeted toward all controls. Its purpose is to open a pop-up window for displaying additional relevant content.
Rating	This control renders a rating system from which end users rate something using images to represent a rating (stars are common).
ReorderList	This ASP.NET AJAX control implements a bulleted, data-bound list with items that can be reordered interactively.
ResizableControl	This extender works with any element on a Web page. Once associated with an element, the *ResizableControl* gives the user the ability to resize that control. The *ResizableControl* puts a handle on the lower right corner of the control.

Continued

TABLE 22-1   Continued

Component	Description
RoundedCorners	The *RoundedCorners* extender may be applied to any Web page element to turn square corners into rounded corners.
Slider	This extender is targeted to the *TextBox* control. It adds a graphical slider that the end user may use to change the numeric value in the *TextBox*.
SlideShow	This extender controls and adds buttons to move between images individually and to play the slide show automatically.
Tabs	This server-side control manages a set of tabbed panels for managing content on a page.
TextBoxWatermark	*TextBoxWatermark* extends the *TextBox* control to display a message while the *TextBox* is empty. Once *TextBox* contains some text, the *TextBox* appears as a normal *TextBox*.
ToggleButton	This extender extends the *CheckBox* to show custom images reflecting the state of the *CheckBox*.
UpdatePanelAnimation	This extender provides a clean interface for animating content associated with an *UpdatePanel*.
ValidatorCallout	*ValidatorCallout* extends the validator controls (such as *RequiredFieldValidator* and *RangeValidator*). The callouts are small pop-up windows that appear near the UI elements containing incorrect data to direct user focus toward them.

Getting Familiar with AJAX

Here's a short example to help get you familiar with AJAX. It's a very simple Web Forms application that shows behind-the-scenes page content updates with the *UpdatePanel* server-side control. In this exercise, you'll create a page with labels showing the date and time that the page loads. One label will be outside the *UpdatePanel*, and the other label will be inside the *UpdatePanel*. You'll be able to see how partial page updates work by comparing the date and time shown in each label.

A simple partial page update

1. Create a new Web site project named *AJAXORama*. Make it a file system Web site. Earlier versions of the AJAX toolkit (for Visual Studio 2005) required a special "AJAX Enabled Web site" template. The template inserted specific entries into the configuration file necessary for AJAX to work. Visual Studio 2008 creates "AJAX Enabled " projects right off the bat. Make sure the default.aspx file is open.

2. Add a *ScriptManager* control to the page. Pick one up off the Toolbox and drop it on the page (you'll find it under a different tab in the toolbox than the normal control tab.). Using the AJAX controls requires a *ScriptManager* to appear prior to any other AJAX controls on the page. By convention, the control is usually placed outside the DIV

Visual Studio creates for you. After placing the script manager control on your page, the <body> element in the *Source* view should look like so:

```
<body>
    <form id="form1" runat="server">
    <asp:ScriptManager ID="ScriptManager1" runat="server">
    </asp:ScriptManager>
    <div>

    </div>
    </form>
</body>
```

3. Drag a *Label* control into the Default.aspx form. From the Properties window, give the *Label* control the name *LabelDateTimeOfPageLoad*.Then drop a *Button* on the form as well. Give it the text *Click Me*. Open the code beside file (default.aspx.cs) and update the *Page_Load* handler to have the label display the current date and time.

```
using System;
using System.Data;
using System.Configuration;
using System.Web;
using System.Web.Security;
using System.Web.UI;
using System.Web.UI.WebControls;
using System.Web.UI.WebControls.WebParts;
using System.Web.UI.HtmlControls;

public partial class _Default : System.Web.UI.Page
{
    protected void Page_Load(object sender, EventArgs e)
    {
        this.LabelDateTimeOfPageLoad.Text = DateTime.Now.ToString();
    }
}
```

4. Run the page and generate some postbacks by clicking the button a few times. Notice that the label on the page updates with the current date and time each time the button is clicked.

5. Add an *UpdatePanel* control to the page (you'll find this control alongside the *ScriptManager* control in the *AJAX Control Toolkit* tab). Then pick up another *Label* from the Toolbox and drop it into the content area of the *UpdatePanel*. Name the label *LabelDateTimeOfButtonClick*.

6. Add some code to the *Page_Load* method to have the label show the current date and time.

```
using System;
using System.Data;
using System.Configuration;
using System.Web;
using System.Web.Security;
```

```
using System.Web.UI;
using System.Web.UI.WebControls;
using System.Web.UI.WebControls.WebParts;
using System.Web.UI.HtmlControls;

public partial class _Default : System.Web.UI.Page
{
    protected void Page_Load(object sender, EventArgs e)
    {
        this.LabelDateTimeOfPageLoad.Text = DateTime.Now.ToString();
        this.LabelDateTimeOfButtonClick.Text =
            DateTime.Now.ToString();
    }
}
```

The following graphic shows the *UpdatePanel*, *Button*, and *Labels* as seen within the Visual
Studio designer (there are some line breaks in between so that the page is readable):

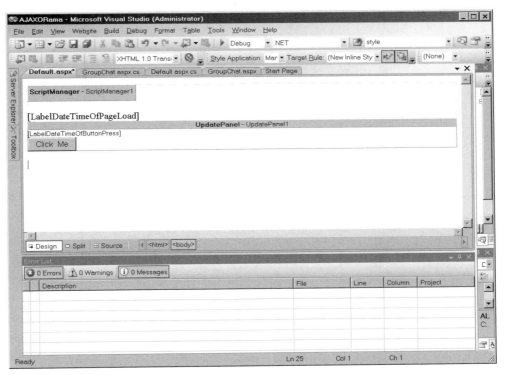

7. Run the page and generate some postbacks by clicking the button. Both labels should
   be showing the date and time of the postback (that is, they should show the same
   time). Although the second label is inside the *UpdatePanel*, the action causing the postback is happening outside the *UpdatePanel*.

The following graphic shows the Web page running without the *Button* being associated with the *UpdatePanel:*

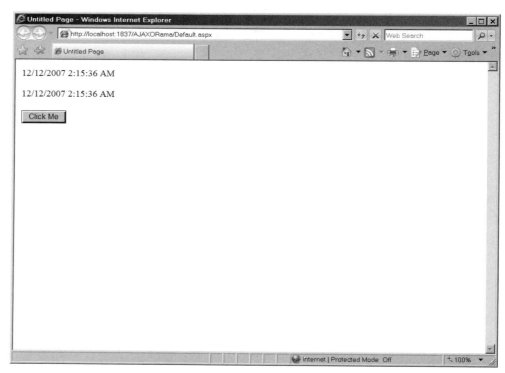

8. Now delete the current button from the form and drop a new button into the *UpdatePanel1* control. Add a *Label* to the *UpdatePanel1* as well. Name the new label *LabelDateTimeOfButtonPress*. Look at the Default.aspx file to see what was produced:

```
<%@ Page Language="C#" AutoEventWireup="true"
CodeFile="Default.aspx.cs" Inherits="_Default" %>

<!DOCTYPE html PUBLIC
"-//W3C//DTD XHTML 1.1//EN"
"http://www.w3.org/TR/xhtml11/DTD/xhtml11.dtd">
<html xmlns="http://www.w3.org/1999/xhtml">
<head runat="server">
    <title>Untitled Page</title>
</head>
<body>
    <form id="form1" runat="server">
        <asp:ScriptManager
         ID="ScriptManager1" runat="server" /><br/>
        <asp:Label ID="LabelDateTimeOfPageLoad"
         runat="server"></asp:Label> <br/>
        <asp:UpdatePanel ID="UpdatePanel1" runat="server">
```

```
                    <ContentTemplate>
                     <asp:Label ID="LabelDateTimeOfButtonPress"
                            runat="server">
                      </asp:Label><br/>
                     <asp:Button ID="Button1"
                            runat="server" Text="Click Me" />
                   </ContentTemplate>
                </asp:UpdatePanel>
          </form>
    </body>
  </html>
```

The new *Button* should now appear nested inside the *UpdatePanel* along with the new *Label*.

9. Run the page and generate some postbacks by pressing the button. Notice that only the label showing the date and time enclosed in the *UpdatePanel* is updated. This is known as a *partial page update*, since only part of the page is actually updated in response to a page action, such as clicking the button. Partial page updates are also sometimes referred to as *callbacks* rather than postbacks. The following graphic shows the Web page running with the *Button* being associated with the *UpdatePanel*.

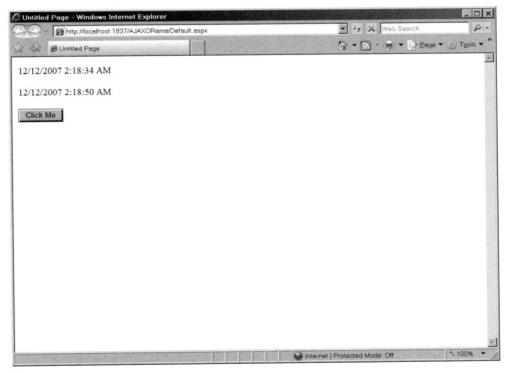

10. Add an UpdatePanel trigger. Because the second label and the button are both associated with the single *UpdatePanel*, only the second *Label* is updated in response to the postback generated by the button. If you could only set up partial page updates

based on elements tied to a single *UpdatePanel*, that would be fairly restrictive. As it turns out, the *UpdatePanel* supports a collection of triggers that will generate partial page updates. To see how this works, you need to first move the button outside the *UpdatePanel* (so that the button generates a full normal postback). The easiest way is to simply drag a button onto the form (making sure it lands outside the *UpdatePanel*).

Because the button is outside the *UpdatePanel* again, postbacks generated by the button are no longer tied solely to the second label, and the partial page update behavior you saw in Step 9 is again non-functional.

11. Update the *UpdatePanel*'s *Triggers* collection to include the *Button*'s *Click* event. With the designer open, select the *UpdatePanel*. Go to the properties Window and choose *Triggers*. This presents a dialog box as shown in the following graphic.

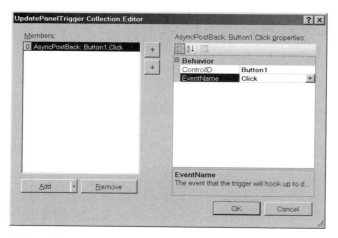

Add a trigger and set the control ID to the button's *ID* and the event to *Click*. (Note that the handy drop-down lists for each property assist you with this selection.) Run the page. Clicking the button should now generate a callback (causing a partial page update) in which the first label continues to show the date and time of the original page load and the second label shows the date and time of the button click. Pretty cool!

Async Callbacks

As you know by this point, standard Web pages require the browser to instigate postbacks. Many times, postbacks are generated by clicking on a *Button* control (in ASP.NET terms). However, most ASP.NET controls may be enabled to generate postbacks as well. For example, if you'd like to receive a postback whenever a user selects an item in a *DropDownList*, just flip the *AutoPostBack* property to *true*, and the control will generate the normal postback whenever the selected item changes.

In some cases, an entire postback is warranted for events such as when the selected item changes. However, in most cases generating postbacks that often will be distracting for the user and lead to very poor performance for your page. That's because standard postbacks refresh the whole page.

ASP.NET's AJAX support introduces the notion of the "asynchronous" postback. This is done using JavaScript running inside the client page. The *XMLHttpRequest* object posts data to server—making an end run around the normal postback. The server returns data as XML, JSON, or HTML and has to refresh only part of the page. The JavaScript running in the page replaces old HTML within the Document Object Model with new HTML based on the results of the asynchronous postback.

If you've done any amount of client-side script programming, you can imagine how much work doing something like this can be. Performing asynchronous postbacks and updating pages usually requires a lot of JavaScript.

The *UpdatePanel* control you just used in this exercise hides all of the client-side code and also the server-side plumbing. Also, because of ASP.NET's well-architected server-side control infrastructure, the *UpdatePanel* maintains the same server-side control model you're used to seeing in ASP.NET.

The Timer

In addition to causing partial page updates via an event generated by a control (like a button click), AJAX includes a timer to cause regularly scheduled events. You can find the *Timer* control alongside the other standard AJAX controls in the Toolbox. By dropping a *Timer* on a page, you can generate automatic postbacks to the server.

Some uses for the *Timer* include a "shout box"—like an open chat where a number of users type in messages and they appear near the top like a conversation. Another reason you might like an automatic postback is if you wanted to update a live Web camera picture or to refresh some other frequently updated content.

The *Timer* is very easy to use—simply drop it on a page which hosts a *ScriptManager*. The default settings for the timer cause the timer to generate postbacks every minute (every 60,000 milliseconds). The *Timer* is enabled by default and begins firing events as soon as the page loads.

Here's an exercise using the *Timer* to write a simple chat page that displays messages from a number of users who are logged in. The conversation is immediately updated for the user typing in a message. However, users who have not refreshed since the last message don't get to see it—unless they perform a refresh. The page uses a *Timer* to update the conversation automatically. At first, the entire page is refreshed. Then the chat page uses an *UpdatePanel* to update only the chat log (which is the element that has changed).

Using the Timer: Creating a chat page

1. Open the AJAXORama application if it's not already open. The first step is to create a list of chat messages that can be seen from a number of different sessions. Add a global application class to the project by clicking the right mouse button in the Solution Explorer and selecting **Add New Item**. Choose *Global Application Class* as the type of file to add. This will add a file named *Global.asax* to your Web site.

2. Update the *Application_Start* method in Global.asax to create a list for storing messages and add the list to the application cache. Using an *Import* statement at the top makes it more convenient to use the generic *List* collection.

```
<%@ Application Language="C#" %>
<%@ Import Namespace="System.Collections.Generic" %>

<script runat="server">

    void Application_Start(object sender, EventArgs e)
    {
        // Code that runs on application startup
        List<string> messages = new List<string>();
        HttpContext.Current.Cache["Messages"] = messages;
    }

    void Application_End(object sender, EventArgs e)
    {
    }

    void Application_Error(object sender, EventArgs e)
    {
    }

    void Session_Start(object sender, EventArgs e)
    {
    }

    void Session_End(object sender, EventArgs e)
    {
    }
</script>
```

3. Create a chat page by adding a new page to the Web site and calling it GroupChat.aspx. This will hold a text box with messages as they accumulate, and it also gives users a means of adding messages.

4. When the messages are coming in, it would be very useful to know who sent what messages. This page will force users to identify themselves first—then they can start adding messages. First, type in the text **Group Chatting...** following the *ScriptManager*. Give it a large font style with block display so that it's on its own line. Following that, type in the text **First, give us your name:**. Then, pick up a *TextBox* control from the Toolbox and drop it on the page. Give the *TextBox* the ID **TextBoxUserID.** Drop a

Button on the page so the user can submit his or her name. Give it the text **Submit ID** and the ID **ButtonSubmitID**.

5. Drop another *TextBox* onto the page. This one will hold the messages, so make it large (800 pixels wide by 150 pixels high should do the trick). Set the *TextBox*'s *TextMode* property to *MultiLine*, and set the *ReadOnly* property to *True*. Give the *TextBox* the ID **TextBoxConversation**.

6. Drop one more *TextBox* onto the page. This one will hold the user's current message. Give the *TextBox* the ID **TextBoxMessage**.

7. Add one more *Button* to the page. This one will let the user submit the current message and should have the text **Add Your Message**. Be sure to give the button the ID value **ButtonAddYourMessage**. The following graphic shows a possible layout of these controls.

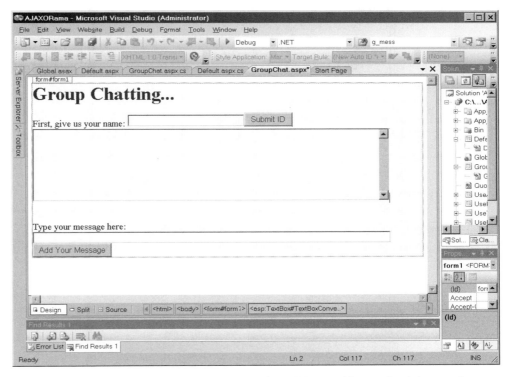

8. Open the code beside file GroupChat.aspx.cs for editing. Add a method that retrieves the user's name from session state. Note you should also add the *using* clause for *System.Collections.Generic* as later we'll need to access the generic list we placed in the application cache (Step 2):

```
using System;
using System.Data;
using System.Configuration;
```

```
using System.Collections;
using System.Linq;
using System.Web;
using System.Web.Security;
using System.Web.UI;
using System.Web.UI.WebControls;
using System.Web.UI.WebControls.WebParts;
using System.Web.UI.HtmlControls;
using System.Xml.Linq;
using System.Collections.Generic;

public partial class GroupChat : System.Web.UI.Page
{
    protected void Page_Load(object sender, EventArgs e)
    {
    }

    protected string GetUserID()
    {
        string strUserID =
          (string) Session["UserID"];
        return strUserID;
    }
}
```

9. Add a method to update the UI so that users may only type messages after they've
identified themselves. If the user has not been identified (that is, the session variable is
not there), then *disable* the chat conversation UI elements and *enable* the user identification UI elements. If the user has been identified, then *enable* the chat conversation UI
elements and *disable* the user identification UI elements.

```
using System;
using System.Data;
using System.Configuration;
using System.Collections;
using System.Linq;
using System.Web;
using System.Web.Security;
using System.Web.UI;
using System.Web.UI.WebControls;
using System.Web.UI.WebControls.WebParts;
using System.Web.UI.HtmlControls;
using System.Xml.Linq;
using System.Collections.Generic;

public partial class GroupChat : System.Web.UI.Page
{
    protected void Page_Load(object sender, EventArgs e)
    {
    }
    // other code goes here...
    void ManageUI()
    {
        if (GetUserID() == null)
```

```
        {
            // if this is the first request, then get the user's ID
            TextBoxMessage.Enabled = false;
            TextBoxConversation.Enabled = false;
            ButtonAddYourMessage.Enabled = false;

            ButtonSubmitID.Enabled = true;
            TextBoxUserID.Enabled = true;
        }
        else
        {
            // if this is the first request, then get the user's ID
            TextBoxMessage.Enabled = true;
            TextBoxConversation.Enabled = true;
            ButtonAddYourMessage.Enabled = true;

            ButtonSubmitID.Enabled = false;
            TextBoxUserID.Enabled = false;
        }
    }
}
```

10. Add a *Click* event handler for the *Button* that stores the user ID (ButtonSubmitID). The method should store the user's identity in session state and then call *ManageUI* to enable and disable the correct controls.

```
using System;
using System.Data;
using System.Configuration;
using System.Collections;
using System.Linq;
using System.Web;
using System.Web.Security;
using System.Web.UI;
using System.Web.UI.WebControls;
using System.Web.UI.WebControls.WebParts;
using System.Web.UI.HtmlControls;
using System.Xml.Linq;
using System.Collections.Generic;

public partial class GroupChat : System.Web.UI.Page
{
    protected void Page_Load(object sender, EventArgs e)
    {
    }
    // other page code goes here...
    protected void ButtonSubmitID_Click(object sender, EventArgs e)
    {
        Session["UserID"] = TextBoxUserID.Text;
        ManageUI();
    }
}
```

11. Add a method to the page for refreshing the conversation. The code should look up the message list in the application cache and build a string that shows the messages in reverse order (so the most recent is on top). Then the method should set the conversation *TextBox*'s *Text* property to the new string (that is, the text property of the *TextBox* one showing the conversation).

```
using System;
using System.Data;
using System.Configuration;
using System.Collections;
using System.Linq;
using System.Web;
using System.Web.Security;
using System.Web.UI;
using System.Web.UI.WebControls;
using System.Web.UI.WebControls.WebParts;
using System.Web.UI.HtmlControls;
using System.Xml.Linq;
using System.Collections.Generic;

public partial class GroupChat : System.Web.UI.Page
{
    // other page code goes here...
    void RefreshConversation()
    {
        List<string> messages = (List<string>)Cache["Messages"];
        if (messages != null)
        {
            string strConversation = "";

            int nMessages = messages.Count;

            for(int i = nMessages-1; i >=0; i--)
            {
                string s;

                s = messages[i];
                strConversation += s;
                strConversation += "\r\n";
            }

            TextBoxConversation.Text =
                strConversation;
        }
    }
}
```

12. Add a *Click* event handler. Double-click on the *Button* and add a *Click* event handler to respond to the user submitting his or her message (ButtonAddYourMessage). The method should grab the text from the user's message *TextBox*, prepend the user's ID to it, and add it to the list of messages held in the application cache. Then the method should call *RefreshConversation* to make sure the new message appears in the conversation *TextBox*.

```
using System;
using System.Data;
using System.Configuration;
using System.Collections;
using System.Linq;
using System.Web;
using System.Web.Security;
using System.Web.UI;
using System.Web.UI.WebControls;
using System.Web.UI.WebControls.WebParts;
using System.Web.UI.HtmlControls;
using System.Xml.Linq;
using System.Collections.Generic;

public partial class GroupChat : System.Web.UI.Page
{
    // Other code goes here...
    protected void ButtonAddYourMessage_Click(object sender,
                                              EventArgs e)
    {
        // Add the message to the conversation...
        if (this.TextBoxMessage.Text.Length > 0)
        {
            List<string> messages = (List<string>)Cache["Messages"];
            if (messages != null)
            {
                TextBoxConversation.Text = "";

                string strUserID = GetUserID();

                if (strUserID != null)
                {
                    messages.Add(strUserID +
                        ": " +
                        TextBoxMessage.Text);
                    RefreshConversation();
                    TextBoxMessage.Text = "";
                }
            }
        }
    }
}
```

13. Update the *Page_Load* method to call *ManageUI* and *RefreshConversation*.

```
using System;
using System.Data;
using System.Configuration;
using System.Collections;
using System.Linq;
using System.Web;
using System.Web.Security;
using System.Web.UI;
using System.Web.UI.WebControls;
using System.Web.UI.WebControls.WebParts;
using System.Web.UI.HtmlControls;
```

```
using System.Xml.Linq;
using System.Collections.Generic;

public partial class GroupChat : System.Web.UI.Page
{
    // Other code goes here...
    protected void Page_Load(object sender, EventArgs e)
    {
        ManageUI();
        RefreshConversation();
    }
}
```

14. Now run the page to see how it works. Once you've identified yourself, you can start typing messages in—and you'll see them appear in the conversation *TextBox*. Try browsing the page using two separate browsers. Do you see an issue? The user typing a message gets to see the message appear in the conversation right away. However, other users involved in the chat don't see any new messages until after they submit messages of their own. Let's solve this issue by dropping an AJAX *Timer* onto the page.

15. Pick up a *ScriptManager* from the AJAX controls and drop it on the page. Then pick up a *Timer* from the AJAX controls and drop it on the page. Although the AJAX *Timer* will start generating postbacks automatically, the default interval is 60,000 milliseconds, or once per minute. Set the *Timer*'s *Interval* property to something more reasonable, such as 10,000 milliseconds (or 10 seconds). Now run both pages and see what happens. You should see the pages posting back automatically every 10 seconds. However, there's still one more issue with this scenario. If you watch carefully enough, you'll see the whole page being refreshed—even though the user name is not changing. During the conversation, you're really only interested in seeing the conversation *TextBox* being updated. Let's fix that by putting in an *UpdatePanel*.

16. Pick up an *UpdatePanel* from the AJAX controls and drop it on the page. Position the *UpdatePanel* so that it can hold the conversation text box. Move the conversation text box so that it's positioned within the *UpdatePanel*. Modify the *UpdatePanel*'s triggers so that it includes the *Timer*'s *Tick* event. Now run the chat pages, and you should see only the conversation text box being updated on each timer tick. The following graphic shows the new layout of the page employing the *UpdatePanel*.

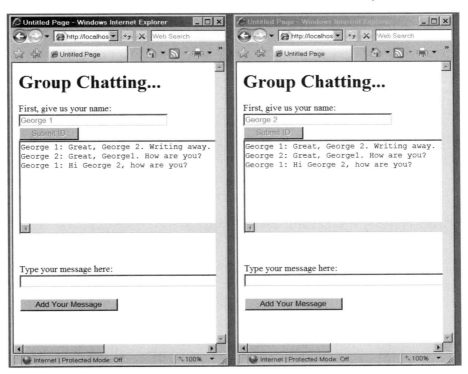

The ASP.NET AJAX *Timer* is useful whenever you need regular, periodic posts back to the server. You can see here how it's especially useful when combined with the *UpdatePanel* doing periodic partial page updates.

Updating Progress

A recurring theme when programming any UI environment is keeping the user updated as to the progress of a long-running operation. If you're programming Windows Forms, you can use the *BackgroundWorker* component and show progress updating using the *Progress* control. Programming for the Web requires a slightly different strategy. ASP.NET's AJAX support includes a component for this—the ASP.NET AJAX *UpdateProgress* control.

UpdateProgress controls display during asynchronous postbacks. All *UpdateProgress* controls on the page become visible when any *UpdatePanel* control triggers an asynchronous postback.

Here's an exercise for using an *UpdateProgress* control on a page.

Using the *UpdateProgress* control

1. **Add a new page.** Add a new page to the AJAXORama site named *UseUpdateProgressControl.aspx*.

2. Pick up a *ScriptManager* from the Toolbox and drop it on the page.

3. Pick up an *UpdatePanel* and drop it on the page. Give the panel the ID **UpdatePanelForProgress** so you can identify it later. Add a *Button* to the update panel that will begin a long-running operation. Give it the ID **ButtonLongOperation** and the text **Activate Long Operation**.

4. Add a *Click* event handler for the button. The easiest way to create a long-running operation is to put the thread to sleep for a few seconds, as shown here. By introducing a long-running operation here, you'll have a way to test the *UpdateProgress* control and see how it works when the request takes a long time to complete.

```
public partial class UseUpdateProgressControl : System.Web.UI.Page
{
    protected void Page_Load(object sender, EventArgs e)
    {

    }

    protected void
        ButtonLongOperation_Click(object sender,
                                    EventArgs e)
    {
        // Put thread to sleep for five seconds
        System.Threading.Thread.Sleep(5000);
    }
}
```

5. Now add an *UpdateProgress* control to the page. An *UpdateProgress* control must be tied to a specific *UpdatePanel*. Set the *UpdateProgress* control's *AssociatedUpdatePanelID* property to the *UpdatePanelForProgress* panel you just added.

6. Add a *ProgressTemplate* to the *UpdateProgress* control—this is where the content for the update display will be declared. Add a *Label* to the *ProgressTemplate* so you will be able see it when it appears on the page.

```
<asp:UpdateProgress ID="UpdateProgress1"
    runat="server"
    AssociatedUpdatePanelID="UpdatePanelForProgress"
    DisplayAfter="100">
    <ProgressTemplate>
        <asp:Label ID="Label1" runat="server"
         Text="What's happening? This takes a long time...">
        </asp:Label>
    </ProgressTemplate>
</asp:UpdateProgress>
```

7. Run the page to see what happens. When you press the button that executes the long-running operation, you should see the *UpdateProgress* control show its content automatically. This graphic shows the *UpdateProgress* control in action.

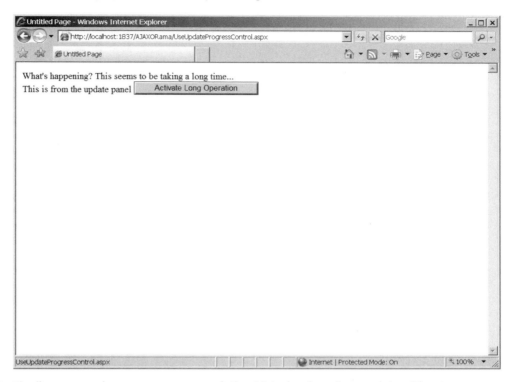

8. Finally, no asynchronous progress updating UI technology is complete without a means to cancel the long-running operation. If you wish to cancel the long-running operation, you may do so by inserting a little of your own JavaScript into the page. You'll need to do this manually because there's no support for this using the Wizards. Write a client-side script block and place it near the top of the page—just before the *<html>* tag. The script block should get the instance of the *Sys.WebForms.PageRequestManager*. The *PageRequestManager* is a class that's available to the client as part of the script injected by the ASP.NET AJAX server-side controls. The *PageRequestManager* has a method named *get_isInAsyncPostBack()* that you can use to figure out whether the page is in the middle of an asynchronous callback (generated by the *UpdatePanel*). If the page is in the middle of an asynchronous callback, use the *PageRequestManager*'s *abortPostBack()* method to quit the request. Add a *Button* to the *ProgressTemplate* and then assign its *OnClientClick* property to make a call to your new *abortAsyncPostback* method. In addition to setting the *OnClientClick* property to the new abort method, insert **return false;** immediately following the call to the abort method, as shown in the following code (inserting "return false;" prevents the browser from issuing a postback).

```
<%@ Page Language="C#"
 AutoEventWireup="true"
CodeFile="UseUpdateProgressControl.aspx.cs"
Inherits="UseUpdateProgressControl" %>

<!DOCTYPE html PUBLIC
"...">

<html xmlns="http://www.w3.org/1999/xhtml">
<head runat="server">
    <title>Untitled Page</title>

<script type="text/javascript">
  function abortAsyncPostback()
  {
    var obj =
        Sys.WebForms.PageRequestManager.getInstance();
    if(obj.get_isInAsyncPostBack())
    {
        obj.abortPostBack();
    }
  }
</script>

</head>
<body>
    <form id="form1" runat="server">
    <div>

        <asp:ScriptManager ID="ScriptManager1" runat="server">
        </asp:ScriptManager>

    </div>
    <asp:UpdateProgress ID="UpdateProgress1"
        runat="server"
        AssociatedUpdatePanelID="UpdatePanelForProgress"
        DisplayAfter="100">
        <ProgressTemplate>
            <asp:Label ID="Label1" runat="server"
             Text="What's happening? This takes a long time...">
            </asp:Label>
            <asp:Button ID="Cancel" runat="server"
              OnClientClick="abortAsyncPostback(); return false;"
              Text="Cancel" />
        </ProgressTemplate>
    </asp:UpdateProgress>
    <asp:UpdatePanel ID="UpdatePanelForProgress" runat="server">
        <ContentTemplate>
            This is from the update panel
            <asp:Button ID="ButtonLongOperation"
              runat="server"
              onclick="ButtonLongOperation_Click"
              Text="Activate Long Operation" />
        </ContentTemplate>
    </asp:UpdatePanel>
```

```
        </form>
    </body>
    </html>
```

> **Caution** *Caveat Cancel:* As you can see, canceling an asynchronous postback is completely a
> client-side affair. Canceling a long-running operation on the client end is tantamount to discon-
> necting the client from the server. Once the client is disconnected from the server, the client will
> never see the response from the server.
>
> Also, while the client is happy that he or she could cancel the operation, the server may *never
> know* that the client canceled. So, the big caveat here is to plan for such a cancellation by mak-
> ing sure you program long-running blocking operations carefully so they don't spin out of con-
> trol. Although IIS 6 and IIS 7 should hopefully refresh the application pool eventually for such
> runaway threads, it's better to depend on your own good programming practices to make sure
> long-running operations end reasonably nicely.

ASP.NET's AJAX support provides a great infrastructure for managing partial page updates
and for setting up other events such as regular timer ticks. Now let's take a look at ASP.NET's
AJAX Extender Controls.

Extender Controls

The *UpdatePanel* provided a way to update only a portion of the page. That's pretty amazing. However, AJAX's compelling features have a very broad reach. One of the most useful
features is the Extender Control architecture.

Extender Controls target existing control to extend functionality in the target. While controls
such as the *ScriptManager* and the *Timer* do a lot of heavy lifting in terms of injecting lots
of script code into the page as it's rendered, the Extender Controls often involve managing
the markup (HTML) in the resultant page.

Here are a couple of examples to familiarize you with ASP.NET AJAX Extender Controls. The
first one we'll look at is the *AutoComplete* Extender.

The *AutoComplete* Extender

This extender attaches to a standard ASP.NET *TextBox*. As the end user types text into the
TextBox, the *AutoComplete* Extender calls a Web service to look up candidate entries based
on the results of the Web service call. The example borrows a component from the chapter on
caching—it's the quotes collection containing a number of famous quotes by various people.

Using the *AutoComplete* extender

1. Add a new page to AJAXORama. Because this page will host the *AutoComplete* Extender, name it *UseAutocompleteExtender*.

2. Add an instance of the *ScriptManager* control to the page you just added.

3. Borrow the *QuotesCollection* class from Chapter 15. Remember, the class derives from *System.Data.Table* and holds a collection of famous quotes and their originators. You can add the component to AJAXORama by creating an App_Code directory under the project node in the Visual Studio Project Explorer, clicking the right mouse button on the *App_Code* directory, selecting **Add Existing Item**, and locating the QuotesCollection. cs file associated with the UseDataCaching example from Chapter 15.

4. Add a method to retrieve the quotes based on the last name. The method should accept the last name of the originator as a string parameter. The *System.Data.DataView* class you'll use for retrieving a specific quote is useful for performing queries on a table in memory. The method should return the quotes as a list of strings. There may be none, one, or many, depending on the selected quote author. You'll use this function shortly.

```
using System;
using System.Data;
using System.Configuration;
using System.Web;
using System.Web.Security;
using System.Web.UI;
using System.Web.UI.WebControls;
using System.Web.UI.WebControls.WebParts;
using System.Web.UI.HtmlControls;
using System.Collections.Generic;

/// <summary>
/// Summary description for QuotesCollection
/// </summary>
public class QuotesCollection : DataTable
{
    public QuotesCollection()
    { }

    public void Synthesize()
    {
        this.TableName = "Quotations";
        DataRow dr;

        Columns.Add(new DataColumn("Quote", typeof(string)));
        Columns.Add(new DataColumn("OriginatorLastName", typeof(string)));
        Columns.Add(new DataColumn(@"OriginatorFirstName",
                typeof(string)));

        dr = this.NewRow();
        dr[0] = "Imagination is more important than knowledge.";
        dr[1] = "Einstein";
```

```
        dr[2] = "Albert";
        Rows.Add(dr);
        // Other quotes added here...
    }

    public string[]
    GetQuotesByLastName(string strLastName)
    {
        List<string> list = new List<string>();

        DataView dvQuotes = new DataView(this);
        string strFilter = String.Format("OriginatorLastName = '{0}'", strLastName)
        dvQuotes.RowFilter = strFilter;

        foreach (DataRowView drv in dvQuotes)
        {
            string strQuote =
                drv["Quote"].ToString();

            list.Add(strQuote);
        }

        return list.ToArray();
    }
}
```

5. Add a class named *QuotesManager* to the Web site's *App_Code* directory to manage caching. The Caching example from which this code was borrowed stores and retrieves the *QuotesCollection* during the *Page_Load* event. Because the *QuotesCollection* will be used within a Web service, the caching will have to happen elsewhere. To do this, add a public static method named *GetQuotesFromCache* to retrieve the *QuotesCollection* from the cache.

```
using System;
using System.Data;
using System.Configuration;
using System.Linq;
using System.Web;
using System.Web.Security;
using System.Web.UI;
using System.Web.UI.WebControls;
using System.Web.UI.WebControls.WebParts;
using System.Web.UI.HtmlControls;
using System.Xml.Linq;

/// <summary>
/// Summary description for QuotesManager
/// </summary>
public class QuotesManager
{
    public QuotesManager()
    {
    }
```

```
public static QuotesCollection GetQuotesFromCache()
{
    QuotesCollection quotes;

    quotes =
        (QuotesCollection)HttpContext.Current.Cache["quotes"];

    if (quotes == null)
    {
        quotes = new QuotesCollection();
        quotes.Synthesize();
    }
    return quotes;
}
}
```

6. Add an XML Web Service to your application. Click the right mouse button on the project and add an ASMX file to your application. Name the service *QuoteService*. The *WebService* and *WebServiceBinding* attributes may be removed but be sure to adorn the XML Web Service class with the *[System.Web.Script.Services.ScriptService]* attribute. That way, it will be available to the *AutoComplete* extender later on. The *AutoCompleteExtender* will use the XML Web Service to populate its drop-down list box.

7. Add a method to get the last names of the quote originators—that's the method that will populate the drop-down box. The method should take a string representing the text already typed in as the first parameter, an integer representing the maximum number of strings to return. Grab the *QuotesCollection* from the cache using the *QuoteManager*'s static method *GetQuotesFromCache*. Use the *QuotesCollection* to get the rows from the *QuotesCollection*. Finally, iterate through the rows and add the originator's last name to the list of strings to be returned if it starts with the prefix passed in as the parameter. The Common Language Runtime's (CLR) *String* type includes a method named *StartsWith* that's useful to figure out if a string starts with a certain prefix. Note you'll also have to add *using* statements for generic collections and data (as shown).

```
using System;
using System.Linq;
using System.Web;
using System.Collections;
using System.Web.Services;
using System.Web.Services.Protocols;
using System.Xml.Linq;
using System.Data;
using System.Collections.Generic;

[System.Web.Script.Services.ScriptService]
public class QuoteService : System.Web.Services.WebService
{

    [WebMethod]
    public string[]
    GetQuoteOriginatorLastNames(string prefixText,
                                int count)
```

```
    {
        List<string> list = new List<string>();

        QuotesCollection quotes =
            QuotesManager.GetQuotesFromCache();

        prefixText = prefixText.ToLower();

        foreach (DataRow dr in quotes.Rows)
        {
            string strName =
                dr["OriginatorLastName"].ToString();

            if (strName.ToLower().StartsWith(prefixText))
            {
                if (!list.Contains(strName))
                {
                    list.Add(strName);
                }
            }
        }

        return list.GetRange(0,
            System.Math.Min(count, list.Count)).ToArray();
    }
}
```

8. Now drop a *TextBox* on the *UseAutocompleteExtender* page to hold the originator's last name to be looked up. Give the *TextBox* an ID of **TextBoxOriginatorLastName**.

9. Pick up an *AutoComplete* extender from the AJAX Toolbox and add it to the page. Point the *AutoComplete*'s *TargetControlID* to the *TextBox* holding the originator's last name, **TextBoxOriginatorLastName**. Make the *MinimumPrefix* length **1**, the *ServiceMethod* **GetQuoteOriginatorLastNames**, and the *ServicePath* **quoteservice .asmx**. This wires up the *AutoComplete* extender so that it will take text from the *TextBoxOriginatorLastName TextBox* and use it to feed the XML Web Service *GetQuoteOriginatorLastNames* method.

```
<cc1:AutoCompleteExtender
    ID="AutoCompleteExtenderForOriginatorLastName"
    TargetControlID="TextBoxOriginatorLastName"
    MinimumPrefixLength="1"
    ServiceMethod="GetQuoteOriginatorLastNames"
    ServicePath="quoteservice.asmx"
    runat="server">
</cc1:AutoCompleteExtender>
```

10. Add a *TextBox* to the page to hold the quotes. Name the *TextBox TextBoxQuotes*.

11. Update the *Page_Load* method. It should look up the quotes based on the name in the text box by retrieving the *QuoteCollection* and calling the *QuoteCollection*'s *GetQuotesByLastName* method.

```
using System;
using System.Data;
using System.Configuration;
using System.Collections;
using System.Linq;
using System.Web;
using System.Web.Security;
using System.Web.UI;
using System.Web.UI.WebControls;
using System.Web.UI.WebControls.WebParts;
using System.Web.UI.HtmlControls;
using System.Xml.Linq;
using System.Collections.Generic;
using System.Text;

public partial class UseAutocompleteExtender :
System.Web.UI.Page
{
    protected void Page_Load(object sender, EventArgs e)
    {
        QuotesCollection quotes =
            QuotesManager.GetQuotesFromCache();
        string[] quotesArray =
            quotes.GetQuotesByLastName(TextBoxOriginatorLastName.Text);

        if (quotesArray != null && quotesArray.Length > 0)
        {
            StringBuilder str = new StringBuilder();
            foreach (string s in quotesArray)
            {
                str.AppendFormat("{0}\r\n", s);
            }
            this.TextBoxQuotes.Text = str.ToString();
        }
        else
        {
            this.TextBoxQuotes.Text = "No quotes match your request.";
        }
    }
}
```

12. To make the page updates more efficient, drop an *UpdatePanel* onto the page. Put the *TextBox* for holding the quotes in the *UpdatePanel*. Put a button in the *UpdatePanel*. This will cause only the *TextBox* showing the quotes to be updated (instead of the whole-page refresh).

13. Add two *asynchPostBack* triggers to the *UpdatePanel*. The first trigger should connect the *TextBoxOriginatorLastName TextBox* to the *TextChanged* event. The second trigger should connect the *ButtonFindQuotes* button to the button's *Click* event.

The following graphic shows the layout of the page using the *AutoComplete* Extender in action.

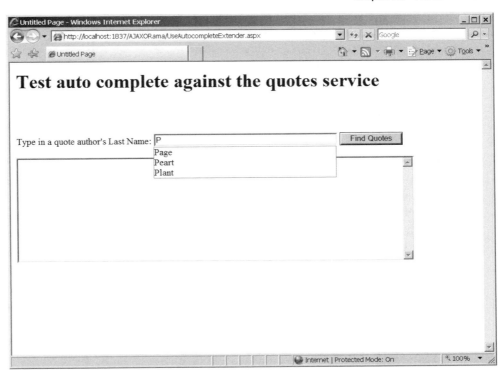

14. Run the page. As you type originator names into the *TextBox*, you should see a drop-down list appear containing candidate names based on the *QuotesCollection*'s contents.

The *AutoComplete* Extender is an excellent example of the sort of things at which ASP.NET's AJAX support excels. Microsoft Internet Explorer has had its own autocomplete feature built into it for quite a while. Microsoft Internet Explorer remembers often-used names of HTML input text tags and recent values that have been used for them. For example, when you go online to buy an airline ticket at some point and go back to buy another one later, watch what happens as you type in your address. You'll very often see Microsoft Internet Explorer's autocomplete feature show a drop-down list box below the address text box showing the last few addresses you've typed that begin with the text showing in the text box.

The ASP.NET *AutoComplete* Extender works very much like this. However, the major difference is that the end user sees input candidates generated by the Web site rather than simply a history of recent entries. Of course, the Web site could mimic this functionality by tracking a user's profile identity and store a history of what a particular user has typed in to a specific input field on a page. The actual process of generating autocomplete candidates is completely up to the Web server, giving a whole new level of power and flexibility to programming user-friendly Web sites.

A Modal Pop-up Dialog-Style Component

Another interesting feature provided by AJAX making Web applications appear more like desktop applications is the *ModalPopup* Extender. Historically, navigating a Web site involves walking down into the hierarchy of a Web site and climbing back out. When a user provides inputs as he or she works with a page, the only means available to give feedback about the quality of the data has been through the validation controls. In addition, standard Web pages have no facility to focus the users' attention while they type in the information.

The traditional desktop application usually employs modal dialog boxes to focus user attention when gathering important information from the end user. The model is very simple and elegant—the end user is presented with a situation in which he or she must enter some data and Click OK or Cancel before moving on. After dismissing the dialog, the end user sees exactly the same screen he or she saw right before the dialog appeared. There's no ambiguity and no involved process where the end user walks up and down some arbitrary page hierarchy.

This example shows how to use the pop-up dialog extender control. You'll create a page with some standard content and then have a modal dialog-style pop-up show right before submitting the page.

Using a *ModalPopup* extender

1. Add a new page to AJAXORama to host the pop-up extender. Call it *UseModalPopupExtender*.

2. As with all the other examples using AJAX controls, pick up a *ScriptManager* from the toolbox and add it to the page.

3. Add a title to the page (the example here uses "ASP.NET Code of Content"). Give the banner some prominence by surrounding it in *<h1>* and *</h1>* tags.

4. Pick up a *Panel* from the toolbox and add it to the page. It will hold the page's normal content.

5. Add a *Button* to the *Panel* for submitting the content. Give the *Button* the ID **ButtonSubmit** and the text **Submit** and create a button *Click* event handler. You'll need this button later.

6. Place some content on the panel. The content in this sample application uses several check boxes that the modal dialog pop-up will examine before the page is submitted.

```
<h1 >ASP.NET Code Of Conduct </h1>

<asp:Panel ID="Panel1" runat="server"
    style="z-index: 1;left: 10px;top: 70px;
    position: absolute;height: 213px;width: 724px;
    margin-bottom: 0px;">
```

```
<asp:Label ID="Label1" runat="server"
    Text="Name of Developer:"></asp:Label>
     <asp:TextBox ID="TextBox1"
    runat="server"></asp:TextBox>

<br />
<br />
<br />
As an ASP.NET developer, I promise to
<br />
<input type="checkbox" name="Check" id="Checkbox1"/>
<label for="Check1">Use Forms Authentication</label>
<br />
<input type="checkbox" name="Check" id="Checkbox2"/>
<label for="Check2">Separate UI From Code</label>
<br />
<input type="checkbox" name="Check" id="Checkbox3"/>
<label for="Check3">Take Advantage of Custom Controls</label>
<br />
<input type="checkbox" name="Check" id="Checkbox4"/>
<label for="Check4">Give AJAX a try</label>
<br />
<asp:Button ID="ButtonSubmit" runat="server" Text="Submit"
        onclick="ButtonSubmit_Click" />
<br />
</asp:Panel>
```

7. Add another *Panel* to the page to represent the pop-up. Give this *Panel* a light yellow background color so that you'll be able to see it when it comes up. It should also have the ID **PanelModalPopup**.

8. Add some content to the new *Panel* that's going to serve as the modal pop-up. At the very least, the popup should have **OK** and **Cancel** buttons. Give the **OK** and **Cancel** buttons the ID values *ButtonOK* and *ButtonCancel*. You'll need them a bit later.

```
<asp:Panel ID="PanelModalPopup" runat="server"
    BorderColor="Black"
    BorderStyle="Solid"
    BackColor="LightYellow" Height="72px"
    Width="403px">
    <br />
    <asp:Label
        Text="Are you sure these are the correct entries?"
        runat="server">
    </asp:Label>
        
    <asp:Button ID="ButtonOK"
        runat="server"
        Text="OK" />
      
    <asp:Button ID="ButtonCancel"
    runat="server" Text="Cancel" />
    <br />
</asp:Panel>
```

9. Add a script block to the ASPX file. You'll need to do this by hand. Write functions to handle the **OK** and **Cancel** buttons. The example here examines check boxes to see which ones have been checked and then displays an alert to show which features have been chosen. The Cancel handler simply displays an alert saying the **Cancel** button was pressed.

```
<script type="text/javascript">

    function onOk() {
        var optionsChosen;
        optionsChosen = "Options chosen: ";

        if($get('Checkbox1').checked)
        {
          optionsChosen =
             optionsChosen.toString() +
             "Use Forms Authentication ";
        }

        if($get('Checkbox2').checked)
        {
          optionsChosen =
             optionsChosen.toString() +
             "Separate UI From Code ";
        }

        if($get('Checkbox3').checked)
        {
          optionsChosen =
             optionsChosen.toString() +
             "Take Advantage of Custom Controls ";
        }

        if($get('Checkbox4').checked)
        {
          optionsChosen =
             optionsChosen.toString() +
             "Give AJAX a try ";
        }
        alert(optionsChosen);
    }

    function onCancel() {
        alert("Cancel was pressed");
    }
</script>
```

10. Pick up the *ModalPopup* Extender from the toolbox and add it to the page.

11. Add the following markup to the page. This will set various properties on the new *ModalPopup* Extender. It will set the *OkControlID* property to **ButtonOK** and it will set the *CancelControlID* property to **ButtonCancel**. It will also set the *OnCancelScript* property to **onCancel()** (the client-side Cancel script handler you just wrote). Set

OnOkScript="onOk()" (the client-side OK script handler you just wrote). Finally, the following markup will set the *TargetControlID* property to be **ButtonSubmit**.

```
<cc1:ModalPopupExtender
    ID="ModalPopupExtender1"
    OkControlID="ButtonOK"
    CancelControlID="ButtonCancel"
    OnCancelScript="onCancel()"
    OnOkScript="onOk()"
    TargetControlID="ButtonSubmit"
    PopupControlID="PanelModalPopup">
    runat="server"
    DynamicServicePath="" Enabled="True"
</cc1:ModalPopupExtender>
```

This graphic shows the layout of the page using the *ModalPopup* Extender within Visual Studio 2008.

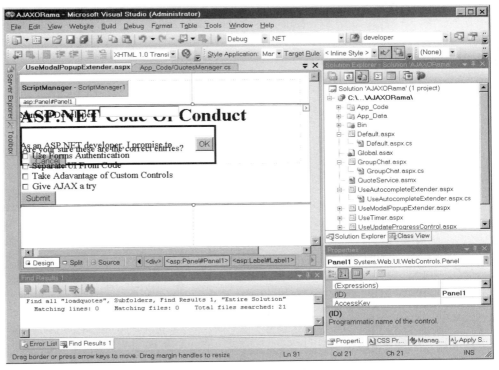

12. Run the page. When you click the *Submit* button, the *Panel* designated to be the modal popup window will be activated (remember, the *Submit* button is the *TargetControlID* of the *ModalPopup* Extender). When you dismiss the popup using **OK** or **Cancel**, you should see the client-side scripts being executed. The following graphic image shows the *ModalPopup* Extender displaying the modal pop-up panel.

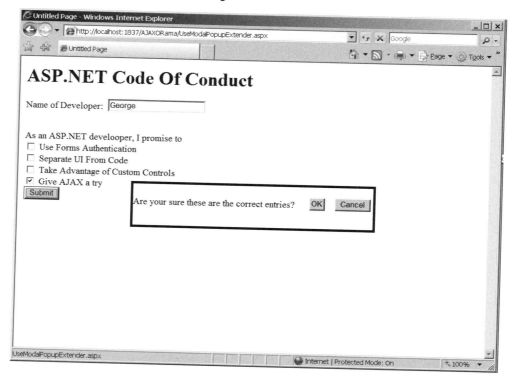

Summary

Without a doubt, supporting AJAX is one of the most important new features of ASP.NET. Using AJAX in your ASP.NET applications helps you improve your Web site's user experience by getting rid of unnecessary postbacks and whole-page refreshes. In addition, AJAX is useful for modifying certain standard server-side controls and HTML elements to change their appearances and behaviors to seem much more "desktop-like." Although many technologies and tricks to improve the user interface experience have been around for a while (DHTML, writing your own client-side script, etc.), AJAX represents the first standard user interface technology available for targeting multiple client platforms. In addition, ASP.NET wraps these capabilities up nice and neatly so they're very convenient to use.

In this chapter, we saw how to use ASP.NET's new *UpdatePanel* to perform partial page updates. We also saw how the *Timer* produces regularly scheduled postbacks and is especially useful in conjunction with the *UpdatePanel*. We saw how the *UpdateProgress* control displays progress information asynchronously. In addition, we got to see how the *AutoComplete* Extender will talk to a Web service to produce an effective "autocomplete" experience, and we saw how the *ModalPopup* Extender allows you to show a *Panel* as though it were a modal dialog box within a desktop application.

If you feel the urge and have the gumption to look at the HTML and script produced by a page using ASP.NET AJAX controls, it's very interesting. You'll also realize the power and convenience of ASP.NET's AJAX support. It's better to have someone else have all that script code packaged within a server-side control than it is to have to write it all by hand.

Chapter 22 Quick Reference

To	Do This
Enable a Web site for AJAX	Normal Web sites generated by Visual Studio 2008's template are AJAX-enabled by default. However, you must add a *ScriptManager* to a page before using any of the AJAX server-side controls.
Implement partial page updating in your page	From within an ASP.NET project, select an *UpdatePanel* from the toolbox. Controls that you place in the *UpdatePanel* will trigger updates for only that panel, leaving the rest of the page untouched.
Assign arbitrary triggers to an *UpdatePanel* (that is, trigger partial page updates using controls and events not related to the panel)	Modify an *UpdatePanel*'s trigger collection to include the new events and controls. Highlight the *UpdatePanel* from within the Visual Studio designer. Select the *Triggers* property from within the property editor. Assign triggers as appropriate.
Implement regularly timed automatic posts from your page	Use the AJAX *Timer* control, which will cause a postback to the server at regular intervals.
Use AJAX to apply special UI nuances to your Web page	After installing Visual Studio 2008, you can create AJAX-enabled sites, and use the new AJAX-specific server-side controls available in the AJAX toolkit. Select the control you need. Most AJAX server-side controls may be programmed completely from the server. However, some controls require a bit of JavaScript on the client end.

Chapter 23
ASP.NET and WPF Content

After completing this chapter, you will be able to

- Understand the benefits of Windows Presentation Foundation (WPF) over traditional Windowing user interfaces

- Add WPF-based content to your Web site

- Understand where Silverlight fits into the picture of Web development

In Chapter 22, we looked at AJAX, which represents a major improvement to Web-based user interfaces (UIs). AJAX adds many elements to Web-based user interfaces that have only been available to desktop applications. For example, AJAX's *AutoComplete* extender allows users typing text into a *TextBox* to select from options generated dynamically from a Web service. The *ModalPopupExtender* allows you to play content in a pane that behaves like a standard Windows modal dialog box at run time.

As rich as these new user interface additions are, there's still room for even more. AJAX still relies fundamentally on HTML, and although HTML includes a huge set of tags that render to standard user interface elements, they stop there. WPF changes that. WPF represents a new way to write user interfaces, and it turns standard Windows- and Web-based user interface programming on its head.

What Is WPF?

Windows-based user interface programming is based on an architecture that has remained fundamentally unchanged for more than a quarter century. Back in the early 1980s and through today, all applications have had the same basic underpinnings. The main application runs a message loop, picking up Windows messages off of the message queue and depositing them into a window handler. Every window is responsible for rendering its own presentation. That's every window—all the way from the top-level window of the application down to the most minor control on the window.

Nearly all Windows applications you see today use the Win32 API at the lowest level—even Visual Basic 6.0 applications. The classic Win32 API has worked well for a long time. However, its design is beginning to show its age. Because every window and control is responsible for its own rendering using the Win32 Graphics Device Interface—GDI, or the GDI+ interface in the case of Windows Forms—we see fundamental user interface limitations that are built into the design of Windows. The GDI and GDI+ interfaces have a huge array of functions. However, it takes a lot of work to do much more than basic drawing and text rendering. That is, special effects such as transformations, transparency, and video play integration are difficult to accomplish using the current Windows graphics interface. Windows does support a richer graphics-based interface named *Direct X*; however, using it is often beyond the scope of most Windows applications and normally reserved for game programmers.

The limitations of the classic Windows API have prompted Microsoft to develop a new programming interface. It's called the *Windows Presentation Foundation* (WPF).

WPF makes programming special effects for a Windows applications (including presenting Web content—as we'll see here) very approachable. The WPF libraries comprise a number of classes that work together very much like the Windows Forms classes work together (on the surface, at least—underneath the goings-on are very different from Windows Forms).

WPF represents a very rich programming interface for developing a user interface. Here's a short list of the kinds of features available through WPF (this is a broad summary and is not exhaustive):

- User interface elements that may be modified in all kinds of ways much more easily than can be done with Win32 and subclassing
- Paths, shapes, and geometries for drawing two-dimensional presentations
- Transforms (scale, translate, rotation, and skewing) that allow consistent and uniform modifications to all user interface elements
- Ability to manage the opacity of individual elements
- Built-in layout panels
- Brushes—image, video, and drawing brushes for filling areas on the screen
- Animations

WPF applications arrange the UI elements using layout panels. Rather than relying on absolute positioning (as is the case for Win32 applications) or flow layout (as is the case for ASP.NET pages), WPF introduces a number of layout options including:

- **Grid**   Elements are placed in a table
- **StackPanel**   Elements are stacked vertically or horizontally
- **Canvas**   Elements are positioned absolutely
- **DockPanel**   Elements are positioned against the sides of the host
- **WrapPanel**   Elements are repositioned to fit when host is resized

The example we'll see a bit later uses the *Canvas*.

A typical WPF application is crafted from files in very much the same way as an ASP.NET application. A stand-alone WPF application includes a main application object (that runs the message loop) and one or more *Windows* (a browser-based WPF application is made up of *Pages*). WPF application components are typically composed from a markup file—just like ASP.NET pages. WPF layouts are defined using eXtensible Application Markup Language (XAML).

XAML files describe a WPF layout's logical tree—a collection of WPF user interface elements. A WPF application is made up of Common Language Runtime (CLR) classes underneath the façade of markup language—very like ASP.NET's object model. XAML files represent instructions for constructing a logical tree of visual elements. In the case of a stand-alone Windows application, the logical tree exists within a top-level window. In the case of a browser-based application, the logical tree exists within a browser pane. The following is a short XAML listing that displays "Hello World" within a button, hosted in a browser pane:

```
<Page
  xmlns="http://schemas.microsoft.com/winfx/2006/xaml/presentation"
  xmlns:sys="clr-namespace:System;assembly=mscorlib"
  xmlns:x="http://schemas.microsoft.com/winfx/2006/xaml" >
<Button Height="100" Width="100">Hello World</Button>
</Page>
```

The code listed here doesn't do a whole lot, but it provides an example of the fundamental structure of a WPF page as expressed in XAML. When run, the XAML you see listed starts a browser session and displays a button with the string "Hello World" as its content (provided the XAML plug-in is installed). In a real application, instead of containing a single button with a string, the top-level WPF node can contain elaborate layouts using the different layout panels available in WPF. We'll see an example of that soon.

How Does It Relate to the Web?

What does this all mean for Web applications? Microsoft Internet Explorer (as well as other browsers running on Windows) is based on the classic Windows architecture. Browsers are responsible for rendering HTML using the graphic interface available to Windows—the Graphics Device Interface (GDI). Consequently, accomplishing special effects via browsers (and normal HTML) is just as difficult as with normal Windows programs.

Web programming is based on submitting HTTP requests to a server, processing the request, and sending the response back to the client. In that sense, any user interface–specific responses are constrained to whatever can be expressed in HTML. The Web is dynamic and HTML is basically a document technology.

What if there were another markup language that provided more than just simple tags that could be interpreted by an HTML browser? Well, that's what XAML is when used within the context of a Web application.

Remember the previous code snippet? Figure 23-1 shows how it appears in Internet Explorer when you load the XAML file into the browser (simply double-click the file name in Windows Explorer).

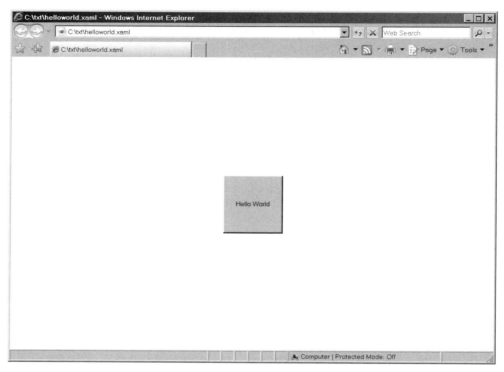

FIGURE 23-1 Button rendered as specified by XAML

When adding WPF-based content directly to a Web site, you have three options: presenting the content through loose XAML files, creating an XAML-based Browser Application (XBAP), or using Silverlight.

Loose XAML Files

As you saw just a moment ago, if you place a properly formatted XAML file within your site and make it available through a Web server, any browser capable of using the XAML plug-in (such as Microsoft Internet Explorer) will pick it up and render it. This is one option for presenting WPF-based content from a Web site. This technique is useful for rendering semi-dynamic content—that is, for rendering anything expressible using pure XAML files.

The WPF programming model marries XAML layout instructions with accompanying code modules—in very much the same way ASP.NET does. Events generated from user interface elements are handled within the accompanying code. Deploying content as loose XAML files precludes adding event handlers and accompanying code.

However, WPF elements are dynamic in the sense that they may be animated, and user interface elements may be tied together using only XAML. That's why WPF content expressed only through XAML is semidynamic. You can hook up some interactive elements using only XAML, but there's a limit. For example, you may render a list of names of images in a list box and allow users to select an image to zoom all through XAML. You may attach slider controls to user interface elements so the end user can change various aspects of the elements through the slider. However, you may not implement event handlers for controls—that requires deploying a WPF application as an XBAP application.

XBAP Applications

XBAPs represent another way to deploy WPF content over the Web. They're a bit more complex than loose XAML files. In addition to expressing layout, XBAP supports accompanying executable code for each page. When you deploy a WPF application over the Web, the client gets the WPF visual layout and the accompanying code downloaded to the client machine. Events occurring within the XBAP application are handled on the client side.

The upside of deploying an application as an XBAP application is that it works in very much the same way that a Windows desktop application works. For example, the application can handle mouse-click movements and can respond to control events all at the client side.

Although XBAP applications are not related directly to ASP.NET, XBAP content may be hosted within ASP.NET-served pages in the same way that loose XAML content may be served. That is, you may make redirects to XBAP files or host XBAP files from within *<iframe>* HTML elements.

Visual Studio includes a Wizard for generating XBAP applications. Using XBAP, you may present WPF content. In addition, the user interface elements contained in the WPF content can respond to events and messages the same way as any other desktop application. When browsers surf to your XBAP application (which will ultimately be deployed via Internet Information Services—IIS), they will have a very desktop-like experience in terms of user interface rendering and responsiveness, even though the application is running in a browser.

WPF Content and Web Applications

WPF content may be served up from an ASP.NET application in much the same way ASP.NET serves up other content. You may include loose XAML files in a Web application, or you may host some specific WPF content within an *<iframe>* HTML element.

Add XAML content to a site

Here's an exercise illustrating how WPF content may be used within an ASP.NET application.

1. Create a new Web site project in Visual Studio. Name the project *XAMLORama*. Make it a File System site.

2. Use Visual Studio to add a new text file to the project. Click the right mouse button on the **XAMLORama** project node within Visual Studio and select **Add New Item**. Select a text file type from the templates.

3. Rename the file so that it has an XAML extension. This file will show a paper airplane drawing, so name the file *PaperAirplane.xaml*.

4. Add some XAML content to the file, starting by defining the top-level layout node. Include the following XML namespaces and make the window 750 units wide:

```
<Page xmlns="http://schemas.microsoft.com/winfx/2006/xaml/presentation"
      xmlns:x="http://schemas.microsoft.com/winfx/2006/xaml" Width="750">

</Page>
```

    All WPF layouts begin with a top-level node. In this case, the node is a *Page* so that it will show up in the client's browser.

5. Add a *Grid* to the page, and add two row definitions and two column definitions.

```
<Page xmlns="http://schemas.microsoft.com/winfx/2006/xaml/presentation"
      xmlns:x="http://schemas.microsoft.com/winfx/2006/xaml" Width="750">
    <Grid>
        <Grid.RowDefinitions>
            <RowDefinition/>
            <RowDefinition Height="100"/>
        </Grid.RowDefinitions>
        <Grid.ColumnDefinitions>
            <ColumnDefinition/>
            <ColumnDefinition Width="25"/>
        </Grid.ColumnDefinitions>
    </Grid>
</Page>
```

6. Now add WPF elements to the grid. Add a *Canvas* to the upper left corner of the *Grid*, and make the *Background* **SkyBlue**. Add two *Slider* controls to the *Grid*, too. The first *Slider* will control the X position of the airplane. Name the *Slider sliderX*. Put the slider into row 1, and use the *ColumnSpan* to stretch the *Slider* across two columns. The maximum value of this slider should be **500**. The second *Slider* should be oriented vertically and should occupy column 1 in the *Grid*. Use the *RowSpan* to stretch the *Slider* across both rows. This slider will control the rotation of the airplane. Name this *Slider sliderRotate*. Its maximum value should be **360**.

```
<Page xmlns="http://schemas.microsoft.com/winfx/2006/xaml/presentation"
      xmlns:x="http://schemas.microsoft.com/winfx/2006/xaml" Width="750">
   <Grid
      <!-- Grid column and row definitions are here... -->
      <Canvas Background="SkyBlue" Grid.Row="0"
            Grid.Column="0">
      </Canvas>
      <Slider x:Name="sliderRotate" Orientation="Vertical"
            Grid.Row="0"
            Minimum="0" Maximum="360"
            Grid.Column="1"></Slider>
      <Slider x:Name="sliderX" Maximum="500"
            Grid.Column="0" Grid.Row="1"
            Grid.ColumnSpan="2"></Slider>
   </Grid>
</Page>
```

7. Now add the airplane and connect it to the sliders using XAML data binding. Here's how. Create the airplane drawing using a WPF *Path*. The *Path* draws a series of line segments using a specific pen. Make the *Stroke* **Black** and the *StrokeThickness* **3**. The *Path* data should connect the following points. Move the cursor to 0,0 and then draw a line to 250,50, and then to 200,75 to 0,0. Then move the cursor to 200,75 and draw a line to 190,115 and another line to 180,85 to 0,0. Then move the cursor to 180,85 and draw a line to 140,105 and then to 0,0. Finally, move the cursor to 190,115 and draw a line to 158,93. Set the *Path*'s relationship to the *Top* of the *Canvas* to be **200**. Bind the *Path*'s relationship to the *Left* of the *Canvas* to *sliderX*'s *Value*. Finally, add a *RenderTransform* to the *Path* and include a *RotateTransform*. Bind the *RotateTransform*'s *Angle* to *sliderRotate*'s *Value*. Set the *Path*'s *RenderTransformOrigin* to **.5, .5**. Here's the *Path* code:

```
<Page xmlns="http://schemas.microsoft.com/winfx/2006/xaml/presentation"
      xmlns:x="http://schemas.microsoft.com/winfx/2006/xaml" Width="750">

   <Grid>
      <!-- Grid column and row definitions are here... -->
      <Canvas Background="SkyBlue" Grid.Row="0"
            Grid.Column="0">
         <Path Stroke="Black" StrokeThickness="2" Fill="White"
            Data="M0,0 L250,50 L200,75 L0,0 M200,75 L190,115 L180,85
               L0,0 M180,85 L140,105 L0,0 M190,115 L158,93"
               RenderTransformOrigin=".5, .5"
               Canvas.Top="200"
               Canvas.Left="{Binding ElementName=sliderX,Path=Value}" >
            <Path.RenderTransform>
               <RotateTransform Angle=
                  "{Binding ElementName=sliderRotate,Path=Value}"/>
            </Path.RenderTransform>
         </Path>
      </Canvas>
      <!--Sliders go here... -->
   </Grid>
</Page>
```

After setting up the *Canvas*, the *Path*, and the *Slider*s in the grid, you should see it appear like this in Visual Studio:

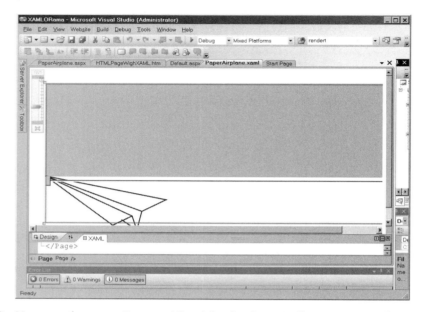

8. Now run the page. Because Visual Studio doesn't allow you to run loose XAML files directly, you'll need to navigate from the default page. Add a *Hyperlink* to the Default .aspx page and set the *NavigationUrl* property to **PaperAirplane.xaml**. Surf to the default page and click on the hyperlink that loads the XAML file in the browser. It should appear like this:

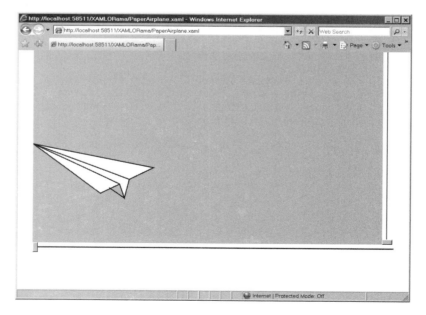

9. Experiment with moving the *Slider*s around. Because the vertical *Slider* controls the angle of rotation, moving it up will cause the airplane to spin in a clockwise direction. Because the horizontal *Slider* is connected to the *Path*'s *Canvas.Left* property, moving the horizontal *Slider* will move the plane along the X axis, like this:

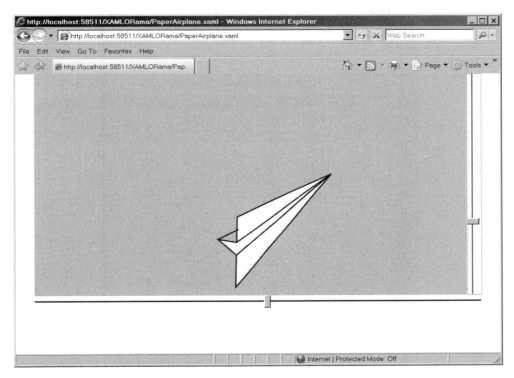

10. Now integrate the new WPF content with some HTML. Add a new Page to the XAMLORama file by clicking the right mouse button on the **XAMLORama** node within the Solution Explorer and adding a new Web page. Name the page *PaperAirplane.aspx*. Add an *<iframe>* tag to the page in between the *<div>* tags Visual Studio provides you with. Set the *<iframe>* height to **500** and the *width* to **750**. Finally, set the *<iframe>* src to **PaperAirplane.xaml**.

```
<%@ Page Language="C#" AutoEventWireup="true" CodeFile="PaperAirplane.aspx.cs"
    Inherits="PaperAirplane" %>

<!DOCTYPE html PUBLIC "...">

<html xmlns="http://www.w3.org/1999/xhtml">
<head runat="server">
    <title>Untitled Page</title>
</head>
<body>
    <form id="form1" runat="server">
    <div>
```

```
        <iframe height="500"
            width="750"
            src="paperairplane.xaml"></iframe> <br />
    </div>
    </form>
</body>
</html>
```

11. Run the page. The PaperAirplane.xaml content will appear in a frame within the page. The XAML content will have the same functionality within the frame as it did when run in the browser:

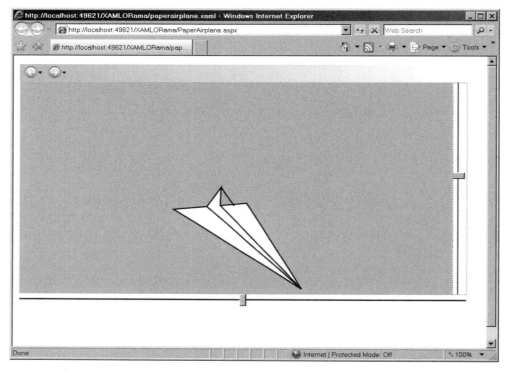

Because this is rendered from a normal ASP.NET page, you could include ASP.NET server controls along with the WPF content.

The previous example illustrates how it's possible to integrate HTML with XAML-based content. Although this lies somewhat outside of the normal ASP.NET pipeline, XAML-based WPF content is still useful in many cases. A full investigation of WPF is beyond the scope of this book. WPF and XAML offer entirely new ways to present content to the end user. Because it is such new technology, the different ways in which it may be exploited are only now being invented and discovered.

What about Silverlight?

As a Web developer, you've probably been unable to avoid hearing the buzz about Microsoft's Silverlight product. Until now, the only effective way to produce dynamic Web content has been through Macromedia Flash. Flash is a plug-in for rendering dynamic content over the Web (i.e., animations). However, with the advent of WPF and its dynamic content capabilities, we now have a markup technology that rivals Flash in raw capability if we can find a way to deliver it to the browser. Although other dynamic content technologies have certainly worked, they've had some serious shortcomings as far as the developer experience is concerned. Microsoft Silverlight changes this.

Microsoft Silverlight is a platform-independent WPF rendering engine. Without Silverlight, the only way to render WPF content within a browser is to run Microsoft Internet Explorer or the Firefox browser with the XAML plug-in. Silverlight is packaged as an ActiveX Control for Microsoft client platforms. For example, the Apple Safari browser is supported by Silverlight.

Silverlight enables animations and rich two-dimensional graphics and video playback. Silverlight applications are not quite as rich as a full-fledged WPF desktop application or an XBAP application, but they provide a richer programming model than is available through AJAX.

The arenas in which Silverlight will probably be most used include multimedia applications, applications requiring rich animations (such as page-turning simulations), and any other applications requiring the richness of the most modern user interface technologies available.

A Silverlight page consists of four basic parts. First is an HTML file describing the overall page. Second, the Silverlight software development kit includes a file named *Silverlight.js* that's used to activate the Silverlight control and get things going. Third, a Silverlight application includes an XAML file for providing WPF-based layout instructions. Finally, a Silverlight application includes several JavaScript code files for handling client-side events.

Hot on the heels of Silverlight version 1.0 is Silverlight version 2.0. Silverlight 2.0 includes a cross-platform CLR engine and support for C#, threading support, Web service client proxy support, and it targets .NET 3.5 and Visual Studio 2008.

Summary

ASP.NET made major improvements to the craft of Web application programming. With the addition of AJAX and Windows Communication Foundation (WCF) into the already rich ASP.NET programming toolset, Web applications for the Microsoft platform are becoming nearly indistinguishable from desktop Windows applications. However, Web-based programming is still fundamentally document based. Web applications are dynamic in that an application can tailor responses to suit the client's request. However, the responses are still in the form of HTML (or XML in the case of a Web service). WPF changes this.

WPF is a new user interface technology that turns Windows programming on its head. For example, it removes the traditional one window handle per user interface element rule. This makes applying stunning visual effects more approachable than with earlier technologies (that is, OpenGL and DirectX). In addition, WPF-style programming draws a clear distinction between visual layout and program logic (in much the same way aspx files do) paving the way for robust design tools tailored toward Human Computer Interface professionals. Finally, the ability to integrate WPF content into Web sites is constantly improving (for example, with the advent of Silverlight). These features combine to open the way for a revolution in rich content. WPF may be integrated into Web sites in several ways. Web sites may expose WPF-based content through loose XAML files. In addition, WPF applications may be deployed over the Web using XBAP technology. Finally, Microsoft Silverlight introduces a platform-independent way to render rich content expressed via XAML.

Chapter 23 Quick Reference

To	Do This
Add an XAML file to your site	Click the right mouse button on the project node within Visual Studio's Solution Explorer. Choose **Add New Item**. Select **Text File** from the available templates. Be sure to name the file with an .xaml extension.
Declare a Page within the XAML file	At the top of the file, add a beginning *<Page>* tag and an ending *</Page>* tag. Using WPF within XAML requires the standard WPF namespace "http://schemas.microsoft.com/winfx/2006/xaml/presentation" and the keywords namespace "http://schemas.microsoft.com/winfx/2006/xaml" (which is often mapped to "x").
Add a *Canvas* to the *Page*	Use the *<Canvas>* opening tag and the *</Canvas>* closing tag. Nest objects you'd like displayed in the canvas between the opening and closing tags.
Add content to the *Canvas*	Nest objects you'd like to appear on the canvas between the *<Canvas>* opening tag and the *</Canvas>* closing tag. Assign positions within the canvas using the *Canvas.Top* and *Canvas.Right* properties.
Add a *Grid* to a *Page*	Declare a *<Grid>* opening tag and a *</Grid>* closing tag on the page. Use the Grid's *RowDefinitions* and the Grid's *ColumnDefinitions* properties to define the rows and columns.
Add content to the *Grid*	Nest objects you'd like to appear on the canvas between the *<Grid>* opening tag and the *</Grid>* closing tag. Assign positions within the grid using the *Grid.Row* and *Grid.Column* properties.

Chapter 24
How Web Application Types Affect Deployment

After completing this chapter, you will be able to

- Recognize ways the Visual Studio project models affect deployment
- Build a Web setup utility

The past 23 chapters focused on how the various features of ASP.NET work. A major theme within ASP.NET has always been to solve the most common use cases as far as developing Web sites is concerned. We saw ASP.NET's

- Rendering model, which breaks down page rendering into small manageable pieces via server-side controls
- Support for data binding, easing the task of rendering collections
- Login controls covering the most common login scenarios
- Session state that makes tracking users manageable
- Navigation and site map support
- XML Web Services as well as Windows Communication Foundation (WCF)-based Web site service support
- Support for creating a common look and feel for an application through Master Pages and Themes
- Support for AJAX-style programming

After building a feature-rich application that streamlines your company operations or drives customers to your business, you need to be able to deploy it and manage it effectively. That's the topic of this chapter—how the various Visual Studio models affect your deployment strategy. In addition, we'll look at building a Web setup project.

Visual Studio Projects

Visual Studio gives you several options when building a Web site project (as opposed to earlier versions that depended on Internet Information Services—IIS). These project models include the HTTP project, the FTP project, and the file project. Here's a summary of how each model works.

HTTP Project

The HTTP project is most like the first ASP.NET project development model available from Visual Studio (that is, pre–Visual Studio 2005). Using the HTTP project model, Visual Studio creates a virtual directory under IIS and uses IIS to intercept requests during development time. Under this model, the solution file (the .sln file) resides in a directory specified under Visual Studio's project settings directory. The source code for the project is stored in the IIS virtual directory (that is, \Inetpub\wwwroot).

You may either have Visual Studio create a virtual directory for you or you may create a virtual directory ahead of time. You may store the code for your Web site in any folder. The virtual directory just needs to point to that location.

Use this option if you want to work as closely as possible with IIS. Using an IIS Web site during development lets you test the entire request path as it will run in production (not just the path through the Visual Studio integrated Web server). This is important if you want to test an application that leverages IIS security or requires ISAPI filters, application pooling, or some other specific IIS features to run effectively. One other reason to create a local Web site is to test your application against a local version of IIS. Using IIS as part of the development environment makes it easier to test these things. Of course, the downside to this approach is that IIS must be installed on your machine (it's not installed automatically on Windows XP—you have to take a deliberate step to install it). Having IIS on your machine may also compromise security. Many company policies prohibit you from running IIS on your development machine for this reason.

FTP Project

The FTP project is meant for those projects you want to manage remotely through an FTP server. For example, this is a good option if you use a remote hosting service to host your Web site. The FTP site option represents a reasonable means of getting files from your development environment to the hosting site.

When creating this type of site, Visual Studio will connect to any FTP server for which you have file and directory read and write privileges. You then use Visual Studio to manage the content on the remote FTP server.

You might use this option to test the Web site on the live-deployed server where it will actually be deployed.

File System Project

The file project is probably the most developer-oriented project (most of the examples in this book use the File System–style Web site). File System projects rely on the Web server integrated with Visual Studio instead of IIS. When you specify a file system Web site, you may tell Visual Studio to put it anywhere on your file system or in a shared folder on another computer.

If you don't have access to IIS, or you don't have administration rights to the system on which you're developing, then you'll want to create a File System–based Web site project. The site runs locally but independently of IIS. The most common scenario in this case is to develop and test a Web site on the file system. Then, when it comes time to expose your site, simply create an IIS virtual directory and point it to the pages in the file system Web site.

Another aspect of developing ASP.NET Web applications, aside from selecting the proper project type, is deciding whether or not to *precompile* your Web app. By default, Visual Studio does *not* precompile your Web application. Once you've developed a site using Visual Studio, you may decide to precompile it for performance reasons. Let's look at this option next.

Precompiling

The earliest versions of Visual Studio automatically built ASP.NET applications when you selected the **Build, Build Solution** menu item. All the source code (the VB and the CS files) was compiled into a resulting assembly named the same as the project. This precompiled assembly went into the project's *Bin* directory and became part of the files used for deployment. ASP.NET will still precompile an application for you. However, now you have two choices with regard to recompilation—using a virtual path (for applications already defined in IIS) and using a physical path (for sites that live on the file system). In addition, you must be deliberate about precompiling. The two precompilation options are precompile for performance and precompile for deployment. Precompiling a Web site involves using command line tools.

Precompiling for Performance

The first option is also known as "precompiling in place." This is useful for existing sites for which you want to enhance performance. When you precompile the source code behind your site, the primary benefit is that ASP.NET doesn't have to run that initial compilation when the site is hit for the first time. If your site requires frequent updates to the code base, you may see a small amount of performance improvement.

To precompile an IIS-based site in place, open a Visual Studio command window. Navigate to the .NET directory on your machine (probably Windows\Microsoft.Net\Framework\ <versionnumber>). In that directory is a program named *aspnet_compiler*. Execute the aspnet_compiler program, with the name of the Web site as known by IIS following the *–v* switch. For example, if IIS has a virtual directory named *MySite*, the following command line will build it. The precompiled application ends up in the Temporary ASP.NET Files directory under your current .NET directory.

```
aspnet_compiler -v MySite
```

If the Web site is a file system Web site without an IIS virtual directory, use the *–p* command line parameter to specify the physical path.

This compilation option precompiles the code and places it in the *Bin* directory for the application.

Precompiling for Deployment

Compiling for deployment involves compiling the code for a site and directing the output to a special directory from which it may be copied to the deployment machine or used in a setup project (as we'll see momentarily). In this case, the compiler produces assemblies from all ASP.NET source files that are normally compiled at run time. That includes the code for the pages, source code within the *App_Code* directory, and resource files.

To precompile a site for deployment, open a Visual Studio command window. Navigate to the .NET directory. Run the aspnet_compiler command line program, specifying the source as either a virtual path or a physical path. Provide the target folder following the input directory. For example, the following command builds the code in the *MySite* virtual directory and puts the resulting compiled version in C:\MySiteTarget:

```
aspnet_compiler -v MySite c:\MySiteTarget
```

If you add a *–u* command line parameter at the end of the command line, the compiler will compile some of the code and leave the page code files to be compiled just in time.

Once the code is compiled, one of the options you have is to build a Web setup program. The following example illustrates creating a Web setup program.

Creating a Web site installer

1. Start by creating a new site. Make it an HTTP site. Name the site *DeployThis*.

2. Create some content for the site. For example, add a few pages to the site, or borrow content from an earlier example. What's important here is that there is at least a page (some content), not what the content entails.

3. Precompile the site for deployment. Tell the aspnet_compiler to use the DeployThis virtual directory as the source and to direct it to a target holding directory. The following graphic illustrates the command line. Use the *–f* option to overwrite the target directory, if existing files are found there. Use the *–u* option at the end of the command line to instruct the compiler to make an updateable Web site. By making this an updateable site, you can modify the site on the remote server. That is, the site files are copied to the target directory. Any changes made in the files on the server will be reflected when the site is run.

```
aspnet_compiler -v DeployThis c:\deploythis -f -u
```

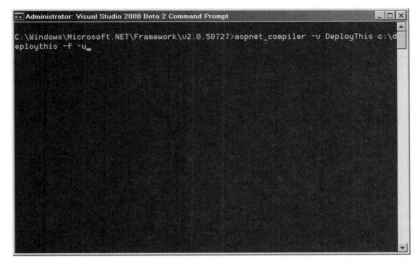

4. After the compiler runs, you'll have a target directory full of compiled code. The following graphic illustrates the results of the compilation.

```
Administrator: Visual Studio 2008 Beta 2 Command Prompt                    _ □ ×

C:\Windows\Microsoft.NET\Framework\v2.0.50727>aspnet_compiler -v DeployThis c:\d
eploythis -f -u
Utility to precompile an ASP.NET application
Copyright (C) Microsoft Corporation. All rights reserved.


C:\Windows\Microsoft.NET\Framework\v2.0.50727>dir \deploythis
 Volume in drive C has no label.
 Volume Serial Number is 74E0-D287

 Directory of C:\deploythis

12/11/2007  01:40 AM    <DIR>          .
12/11/2007  01:40 AM    <DIR>          ..
12/11/2007  01:40 AM    <DIR>          bin
12/11/2007  01:40 AM             1,775 Default.aspx
12/11/2007  01:40 AM             1,772 Page1.aspx
12/11/2007  01:40 AM             1,770 Page2.aspx
12/11/2007  01:40 AM                49 PrecompiledApp.config
12/11/2007  01:27 AM             8,832 web.config
               5 File(s)         14,198 bytes
               3 Dir(s)  75,675,738,112 bytes free

C:\Windows\Microsoft.NET\Framework\v2.0.50727>
```

5. Add a second project to the solution. Make it a Web Setup Project, as shown in the following graphic. Name the project *SetupDeployThis*.

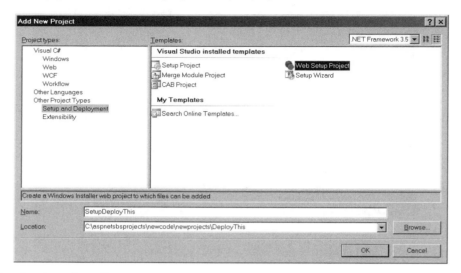

6. Visual Studio will generate a new setup project for you. You should see a screen like the following after Visual Studio is done churning.

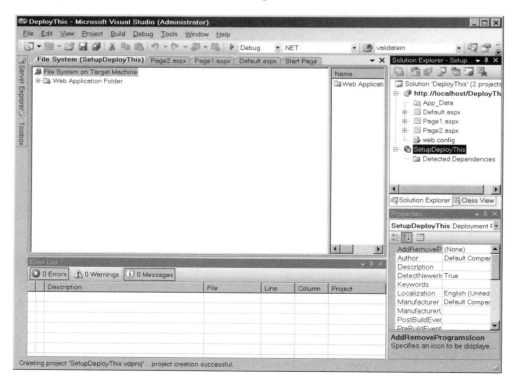

7. Click the right mouse button on the **Web Application Folder** to add the Web files. Navigate to the target directory containing the site code. This will be the precompile directory.

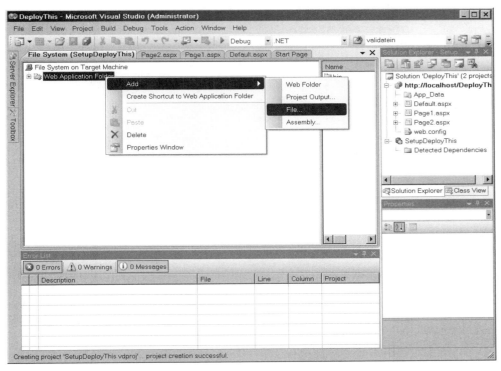

8. Add the Web files from the precompile directory by clicking **Open**.

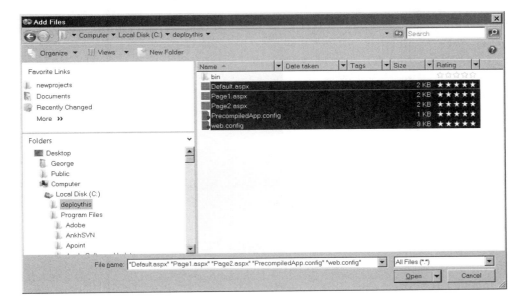

9. Add the DLLs to the *Bin* directory by clicking the right mouse button on the **Bin** node to get the **File Open** dialog box. Then search for and select all the files in the target directory's *Bin* directory. Click **Open**.

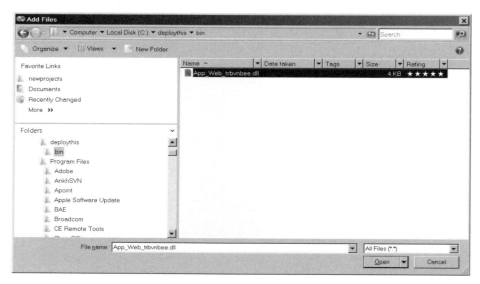

10. After adding all the files, the directory structure should look like this. The *Bin* directory will have the site DLLs.

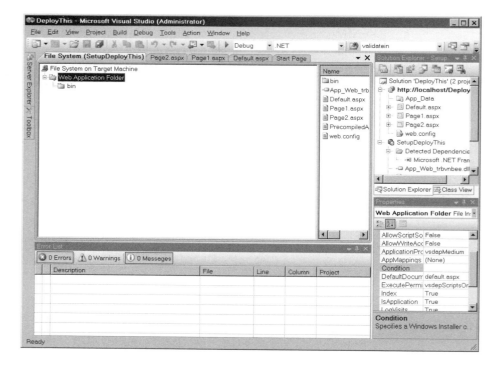

11. The Setup project properties include a prerequisite dialog box that you may review to ensure that certain prerequisites are installed on the end computer. To access the **Prerequisites** dialog box, click the right mouse button on the **SetupDeployThis** project to access the project's master property page collection. In the main property page (*Build*), click the **Prerequisites** button. The following graphic illustrates the prerequisites dialog box. Notice that the .NET Framework box is checked, as is Windows Installer. Assign any other prerequisites that may be required (none in this case) and click **OK**.

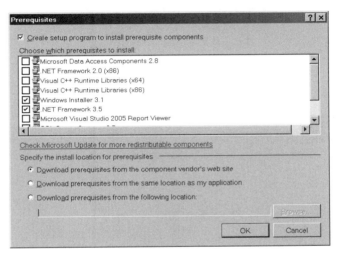

12. Click the right mouse button on the **SetupDeployThis** project and select **Build**. The resulting MSI file goes in the debug directory of the project.

13. Try running the Microsoft Installer file (the MSI file). The MSI file will guide you through several steps as it installs the Web site, as shown in the following graphics.

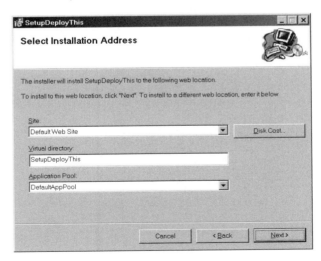

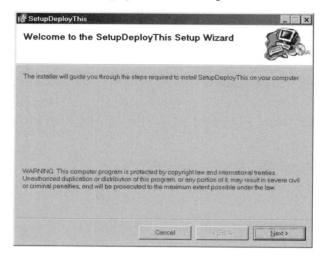

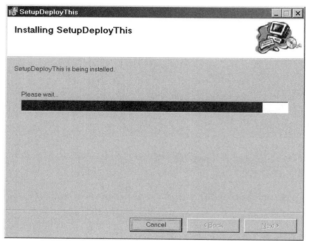

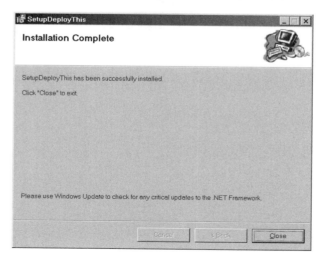

14. Now examine IIS. Refresh the Default Web Site node and look for the DeployThis virtual directory (unless you named it something else during the install process). IIS will have the DeployThis site.

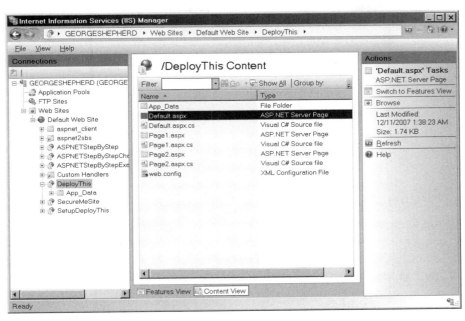

15. After the site is installed, you can surf to it as you can any other site.

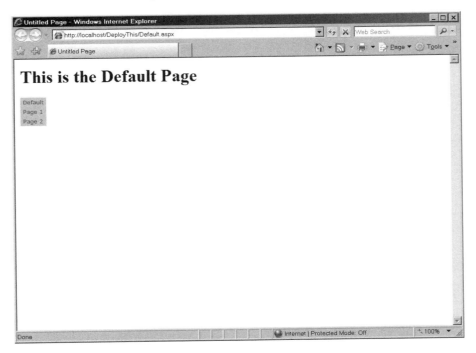

Setting up installation packages is a good way to distribute a Web application across a set of servers. You can push the MSI file to the server as necessary and run it. However, using an installation package isn't the only way to distribute the application. You may also literally copy the entire directory from a development machine to the server (XCOPY deployment), or you may use some other file transfer mechanism to move the bits. The next exercise demonstrates *Publishing* a Web site.

> **Note** The term *XCOPY deployment* refers to the installation strategy available during the late 1980s, when MS-DOS 3.x–5.x ran on most systems. The basic idea was to copy an entire directory structure and place it on the target machine, which you could do with the old MS-DOS *xcopy* command. The directory structure in those days was pretty isolated and transferring entire directory structures was reasonable.

Publishing a Web Site

A Web setup project is useful for distributing your site to several servers via distributable media (a CD or DVD). Another option for deploying your site is to *Publish* it using Visual Studio. There's an option within Visual Studio for publishing the site under the Build menu. Here's an exercise showing how to publish a Web site.

Publishing a Web site

1. Start by creating a new site. Make it a File System–type site. Name the site *PublishMe*.

2. Add a Master page to the site.

3. Delete the Default.aspx page from the site. Add a new Web page to the site and select the new master page. Visual Studio will name the new page *Default.aspx*.

4. Then add two more pages to the site (selecting the master page). Name the pages *Page1.aspx* and *Page2.aspx*.

5. Put labels on each of the pages to distinguish them. Make Page1's label say **This is Page 1** and make Page2's label say **This is Page 2**. Make the label for Default.aspx say **This is the Home page**.

6. Add a menu to the master page so that users may nagivate through the page. Edit each of the menu items. The first menu item's *Text* property should say **Home** and the *NavigateUrl* property should point to **Default.aspx**. The second menu item's *Text* property should say **Page 1** and the *NavigateUrl* property should point to **Page1.aspx**. The third menu item's *Text* property should say **Page 2** and the *NavigateUrl* property should point to **Page2.aspx**.

Go to Visual Studio's **Build** menu and select **Publish**. Visual Studio will show this dialog box:

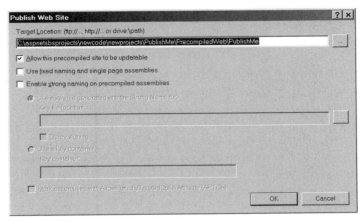

7. Type the name of the directory into which you'd like Visual Studio to place the files. After this step is complete, you may create an IIS virtual directory that points to the newly created directory and start surfing. Keep in mind that the published location need not be on your local system. However, to publish a Web site in this manner requires you to have access permissions on the remote server, and in the case of HTTP publishing, Front Page Extensions must be present and correctly configured on the remote server as well.

8. Click **OK** to publish the site.

Summary

In this chapter, we looked at how the various Visual Studio projects affect the deployment strategy for your Web site. Visual Studio provides several models, including

- HTTP sites that use IIS on the development machine
- File system sites that exist in the development file system, using the Web server built into Visual Studio
- FTP sites, where the bits are transferred to the target server via FTP

In addition to copying the software directly to the deployment machine, you may also precompile the application before copying it. By precompiling, you save the first end user to hit your site the few seconds it takes to compile the site. Of course, the subsequent hits take a much shorter time. However, if you foresee the site churning a lot, it may be worthwhile to precompile for performance. In addition, you may precompile the application so as to deploy it using an installer or a copying technique.

Chapter 24 Quick Reference

To	Do This
Work on a Web site locally without going through IIS	Create a File System Web site.
Work on a Web site using IIS	Create an HTTP Web site.
Work on a Web site by copying files over to the server FTP	Create an FTP site.
Precompile for performance or for deployment	Use the aspnet_compiler utility to precompile the code or publish it using Visual Studio.
Publish a Web application	Use Visual Studio's **Build, Publish** option. Visual Studio will push the files to the directory you specify (which may be an IIS virtual directory.
Create an Installer for your Web application	Add a second project to your solution. Make it a Web Setup Project. Add the necessary files to the project to make it work. Build the installer.

Glossary

ADO.NET (ActiveX Data Objects for .NET) Libraries providing Managed Code access to data services within Microsoft .NET.

AJAX (Asynchronous JavaScript and XML) A Web-based programming style in which requests for data from a Web Server are made out of band rather than through the normal HTTP request mechanism.

ASP.NET (Active Server Pages for .NET) Libraries for handling incoming HTTP requests running under Microsoft .NET.

Assembly The files that make up a Microsoft .NET application. This includes the manifest and deployment information as well as the MSIL code to be executed by the runtime.

Authentication The process of proving an end user's identity.

Authorization The process of allowing or disallowing system features based on a specific user's identity.

C# An object-oriented and type-safe programming language supported by Microsoft for use with the .NET framework.

Caching A widely used performance-enhancing technique in which commonly used data or content that is expensive to create is stored in memory for quick access.

Client An application requesting information or services from a server.

CLR (Common Language Runtime) The .NET infrastructure responsible for executing the MSIL code generated by multiple language syntaxes.

Handler The component within the ASP.NET pipeline that actually handles an HTTP request.

HTML (HyperText Markup Language) Commonly used document layout language that supports hyperlinks.

HTTP (HyperText Transfer Protocol) A standard Internet protocol used to transport content and control information across the World Wide Web (WWW).

HttpApplication A class within the ASP.NET framework representing the central rendezvous point for the application.

HttpContext A class within the ASP.NET framework representing the entire state of an HTTP request, including references to session state and the Response object.

Internet A collection of arbitrary heterogeneous computers loosely connected throughout the world.

Managed Code Code executed by the CLR.

Master Page A type of ASP.NET Web page that defines the common look and feel for a set of pages.

Method A member function defined within a .NET class or struct.

Module Within the context of ASP.NET, modules represent a way to do pre- and postprocessing within the ASP.NET pipeline.

MSIL (Microsoft Intermediate Language) Machine-independent representation of executable code resulting from compiling a language such as C# or Visual Basic.

Property A CLR convention for exposing a class or structure's member data (implicit getters and setters for the member data).

Request A class within the ASP.NET framework representing state coming from the client.

Response A class within the ASP.NET framework representing state going to the client.

Server A program for providing information for clients.

Session State A state that is associated with a specific client.

SOA (Service-Oriented Architecture) An approach to software architecture in which information is processed over a loosely connected network.

SOAP A commonly used network wire format for Web Services.

WCF (Windows Communication Foundation) Microsoft technology for unifying Web service–style remoting and .NET-style remoting.

Web Colloquial term representing all the nodes on the Internet.

Web Service A program running through a Web server typically providing information and services.

WPF (Windows Presentation Foundation) High-performance graphics and presentation technology useful for writing Windows programs and presenting content in the browser.

XML (eXtensible Markup Language) A flexible markup language useful for describing any type of structured data in a platform-independent way.

Index

A

access rules, 224–225
Accordion extender, 485
AcquireRequestState event, 401
Active Data Objects (ADO).NET, 241–242, 244
ActiveX controls, 62–63
add attribute, 418
Add New Item, in Visual Studio, 53–54
address, Windows Communication Foundation, 460
ADO.NET, 241–242, 244
AJAX. *See* Asynchronous Java And XML programming model (AJAX)
AlwaysVisibleControl extender, 485
Animation extender, 485
anonymous authentication, 208. *See also* authentication
anonymous personalization, 289–290. *See also* personalization
anonymous user profiles, 289. *See also* user profiles
AppearanceEditorPart control, 149, 154
AppendCacheExtension, 360
Application class, 395
application pooling, 31
application settings management, 202
application state
  caveats, 399
  management, 397–399
application tracing, 379–383
Application_End event, 400–401
Application_Error event, 400
applications
  debugging in Visual Studio, 383–386
  desktop vs. Web-based, 3
  Web parts, 147
Application_Start event, 400–401
application-wide events, 395, 396, 399–404
ASP (classic)
  consistency considerations in, 169
  dynamic content, 61
  processing in, 46
  Response object in, 32
  script blocks in, 35

ASP.NET 1.x
  code style, 43–44
  configuration management, 194
ASP.NET architecture, 35–40
ASP.NET compilation model, 41–42
ASP.NET Web Site, in Visual Studio, 52
.aspx page, compiling, 41
assemblies, viewing, 41–42
Asynchronous Java And XML programming model (AJAX)
  Accordion extender, 485
  AlwaysVisibleControl extender, 485
  Animation extender, 485
  AutoComplete extender, 485, 505–511
  browser support, 480, 483
  Calendar extender, 485
  CascadingDropDown extender, 485
  client-side support, 483–487
  CollapsiblePanel extender, 485
  ConfirmButton extender, 485
  Control Toolkit, 484
  definition, 478–479
  DragPanel extender, 485
  DropDown extender, 485
  DropShadow extender, 485
  DynamicPopulate extender, 485
  efficiency and, 480
  extender controls and, 480, 485–487
  FilteredTextBox extender, 486
  HoverMenu extender, 486
  ListSearch extender, 486
  MaskedEdit extender, 486
  ModalPopup extender, 486, 512–515
  MutuallyExclusiveCheckBox extender, 486
  networking layer, 484
  NumericUpDown extender, 486
  overview, 479–482
  PagingBulletedList extender, 486
  PasswordStrength extender, 486
  PopupControl extender, 486
  Rating control, 486
  in real world, 481
  reasons to use, 480–481
  ReorderList control, 486
  ResizableControl extender, 486

  rise of, 63
  RoundedCorners extender, 487
  ScriptManager control, 482
  ScriptManagerProxy control, 482
  server-side support for, 482–483
  Slider extender, 487
  SlideShow extender, 487
  Tabs control, 487
  TextBoxWatermark extender, 487
  Timer control, 483, 493–501
  ToggleButton extender, 487
  UpdatePanel control, 483
  UpdatePanelAnimation extender, 487
  UpdateProgress control, 483
  user interface and, 480
  ValidatorCallout extender, 487
  Web Services and, 479
asynchronous method calls, 451–454
asynchronous postbacks, 492–493
attributes
  add, 418
  CacheProfile, 355
  defaultRedirect, 387
  Duration, 355
  Inherits, 44
  Language, 64
  Location, 355
  in Master Pages, 171
  NoStore, 355
  on/off, 387
  remoteOnly, 387
  runat, 34
  runat=server, 64
  Shared, 356
  SqlDependency, 356
  Src, 44
  Trace, 65–66
  type, 418
  validate, 418
  VaryByContentEncoding, 356
  VaryByControl, 359
  VaryByCustom, 356, 359
  VaryByHeader, 356, 359–360
  VaryByParam, 356, 359, 360
  verb, 418
  WebMethod, 439
Authenticate, 215
AuthenticateRequest event, 401

SetCacheAbility, 360
SetETag, 360
SetExpires, 360
SetLastModified, 360
SetMaxAge, 360
SetRevalidation, 360
SetValidUntilExpires, 360
SetVaryByCustom, 360
Shared attribute, 356
SharePoint, 146
shopping carts, 304
"shout box," 493
side-by-side mode, Windows
    Communication Foundation,
    462
SignOut, 215
Silverlight, 529
site map configuration, 269–270
site maps, 264–266
SiteMap class, 265
SiteMapNode, 266, 275–277
SiteMapPath control, 263–264, 268
SiteMapProvider, 265
SiteMapResolve event, 266, 274–275
Skins, 185–186
Slider extender, 487
SlideShow extender, 487
sliding expirations, 340–341
SlidingExpiration property, 215
SOA (Service-Oriented
    Architecture), 454–455, 459
SOAP, 417, 437, 459
social networking sites, 145
Split tab, Visual Studio, 69
SplitMe class, 45
SQL (Structured Query Language),
    243
SQL Server dependency, 344–345
SqlDependency attribute, 356
Src attribute, 44
state
    application. *See main heading*
    caching. *See* data cache and
        caching
    control, 98–101
    session. *See main heading*
    storage in modules, 410–413
    view, 98–101, 396
state servers, 312–313
stateNetworkTimeout, 317
Static value of *Display* property, 130
Structured Query Language (SQL),
    243
stub handlers, 399–404
style sheets, 182
Substitution control, 357
supply chain management, 454
System.Web.UI.Control class, 79–80

System.Web.UI.Page class
    composite controls, 104
    rendered controls, 80
System.Web.UI.UserControl class,
    112
System.Web.UI.WebControl class,
    83
System.Diagnostics.Debug, 382
System.Diagnostics.Trace, 382

T

Tabs control, 487
tags
    in Master Pages, 170
    rendering controls as, 59–61
TCP monitors, 5
TcpTrace, 5
TELNET, 5
TEMP variable, 190
TextBoxWatermark extender, 487
Themes, 181–184, 286
Threads window, in Visual Studio,
    386
timeouts, session state, 317
Timer control, 483, 493–501
timing modules, 406–408
ToggleButton extender, 487
Trace handler, 419
TraceFinished event, 381
Trace.Warn, 376–378
Trace.Write, 376–378
tracing
    application, 379–383
    compiler, 382
    configuration file values,
        379
    data cache, 333
    enabled, 379
    localOnly, 379
    message piping, 382
    mostRecent, 379
    pageOutput, 379
    programmatic enabling,
        381
    requestLimit, 379
    self-supplied, 375–377
    session state, 374
    statements, 375–377
    turning on, 372–374
    writeToDiagnosticsTrace,
        379
tracking session state, 314–317
trapping exceptions, 390–391
TreeView control, 134–137, 235,
    263–264, 267
trimming, security, 278
type attribute, 418

U

UI. *See* user interface (UI)
unhandled exceptions, 390–391. *See
    also* debugging; error pages
Uniform Resource Locator (URL)
    mangled, 289
    mapping, 278–282
    session state tracking, 316
United Parcel Service (UPS), 454
Universal Resource Indicator (URI)
    authentication, 210
    session information, 191
update progress, 501–505
UpdatePanel control, 483, 487–492,
    501–505
UpdatePanelAnimation extender,
    487
UpdateProgress control, 483,
    501–505
UpdateRequestCache event, 401
URI. *See* Universal Resource
    Indicator (URI)
URL. *See* Uniform Resource Locator
    (URL)
user authentication. *See also*
    authorization; security
    anonymous, 208
    ASP.NET services, 214–219
    cookies, 217
    definition, 207
    forms, 209–214
    in Internet Information Services
        (IIS), 209
    login pages, 211–213
    optional login page, 215–219
    Passport, 214
    Windows, 214
    Windows network, 208
user authorization, 229–231
User controls, 112–118, 170. *See also*
    controls
user data, validation of, 121–122
user interface (UI)
    ActiveX controls, 62–63
    AJAX and, 480
    control tags for, 59–61
    controls history, 62–63
    packaging as components, 62–67
    System Web.UI.Control class,
        79–80
user management, 219–225
user profiles. *See also*
    personalization
    anonymous, 289
    definition of, 286
    information, 287–288
    saving changes, 288

George Shepherd

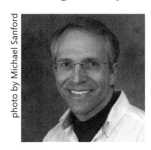

George Shepherd is a software consultant who specializes in Microsoft .NET technologies. As an instructor for DevelopMentor, George delivers short seminars that cover .NET, ASP.NET, and WPF. George is the author and co-author of several other books on software development, including *MFC Internals* (Addison-Wesley) and *Programming Visual C++ .NET* (Microsoft Press). He has served as contributing editor for *MSDN Magazine* and *Dr. Dobb's Journal* and is a contributing architect for Syncfusion's Essential .NET toolset.

What do you think of this book?

We want to hear from you!

Do you have a few minutes to participate in a brief online survey?

Microsoft is interested in hearing your feedback so we can continually improve our books and learning resources for you.

To participate in our survey, please visit:

www.microsoft.com/learning/booksurvey/

...and enter this book's ISBN-10 or ISBN-13 number (located above barcode on back cover*). As a thank-you to survey participants in the United States and Canada, each month we'll randomly select five respondents to win one of five $100 gift certificates from a leading online merchant. At the conclusion of the survey, you can enter the drawing by providing your e-mail address, which will be used for prize notification only.

Thanks in advance for your input. Your opinion counts!

* Where to find the ISBN on back cover

ISBN-13: 000-0-0000-0000-0
ISBN-10: 0-0000-0000-0

Example only. Each book has unique ISBN.

Microsoft®
Press

No purchase necessary. Void where prohibited. Open only to residents of the 50 United States (includes District of Columbia) and Canada (void in Quebec). For official rules and entry dates see:

www.microsoft.com/learning/booksurvey/